T0030143

The BITTER END

THE
BITTER
END

The 2020 Presidential Campaign
and the Challenge
to American Democracy

John Sides,
Chris Tausanovitch,
and Lynn Vavreck

With a new preface by the authors

PRINCETON UNIVERSITY PRESS
PRINCETON & OXFORD

Published by Princeton University Press
41 William Street, Princeton, New Jersey 08540
99 Banbury Road, Oxford OX2 6JX

press.princeton.edu

All Rights Reserved

First paperback edition, 2023
Paperback ISBN 9780691243733
Cloth ISBN 9780691213453
ISBN (e-book) 9780691253985

Library of Congress Control Number: 2023930548

British Library Cataloging-in-Publication Data is available

Editorial: Bridget Flannery-McCoy, Alena Chekanov
Jacket/Cover Design: Karl Spurzem
Production: Erin Suydam
Publicity: James Schneider, Kate Farquhar-Thomson

Jacket/Cover photograph: Shutterstock

This book has been composed in Arno Pro

Printed in the United States of America

To
Rick and Elizabeth Sides,
Stephanie Carrie,
and
Abigail and William Lewis,
Our families.

CONTENTS

PREFACE TO THE PAPERBACK EDITION

JANUARY 6, 2023, marked the second anniversary of the attack on the U.S. Capitol by supporters of Donald Trump. President Joe Biden gave a speech in the Statuary Hall of the Capitol, which had been occupied by attackers two years earlier as they sought to stop Congress from certifying Biden's victory in the 2020 presidential election. Biden singled out Trump for spreading a "web of lies" about the election and said, "You can't love your country only when you win." In the House chamber, Speaker Nancy Pelosi also offered remarks after a moment of silence. Just one Republican member of Congress, Rep. Liz Cheney, was in attendance. The only other Republican members to speak about the attack that day were ardent Trump supporters Rep. Marjorie Taylor Greene and Rep. Matt Gaetz, who claimed without evidence that the FBI was behind the attack.[1]

Meanwhile, Greene, Gaetz, and other House Republicans were in the middle of an unusually protracted effort to elect a new Speaker. The party's challenge had its roots in the 2022 midterm election. Despite many confident predictions of a "red wave," Republicans gained only nine seats in the House, giving them a slim nine-seat majority. The Speaker election could thus be delayed if only a small number of Republicans refused to back the minority leader and presumptive Speaker, Rep. Kevin McCarthy of California.

That is exactly what happened over five dramatic days—the longest Speaker election since 1860. A group of roughly twenty Republicans, including Gaetz and other hardliners, refused to support McCarthy.

Only after McCarthy agreed to a series of concessions did he emerge victorious on the fifteenth vote. Those concessions were widely seen as complicating McCarthy's ability to lead and exposing him to even more challenges from hardliners.

This discord within the Republican Party quickly gave way to a more familiar pattern, however. Two days after McCarthy's election, the very first House vote saw a united Republican majority rescind $70 billion in funding for the Internal Revenue Service over the opposition of a united Democratic minority. The next day, after another party-line vote, Republicans created a select committee on the "weaponization of government" that would investigate executive branch agencies like the FBI, largely because of previous and ongoing government investigations of Trump. Not every vote was so contentious; the same day, a bipartisan majority created another select committee "on the strategic competition between the United States and the Chinese Communist Party." But, overall, congressional politics reverted to its norm of strong partisanship. This is why Republican leaders would rather suffer an embarrassing Speaker election and appease hardliners in their party than pursue a deal with moderate Democrats.

This book was first published in the fall of 2022, just before the midterm election. But that election and its aftermath showed that even with a new Republican majority in the House, much of American politics had not changed. Not only were the two parties far apart on many issues, but the Biden presidency and the midterm election showed the continuing importance of both *calcification* and *partisan parity*—two of the key ideas that we explore in this book. Although Americans' opinions of Biden were strongly linked to their opinions of the economy— a pattern that did not exist for Obama or Trump—both presidential approval and voting in the midterm manifested the partisan loyalty that is characteristic of calcification, in which relatively few Democrats or Republicans oppose their own side. Indeed, rates of split-ticket voting in 2022 were lower than in any midterm in over thirty years.

The parity between the parties, however, ensures that even small changes—in party loyalty, in other factors—can have important effects on who wins elections and who governs the country. And the question of "who governs" takes on additional significance in an era where the essential components of democracy remain at stake.

THE BIDEN PRESIDENCY

The Republicans were not alone in facing challenges. Joe Biden faced some as well. Most significant was a large spike in inflation that began in early 2021. At its peak in the summer of 2022, prices were over 8 percent higher than they had been the previous year.[2] These were the highest numbers since the "stagflation" of the late 1970s and early 1980s. One possible cause was a piece of legislation that Biden himself had championed: the American Rescue Plan of 2021. This plan provided another round of economic stimulus, including checks to individual Americans, as part of the government's response to the COVID-19 pandemic and resulting economic downturn. By helping Americans spend money when supply constraints hindered the availability of many goods, this legislation may have pushed prices higher.[3]

To be sure, not all of the economic news was negative: for most of 2021 and 2022, the economy was expanding, as measured by changes in gross domestic product. Job growth was robust, and the unemployment rate remained low. There was inflation, but not stagflation. However, as research has shown, negative economic information tends to be more prevalent in news coverage and therefore in the minds of Americans.[4] One long-standing measure of people's economic perceptions, the University of Michigan's Index of Consumer Sentiment, bottomed out in the summer of 2022 at a level actually lower than in the stagflation period and in the Great Recession of 2008–9. This shows just how large inflation loomed in the minds of Americans.

As their views of the economy worsened, so did Americans' views of Biden. This set Biden apart from both Barack Obama and Trump. During Obama's and Trump's presidencies, economic indicators, including consumer sentiment, did not have much relationship to their approval ratings. One ready explanation was partisanship: Americans' party loyalties kept presidential approval from changing very much, as expected in an increasingly calcified politics. The president's own partisans would not punish him for an economic downturn, the story went, nor would opposite partisan give him any credit for an economic boom. The power of partisanship makes sense given how much the parties differ on many issues—including, increasingly, on potent issues related to racial, ethnic, and gender identities.

By contrast, Biden's approval rating in the first two years of his presidency was correlated with consumer sentiment, much as it was for presidents prior to Obama (figure 1). As a result, Biden's approval ratings dropped to the level of Trump's at the same point in his presidency. The economy was not the only factor that mattered, of course. The percentage who disapproved of Biden initially increased before consumer sentiment worsened, which likely reflected the end of the "honeymoon" that presidents typically experience at the beginning of their first term. Biden's approval rating worsened during the chaotic withdrawal of U.S. forces from Afghanistan in August 2021, although consumer sentiment was also dropping at that time. Regardless, the importance of the economy stands out: by itself, consumer sentiment predicted 88 percent of the variation in Biden's approval rating between February 2021 and December 2022.

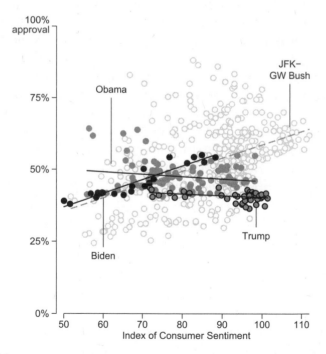

Figure 1.

The Relationship between Consumer Sentiment and Presidential Approval.

Source for Index of Consumer Sentiment: University of Michigan Survey of Consumers.

At the same time, calcification was evident in these two years. Like Trump's approval rating, Biden's did not fluctuate very much. When he was inaugurated, only about 55 percent of Americans approved of Biden—a much smaller honeymoon bump than presidents typically receive, thanks largely to high disapproval among Republicans. Indeed, comparing Biden's and Trump's approval ratings in figure 1, it stands out just how little their ratings varied despite the wide range in consumer sentiment during their presidencies. Almost all of Trump's presidency was spent with approval ratings between 37 and 50 percent. The same was true for Biden in the second half of 2021 as well as 2022.

Calcification is even more apparent when comparing Biden to a president in similar circumstances: Jimmy Carter in 1979. At that point, Carter was presiding over even higher inflation. It was already 9 percent in January 1979, on its way to a peak of 15 percent in early 1980. Consumer sentiment levels were low, although not as low as under Biden.

Nevertheless, Biden was more popular than Carter despite facing lower consumer sentiment. The central reason was greater party loyalty among Democrats. According to Gallup polls in 2021–22, the vast majority of Democrats—no fewer than 78 percent—approved of Biden's performance. But for much of 1979, up until the Iran hostage crisis began in November, only half of Democrats, and sometimes less, approved of Carter. Reflecting the lower polarization of that time, Carter's approval among Republicans was higher than Biden's. Thus, Biden's support among Democrats was even more crucial. Democrats' willingness to stick with Biden despite high gas and food prices buoyed his approval rating.

THE 2022 MIDTERM ELECTION

Although Democratic loyalty kept Biden from lower approval ratings, those approval ratings still did not bode well for Democrats running in the 2022 midterm election. Of course, the president's party typically loses seats in the midterm election, but some forecasting models suggested that a real "red wave" was brewing. For example, one model based on three factors—Biden's approval rating, the change in real personal incomes (which were shrinking because of inflation), and the number of seats Democrats already controlled in the House—predicted that the party could lose forty-five seats. Forecasts that incorporated race ratings by political experts were only a little more optimistic, suggesting that Democrats would lose between thirty-seven and forty-four seats.[5]

There were at least two countervailing factors at work, however. One, perhaps surprisingly, was the redrawing of U.S. House boundaries after the 2020 census. After the 2010 census, Republican majorities in a number of states drew quite severe gerrymanders. But analyses of the new maps found a more modest GOP advantage, perhaps amounting to as little as an additional seat or two compared to nonpartisan alternatives.[6]

More notable in the new maps was the declining number of competitive seats. One analysis found that nonpartisan redistricting would have produced about 50 competitive U.S. House seats out of 435, where "competitive" is defined as an expected vote margin within 2.5 points of fifty-fifty. The actual number of competitive seats was only thirty-four. This result was driven in particular by an increase in safe Republican seats.[7] Thus, there was less potential for a large seat swing in Republicans' favor.

Another factor was Supreme Court's June 2022 decision in *Dobbs v. Jackson Women's Health*, in which five conservative justices struck down the constitutional right to an abortion established in *Roe v. Wade* in 1973. That this decision might elicit a backlash was anticipated by our analysis: we show that abortion—and specifically opposition to abortion bans—was already a central issue for Democrats, even before the Supreme Court's ruling.[8] After the ruling, the "generic ballot" polls that capture voters' intentions in U.S. House races shifted, putting Democrats even with or even ahead of Republicans. Forecasts based on the historical relationship between these polls and congressional election outcomes suggested that the Democrats would do much better, losing fewer than twenty seats if the generic ballot gave Republicans a two-point advantage or less.[9]

That is exactly what happened. The Republicans' nine-seat gain was small by historical standards, especially given Biden's low approval rating. And Democrats actually expanded their margin in the Senate by one seat, thanks in part to incumbent Senator Raphael Warnock's defeat of Republican Herschel Walker in a Georgia runoff election. The upshot was a continuation of the partisan parity that has come to characterize American politics, with not only narrow margins in presidential elections but also small and temporary congressional majorities.

Given this parity, small changes in vote margins can have big consequences for political power. In 2022, Republicans may have lost key races because they nominated weak candidates whose viewpoints or backgrounds earned them unwanted controversy. In some cases, these were also candidates whom Trump endorsed in the primary election campaign. Walker was one—a former college and professional football player who drew particular attention because of children he had fathered out of wedlock and never acknowledged publicly, as well as claims by two former girlfriends that he had pressured them to obtain abortions. A series of postelection analyses suggested that, just as in the 2018 midterm election, Trump-endorsed candidates as well as candidates clearly identified with Trump's wing of the GOP ran several percentage points behind other Republican candidates. Walker was a good example. He ran behind the Republican gubernatorial candidate, Brian Kemp, who beat Stacey Abrams by seven points, while Walker lost to Warnock by one point in the November election. Another analysis found that Walker ran six points behind what one would predict based on Georgia's demographics, Warnock's status as an incumbent, and other factors.[10]

But the possibility that some voters in Georgia and elsewhere split their tickets should not obscure this fact: there was actually *less* apparent ticket-splitting in 2022 than in recent midterms (figure 2). The gap between the outcomes in Senate races and gubernatorial races was only seven percentage points in 2022, compared to seventeen points in 2014. Moreover, only one senator won an election in a state where the opposing party had won the 2020 presidential vote (Wisconsin Republican Ron Johnson). These are exactly the expected patterns if voters' choices reflect calcification and a stubborn refusal to vote for the opposite party's candidate. Thus, two things are true simultaneously: voters who are willing to split their ticket can help decide key elections, even as split-ticket voting becomes increasingly rare in a calcified era.[11]

Median percentage-point gap between each state's senatorial and gubernatorial election results

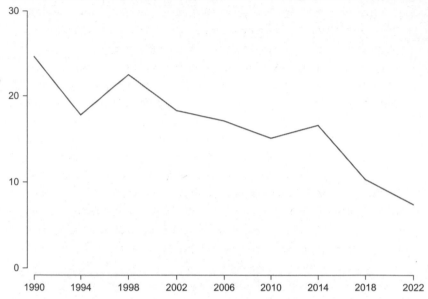

Figure 2.
The Decline of Split-Ticket Voting in Midterm Elections. Only races between a Republican and a Democrat are included. *Source*: Data compiled by *Politico* from MIT Election Data and Science Lab, Associated Press, and state election results.

After the election, there was little sign of anything that could weaken partisan alignments. The political agenda and positions of the two parties did not change much. Although Biden pivoted toward a more stringent policy at the U.S.-Mexico border, which had been experiencing a large influx of asylum-seekers and other immigrants, he largely defended his administration's record, including the American Rescue Plan. Meanwhile, the GOP House majority pursued typical conservative positions—anti-tax, anti-spending—alongside its effort to investigate the Biden administration. And despite the challenges of Trump-backed candidates, there was no sign the Republican Party would purge Trump or Trumpism from its ranks. Trump himself entered the 2024 presidential race immediately after the midterm election. Although polls suggested that he would not sew up the nomination, neither did they suggest that he would clearly fail. Indeed, Trump's problem is not so much that the GOP has rejected him but that there are now too many Trumps in the party. Candidates like Florida governor Ron DeSantis, who won reelection easily in 2022, are poised to challenge Trump precisely because they emulate his politics and style.

CONCLUSION

The midterm election ended without the violence of January 6, 2021. Unlike Trump, most losing Republican candidates did concede defeat. Although a few candidates filed suit to challenge the results, there was no systematic campaign to undermine confidence in the outcome. As a result, views of the electoral system were much more positive among Republicans. After the 2020 election, only 21 percent of Republicans said that it was "run and administered" well in the United States. That rebounded to 53 percent after 2022.[12]

However, that 53 percent figure was far below the 78 percent of Republicans who expressed confidence in the electoral system after the 2016 election, and below the 73 percent of Democrats who expressed confidence in 2016 even though they lost the presidential election. Thus, Republican voters manifested a lingering willingness to question the election results, even without Trump and his allies leading a weeks-long effort to delegitimize the outcome.

Election denial also remained alive and well among Republicans in Congress. After the 2020 election, a total of 139 House Republicans voted not to certify the results. In 2022, 127 of them ran for reelection, and almost all of them won, many in uncompetitive districts that the redistricting process had produced. In total, the *Washington Post* counted 155 Republicans in the next Congress, including incumbents and those newly elected, who had voted not to certify the 2020 election, voiced skepticism about Biden's victory, or both. In a separate count, the *New York Times* identified twenty more. Of course, there were election deniers who lost, including in races for key statewide offices with oversight over elections. Regardless, the sentiments that led to the January 6 attacks grew more prevalent within Congress itself.[13]

This book tells the story of the 2020 election, including the Trump presidency, the Democratic primary, the COVID-19 pandemic, the murder of George Floyd, and the election itself. It also tells the story of election's aftermath and a tragic challenge to American democracy. Ultimately, as Biden said in his speech on the January 6 anniversary, "Our democracy held." However, the two years after the attack showed that the challenge of upholding democracy remains.

NOTES

1. Annie Linsky, "Biden Goes After Trump for Lies and Self-Aggrandizement in Jan. 6 Insurrection Anniversary Speech," *Washington Post*, January 6, 2022, https://www.washingtonpost.com/politics/biden-goes-after-trump-for-lies-and-self-aggrandizement-in-jan-6-insurrection-anniversary-speech/2022/01/06/fdb39c14-6eff-11ec-aaa8-35d1865a6977_story.html.

2. See this St. Louis Federal Reserve graph: https://fred.stlouisfed.org/graph/?g=8dGq.

3. An overview of the debate about the impact of the ARP on inflation is David J. Lynch, "Biden's Rescue Plan Made Inflation Worse but the Economy Better," *Washington Post*, October 9, 2022, https://www.washingtonpost.com/us-policy/2022/10/09/inflation-economy-biden-covid.

4. Stuart N. Soroka, *Negativity in Democratic Politics: Causes and Consequences* (New York: Cambridge University Press, 2014); and Stuart N. Soroka, "The Gatekeeping Function: Distributions of Information in Media and the Real World," *Journal of Politics* 74, no. 2 (2012): 514–28.

5. The forty-five-seat forecast is discussed in Gary C. Jacobson, "The 2022 U.S. Midterm Election: A Conventional Referendum or Something Different?," https://www.dropbox.com/s/95s7hip8bzg5x8n/Jacobson%202022%20Essay.pdf?dl=0. The other forecasts are Charles Tien and Michael S. Lewis-Beck, "Forecasting 2022 Using the Fundamentals: The Structural and Structure X Models," Center for Politics, September 8, 2022, https://centerforpolitics.org/crystalball/articles/forecasting-2022-using-the-fundamentals-the-structural-and-structure-x-models; and James E. Campbell, "The Seats-in-Trouble Forecasts of the 2022 Midterm Congressional Elections," Center for Politics, September 8, 2022, https://centerforpolitics.org/crystalball/articles/the-seats-in-trouble-forecasts-of-the-2022-midterm-congressional-elections.

6. Analyses of the 2010–11 redistricting include Nicholas Stephanopoulos and Eric McGhee, "Partisan Gerrymandering and the Efficiency Gap," *University of Chicago Law Review* 82 (2015): 831–900; and Anthony J. McGann, Charles Anthony Smith, Michael Latner, and Alex Keena, *Gerrymandering in America* (New York: Cambridge University Press, 2016). On the 2020–21 redistricting, see Christopher Warshaw, Eric McGhee, and Michal Migurski, "Districts for a New Decade—Partisan Outcomes and Racial Representation in the 2021–-22 Redistricting Cycle." *Publius* forthcoming; and Christopher T. Kenny, Cory McCartan, Tyler Simko, Shiro Kuriwaki, and Kosuke Imai, "Widespread Partisan Gerrymandering Mostly Cancels Nationally,

but Reduces Electoral Competition," ALARM Project, August 15, 2022, https://alarm-redist.org /posts/2022-08-14-gerrymandering-mostly-cancels-nationally.

7. Kenny et al., "Widespread Partisan Gerrymandering."

8. See also John Sides, Chris Tausanovitch, and Lynn Vavreck, "How Americans' Priorities Explain Abortion Politics," Princeton University Press Ideas, October 28, 2022, https://press .princeton.edu/ideas/how-americans-priorities-explain-abortion-politics.

9. Alan Abramowitz, "Are Democrats Headed for a Shellacking in the Midterm Election?," Center for Politics, April 12, 2022, https://centerforpolitics.org/crystalball/articles/are -democrats-headed-for-a-shellacking-in-the-midterm-election.

10. On Trump's endorsements in 2018, see Andrew O. Ballard, Hans J. G. Hassell, and Michael Heseltine, "Be Careful What You Wish For: The Impacts of President Trump's Midterm Endorsement," *Legislative Studies Quarterly* 46, no. 2 (2021): 459–91. On the impact of Trump in 2022, see Nate Cohn, "Trump's Drag on Republicans Quantified: A Five-Point Penalty," *New York Times*, November 16, 2022, https://www.nytimes.com/2022/11/16/upshot/trump-effect -midterm-election.html. On Walker, see Lakshya Jain and Leon Sit, "Our 2022 Senate Wins above Replacement Model," Split Ticket, January 25, 2023, https://split-ticket.org/2023/01/25 /our-2022-senate-wins-above-replacement-model.

11. The data in figure 2 are presented in Lisa Kashinsky and Jessica Piper, "Voters Who Backed GOP Governors Helped Keep the Senate Blue," *Politico*, November 19, 2022, https:// www.politico.com/news/2022/11/19/ticket-splitting-senate-democrats-00069574. The statistic about Senate winners is from Drew DeSilver, "In 2022 Midterms, Nearly All Senate Election Results Again Matched States' Presidential Results," Pew Research Center, December 8, 2022, https://www.pewresearch.org/fact-tank/2022/12/08/in-2022-midterms-nearly-all -senate-election-results-again-matched-states-presidential-votes.

12. Pew Research Center, "Public Has Modest Expectations for Washington's Return to Divided Government," December 1, 2022, https://www.pewresearch.org/politics/2022/12/01 /public-has-modest-expectations-for-washingtons-return-to-divided-government.

13. The *New York Times* tabulation is here: https://www.nytimes.com/interactive/2022/11 /09/us/politics/election-misinformation-midterms-results.html. The *Washington Post* tabulation is here: https://www.washingtonpost.com/politics/interactive/2022/election-deniers -midterms.

The BITTER END

1

The Storm Is Here

"WHEN DO WE START WINNING?"

That was what a friend of Ashli Babbitt's asked on Twitter the week before Congress met to certify the 2020 presidential election. Babbitt replied, "January 6, 2021."

Babbitt was a thirty-five-year old Air Force veteran who lived outside San Diego with her husband. She owned a struggling pool-supply company. She also was an ardent supporter of Donald Trump and his crusade to overturn the results of the 2020 election. On January 5 she had tweeted, "Nothing will stop us. They can try and try and try but the storm is here and it is descending upon DC in less than 24 hours . . . dark to light!"[1] The next day, with a Trump flag tied around her neck, Babbitt joined a mob that breached the U.S. Capitol and interrupted the certification of the election.

Babbitt had traveled to Washington to attend a "Save America" rally that Trump and his allies organized for that morning. At the rally, multiple people spoke in violent terms about what needed to happen. Rep. Mo Brooks, a Republican from Alabama, said, "Today is the day American patriots start takin' down names and kickin' ass. Are you willing to do what it takes to fight for America?" One of Trump's sons, Donald Jr., said that "red-blooded, patriotic Americans" should "fight for Trump." Trump adviser Rudy Giuliani called for "trial by combat." At noon,

Trump himself spoke for an hour, declaring that he would "never concede" the election and telling supporters, "We fight like hell and if you don't fight like hell, you're not going to have a country anymore." He called on supporters to go to the Capitol and "demand that Congress do the right thing."[2]

Thousands of his supporters heeded Trump's call. By 1:00 p.m., some breached the temporary fences on the Capitol grounds and clashed with Capitol Police officers. A little after 2:00 p.m., protesters broke a window and began to enter the Capitol. At 2:30, the Senate, including Vice President Mike Pence and several members of his family, was evacuated. Protesters, including a few who were armed or carried zip-tie restraints, soon occupied the Senate chamber. Approximately 800 eventually entered the Capitol. The protest had become a riot—or, as some would later say, an insurrection.

Babbitt was among a group that targeted the House chamber, where some members of Congress still remained, hiding under desks. The rioters attacked the glass doors that opened into the Speaker's Lobby, a room just outside the chamber. One yelled "Fuck the blue!" at the officers standing there. The group hit the doors with their hands, flagpoles, and other objects.

When one door broke, Babbitt tried to climb through. Michael Byrd, a Capitol Police officer standing on the other side, shot her. Babbitt received medical attention on the scene from police and was transported to a local hospital, where she died of her injuries.[3]

Babbitt was the only rioter to be killed that day, but she was otherwise similar to the types of people who entered the Capitol. Most who were charged with a crime had no connection with far-right groups, militias, or white nationalist organizations, although such groups, including the Proud Boys and the Oathkeepers, were represented among the rioters. Court records showed that most of these people said they were only doing what Trump had told them to do: defend him and keep Biden from winning a "stolen" election. This was Babbitt's goal, too.[4]

Trump welcomed their efforts. Indeed, he had long been willing to downplay, countenance, or even encourage violence on his behalf. In his first presidential campaign he praised supporters who assaulted protestors at his rallies, offering to pay their legal bills. In his second campaign, rather than disavowing the support of extremist groups, he encouraged them. In the presidential debate on September 29, 2020, he told the Proud Boys to "stand back and stand by."

And so it was no surprise that Trump was "initially pleased" when his supporters stormed the Capitol, according to White House officials who later spoke with reporters. The violence was well underway before Trump finally tweeted, at 2:47 p.m., "Please support our Capitol Police and Law Enforcement. They are truly on the side of our Country. Stay peaceful!" Even then, one official said that Trump had not wanted to include "stay peaceful."[5]

Members of Congress and White House aides implored Trump to speak out more forcefully. Trump sent a second tweet at 3:25, calling for people to "remain peaceful" and saying, "No violence!" But he refused to condemn the violence outright or tell his supporters to leave the Capitol. At 4:22 p.m. he published a video message in which he said that "we have to have peace" and told his supporters to "go home." But he also said that "we love you, you're very special" and repeated his false claim of election fraud. At 6:25 p.m., after the rioters had finally been cleared from the Capitol, Trump praised them again, tweeting, "These are the things and events that happen when a sacred landslide election victory is so unceremoniously & viciously stripped away from great patriots who have been badly & unfairly treated for so long." He added, "Go home with love & in peace. Remember this day forever!"[6]

It was a jarring sentiment even at that point, and it would become more so when the full toll of that day was clear. Ashli Babbitt was dead; the Capitol building had been damaged extensively; and the Capitol Police had suffered devastating harm and loss—approximately 140 officers were injured by rioters, who beat them with baseball bats, flagpoles, and pipes. One officer, Brian Sicknick, died the following day of a stroke that was possibly linked to the injuries he had received when a rioter pepper-sprayed him. Four officers committed suicide in the months following the riot.[7]

Beyond the toll on people and property was the cost to American democracy itself. A hallmark of democracies is the peaceful transfer of power after an election. That did not happen. Another hallmark is the willingness of election losers to consent to the outcome, thereby upholding the legitimacy of the system even as they regroup and seek to win next time. That did not happen, either. Not only did Trump continue to insist that the election was stolen, but on the night of January 6 he was joined by eight Senate Republicans and 139 House Republicans, all of whom voted to object to the election results when Congress reconvened only hours after members were forced to flee for their lives.[8]

The 2020 election and the attack on the Capitol were the culmination of a long year of casualties and crisis in the United States. There was the COVID-19 pandemic, which took the lives of over 350,000 Americans in 2020 alone and put at least 14 million people out of work,[9] and there were yet more deaths of African Americans at the hands of police officers, most notably the murder of George Floyd by Minneapolis police officer Derek Chauvin, on May 25, 2020, which led to massive protests. The Trump White House saw its own series of crises, culminating in Trump's impeachment in early 2020 and then a second impeachment in early 2021 because of his actions—and then inaction—during the insurrection.

These extraordinary events seemed initially as if they might transcend the powerful partisanship that usually characterizes American politics. Perhaps Americans would come together to beat a deadly virus; as one *Washington Post* columnist noted in February 2020, "a global crisis . . . could unite the planet and encourage everyone to pull together." Or perhaps they would be united by the gruesome spectacle of a police officer kneeling on the neck of a man for nine minutes. As one headline after Floyd's murder put it: "Will This Be the Moment of Reckoning on Race That Lasts?" But anything like unity or a reckoning proved fleeting at best. Political leaders stoked partisan divisions with predictable, even violent, consequences. Thus, politics shaped how the central events of the election year played out as much, if not more, than these events shaped politics.[10]

In turn, this had important consequences for the presidential election. For an incumbent like Trump, the combination of impeachment, a pandemic, and a recession seemed like a recipe for a landslide defeat.

It was not. In the national popular vote, Biden's margin of victory was only about 2 points greater than Hillary Clinton's in 2016. In the key battleground states, the margins were even closer than in 2016.

Of course, Trump still lost, and the attempts by his supporters and allies in Congress to overturn the election failed. Joseph R. Biden Jr. became the forty-sixth president of the United States. In his inaugural address, Biden expressed his own hopes of unifying the country, saying, "We can join forces, stop the shouting and lower the temperature. For without unity there is no peace, only bitterness and fury. No progress, only exhausting outrage. No nation, only a state of chaos. This is our historic moment of crisis and challenge, and unity is the path forward."[11]

But how leaders responded to the events of 2020—and especially how Trump and his allies responded to the election and its aftermath— only exacerbated divisions that had been years in the making. Understanding those divisions helps explain why the election came to such a bitter end, and why this bitter end may only signal the beginning of a new democratic crisis in American politics.

A CALCIFIED POLITICS

That Americans are politically divided is obvious, but it is important to clarify what this means. Generalizations about a divided America do not tell us what issues are most divisive, when those divisions emerged, and whether we are deeply divided or merely closely divided. This makes it hard to say what has happened in American politics, what is causing it, and what it implies for the future. We seek to push beyond simple generalizations to identify the facts and trends that provide insight into the politics of the Trump presidency, the 2020 election, and the election's aftermath.

Our argument centers on three elements. First, long-term *tectonic shifts* have pushed the parties apart while making the views within each party more uniform. This is the familiar trend toward gradually increasing partisan polarization. Second, shorter-term *shocks*, catalyzed especially by Trump, have sped up polarization on identity issues—those related to race, ethnicity, religion, and gender. And third, it is precisely these identity issues that voters in both parties care more about—exacerbating divisions even further and giving politicians every incentive to continue to play to them.

The upshot is a more *calcified politics*. As it does in the body, calcification produces hardening and rigidity: people are more firmly in place and harder to move away from their predispositions. Growing calcification is a logical consequence of growing polarization, but the concepts are not identical. Polarization means more distance between voters in opposing parties in terms of their values, ideas, and views on policy. Calcification means less willingness to defect from their party, such as by breaking with their party's president or even voting for the opposite party. There is thus less chance for new and even dramatic events to change people's choices at the ballot box. New events tend to be absorbed into an axis of conflict in which identity plays the central role. And this means smaller fluctuations from year to year in election outcomes.

But perhaps paradoxically, a more calcified politics does not produce the same winner year after year. This is because increasing partisan polarization has coincided with increasing *partisan parity*. In sheer numbers, Democrats and Republicans are more narrowly divided than they used to be, meaning that any movement in elections from one year to the next could change who governs the country. This combination of calcification and parity raises the stakes of politics—and makes them more explosive.

Tectonic Shifts in Partisan Attitudes

Over the long term, the Democratic and Republican parties have become more internally homogeneous and more different from each other in political ideology, certain demographic characteristics, and certain policy issues. They have increasingly unfavorable views of each other, too.

It is worth unpacking this trend. First, the "long term" refers to a period that is measured in decades. This means that certain partisan divisions were visible at least by the 2000s and in many cases by the

1990s or even 1980s. "Internally homogeneous" means that each party is more consistently on "one side" of an issue—that is, Democrats are more consistently liberal and Republicans more consistently conservative. "More distant" means that, on average, Democrats and Republicans have become more different from each other or farther apart on some underlying ideological dimension.

These changes are tectonic in the sense that they are slow-moving and, like the shifts of tectonic plates in the earth's crust, accumulate to alter the landscape. These changes travel under different labels, such as "partisan sorting" or "partisan polarization," but the upshot is the same: a growing alignment between people's party identification and certain demographic attributes and political views.

For example, political science research and public opinion data shows that Democrats and Republicans increasingly diverge in their self-described political ideology. Between 1994 and 2020, the percentage of Democrats who called themselves liberal increased from 25 percent to 51 percent, and the percentage of Republicans who called themselves conservative increased from 58 percent to 75 percent—although substantial fractions of both parties still call themselves "moderates" (as of 2020, 35% of Democrats and 20% of Republicans).[12]

Moreover, Democrats and Republicans increasingly differ demographically, including by gender, race, and religiosity. For example, compared to earlier periods of time, men have become less likely, and women more likely, to identify with the Democratic Party. African Americans, Hispanic Americans, and Asian Americans have also become more likely to identify with the Democratic Party. And especially among white Americans, religiously observant people and evangelical Protestants (not mutually exclusive groups, to be sure) have become more likely to identify as Republican. The exact magnitude and timing of these trends differs; for instance, the shifts among African Americans were larger and occurred much earlier than shifts among Hispanic Americans.[13]

Democrats and Republicans increasingly diverge on many political issues, too. Between 1972 and 2016, for example, Democrats and Republicans came to take more distinctive positions on the role of government in the economy—visible in issues including the overall size of government, whether it should spend more or less on various policy areas, and whether it should play a larger role in regulating economic markets, such as by guaranteeing people jobs or providing health care or health insurance. Polarization on these issues has been driven primarily by growing conservatism in the Republican Party. The parties have also diverged on noneconomic issues. The most obvious one is abortion, with Democrats shifting to the left and Republicans to the right.[14]

These various and growing partisan differences are related, unsurprisingly. One's self-described ideology and views on policy issues are not synonymous—not every person who identifies as "conservative" favors cuts to government spending, for example—but it makes sense that they both exhibit partisan polarization. Polarization by demography and ideology are also linked: the gender gap in party identification has grown because men and women have different views of certain policies, the parties have polarized around those same policies, and thus men and women now differ more in their partisan loyalties.[15]

But this pattern of polarization or sorting does not characterize everything. Catholicism used to be more strongly correlated with party when Catholics were a linchpin of the Democratic-leaning New Deal coalition. Now, Catholics are evenly split between the parties.[16]

Partisan polarization in the public has been led by polarization among politicians and activists. In the first half of the twentieth century, both political parties had an ideologically diverse mix of elected officials and interest group leaders. The Democratic Party had its northern liberals and its southern conservatives; the GOP had its Goldwater conservatives and its liberal Rockefeller Republicans. As time went on, conservative southern Democrats were replaced by Republicans. Ronald Reagan's support of tax cuts and deregulation and opposition to abortion helped to position the GOP more firmly as a party of the right.

As leaders became more ideologically similar within each party, many rank-and-file partisans did too, especially people attentive enough to politics to know where leaders stood. However, because many people are not political junkies, party polarization among citizens has always

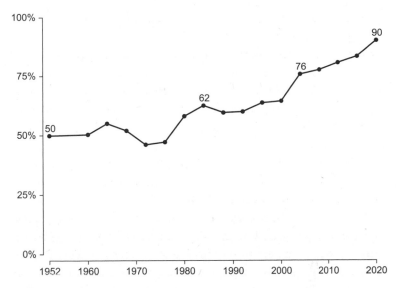

Figure 1.1.

A Growing Number of Americans Perceive Important Differences between the Parties.
Source: American National Election Studies conducted in presidential election years.

been more modest than among political leaders. Many ordinary voters continue to have at least some views that are out of step with the reigning ideas in their party.[17]

Nevertheless, partisan polarization is meaningful and, crucially, it is visible to Americans. When asked, "Do you think there are any important differences in what the Republicans and Democrats stand for?," Americans increasingly say yes (figure 1.1). In 1952, only 50 percent did; by 1984 it was 62 percent, by 2004 it was 76 percent, and in 2020 it was 90 percent. These trends were apparent among men and women, different racial and ethnic groups, both Democrats and Republicans, and so on. In other words, the trend in perceptions of the parties is not due to changes in the demographic composition of the American public, such as its growing racial and ethnic diversity; it is more the result of changes in the parties themselves. As a result, the vast majority of Americans— as well as all kinds of Americans—now reject the old George Wallace quote that there is not a "dime's worth of difference" between the two major parties.[18]

An increasing percentage of voters can place the two parties on the liberal-conservative spectrum with basic accuracy—meaning, they place the Democrats to the left of the Republicans. Moreover, voters tend to see an increasing distance between the parties on various issues, and especially to see the opposing party as more distant from their preferred party.[19]

As the parties have polarized and as people have perceived those differences, they have also come to *feel* differently about the two parties. Thus, partisan divides are not only about substantive political issues—more taxes or fewer taxes, say—but about whether the other party and those who support it are fundamentally good or bad.[20] In a 2019 Pew Research Center survey, substantial fractions of Democrats and Republicans said that members of the other party are more closed-minded, unintelligent, immoral, or unpatriotic than other Americans. For example, 55 percent of Republicans said that Democrats were more immoral than other Americans, and 47 percent of Democrats said this of Republicans.

This dislike of the opposing party has become more prevalent over the past decades—a phenomenon known as "affective polarization" or "negative partisanship."[21] The trend only continued into 2020. In particular, when asked to evaluate the two parties on a 0–100 scale, where 100 indicates the most positive feelings, Americans increasingly rate the opposing party unfavorably—that is, below 50 (figure 1.2). Data from American National Election Study (ANES) surveys shows this trend since the question was introduced in 1978. Between 1978 and 2016, the average rating of the opposing party declined from 48 to 31, while the average rating of a person's own party was largely stable. In online surveys conducted by the ANES since 2012—including in 2020, when the pandemic prevented face-to-face interviewing—unfavorable feelings were even more prevalent, in part because people appear to feel more comfortable expressing negative opinions when they are not being interviewed by another person.[22] In 2012 the average rating of the opposing party among online respondents was 25; in 2020 it was 19. And

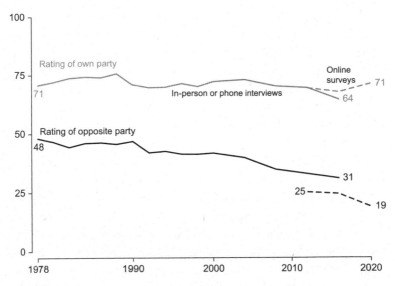

Figure 1.2.
Views of the Opposing Party Are Increasingly Unfavorable. The lines represent average ratings on a 0–100 scale among Democratic and Republicans (including those who lean toward a party). *Source:* American National Election Studies.

because views of respondents' own party rebounded, 2020 saw a record level of affective polarization.

These trends in polarization are significant enough on their own. But they take on even greater significance in the minds of ordinary Americans, whose perceptions of the parties are often exaggerated and stereotyped. For example, Americans see the parties as farther apart on issues than they really are, as well as more demographically distinct from each other. Republicans think that almost half of Democrats are Black, about twice the real number. Democrats think that about 45 percent of Republicans are very wealthy, making $250,000 or more a year; the true number is more like 2 percent. Partisans also exaggerate the extent of affective polarization itself: they think the other party feels more prejudice against their own party than is really true. One reason for these rampant misperceptions seems to be that Americans' mental picture of the political parties includes mainly party leaders, activists, and ideologues—that is, the type of partisans who are most likely to illustrate the pattern of polarization.[23]

These trends in polarization have important implications for elections. One is higher levels of partisanship in presidential approval and voting behavior. Most partisans approve of their own party's president but disapprove of the opposing party's president. Similarly, most partisans vote for their party's candidates up and down the ballot. Presidential candidates typically win 90 percent or more of their party's voters. And split-ticket voting—such as voting for the Republican presidential candidate and the Democratic congressional candidate—is in decline.[24]

A second, and related, implication is the weakening power of other factors that have traditionally affected evaluations of presidents and voting in presidential elections. Most important is the state of the national economy. In the past, incumbent presidents benefited from economic growth and suffered from economic downturns. But strong partisanship has weakened the relationship between the economy and presidential approval, in part because people are loath to give the opposing party's president credit for a growing economy or to punish their own party's president when the economy goes south. Similarly, a more polarized political environment may make presidential election outcomes less sensitive to changes in the economy because so many partisans are unwilling to support the opposing party's candidate under any circumstances.[25] In short, recent election outcomes seem to depend less on achieving shared goals, like peace and prosperity, and more on the clashing views increasingly visible in party politics.

A third implication is that there are smaller shifts in presidential election outcomes from year to year. If factors like the economy do not affect presidential approval or elections as much, and if partisan loyalty is strong, then one year's election outcome is not likely to differ much from the previous outcome.[26]

But smaller shifts do not mean no shifts—and even small shifts can be consequential given partisan parity. In the 1952 ANES survey, 59 percent of Americans identified with or leaned toward the

Democratic Party but only 36 percent identified with or leaned toward the Republican Party—a Democratic advantage of 23 points. But this advantage declined over the years, and by 2016 it was only 7 points (46% vs. 39%). This parity is visible not just at the national level but also in crucial battleground states; in 2016, the outcomes in Pennsylvania, Michigan, and Wisconsin were all decided by less than 1 percentage point. This increasing party parity matters all the more because American elections tend to use winner-take-all rules. A narrow win gets you four years in the White House or a House or Senate seat, but a narrow loss gets you nothing.[27]

It makes sense, then, that these long-term changes are crucial to explaining the dramatic events of 2020 and the violent aftermath of a narrowly decided election.

Sudden Shocks in Identity Politics

Over the short term—years, not decades—the Democratic and Republican parties have rapidly divided on issues related to identity, especially race, ethnicity, nationality, religion, and gender. Of course, some party divisions on these issues were apparent years ago. But recently there has been a sharp increase in the magnitude of these divisions. If the process of partisan sorting or polarization was tectonic, like the slow creep of the earth's crust, the pace of partisan polarization on identity-inflected issues more resembles the shocks of an earthquake. These shocks stem directly from the identity, rhetoric, and decisions of political leaders and how the public has reacted to them. A central part of this story is Trump himself.

One example of an "identity shock" concerned immigration. Since 1965, Gallup has asked Americans, "In your view, should immigration be kept at its present level, increased, or decreased?" From 1965 to 1993, restrictive views became increasingly common, as more and more Americans wanted to decrease immigration (figure 1.3). Since the mid-1990s, restrictive views have receded overall, although there have been occasional spikes in the percent who favored decreasing immigration, such as after the terrorist attacks on September 11, 2001.

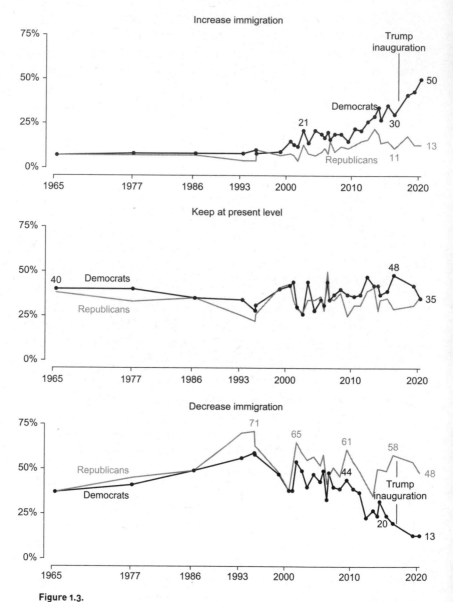

Figure 1.3.
Trends in Democratic and Republican Views of Immigration Levels. *Source*: Gallup polls.

More notable, though, is the pattern of partisan polarization. Early on, there was almost none. In the 1965 poll, which was conducted right before Congress passed the Immigration and Nationality Act of 1965, the views held by Democrats and Republicans were almost identical. That matched the signals that party leaders were sending, as large bipartisan majorities in both the House and Senate voted for this bill. The 1977 poll and the 1986 poll likewise showed little division between parties. But in the mid-1990s, a partisan gap opened up—visible mostly in the larger percentage of Republicans who wanted to decrease immigration—though it disappeared within a few years. In a February 1999 poll, for example, roughly equal numbers of Democrats (7%) and Republicans (9%) wanted to increase immigration. Only beginning in the early 2000s was there any consistent partisan gap, with Democrats generally being more open to immigration than Republicans. For example, in a poll conducted in June 2016, 30 percent of Democrats wanted to increase immigration, compared to 11 percent of Republicans.

In the four years since that 2016 poll, however, there has been a sea change in Democratic attitudes. While Republican support for increasing immigration moved up only slightly, to 13 percent in 2020, the percentage of Democrats who wanted to increase immigration shot up from 30 percent in 2016 to 50 percent in 2020. This produced much more polarization in a very short time. The gap in Democratic and Republican support for increasing immigration was 2 points in 1999 and 19 points in 2016—a 17-point increase in polarization. Between 2016 and 2020, there was a 20-point increase (from 17 to 37). In other words, more polarization occurred in those four years then in the previous seventeen. That is what a sudden shock looks like.

The same pattern characterized attitudes on other immigration topics and identity-inflected issues: any longer-term partisan gap quickly became much larger. One set of survey questions that captured this gap focused on how Americans explain the disadvantages facing Black Americans and specifically whether they attribute those disadvantages more to Black Americans' lack of effort or to structural forces like slavery or discrimination. For example, one question asks whether people agree or disagree that "Generations of slavery and discrimination have created conditions that make it difficult for Blacks to work their way out of the lower class."[28] Since the 1990s, white Democrats have been more likely than white Republicans to attribute racial inequality to structural forces. Thus, party differences on these questions are not brand new. Nevertheless, in surveys conducted in 2016 and after, there was a sharp increase among Democrats in their endorsement of structural explanations for racial inequality, but virtually no change among Republicans. Democrats also became more liberal on other questions related to civil rights for African Americans. And they became more favorable to Islam and Muslims.[29]

On other identity issues, recent partisan polarization has been more symmetrical, with both parties moving away from each other. For instance, Democrats have become more sympathetic to claims of sexual harassment while Republicans have become less so. For example, in 2008, 73 percent of Democrats disagreed with the statement "Women who complain about harassment cause more problems than they solve." By 2018, that had increased to 82 percent. By contrast, the percentage of Republicans who disagreed dropped from 52 percent to 39 percent. There was also an increase in the percentage of Democrats who disagreed with the statement "When women demand equality these days they are actually seeking special favors" (from 71% to 78%). Republicans went in the opposite direction (from 49% to 39%).[30]

Meanwhile, on many other issues not as closely tied to racial, ethnic, and gender identities, partisan polarization over this period was more muted. In 2016, the two parties were 63 points apart on the question of whether the government should provide universal health care and in 2020 they were 71 points apart. Polarization increased even less on the question of whether abortion should be legal. In 2016, 51 percent of Democrats said abortion should be legal in all cases, compared to 9 percent of Republicans; in 2020 those fractions were nearly the same, 53 percent and 9 percent.[31]

What has brought about this partisan polarization specifically on identity-inflected issues? The chief explanation, as it was for the more general pattern of partisan polarization, has to do with the political leaders who provide cues for ordinary voters. Dating back to the 1930s, activists and leaders within the Democratic and Republican parties diverged on civil rights for African Americans. In the 1980s, activists and leaders within the parties diverged on immigration as well. In 1986, when Congress passed the Immigration Reform and Control Act—which, among other things, legalized undocumented immigrants who had arrived in the country before 1982—there was much more Republican opposition than there was when Congress passed the 1965 immigration bill. Even though Ronald Reagan supported and ultimately signed the bill, the majority of House Republicans opposed it. Although it took time, those differences among political elites were gradually reflected in public opinion, such as opinion on immigration in the 1990s and early 2000s.[32]

The more recent and rapid transformation began with the campaigns and presidency of Barack Obama. Obama's status as the first African American president helped clarify the partisan politics of race in a new way, despite years of partisan debates about racialized issues ranging from affirmative action to welfare programs. Even though scholars found that Obama actually talked about race less than other recent Democratic presidents, his mere presence in the Oval Office changed how Americans perceived the parties' positions on racial issues. They came to see larger differences between the Democratic and Republican parties and, in particular, to believe that the Democratic Party was more supportive of government action to help African Americans. Moreover, people's racial attitudes became significant predictors of Americans' attitudes toward almost anything connected to Obama. For example, racial attitudes were much more strongly associated with support for Obama's health care reform proposal than the one Bill Clinton had proposed in 1993. Racial attitudes also predicted attitudes toward figures in his administration, such as Hillary Clinton, as well as Americans' party identification and their votes in both the presidential and midterm elections during Obama's tenure. During his tenure, police killings of African Americans and the resulting Movement for Black Lives also helped push the Democratic Party (and perhaps Obama himself) toward more liberal positions on racial issues.[33]

The rise of Donald Trump was even more consequential for polariza-tion on identity-inflected issues. Trump put these issues at the center of his presidential campaign and talked about them in a more inflamma-tory way than most politicians. During his campaign he was con-demned, including by fellow Republicans, when he called for a ban on Muslims traveling to the United States and a database of Muslims living in the country, when he declined to disavow the support of Ku Klux Klan grand wizard David Duke and other white nationalists, and when he said he would not get fair treatment in a lawsuit because the judge was of Mexican descent—a remark that House Speaker Paul Ryan said was "the textbook definition of a racist comment."[34] Trump's casually sexist treatment of women emerged multiple times during the cam-paign, most infamously in the *Access Hollywood* tape in which Trump was recorded describing kissing women and grabbing their genitalia without their consent.

Hillary Clinton's campaign made the contrast with Trump very clear. Her positions on racial issues were more explicit and liberal than Obama's—one of her first speeches as a candidate discussed systemic racism—and she frequently criticized Trump for his treatment of women. As a result, voters came to see even larger differences between the parties on racial issues than they had under Obama. And Americans' attitudes on issues like immigration, the treatment of Muslims, racial inequality, and sexual harassment were more strongly associated with voting for Trump in the primary and general elections than in other recent elections. In short, political cues, especially from Trump, helped make identity-inflected issues a more polarizing force.[35]

That only continued into Trump's presidency. Indeed, the rapid shifts among Democrats, such as their increasingly positive views of immigra-tion, were likely due to President Trump's push for restrictions on im-migration. As political science research has shown, people form political opinions not only by taking cues from their political allies but also by reacting against their political enemies.[36] Democrats' extraordinary ani-mosity toward Trump meant that any Democrats with conservative positions on issues like immigration confronted the incongruity of op-posing Trump but sharing, at least to some degree, his positions on identity-inflected issues. The easiest way for these Democrats to resolve this incongruity was to shift their positions away from Trump's. Indeed, even before he became president, Trump's push for a U.S.-Mexico border wall appeared to make it less popular among Democrats.[37]

This increasing alignment of partisan politics and identity politics has transformed the Democratic Party. For many years, Democratic politicians had to manage tensions within its coalition between African Americans and white Democrats with liberal views on racial issues on the one hand and a significant number of white Democrats with conservative views on the other. Politicians did this by maintaining support for civil rights but also sending racially conservative signals—for instance, presidential candidate Bill Clinton's 1992 criticism of the rap artist and political activist Sister Souljah for her comments about white people, including a song in which she said, "If there are any good white people, I haven't met them." Even in 2012, a large number of white Obama voters expressed conservative views on identity-inflected issues, attributing racial inequality to African Americans' lack of effort or opposing a path to citizenship for undocumented immigrants. But the defection of those voters to Trump in 2016, as well as the subsequent shifts in Democratic attitudes during Trump's presidency, lessened the intraparty coalitional tension for Democrats. Democratic candidates could support immigration or express concern about the Black Americans killed by police officers with less fear of alienating many Democratic voters. This is not to say that Democrats speak with one voice or are uniformly progressive on identity-inflected issues. Nevertheless, the contemporary Democratic Party is much different than the one that Bill Clinton or even Barack Obama led.

Political Priorities

The third element of our argument centers on Americans' *political priorities*. As early as 2019, Americans prioritized the same identity-inflected issues that have come to define our politics. Here, political priorities refer to the issues that people think are important. People have opinions on many issues, of course, but do not care equally about all of them. When an issue is important to people, they are more likely to take action on that issue, vote based on candidates' positions on the issue, and so on. The importance attached to issues is relevant not just to individual voters but also to the shape of political conflict overall. If the most important issues are the ones Americans disagree on, then more conflict is likely to result. Politics gets angrier when people deeply care about their disagreements.[38]

To gauge Americans' political attitudes and priorities throughout the 2020 campaign, we conducted one of the largest survey projects fielded during an election campaign. This project, called Nationscape, interviewed about 500,000 Americans between July 2019 and January 2021. We will draw on this project throughout the book—to map trends, compare opinions among groups of Americans, shed light on what factors affected choices at the ballot box, and ascertain political priorities.

It can be challenging to measure political priorities, however. Surveys routinely ask people to rate the importance of various issues, but it is not clear that this approach generates meaningful responses. People who rate an issue as more important, for example, do not appear to rely more on that issue when they choose between candidates.[39]

A better way to measure political priorities is what we might call a "show, don't tell" strategy. Within Nationscape, we designed an experiment that allowed people to reveal, or show, which issues they care about rather than simply asking them to tell us.[40] In this survey, we asked people whether they supported or opposed forty-four policies, such as instituting universal background checks for gun purchases, raising the minimum wage to $15 an hour, and providing a path to citizenship for undocumented immigrants. We also asked about some non-policy considerations, such as impeaching Trump and electing a woman or gay man to the White House. Then we randomly selected items from that list and presented respondents with two competing "packages" of between two and four policies. One package could have been instituting universal background checks, raising the minimum wage, and not providing a path to citizenship. The other package would have the opposite positions on those three issues. The packages sometimes had exclusively liberal or conservative positions and sometimes a mix (as in this example). The point is that respondents had to choose which package they preferred. Respondents saw ten sets of packages and had to make ten choices. (More information on the survey and the experiment appears in the appendix to this chapter.)

By examining these choices across respondents, we generate the "revealed importance" of each issue. Revealed importance captures how much more likely people are to choose a set of policies when the set includes that particular issue. The higher the importance, the higher the priority Americans attach to that issue.

So what issues do Americans care about? It is instructive to focus initially on the salient issues during the Trump presidency: whether to impeach Trump, immigration policy, taxes for both the middle and upper classes, the role of the government in health care, whether transgender people should be able to serve in the military, trade policy, and paid maternity leave. All of these reflect priorities for Trump and were the subject of debate between Trump and Democrats. Altogether, there were sixteen specific policies included in the Nationscape survey experiments that were relevant to these issues.

Figure 1.4 presents the revealed importance of these sixteen issues. Specifically, this figure shows the increase in the share of people who choose a package of issues when their position on a particular issue is included in the package. For example, the revealed importance of "impeaching Trump," 0.35, means that when a set contained the respondents' position on this issue (whether for or against impeaching Trump), 67.5 percent of people chose that set and 32.5 percent did not, for a difference of 35 percent.

The results from the 2019 surveys show that in the run-up to the election year, far and away the most important issue to Americans—Democrats and Republicans alike—was the impeachment of Trump (figure 1.4). Below impeachment were a number of policies related to immigration: whether to deport all undocumented immigrants, build the border wall with Mexico, separate children from undocumented

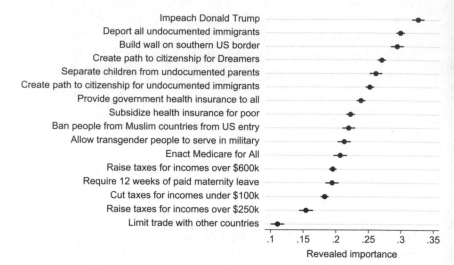

Figure 1.4.

Revealed Importance of Selected Salient Issues during the Trump Presidency. The graph displays estimates of revealed importance and 95% confidence intervals. *Source:* Democracy Fund + UCLA Nationscape surveys (July–December 2019).

parents at the border, and create a path to citizenship. Different policies for the government's role in health insurance, all of which were debated in the Democratic primary, follow next. Everything else was less important, including tax policy and trade, despite the debates over the 2017 tax cuts passed by Republicans and the tariffs and other restrictions on trade enacted by the Trump administration.

Thus, Americans' political priorities as of 2019 were focused on some of the most partisan and divisive issues of that time, and especially those with the additional emotional charge of identity politics. Indeed, the full results from the experiment—presented in the appendix to this chapter—show that these issues were as important as, if not more important than, radical policies that we included for comparison, including complete bans on abortion and guns. Of course, we do not know how long these issues have been important, since our experiments began only in 2019. But in the year and a half that the Nationscape survey was in the field, these priorities were remarkably stable. This suggests that these priorities are long standing and some may even have predated the Trump presidency.

One implication is that existing partisan divisions were magnified by how people defined their priorities. The types of policies where Democrats and Republicans might find some common ground were not as important as those where they strongly disagreed. When we compared the revealed importance of all forty-four issues to the partisan polarization in opinion on those issues, the relationship was positive: the farther apart Democrats and Republicans were, the more important the issue was to Americans overall.

A second implication, which we explore in later chapters, is that people whose issue positions aligned with their party's ideology—Democrats who took a liberal position, Republicans who took a conservative position—tended to care more about those issues than did people whose positions were out of step with their party. This also helped lock in partisan divisions. If partisans who were out of step, such as the substantial number of Republicans who favored tax increases on the wealthy or raising the minimum wage, cared deeply about those issues, then there would have been more potential for cross-party coalitions or for an enterprising Democratic candidate to steal away those voters and weaken partisan loyalty. But instead, the issues that Democrats and Republicans cared about tended to keep them in the party's fold—and intensify conflict between the parties.

A CALCIFIED 2020

It was far from obvious that the idea of "calcified politics" would ultimately apply to the 2020 presidential campaign. The events leading up to the election seemed like they could create big political changes. After Trump's unexpected victory in 2016, his presidency brought continuous chaos and controversy, culminating in impeachment in early 2020. As Democrats stepped up to challenge him, the party faced a crowded primary field but no dominant front-runner. Then came a global pandemic and economic recession. In the midst of all that, a brutal murder led to historic protests for racial justice. To many, the election year was one of superlatives—"the worst," "the craziest," and so on.[41]

And yet these events did not create the expected political changes. People's attitudes toward Trump shifted only slightly, the Democratic primary resolved quickly, and much of the impact of the racial justice protests on public opinion proved ephemeral. In key battleground states, the election was closer than in 2016. In short, the drama coincided with a great deal of political stasis. But at the same time, one big thing did change: the person who is the nation's president.

Thus, a story about the 2020 election has to address two questions: why Trump lost, but also why the election was so close. The tectonic shifts in the two political parties, the identity shocks of the past decade, and Americans' political priorities all help to answer those questions.

The story begins with the Trump presidency (chapter 2). When Trump took office there was speculation that he would not be a conventional Republican but instead an economic populist willing to embrace heterodox ideas like raising taxes on the wealthy or enacting new spending for the country's infrastructure. But in fact, he governed mostly like a traditional conservative. He cut taxes, especially on the wealthy; he weakened and hollowed out the federal bureaucracy; and he proposed increases in defense spending but large cuts in other discretionary spending. In other words, Trump did not disrupt the ongoing tectonics of partisan polarization—instead, he reinforced them.

If President Trump seemed to cast aside the economic populism implicit in his campaign, he certainly embraced his campaign's other focus: a hard-line agenda around identity. Trump moved quickly to limit travel from certain Muslim-majority countries, ramp up deportation of undocumented immigrants, and build a wall at the Mexican border. He pursued controversial measures like the separation of immigrant children from their families. When opportunities arose to pursue less restrictive policies—even popular ones like providing a pathway to citizenship for undocumented immigrants who were brought to the country as children—Trump sided with the hard-liners in his party and rejected those opportunities. Ultimately, Trump's actions as president furthered what his campaign had already started to accomplish: coupling partisanship with views on identity-inflected issues.

Trump's actions helped ensure that he remained a chronically unpopular president, which was an important impediment to his reelection (chapter 3). Even before his election, he was an unpopular person and candidate. His tenure in the White House did little to change that. Because he governed as a representative only of the GOP and especially its hard-line faction, he did little to increase his appeal beyond his party, which he was probably going to need, given his narrow victory in 2016. Of course, partisan polarization limits how popular any contemporary president can hope to be. But small and potentially consequential shifts in popularity are possible, and Trump was never able to lift his popularity even above the 50 percent mark.

But at the same time, Trump's approval rating showed no major decline, despite his many scandals, incendiary remarks, and governing missteps. In fact, Trump's approval was more stable than any other president's in the age of opinion polling. Two reasons were partisan polarization and Republicans' political priorities. Partisan polarization helped ensure that Republicans stuck by Trump's side through the scandals and through impeachment—especially because Trump's conventional conservatism satisfied most Republicans and because few Republicans wanted to do anything to help the Democratic Party. As Paul Ryan said when he called Trump's remark about the Hispanic judge "racist" but then backed Trump over Hillary Clinton anyway, "I believe that we have more common ground on the policy issues of the day and we have more likelihood of getting our policies enacted with him than with her."[42]

Republicans' political priorities mattered, too. Not only did most Republicans oppose Trump's impeachment and favor the linchpins of his identity agenda, but they also considered these issues to be top priorities. The smaller number of Republicans who opposed Trump's agenda did not appear to care as deeply about the issues on which they disagreed with Trump. Trump did not necessarily make the party more conservative on immigration in the sense of shifting overall GOP opinion. But he was clearly more responsive to the party's hard-liners, who cared most about the issue. The party's more moderate voices were increasingly marginalized.

By the beginning of the election year, then, Trump was not in an ideal position for reelection. Despite a robust economy, his approval rating was lower than that of all the incumbent presidents who went on to reelection. But steadfast support within the GOP kept him from being a massive underdog.

A lot, then, turned on whom the Democrats would nominate to challenge him (chapter 4). With the largest field of candidates in any modern primary, no clear front-runner, and tensions between the party's moderate and progressive wings, the scene was set for a protracted and ideologically polarizing battle. But this did not happen. Like Hillary Clinton before him, Biden showed that a multiracial coalition of supporters could help him withstand stumbles in the early caucus and primary states. The ideological battle mostly fizzled as many Democrats, including eventually Biden's opponents, were willing to back Biden if it meant getting rid of Trump.

Again, partisan polarization and Democratic priorities helped the party achieve a quicker resolution to the primary than many anticipated. The growing ideological homogeneity within the party meant that there was actually a great deal of consensus on policies. Most Democratic primary voters took liberal positions on most issues, regardless of which candidate they supported. Moreover, Democrats' political priorities reflected their deep dislike of Trump and their overwhelming opposition to his agenda and especially to his identity agenda. This made the party even more committed to defeating Trump.

As Biden sewed up the nomination, two things happened that seemed destined to reshape the election: the COVID-19 pandemic (chapter 5) as well as the murder of George Floyd by Minneapolis police officer Derek Chauvin and the national protests that resulted (chapter 6). Politically speaking, the pandemic was a potential risk to Trump's reelection bid, but it also offered him an opportunity: to rally the country and work together to defeat a deadly virus. It was an opportunity he did not take. After a brief period in March 2020 during which he warned

Americans of the pandemic's seriousness and helped create truly bipartisan concern about the virus, he pivoted and began downplaying the virus, opposing countermeasures, and pushing to reopen businesses even as cases mounted. This ensured that the partisan polarization that characterized so many other issues came to characterize COVID-19 as well. It also meant that Trump, unlike many state governors and world leaders, did not see his approval rating increase. Moreover, his intended case for reelection—the country's economy under his tenure—became much harder to make.

The consequences of Floyd's murder for politics and public opinion followed a similar trajectory. Immediately after Floyd's killing on May 25, 2020, there was a bipartisan consensus condemning Chauvin. This led to sharp shifts in public opinion: more favorable views of African Americans and the Black Lives Matter movement and less favorable views of the police. But two things changed. First, Floyd's murder stayed in the news only as long as the national protests continued. By the end of July, the protests had dwindled and the news coverage with it. Second, Trump and his allies seized on the few instances of violence at the protests to change the subject and portray the protestors themselves as the threat. And so, as with COVID-19, the consensus disappeared and Democrats and Republicans moved farther apart once again. This only increased the ongoing alignment between partisan politics and identity politics.

That polarization continued into the fall campaign (chapter 7). While Biden's message centered on the pandemic and country's economic struggles, Trump sought to portray the country as on an upswing, one threatened by Biden and the "Radical Left." Little altered the basic state of the horse race. Partisans solidly backed their party's candidate throughout the fall. The usual campaign events, such as the candidate debates, did not shift Biden's lead. Neither did the more dramatic events, such as the death of Supreme Court justice Ruth Bader Ginsburg, her replacement by Amy Coney Barrett, and Trump's serious battle with COVID-19. But there was a widening gap between the candidates in another respect: money. Trump struggled to match Biden's spending, which meant that Biden's ads dominated the airwaves.

When the votes were finally counted, one thing was clear: calcified politics had produced a surprisingly close outcome, despite a surge in voter turnout (chapter 8). Party loyalty kept the election much closer than the Biden landslide that preelection polls suggested. Across counties and states, the 2020 results were strongly correlated with the 2016 results. To be sure, the small differences between the 2016 and 2020 results were enough to make Biden the winner, and Trump's low approval rating was undoubtedly important here. But several things kept the election close. One was the unusual state of the economy. By Election Day, the worst of the recession had passed. Although the country's employment numbers and economic output had not fully recovered, people's incomes were up thanks to large stimulus checks from the federal government. The implications of the economy for the election were therefore ambiguous. Additionally, the outcome of the election did not appear much affected by local conditions that could have increased Biden's lead, such as the size of his advertising advantage on television or the number of COVID-19 deaths in a county. Another factor was Trump's support among conservatives of all stripes, including, to many observers' surprise, conservative Latinos and African Americans.

To many, the closeness of Biden's win stemmed from the racial justice protests. People blamed the fact that a small number of protests were accompanied by violence, or the fact that some progressives seized on George Floyd's murder to push for "defunding" the police. But there is little clear evidence for this. If anything, it appears Biden did better in counties with protests, even ones at which there were injuries, arrests, or property damage. And views of the police and of the protests seemed more a consequence of partisanship than a cause of how people voted.

The election's aftermath turned a contentious race into a full-blown crisis (chapter 9). Trump had long promised to challenge the outcome if he lost and he followed through, filing dozens of long-shot lawsuits that gained little traction in court. He unsuccessfully pressured state election officials to "find votes" for him and unsuccessfully pressured the Department of Justice to investigate what he claimed was massive election fraud. But if Trump was wrong in thinking these officials would back him, he was right in betting that rank-and-file Republicans would.

It appeared that GOP fealty to Trump might change after the riot. Trump's approval rating among Republicans finally dropped and a larger number of congressional Republicans supported the second impeachment effort than had the first. But with time, sentiment in the party shifted. Ashli Babbitt became a martyr as Trump and his allies sought to rewrite the history of January 6. Republican support for prosecuting the rioters declined. Once again, a singular and tragic event—an attack on the U.S. Capitol—could not transcend partisan politics. Meanwhile, Republican leaders in the states enacted new obstacles to voting and rewrote laws to take power away from the kinds of local election officials who did not cave to Trump's pressure after the election.

The GOP's actions illustrate the incentive created by an era of calcified politics and partisan parity: find any way possible to bend the rules in your favor and target your opponents. When elections and even control of the government hinge on a few states or a few thousand votes, and you think the other party is not just wrong on policy but also immoral and unpatriotic, it becomes easier to justify doing whatever it takes to win, regardless of its democratic merit. Many partisans will countenance any measure targeted at the opposition, perhaps even violence. When the 2020 election came to its bitter end, Republicans chose this route rather than reckon with the party's loss and rethink its direction.

But it did not have to be that way. Far more Republicans accepted Mitt Romney's loss in 2012, and far more Democrats accepted Clinton's in 2016. No one was told to "fight like hell" and then invaded the Capitol. Violence and democratic decay are not an inevitable consequence of calcified politics. The future depends on what political leaders do when the losses are especially bitter—and whether they will uphold democracy when the bitterness has no end in sight.

2

The Fight

If you think they're going to give you your country back without a
fight, you are sadly mistaken.

—STEVE BANNON, WHITE HOUSE CHIEF STRATEGIST, 2017

IN DECEMBER 2016, Donald Trump finally got something he had
wanted for a long time: he was named *Time* magazine's Person of the
Year. Trump had hung fake pictures of himself on a *Time* cover in his golf
clubs for years and complained vociferously in 2015 when *Time* had named
German chancellor Angela Merkel as Person of the Year instead of him.[1]

When he sat for an interview as part of the 2016 *Time* cover story, the
reporter, Michael Scherer, read Trump what Scherer called "one of
Obama's oft-stated quotes about trying to appeal to the country's better
angels and to fight its tribal instincts." Trump immediately stopped
the interview, went to another room, and returned a minute later with
that morning's copy of the Long Island tabloid *Newsday*. On the front
was an article with the headline "'EXTREMELY VIOLENT' GANG
FACTION." Trump said, "They come from Central America. They're
tougher than any people you've ever met. They're killing and raping
everybody out there. They're illegal. And they are finished." Scherer
noted that Trump sounded like Philippines president Rodrigo Duterte,
who had overseen the extrajudicial killing of thousands of alleged crimi-
nals. Trump responded, "Well, hey, look, this is bad stuff. . . . What are
we supposed to do? Be nice about it?"[2]

This conversation, conducted before Trump took the oath of office,
previewed the tone and approach he would use as president. Trump

arrived in Washington, DC, after years of growing polarization, and his presidency would produce even more polarization. He had just spent months on the campaign trail making inflammatory statements about immigrants and other racial and ethnic minority groups, and then he oriented his presidency around exactly the same issues and rhetoric. "Tribal instincts" were his bread and butter.

Trump had an alternative course of action available to him. His campaign promises also included policies, such as infrastructure investment, that were popular with the broader electorate and had the potential to attract Democratic support. Indeed, these campaign promises had often alarmed mainstream Republicans and traditional conservatives precisely because they flouted party orthodoxy and made common cause with the opposition. But as president, Trump pushed policies that were popular mainly with his own party and, at times, only with the most conservative faction of his party. This was particularly true on immigration, where Trump's hard-line policies earned him plaudits from Fox News personalities but opposition from most Americans. Trump ensured that the political trends we highlighted in chapter 1 would continue: the long-term tectonic polarization in American politics as well as the catalytic "identity shocks" created by his 2016 campaign.

Of course, presidents routinely pursue the priorities of their party rather than those of Americans generally.[3] In this sense, presidents are often reliable partisans and even agents of polarization. Our argument is not that Trump was the first president to pursue policies more popular among his party than among Americans overall. We argue that Trump's policy goals—as reflected in his executive actions and legislative agenda—were *distinctively* unpopular and *distinctively* polarizing compared to those of past presidents.

Moreover, Trump was distinctive in how much he eschewed even lip service to the idea that presidents should signal inclusiveness and seek to represent the country as a whole. Instead, Trump lashed out at anyone he perceived as insufficiently supportive. He attacked opponents with insults, false accusations, and tactics that led to a federal investigation and to his first of two impeachments. He responded to racially charged and even racist events with his own inflammatory language, even when a conciliatory gesture or a rote condemnation of bigotry would have been easy.

Trump's ethos was summed up by his strategist Steve Bannon, speaking a month into his presidency at the Conservative Political Action Conference. Referring to liberals and the media, Bannon said, "If you think they're going to give you your country back without a fight, you are sadly mistaken."

For the first three years of Trump's presidency, the fight was often the point.

"A GOVERNING PARTY"

Trump had ambitious plans for his first 100 days in office. In late October 2016, he outlined a broad legislative agenda, including the Middle Class Tax Relief and Simplification Act, the American Energy and Infrastructure Act, the Repeal and Replace Obamacare Act, and the End Illegal Immigration Act. His agenda combined long-standing GOP priorities with his signature focus on immigration and one issue, infrastructure, that had potential bipartisan appeal. With Republican majorities in both the House and Senate, Trump seemed poised to make progress on this agenda. Although unified government does not necessarily reduce gridlock, especially in an age of polarized parties, it at least gives presidents more influence on legislation.[4]

But Trump also confronted significant obstacles. The Republican majorities in Congress were narrow—typical of an era of partisan parity—which meant the party would have to stick together to pass legislation while simultaneously protecting vulnerable members in the upcoming midterm, when the president's party usually loses seats. Moreover, the GOP was struggling with significant internal divisions. Operating in the opposition under Obama helped make those divisions less apparent at times. But as House Speaker Paul Ryan put it in March 2017, "We have to go from being an opposition party to a governing party." Part of the challenge was that congressional Republicans' agenda, which they called "A Better Way," only partially overlapped with Trump's. It included things like repealing Obamacare and tax cuts, but nothing about immigration or infrastructure.[5]

The obstacles confronting Trump went beyond uniting the GOP. Despite the growing polarization in Congress, most major legislation is still the product of bipartisanship; a bill like the Patient Protection and Affordable Care Act (aka Obamacare), which passed with no Republican votes, was the exception, not the rule.[6] The fifty-two-seat Senate majority meant that Trump could lose only two Republican senators to pass a bill without Democratic support. And that would work only in the confines of the budget reconciliation process. The Senate's sixty-vote filibuster threshold meant that Trump needed support from eight Democratic senators to pass other legislation, unless he could convince the Senate to end the filibuster rule.

Like many presidents before him, Trump had two strategic imperatives. The first was to focus on issues where Trump's position was already popular with voters, which would then put pressure on lawmakers to support the president's agenda. Most presidents have tried to do this. A study of over forty years of public appeals by presidents found they tended to focus on issues where the president's position was already supported by a majority of Americans. The same has been true for executive actions; on average, presidents have taken unilateral steps when their goal was already popular.[7]

The second imperative for Trump was to win over members of Congress and executive branch officials. In a famous passage, the political scientist Richard Neustadt wrote that "the essence of a president's persuasive task is to convince such men that what the White House wants of them is what they ought to do for their sake and on their authority."[8] The logic is straightforward: the president cannot simply command legislators to obey him. Trump would need to cultivate relationships with his allies and use the carrots and sticks at his disposal.

Trump largely ignored these imperatives, however. Instead, he focused on policies that were popular mainly among Republicans. At times, the unpopular agenda was Trump's own doing, especially when it came to issues like immigration. At other times, Trump seemed willing to consider a more popular idea—such as allowing undocumented immigrants brought to the United States as children to live and work here without fear of deportation—but allowed himself to be steered away from it by die-hard conservatives within the Republican Party.

Trump's policy agenda showed how an us-versus-them politics was not just his brand but also his mode of governance. As a result, he did not achieve very much legislatively, especially given the opportunity afforded by unified Republican government. What he did achieve was often unpopular. In fact, he could have ended up with an even less popular policy record if not for instances when Republicans in Congress ignored policies that Trump was pushing and, in essence, tried to save Trump from himself. This was a central irony of Trump's presidency: the missteps that kept him from building a more popular record also kept him from building an even more unpopular one.

How Popular Was Trump's Agenda?

A simple visualization shows public opinion about the policy choices Trump could have made relative to those he did make (figure 2.1). The figure is based on a March 2017 Gallup poll that asked Americans whether they supported or opposed these Trump agenda items:

- Require companies to provide family leave for parents after the birth of a child
- Enact a $1 trillion program to improve U.S. infrastructure, such as roads, bridges, and tunnels
- Significantly cut federal income taxes for the middle class
- Provide federal funding for school-choice programs that allow students to attend any private or public school
- Increase military spending by $54 billion
- Replace the Affordable Care Act, also known as Obamacare, with a new health care plan
- Impose a 90-day ban on issuing new U.S. travel visas for citizens of six Muslim-majority nations
- Stop all refugee resettlement in the U.S. for 120 days
- Reduce the corporate income tax rate
- Begin the construction of a wall between the U.S. and Mexico
- Authorize construction of the Keystone XL and Dakota Access pipelines

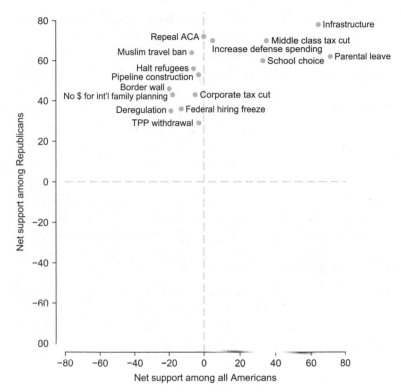

Figure 2.1.
Views of Trump's Agenda among All Americans and Only Republicans. *Source:* Gallup Poll, March 9–29, 2017.

- Eliminate U.S. funding for international organizations that promote or provide abortions
- Put a hiring freeze on most civilian jobs in the federal government
- Require that for every new federal government regulation put in place, two existing regulations must be eliminated
- End U.S. participation in the Trans-Pacific Partnership or TPP

The figure compares net support among Republicans (the vertical axis) to net support among all Americans (the horizontal axis), where net support is the percent supporting minus the percent opposing each proposal.[9] All of these policy items were more popular than unpopular among Republicans, which places them at the top of the figure.

By contrast, among all Americans, there was wide variation in the popularity of these policies. Most Americans favored parental leave (81% supported and 10% opposed) and an infrastructure program (76% to 12%). Americans also tended to favor a middle-class tax cut (61% to 21%) and federal funding of school choice programs (59% to 26%). Americans were roughly evenly divided on increasing military spending and replacing Obamacare. On everything else, Americans were more opposed than supportive, including on Trump mainstays such as building a border wall, restricting immigration from certain Muslim-majority countries, and halting resettlement of refugees. The border wall actually became unpopular because Trump advocated for it in his presidential campaign, which led many Democrats to oppose it.[10] Trump could have steered around divisive issues like the border wall and pursued policies, especially infrastructure and parental leave, that united both his party and all Americans. Or he could have tried to do both. Instead, he focused on the things that mainly Republicans wanted instead of the things that most Americans wanted.

Executive Actions and Rule-Making

This tendency was visible in Trump's executive actions. Before he became president, Trump had criticized Obama's use of unilateral action. But once in office presidents are always tempted by unilateralism, which gives them an avenue for policymaking when Congress is stalemated and enables them to centralize policymaking in the White House rather than delegate it to federal agencies.[11]

Thus, Trump began his presidency with a string of executive actions. On January 20, the day he was inaugurated, Trump issued an executive order that allowed the Department of Health and Human Services to waive or defer Obamacare requirements. On January 23, he withdrew the United States from the TPP, issued a federal hiring freeze, and prohibited giving U.S. foreign aid to any health provider who discussed abortion as a family planning option. On January 24, he announced his intent to allow the construction of the Keystone and Dakota pipelines. On January 25, he issued an executive order directing the construction of the border wall. On January 27, he ordered reductions in refugee admission and suspended entry of citizens from Iran, Iraq, Libya, Somalia, Sudan, Syria, and Yemen. On January 30, he ordered federal agencies to repeal two existing regulations for every new regulation they implemented.

What these orders had in common was their popularity among Republicans and unpopularity among the general public. The unpopularity was evident not only in the March 2017 poll but also in polling that was conducted around the time the orders were issued. For example, in a February 2017 Quinnipiac poll, the majority of Americans opposed suspending travel from these mostly Muslim countries (46% support vs. 51% oppose) and suspending the refugee program (37% to 60%).

This same pattern characterized Trump's later executive orders as well as rule-making directed by his appointees at federal agencies. A good illustration of Trump's decision not to pursue broadly popular policies opposed by a hard-line faction of his party was his administration's immigration policy. One immediate question for Trump concerned the fate of the Obama-era program called Deferred Action for Childhood Arrivals (DACA). The program allowed undocumented immigrants who were brought to the country as children and met other criteria to receive renewable two-year relief from the threat of deportation and apply for a work permit. Obama created DACA in 2012 via executive order after Congress had failed to take legislative action. A group of Republican state attorneys general sued to overturn the program and a federal court suspended the program in 2015. Trump appeared to agree. When he announced his candidacy in June 2015, he said he would "immediately terminate President Obama's illegal executive order on immigration."

Initially, Trump waffled when it came to actually ending DACA. Its beneficiaries, known as Dreamers, are a sympathetic group because they came to the United States through no decision of their own and, after years in the country, had integrated into American life and often had no place to return to in their country of origin. Some have no memory of their country of origin and do not speak the common language spoken there. Trump seemed to recognize this, saying not long after his election that Dreamers "got brought here at a very young age, they've gone to school here. Some were good students. Some have wonderful jobs. And they're in never-never land because they don't know what's going to happen." Soon after his inauguration, he pledged to "deal with DACA with heart."[12] This was the politically popular thing to do. In a March 2017 Suffolk University poll, 66 percent of Americans wanted Trump to continue to protect the Dreamers from deportation and only 22 percent wanted him to remove this protection.

But Trump bowed under pressure from conservative hard-liners. In June 2017, a group of state attorneys general sent Trump a memo asking him to rescind DACA. In August, Trump's attorney general, Jeff Sessions, said that the Justice Department would not defend the program in court. On September 5, Trump rescinded DACA.

The very next week, however, he discussed an agreement with Democratic leaders Nancy Pelosi and Chuck Schumer that would protect Dreamers in exchange for additional border security measures—but, crucially, not a border wall. Once again, this was a popular compromise. In a Quinnipiac poll that asked whether Trump was right or wrong to "agree to work with Democrats to pass a law to grant legal status and work permits to undocumented immigrants who were brought to the U.S. as children in exchange for increased border security," 72 percent said that he was right to work with Democrats. In fact, 76 percent of Republicans thought so, too.[13] However, a potential DACA deal outraged the most anti-immigration figures in politics and media. Rep. Steve King declared that Trump's base was "disillusioned beyond repair." The commentator Ann Coulter suggested that Trump should be impeached. The right-wing website Breitbart called Trump "Amnesty Don."[14] The hard-liners carried the day. Trump immediately downplayed the significance of his conversations with Schumer and Pelosi, and no such deal was cut.

Four months later, Trump was on the brink of another DACA deal. This proposal was put together by a bipartisan group of senators and included a pathway to citizenship for Dreamers as well as $2.7 billion for border security, this time including $1.6 billion for a border wall. When these senators came to meet Trump at the White House, they found that he had invited a number of conservative allies, who then proceeded to push back on the deal. Trump pushed back himself because the deal continued a program that gave "temporary protected status" to immigrants who could not return to their countries because of conditions like civil war. "Why do we want all these people from shithole countries coming here?" Trump asked. He countered with a plan that paired a path to citizenship for Dreamers with $25 billion for a border wall and reductions in legal immigration. The bipartisan group then revised its plan to incorporate the $25 billion figure.[15]

For Trump, the situation at this point was win-win. The bill would have allowed him to credibly claim that he had enacted one of his major campaign promises—securing the border—and passed the sort of immigration reform bill that had eluded past administrations. Trump's recalcitrance had proved valuable, multiplying the amount of spending on border security by a factor of ten. The bill also promised to attract support from Democrats and Republicans in the Senate. By passing the bill, Trump could argue to voters that he really was a deal-maker.

To hard-liners, however, the bill was still unacceptable. They could not countenance citizenship for any group of undocumented immigrants. It was "an amnesty bill," said the conservative group Heritage Action.[16] Trump ultimately agreed with them, calling the compromise a "catastrophe." He refused to support it.

After Trump opposed the deal, it failed in the Senate, six votes short of a filibuster-proof majority. Even Republican senators were disappointed. South Carolina senator Lindsey Graham, normally a defender of Trump, said, "I'm looking for leadership from the White House, not demagoguery." But there was no White House leadership forthcoming, and no further legislative progress on immigration reform in 2018 or 2019.[17] Trump chose to side with a faction of his party rather than pursue policies that were popular with the majority of Americans.

If DACA was a case where certain Republicans pushed Trump toward a more conservative and unpopular position, other parts of Trump immigration policy pushed Republicans toward the same. A good example was Trump's policy of "family separation." Like previous presidents, Trump faced the question of what to do with immigrants apprehended when they crossed the U.S-Mexico border. Unlike previous presidents, Trump ultimately adopted a policy in which every undocumented immigrant adult would be charged and jailed, with children taken from their parents and sent to separate facilities. Even families who arrived at the border lawfully seeking asylum could be separated. Family separation was intended to be a "tough deterrent," said Trump's chief of staff, John Kelly. When asked if separating children from their parents was cruel, he said, "I wouldn't put it quite that way. The children will be taken care of—put into foster care or whatever." Ultimately, more than 5,500 children were separated and forced to live amid poor conditions. Later reports from the Office of the Inspector General at the Department of Health and Human Services described how separation and detention had damaged the mental health of the children. Six children even died in U.S. custody in only six months, even though there had been no deaths in the previous decade. Over two years later, the process of reuniting children and their parents was tragically incomplete. As of October 2020, the parents of 545 children had not been found.[18]

Like the border wall and other Trump immigration policies, family separation was unpopular. In a June 2018 CNN poll, 67 percent disapproved of criminally charging more undocumented immigrants and increasing separations of children from families. In a CBS poll from the same time, 67 percent said that the separation of parents and children was "unacceptable," while only 17 percent said it was acceptable. In an August 2018 CNN poll, Americans were asked whether the government should "do everything to keep families together even if it means that fewer face criminal prosecution." Two-thirds (66%) favored keeping families together, while only 27 percent prioritized prosecution. In a June Quinnipiac poll, 60 percent said the policy was "a violation of human rights." In that poll, only 38 percent approved of Trump's handling of immigration, while 58 percent disapproved.

Taken together, Trump's executive actions were exceptionally unpopular when compared to the executive actions of both Obama and

George W. Bush. On average, the actions of Obama and Bush—at least the ones that were important enough to be polled—elicited more support than opposition. But among sixteen Trump executive actions, fifteen elicited more opposition than support. In fact, thirteen of Trump's executive actions were more unpopular than the least popular executive action taken by either Obama (an attempt to close the facility housing suspected terrorists at the Guantanamo naval base) or Bush (banning the use of federal funds for abortion services abroad). As the political scientists Dino Christenson and Douglas Kriner have written, Trump was "a president who cannot anticipate or does not care about the aggregate public response to his unilateral moves."[19]

Legislative Actions

This same indifference to overall public opinion was evident in the legislative priorities of Trump and congressional Republicans. Instead of focusing on popular policies like infrastructure investment and parental leave, they began the legislative session in 2017 with one paramount goal: repeal Obamacare. Republicans in Congress had, of course, voted to repeal Obamacare many times under Obama, and, of course, Obama had vetoed any such bill that reached his desk. Under Trump, the GOP finally had a real chance. But repealing a policy is one thing and coming up with a new one is another. Research on the administrations of both Ronald Reagan and Margaret Thatcher shows that is especially true when repealing expansions to social welfare policies, which often survive conservative attacks.[20]

Part of the challenge for Trump and congressional Republicans was that the broader party was divided on health care. Few Republicans liked Obamacare specifically, but ordinary Republicans and the GOP donor class disagreed about the government's role in health care generally. In a 2017 survey, 52 percent of GOP donors strongly disagreed that the government should make sure all Americans have health insurance. Only 23 percent of Republican voters disagreed, however. And although Trump had campaigned on Obamacare repeal, his earliest supporters, dating back to the 2016 Republican primary, included a disproportionate number of the Republicans who actually wanted more government involvement in health care. A few weeks after Trump's inauguration, former Republican House Speaker John Boehner, who was in Congress for many of the attempted Obamacare repeals, summarized the party's divisions succinctly: "In the 25 years that I served in the United States Congress, Republicans never, ever, one time agreed on what a health care proposal should look like. Not once."[21]

That comment proved prescient. The first attempt by House Republicans to generate a repeal bill failed because moderates and conservatives in the party could not agree. Trump initially blamed Democrats, but later admitted the real problem was his own party: "You have certain factions. You have the conservative Republicans. You have the moderate Republicans. So you have to get them together, and we need close to a hundred percent. That's a pretty hard thing to get." When the House managed to pass a bill on May 4, 2017—the American Health Care Act (AHCA)—the vote was extremely close (217 to 213) because twenty Republican members joined with all the Democrats to oppose it.[22]

Remarkably, however, Trump undercut House Republicans a few weeks later by criticizing the AHCA. In a lunch with Senate Republicans, who were considering their own bill, he called the House bill "mean" and suggested that it did not do enough to protect Americans who had bought health insurance through the marketplaces created by Obamacare. Trump appeared to want a bill that spent more money and would be "generous" and "kind." This illustrated the challenge of working with Trump, whose wavering positions often left legislative allies in the lurch.[23]

The Senate could not agree on a bill. It rejected several versions before a climactic July 27 vote on a slimmed-down bill known as "skinny repeal." It would have repealed the individual mandate to buy health insurance by zeroing out the penalty for failing to do so, but it would not have altered many other aspects of Obamacare, including the expansion of Medicaid. Nevertheless, all Senate Democrats, even those representing states where Trump had won, as well as three Republicans (Susan Collins, John McCain, and Lisa Murkowski) voted against it, leaving the bill one vote short of passage. The health care push had cost Trump half of his first year in office with nothing to show for it.

Indeed, during the GOP's campaign to repeal Obamacare, the program actually became more popular. In polling by the Kaiser Family Foundation throughout 2016, more Americans opposed Obamacare than supported it. In December 2016, for example, 40 percent supported and 43 percent opposed it. But by August 2017, right after the Senate vote, 52 percent supported and 39 percent opposed it. This net positive rating would continue throughout Trump's term. Dean Rosen, a Republican health care strategist, summed up the party's failure this way: "There was an intellectual simplicity or an intellectual laziness that, for Republicans in health care, passed for policy development. That bit us in the ass when it came to repeal and replace."[24]

After this failure, the GOP turned to tax cuts. There was a clearly popular path here: a tax cut focused on the middle class, as opposed to, say, corporations (see figure 2.1). Trump had signaled his willingness to support a progressive tax bill, even saying during his presidential campaign that he would support raising taxes on the wealthy (although the actual tax plan his campaign released would have reduced taxes on the wealthy). In the Trump White House, Steve Bannon also pushed to increase the top income tax bracket to pay for tax cuts for the middle class and poor. Public opinion polling has shown for years that tax increases on the wealthy are popular. And Trump's success in the 2016 GOP primary was due partly to the roughly one-third of Republicans who supported his unorthodox view and wanted to increase taxes on the wealthy. This was another issue on which GOP voters were far less conservative, on average, than Republican donors and other elites.[25]

But cutting taxes on the wealthy had been Republican orthodoxy for decades. Both Ronald Reagan and George W. Bush pushed for tax cuts that included reductions in taxes on the wealthy. And when George H. W. Bush signed tax increases into law in 1990, it led to a significant backlash within the GOP and motivated the conservative Patrick Buchanan to challenge Bush in the 1992 Republican primary.

It was no surprise, then, that in the GOP tax plan the largest income tax cuts went to the wealthiest Americans. The tax plan also exempted a larger amount of income from federal estate taxes, which would benefit the heirs of wealthy individuals. Furthermore, the plan enacted the largest corporate income tax cut in U.S. history. And unlike with the individual income tax cuts, which expire after ten years, the plan made this corporate tax cut permanent. Perhaps the only popular thing in the bill was something the GOP could not accomplish with the AHCA: the elimination of the individual mandate.[26]

Despite concerns about the benefits for corporations and the wealthy, the bill moved from its initial introduction in the House to Trump's signature in less than two months. On the key roll call votes in the House, no Democrats supported it and roughly a dozen Republicans broke with their party. In the final vote in the Senate, Democrats were again united in opposition while all Republicans voted in favor. When he signed the bill on December 22, Trump said, "It's going to be a tremendous thing for the American people."[27]

Most American people did not think so, however. Polls taken throughout the fall showed that on average only 31 percent of Americans supported the tax bill. Even fewer Americans thought the middle class would benefit from the bill. According to a December 2017 Marist poll, only 21 percent said the bill mostly helped the middle class and even fewer (4%) said it mostly helped the poor. The majority (60%) said it mostly helped the wealthy.

Indeed, both the AHCA and the tax plan stand out as distinctively unpopular compared to many major initiatives from Trump's predecessors (see figure 2.2).[28] This includes various gun control efforts of the early Clinton administration, environmental initiatives such as amendments to the Clean Air Act in 1990 and the cap-and-trade bill that failed in 2009, and economic measures such as increasing the federal minimum wage, the 2009 stimulus, and the tax cuts pushed by President George W. Bush. The Trump-era health care and tax plans were even less popular than more controversial measures, like the Troubled Assets Relief Program (aka the "bank bailout") and the Affordable Care Act.

Perhaps most remarkably, at the time of their passage the 2017 tax cuts were about as unpopular as the tax *increases* that George H. W.

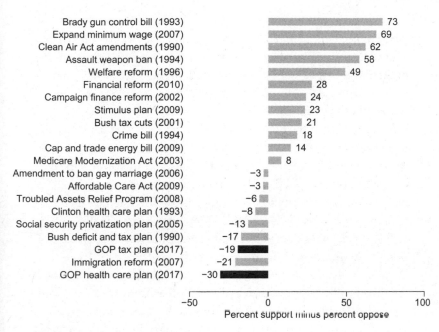

Figure 2.2.
Public Support for Major Legislative Initiatives. Source: Averages from various public polls conducted before and after the passage or debate over each initiative.

Bush supported in 1990. In the months after passage, the tax cuts did become a bit more popular, but not popular in the absolute. An April 2019 Gallup poll found that only 40 percent supported the tax cuts while 49 percent opposed them and 11 percent were uncertain—a level of popularity similar to Bill Clinton's ill-fated 1993 health care plan.

The pattern established in Trump's first year in office did not change that much in the subsequent years of his term. The more popular items on his agenda, infrastructure and parental leave, languished, even as these ideas attracted interest from Democrats on Capitol Hill. For example, after the White House launched what it called "Infrastructure Week" in June 2017, Democratic senator Brian Schatz said that if the Trump administration "had been willing to do a real infrastructure package, then I would have been willing to participate." But Schatz's reference to a "real" package hints at part of the problem: Trump and Democrats did not agree about how to fund such a package, with Democrats objecting to Trump's emphasis on private investment as opposed to federal funding. Congressional Republicans objected as well, particularly to the amount of federal funding that would be required to fund a major infrastructure plan or paid parental leave. Once again, Trump's own party resisted the popular parts of his agenda. Paid parental leave was eventually extended only to federal employees, not the broader workforce. And as infrastructure plans came and went with little progress, "Infrastructure Week" became a running joke among political reporters and commentators—"less a date on the calendar than . . . a 'Groundhog Day'–style fever dream doomed to be repeated."[29]

If Republican resistance to Trump's agenda hindered popular legislation, it also hindered Trump's less popular goals as well. There were many examples. For one, although the GOP could not unilaterally overturn Trump's trade policy, such as the tariffs that he enacted, many congressional Republicans pushed for more-modest tariffs, which were not very popular with Americans anyway. For another, Republicans rejected Trump's more conciliatory approach to Russia, passing new sanctions in July 2017 and criticizing Trump when he stood beside Putin after a 2018 meeting and said he believed Putin's false claims that Russia did not attempt to influence the 2016 U.S. election. Unlike Trump, most Americans favored limiting Russia's power, not cooperation and engagement. A third example was Trump's budget proposals, which routinely proposed large cuts to discretionary spending, including social safety net programs, science research, and education, that went far beyond what congressional Republicans could stomach. Tiny minorities of Americans thought that the government was spending too much on programs like education (6%) or scientific research (9%).[30]

Trump did, however, want the government to spend more on one thing in particular: the border wall. The resulting saga included moments when some congressional Republicans pushed back against Trump, when conservative hard-liners pushed Trump and other Republicans to support the wall, and when Trump's own intransigence put him, and his party, in a damaging situation.

Trump's 2017 executive order could direct the government to use only existing funding to begin constructing a border wall. To do more, Trump needed Congress to appropriate new funding. But Republicans were wary of the border wall's cost. Trump was adamant, saying in August 2017 that he would "close down our government" in order to build the wall. He made the same threat in December 2018 as Congress was rushing to finalize a bill that would fund the government, saying "I will take the mantle" and "I will be the one to shut it down" if the bill did not contain the border wall funding he wanted.[31]

When the funding bill failed in the Senate, the resulting stalemate led to the longest government shutdown on record—thirty-five days, from December 22 to January 25, 2019. And if Trump wanted "the mantle" for the shutdown, Americans certainly gave it to him. In a January 2019 CNN poll, 55 percent said Trump was more responsible for the shutdown, while only 32 percent blamed Democrats in Congress. Trump's net approval rating went from an average of −10 on December 10 (42% approve, 52% disapprove) to 17 on January 26 (39%–56%). His approval rating would improve only after the shutdown ended.[32]

The border wall saga continued after the shutdown. Impatient with Congress, Trump once again resorted to unilateral action, declaring a national emergency in February 2019 so that he could take money approved for other purposes and use it for the wall. This decision was challenged in Congress, where it attracted even some Republican opposition, and in the courts. Although Trump ultimately prevailed, progress was slow. Nearly all of the border wall constructed under Trump just replaced older wall.[33]

The border wall was emblematic of Trump's governing agenda: it was an unpopular goal that Trump struggled to achieve, even with conservative majorities in the House, Senate, and Supreme Court. Indeed, Trump's legislative accomplishments were unusually limited for presidents who benefited from unified control of government for at least part of their term (see figure A2.1).[34]

This is not to say that Trump or the GOP accomplished nothing. Of course, Trump's unilateral efforts changed federal policy, particularly on immigration and trade. Trump and Senate Republicans appointed and confirmed a large number of federal judges—roughly a quarter of the federal judiciary, including three Supreme Court justices.[35]

However, Trump did not accomplish much of what said he wanted to accomplish. And even some of what he and congressional Republicans did accomplish did not have its intended effect. Most notably, eliminating penalties for not purchasing health insurance—a core part of Obamacare's individual mandate—did not lead to the collapse of the law or a massive exodus from the health insurance marketplaces that the law created. Like other expansions of the American welfare state, Obamacare has proven tough to kill.[36]

Clearly the opposition of Democrats played an important role in limiting Trump's ambitions. But divisions among Republicans were also important. This is apparent in how the politics of trade, immigration, and foreign policy played out and in the party's challenges in repealing Obamacare or cutting spending.[37] Trump's priorities and decisions often exacerbated those divisions, particularly on immigration.

The alternative policy agenda for Trump—the one that simultaneously appealed to Republicans and to Americans as a whole, the one that could have attracted Democratic support in Congress and given Trump more legislative success—was not his priority.

LET TRUMP BE TRUMP

Early in the 2016 presidential campaign, Trump's then-campaign manager Corey Lewandowski famously coined the phrase "Let Trump Be Trump." This was not so much a strategy as a capitulation to his boss's refusal to be reined in. After winning the election, however, Trump suggested that he would change. "I can be the most presidential person ever," he said when he took office.[38]

But the office of the presidency had little effect on Trump. Just as in the campaign, Trump's mentality was always "us versus them" and sometimes just "me versus them." Trump's attacks on "them"—his political opponents, women, racial and ethnic minority groups, the media—stoked the country's identity-based divisions and showed Trump's disdain for basic democratic norms.

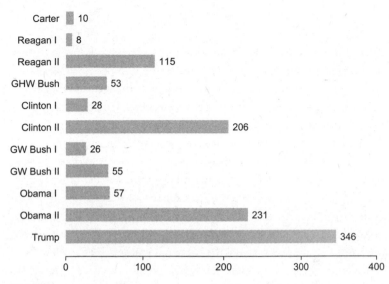

Figure 2.3.
Number of Major *Washington Post* Stories about Presidential Administration Scandals.

Trump's behavior led him to receive more news coverage about administration scandals than any president since Watergate, as measured by stories in the *Washington Post* (figure 2.3). This simple measure generates intuitive findings, such as the increase in stories in the second term of Ronald Reagan, when he was dealing with the Iran/*contra* scandal; a similar spike in Bill Clinton's second term amid the Monica Lewinsky scandal; and a spike in Obama's second term because of the attack on the U.S. embassy in Benghazi and a scandal at the Veterans Administration.[39] But no president, and especially no first-term president, received as much *Washington Post* coverage about scandals as Trump did—346 articles in total, or nearly one every four days. And this was only one news outlet. For average Americans paying at least some attention to the news, a lot of what they heard about Trump was arguably bad publicity.

Summarizing these controversies and scandals would require a book unto itself. But many of them stemmed from Trump's proclivity to attack both his opponents and democratic values.

Attacking Opponents

Trump appeared to thrive off attacking his perceived enemies, and especially liked to attack them in personal terms. This penchant for insults and attacks inspired news organizations to tally them comprehensively. A *New York Times* compendium of the insults that Trump tweeted numbered between 6,000 and 10,000, depending on how one counted them, or at least about four tweeted insults per day of his presidency.[40] He coined schoolyard nicknames for Democratic leaders, like "Crazy" Nancy Pelosi and "Sleepy" Joe Biden. He attacked many other Democrats and liberals as well, such as Supreme Court justice Ruth Bader Ginsburg ("Her mind is shot"), Rep. Eric Swalwell ("Radical Left Hater"), and Senator Dianne Feinstein ("a disgrace"). He targeted media outlets and reporters with his usual epithets ("Fake News") as well as more bespoke insults: "nasty lightweight reporter" (the *Washington Post*'s Philip Rucker) or "a third-rate reporter who has nothing going" (the *New York Times*'s Maggie Haberman). He called MSNBC's Joe Scarborough "Psycho Joe" and falsely insinuated that Scarborough was involved in a murder. Anyone who criticized him—actors, athletes, comedians, you name it—seemed to be fair game: the mixed martial artist Ronda Rousey was "not a nice person" and the actress Debra Messing was "Debra The Mess Messing."

Members of Trump's own party were fair game, too. Although Republicans in Congress were able to push back on certain parts of Trump's agenda, direct criticisms of Trump were met with a harsh reprisal from Trump and then a drop in support among Republican voters. For example, amid the Republicans' challenges in repealing the Affordable Care Act in 2017, Senate majority leader Mitch McConnell said that Trump had "excessive expectations" about how quickly Congress could move. Trump responded by saying he was "very disappointed" in McConnell and then tweeted: "Can you believe that Mitch McConnell, who has screamed Repeal & Replace for 7 years, couldn't get it done. Must Repeal & Replace ObamaCare!" After Trump's attack, McConnell's favorability among Republicans dropped 16 points in a single week.[41]

Trump's eagerness to take down his political opponents also led him to take questionable and possibly criminal actions. One example involved his 2016 presidential campaign's entanglement with Russia. Russia sought to help Trump win the 2016 election through various means, including hacking and disseminating emails associated with the Democratic National Committee and Hillary Clinton's campaign. The Trump campaign's contact with Russians raised suspicions that the campaign had cooperated or colluded with Russian actors. For example, in June 2016 Trump's son-in-law, Jared Kushner, campaign manager Paul Manafort, and son Donald Trump Jr. met with a Russian lawyer under the belief that they would receive damaging information about Hillary Clinton. The FBI had already opened an investigation into Russia and the Trump campaign when Trump was elected.

As president, Trump interfered with the FBI investigation into Russia's conduct, first asking FBI director James Comey for his "loyalty" and then firing him and bragging about it to a group of visiting Russian officials. The investigation continued under a special counsel, former FBI director Robert Mueller, which led to the convictions of six people with direct ties to Trump. Mueller's report, released in March 2019, did not find that contacts between Russia and the Trump campaign met the formal definition of a criminal conspiracy, although Mueller noted that the investigation was hampered by witnesses who had deleted communication, invoked their Fifth Amendment right against self-incrimination, or provided false testimony. Mueller also found evidence of obstruction of justice by Trump but chose to abide by a 2000 Department of Justice opinion that a sitting president cannot be indicated for a federal crime. Of course, Trump declared that the report fully vindicated him. Only three months after the Mueller report was released, ABC News anchor George Stephanopoulos asked the president, "If foreigners, if Russia, if China, if someone else offers you information on an opponent, should they accept it or should they call the FBI?" Trump said, "I think maybe you do both. I think you might want to listen. I don't. There's nothing wrong with listening."[42]

Trump then sought to help his reelection effort and tar another opponent by pressuring the government of Ukraine to investigate Joe Biden's son. Hunter Biden had previously served on the board of directors of a Ukrainian energy company, which Trump alleged had biased both the Obama administration's policy toward Ukraine and Biden's

actions as vice president. Trump's efforts came to light after a government whistle-blower stated that Trump and several associates had pressured the Ukrainian president, Volodymyr Zelensky, for information
that could potentially hurt Biden's presidential campaign and suggested
that U.S. support for Ukraine was conditional on that information. On
September 24, House Speaker Nancy Pelosi launched an impeachment
inquiry. In response, Trump defended the call and accused Pelosi of
"treason."[43]

During the impeachment inquiry, a series of administration officials,
such as National Security Council staff Fiona Hill and Alexander Vindman,
testified to Trump's pressure campaign in Ukraine. After the congressional inquiry, House Democrats introduced articles of impeachment
for abuse of power and obstruction of Congress.[44] On December 18, 2019,
the House voted in favor of impeachment (229–198), with nearly unanimous Democratic support and no Republican support. Trump thus became the third president to be impeached, after Andrew Johnson and Bill
Clinton. On February 5, 2020, the Senate voted to acquit Trump on both
counts (52–48 and 53–47), although Utah senator Mitt Romney did vote
to convict Trump on the first count, becoming the first senator to vote to
convict a president in his own party.

Attacking Groups

Trump's political career was built on provocations that targeted racial,
ethnic, and religious minority groups. Before his presidential campaign,
his rise in Republican and conservative circles came after he falsely
claimed that Barack Obama was not born in the United States. During
his presidential campaign, he falsely claimed that Muslims were ap-
plauding the destruction of the World Trade Center on September 11,
2001, and tweeted an anti-Semitic meme involving Hillary Clinton, the
Star of David, and a pile of money—among many examples.[45]

When Trump became president, nothing really changed. He continued to make ugly comments about nonwhite people. In addition to the
comment about "shithole" countries, he reportedly said that Haitian
immigrants "all have AIDS" and that Nigerian immigrants would never

"go back to their huts" (the White House denied this). He told four female members of Congress, each of whom was also not white, to "go back" to their countries, even though all of them were native-born or naturalized Americans. He called Elizabeth Warren "Pocahontas" after she faced a controversy for having claimed Native American ancestry.

Perhaps the most infamous incident, however, came after a group of white supremacists and neo-Nazis gathered for a "Unite the Right" rally in Charlottesville, Virginia, on August 11–12, 2017, to protest the potential removal of a statue of the Confederate general Robert E. Lee. White supremacist leaders explicitly credited Trump for emboldening them. For example, Richard Spencer said, "There is no question that Charlottesville wouldn't have occurred without Trump. It was really because of his campaign and this new potential for a nationalist candidate who was resonating with the public in a very intense way."[46] The weekend turned violent, as many had feared; one participant killed a woman and injured others after deliberately ramming his car into a crowd of counterprotestors.

Moments such as this give presidents a straightforward task: decry the violence and prejudice, acknowledge the tragic death, and use the office's perquisites to serve as a unifying and constructive force. Yet for Trump to condemn neo-Nazis would mean criticizing people who supported him, and even more important, it would mean *not* criticizing people who opposed him.

Initially, Trump said that "we condemn in the strongest possible terms this egregious display of hatred, bigotry and violence on many sides. On many sides." The apparent suggestion that somehow both the white supremacists at the rally and those opposing them were equally bigoted or violent was criticized by both Democratic and Republican leaders. Republican senator Cory Gardner said, "Mr. President—we must call evil by its name. These were white supremacists and this was domestic terrorism." But white supremacists took note of Trump's silence about their role. Andrew Anglin, editor of the neo-Nazi *Daily Stormer*, said, "He refused to even mention anything to do with us. When reporters were screaming at him about White Nationalism he just walked out of the room."[47]

Trump would continue saying this. Three days after the rally, Trump said there "were many fine people, on both sides," called the Lee monument "a very, very important statue," and said that those opposed to the statue were "changing history" and "changing culture." On August 22, Trump told an audience at a Phoenix rally, "They're trying to take away our culture. They're trying to take away our history."[48]

These actions did more than embolden the small minority of Americans who actively identify as white supremacists or neo-Nazis. Trump's statements about racial and ethnic minorities also made it more likely that average Americans would express unfavorable views of these groups themselves. In one experiment, people exposed to the statement Trump made when he announced his candidacy, that many Mexican immigrants were "rapists" and "bringing drugs" and "bringing crime," became more likely to say something offensive when invited to write their own open-ended comments about Mexicans. This was particularly likely among Trump supporters. In short, when political leaders signal that prejudice is acceptable, ordinary people feel freer to express prejudice themselves.[49]

Attacking Democratic Values

There was a troubling backbeat to these scandals and controversies: Trump seemed ambivalent at best toward the basic values that are important to a functioning democracy and the rule of law. Trump's brand of identity politics underscored this concern: in relentlessly dehumanizing his enemies, Trump acted as if that the rights and privileges of democratic citizenship belonged only to his supporters, not to his opponents.

For one, although tensions between politicians and the news media are nothing new, Trump escalated these tensions by attacking the news media in inflammatory terms that went well beyond his mantra of "Fake News." He routinely referred to journalists as the "enemy of the people," and journalists were often personally threatened by Trump supporters at his speeches or rallies. Trump praised this behavior and seemed to delight in episodes where reporters were physically attacked. At one

2020 rally, he regaled supporters with a story of security forces removing a reporter from a protest, saying, "They threw him aside like a bag of popcorn. But honestly, when you watch the crap we've all had to take so long . . . when you see it, it's actually a beautiful sight."[50]

His attacks on his opponents were equally inflammatory. He portrayed leading Democrats—Hillary Clinton, Obama, Pelosi, and others—as guilty of heinous crimes ("treason") that deserved imprisonment. The "Lock her up!" chants directed at Clinton during the 2016 campaign were a fixture of Trump rallies even during his presidency. Trump supporters echoed and even appeared to act on this rhetoric. One supporter, Cesar Sayoc, was arrested after mailing sixteen packages containing pipe bombs to prominent Democrats, including Obama, Biden, Clinton, Kamala Harris, and others. He also sent a package to CNN. Trump condemned Sayoc's actions but continued to attack the very people whom Sayoc targeted.[51]

Trump not only attacked his perceived enemies but also threatened them with arrest. A leader's use of the government's power to imprison his enemies is usually the stuff of authoritarian governments. But starting in his presidential campaign, Trump routinely threatened to make "lock her up" a reality. In an October 2016 debate, he said he would "instruct my attorney general to get a special prosecutor to look into" Clinton's use of a private email server when she was secretary of state, and Trump went on to say that when he was president, Clinton would be in jail. Nothing changed once Trump became president. In fact, four years later, almost to the day, Trump railed at his attorney general, William Barr, wondering why Clinton, Obama, and Biden were not in prison and asking, "Where are all the arrests?"[52]

Trump's willingness to politicize the Department of Justice, federal law enforcement, and the military went further. He frequently made statements or took actions that subverted these institutions, eroded the rule of law, and signaled his support for violence that served his political goals. He pardoned or promoted military officers who had been convicted in military court of war crimes. He pardoned former Maricopa County (AZ) sheriff Joe Arpaio, who had been convicted of defying a court order to stop racially profiling immigrants. Trump told the head of Customs and Border Patrol that he would pardon him if immigration agents defied U.S. law and blocked immigrants seeking asylum. These actions echoed his campaign promises to pay the legal fees of supporters who physically attacked protesters at his rallies.[53]

Perhaps it was no surprise that Trump's actions seemed taken from the playbook of authoritarian leaders: he frequently praised such leaders publicly. Trump called North Korea's Kim Jong-un "somebody that I've gotten to know very well and respect." About Turkey's Recep Erdoğan: "He's doing a very good job." About China's Xi Jinping, "I like him a lot. . . . He's a strong guy, tough guy." About Putin: "He's been a leader." Harkening back to his *Time* magazine interview, Trump praised Philippines president Rodrigo Duterte for doing "an unbelievable job on the drug problem," even though Duterte had sanctioned violence that led to the deaths of more than 6,000 alleged drug dealers with little regard for due process of law. Comments like these seemed to confirm Trump's weak commitment to the laws and norms necessary for healthy democracy.[54]

CONCLUSION

When the Conservative Political Action Conference (CPAC) convened again in 2018, it was a who's who of Trump staffers, appointees, and die-hard supporters, with some cameos from international anti-immigrant figures such as Marion Maréchal-Le Pen of France and Nigel Farage of the United Kingdom. As CNN put it, "CPAC Goes Full Trump for 2018."[55]

Trump's keynote address included plenty of red meat for the likes of Maréchal-Le Pen and Farage. Trump likened immigrants coming to America to a snake that is taken in by a kindly woman and then bites and kills her. Once again, he promised that he would build his signature wall on the southern border. At one point, Trump bragged that "my administration, I think, has had the most successful first year in the history of the presidency. I really believe that. I really believe it. I really believe it."

The problem for Trump was that many Americans did not believe it. Throughout the three years leading into 2020, Trump was much more successful at appealing to a die-hard audience, such as the one at CPAC, than building a more broadly popular record. In many ways, he treated the presidency like his 2016 campaign—attacking opponents, attracting controversy, stoking animosity toward immigrants and other groups, and generally fomenting division even when there was an opportunity for some degree of consensus.

In short, Trump inherited a divisive politics and then made it even more so. There was some irony in this, given that Trump had campaigned as an outsider and a disrupter of an entrenched Washington establishment. But Trump did not disrupt preexisting political alignments, he helped to cement them—including the long-term polarization of the two parties and the more recent alignment of partisanship and attitudes on identity-inflected issues. Little that Trump did was likely to make politics any less calcified.

But governing this way failed to address Trump's central challenge: he was a historically unpopular president when he took office, and that did not improve during his first three years in the White House. His reelection bid was in question, and it was not clear if Trump appreciated his predicament.

3

Somewhere between "Landslide" and "Oh, Shit"

Based on the economy, I should be up 15 or 20 points higher.

—DONALD TRUMP, JUNE 2019

THE DAY AFTER HIS INAUGURATION, Donald Trump gave a speech at the headquarters of the Central Intelligence Agency. Standing in front of a memorial to the 117 CIA agents who had died in service, Trump talked about himself: "Probably almost everybody in this room voted for me. But I will not ask you to raise your hands." He said his inauguration speech had earned "good reviews." Most famously, he exaggerated the size of the inauguration crowd: "I looked out, the field was—it looked like a million, million and a half people." He criticized the media for showing "an empty field" and reporting a smaller crowd size. Administration figures rushed to defend Trump's falsehood, with Press Secretary Sean Spicer calling the inauguration crowd "the largest audience ever to witness an inauguration—period—both in person and around the globe." White House adviser Kellyanne Conway defended Spicer's use of "alternative facts."[1]

Trump's remarks at the CIA manifested one of his abiding concerns: his own popularity. Of course, all presidential administrations monitor the president's popularity—conducting surveys, discussing trends, and tracking key groups in the electorate. More unusual was how frequently and how publicly Trump discussed his poll numbers, highlighting the polls that suggested greater popularity and attacking polls and pollsters whose facts were not "alternative" enough.[2]

If it seemed as if Trump protested too much, there was good reason. Throughout his presidency, Trump's standing with the American public had two key features. First, it was low: not once during Trump's tenure did a majority of Americans approve of the job he was doing as president. Trump was the only president in the era of polling for whom this was true.

Second, Trump's public standing stuck at this low level. Although other presidents have had lower approval ratings than Trump at some point in their presidencies, they have had higher ratings, too. But Trump's approval rating varied less than that of any previous president's. In short, Trump stood out for having an extraordinarily stable approval rating as well as a low one.

These features of Trump's poll numbers derived both from Trump's own decisions and from the broader political trends we identified in the first chapter. Trump's chronic unpopularity may have stemmed in part from his unpopular governing agenda and the news coverage of his administration's scandals. In addition, the tectonic shifts that have strengthened party loyalty mean that presidential approval may not vary as much depending on economic conditions. This was not unique to Trump, but it mattered for him. The growing economy in 2017–19 did not appear to lift Trump's approval rating, which was why Trump was not "up 15 or 20 points higher," as he complained in the summer of 2019.

The stability of Trump's approval can be traced to two other factors. One, again, is the power of party loyalty. Despite his struggles, Trump received steady support from Republican voters. This support was sometimes characterized as rapturous, but in reality, many, if not most, Republican voters had both positive and negative feelings about Trump. Nevertheless, they continued to support him overall. Much of Trump's agenda was popular with Republicans, as we noted in chapter 1. This helped keep Republican voters on his side.

The second factor was the political priorities of Republican voters. At the top of their list was not only Trump's impeachment, which they overwhelmingly opposed, but also key items on Trump's identity agenda, such as the border wall, which they overwhelmingly supported.

Republicans' political priorities also help explain why Trump did not face any consequence for backing away from economic populism. Even Republican voters who supported economically populist policies were more likely to reward Trump for his immigration policies than punish him for abandoning economic populism. For these Republicans, identity politics took precedence over economics.

The upshot of these two factors was this: although plenty of Republican leaders and voters expressed reservations about Trump, they were willing to overlook or downplay his missteps and scandals. This kept his approval rating from taking an outright nosedive. In a polarized era, it appears harder to criticize your own side without seeming like you are defecting to the other side.

Public attitudes toward Trump showed what a calcified politics looks like. Fewer people appear willing to change their minds about a president, and this makes presidents less accountable for conditions in the country and for their own missteps. As a result, Trump did not experience a clear drop in approval because he pursued policies that were unpopular, or because his words and actions created a stream of controversies.

But Trump's stubborn unpopularity made his prospects for reelection decidedly mixed as the election year approached, despite the growing economy. Trump was not a clear underdog, but neither was he a clear favorite.

AN UNPOPULAR PERSON AND PRESIDENT

Trump's unpopularity began well before he became president. The earliest poll to ask people's views of Trump, a July 1990 NBC News/*Wall Street Journal* poll, found that only 14 percent had a positive view but 49 percent had a negative view. The rest were neutral (28%) or had no opinion (9%). Over the following two decades, Americans' opinions of him were evenly divided at best, and often highly unfavorable when he entered politics. After Trump ran for the presidential nomination of the Reform Party in 1999, his net favorability—the percentage with a favorable view minus the percentage with an unfavorable view—dropped from −6 points in September to an average of −50 across six polls conducted between October 1999 and January 2000. In March 2011, when Trump flirted with running for president, the same thing happened. The handful of public polls about Trump from 2005 to 2010 again showed mixed opinions (an average favorability of −2). But after March, Trump's favorability dropped to an average of −25 in the remaining polls that year.

Of course, public figures often lose popularity when they enter politics, and especially electoral politics. But Trump was less popular than a typical political figure in his position. In fact, when he ran for president in 2016, he was the least popular major-party presidential candidate in Gallup polls dating back to 1956. In the closing week of the election, only 35 percent of Americans had a favorable opinion of him, while 62 percent had an unfavorable opinion—a net of −27.[3] After the election, Trump's standing improved, but he remained unpopular. In an early January 2017 Gallup poll, only 40 percent viewed Trump favorably and 55 percent viewed him unfavorably (a net of −15).

After his inauguration, Trump went from being an unpopular person and candidate to being an unpopular president. In his first three years as president, Trump's approval rating was both unusually low and unusually stable (figure 3.1).

Right after inauguration, in late January and February 2017, Trump's average net approval rating was −7 percentage points (43% approve vs. 50% disapprove). This negative rating was, again, unusual. Dating back to the Eisenhower administration, every president has had a positive net approval rating in their first month in office—a sort of "inauguration bounce." For example, in this period in 2009, Obama's net approval rating was +41 (64% approval vs. 23% disapproval); George W. Bush's was +34 in early 2001. The average among elected presidents from Eisenhower to Obama was +49.[4]

For the first three years of his presidency, Trump's approval rating moved up or down only a bit. It continued to be negative, averaging −13, and it ranged from −21 to −7. That 14-point range is the smallest of any elected president during the same period of their presidency. For example, Obama's net rating ranged from −10 to +41. Reagan's ranged from −8 to +49. Even though Trump's scandals did not appear to lower his

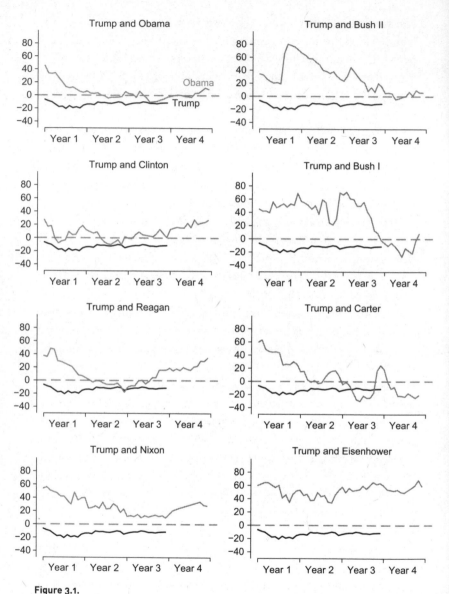

Figure 3.1.

Monthly Net Job Approval Ratings for Trump in Years 1–3 vs. Other Elected Incumbent Presidents. Lines depict the percent approving minus the percent disapproving. Months with no approval polling data are linearly interpolated. *Sources*: George Edwards, Gary Jacobson, Huffington Post/Pollster, FiveThirtyEight.

popularity, his approval ratings never increased even to the average for a typical president.

His unpopularity was unusual in another sense. Trump was, as he often reminded people, presiding over a relatively strong economy. Given how favorably people felt about the economy, his approval rating should have been much higher. This is clear when comparing presidential approval ratings to a long-standing measure of how Americans view the economy, the Index of Consumer Sentiment. The index is constructed from responses to five questions that have been asked in the University of Michigan's Survey of Consumers since 1952. These questions capture both how people think the economy has been doing and how they think it will do in the future.[5] Higher values of the index mean that Americans feel better about the economy. Typically, higher consumer sentiment has meant better approval ratings for the incumbent president.

But not for Trump in his first three years in office (figure 3.2). Trump experienced high consumer sentiment and *low* approval ratings. For example, from 2017 to 2019, consumer sentiment averaged 97—roughly equal to the average during Bill Clinton's presidency. But Clinton's average net approval rating was +17 compared to Trump's −13. Similarly, when consumer sentiment hit the same level under Ronald Reagan in February 1984, Reagan's net approval rating was +18. Despite a strong economy, Trump's approval ratings languished.

This disjuncture between consumer sentiment and presidential approval predated Trump's presidency. It appears to be the consequence of Americans' increasingly powerful party loyalties, which have become stronger predictors of how they evaluate both the economy and the incumbent president. If their party controls the White House, Americans tend to say the economy is doing well and the president is doing a good job. If the other party controls the White House, Americans tend to say the opposite. Partisan polarization has led to growing partisan biases in economic perceptions and made it harder for presidents to garner support from the opposite party when the economy is doing well.[6]

Because of this, perhaps the closest analog to Trump—no doubt to his chagrin—is Barack Obama.[7] During Obama's presidency, consumer sentiment increased sharply as the country recovered from the Great

Recession, but Obama's approval rating did not increase until the very end of his presidency. As a consequence, Obama was also less popular than many other presidents who experienced similarly high levels of consumer sentiment.

But under Trump, partisan polarization in economic perceptions and presidential approval was even greater than under Obama.[8] In early 2019, 75 percent of Republicans said that the economy was excellent or good, but only 32 percent of Democrats agreed. At the end of Obama's presidency, the partisan gap in positive economic perceptions was much smaller (46% among Democrats and 14% among Republicans). In terms of job approval, the average partisan gap in approval of Trump was 79 points as of 2020: 87 percent of Republicans approved of Trump but only 6 percent of Democrats did. That set a record for modern presidents. Under Obama, the gap was large but not as large: on average, 81 percent of Democrats approved of Obama compared to 14 percent of Republicans. Trump was even less popular than one would expect given Obama's situation. For example, in Obama's last year in office, consumer sentiment was actually slightly lower than in Trump's first three years (91 vs. 96), and yet Obama's net approval rating (+6) was nearly 20 points better than Trump's.

Trump's unpopularity extended beyond his job approval to how Americans perceived him as a person. Trump stands out compared to recent presidents in how frequently evaluations of him as a person were *lower* than evaluations of his job performance. For example, in 2018 and 2019 polls, when Trump's approval was in the low 40s, even fewer perceived him as "honest and trustworthy" (34%) or "likable" (37%) or agreed that he "shares your values" (38%) or "is a person you admire" (35%). Only when asked if Trump was a "strong and decisive leader" did positive perceptions exceed his job approval. In many cases, these poor perceptions

---

Figure 3.2.

The Relationship between Monthly Net Job Approval Ratings and Consumer Sentiment for Trump in Years 1–3 vs. Other Elected Incumbent Presidents. Data points are months, with least squares fit lines. Data includes 2017–19 for Trump and all months for other presidents. *Source for Index of Consumer Sentiment*: University of Michigan Survey of Consumers.

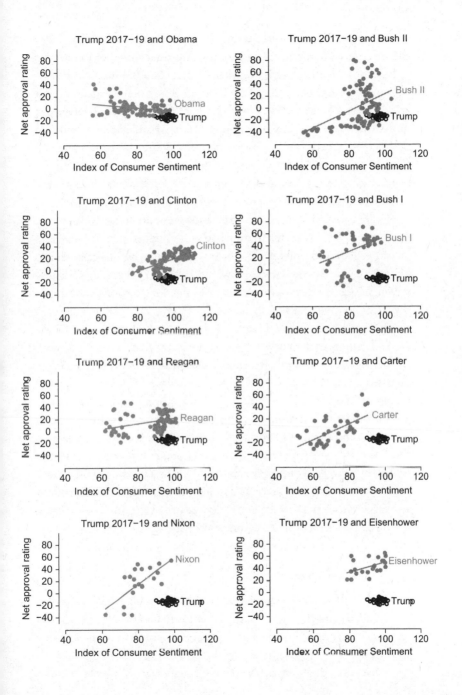

Trump 2017–19 and Obama

Trump 2017–19 and Bush II

Trump 2017–19 and Clinton

Trump 2017–19 and Bush I

Trump 2017–19 and Reagan

Trump 2017–19 and Carter

Trump 2017–19 and Nixon

Trump 2017–19 and Eisenhower

of Trump predated his presidency. But his many scandals arguably helped ensure those perceptions did not improve throughout his term.[9]

By contrast, other recent presidents did not have such unusually low personal popularity in their first term. In June 2012, when a modest 46 percent of Americans approved of Barack Obama's job performance, more Americans said that he was honest (60%) and likable (81%) and shared their values (53%).[10] Perceptions of George W. Bush's and Bill Clinton's personal qualities often matched or exceeded their job approval ratings as well. And in absolute terms, all three of these recent presidents were far more personally popular than Trump.

Negative perceptions of Trump extended into other domains as well. A majority (54%) said that Trump had "emboldened people who hold racist beliefs." And a slender majority (51%) outright said that Trump himself was "racist." Perhaps as remarkable as the 51 percent figure is that it would even be relevant for a pollster to ask the question about a U.S. president in the first place.[11]

Clearly, then, President Trump's challenges had a lot to do with being Donald Trump. Presidents who were as unpopular as or more unpopular than Trump usually experienced an economic recession or a long, punishing war, or both. These kinds of events helped drag the approval ratings of George W. Bush, Jimmy Carter, Lyndon Johnson, and Harry Truman lower than Trump's. Trump's unpopularity over the first three years of his presidency stands out because it occurred during a level of peace and prosperity that many presidents would have coveted. But the similarity between Trump's situation and Obama's—presidents whose popularity rating did not increase despite consistent economic growth— also suggests that Trump's challenges derived in part from broader political trends, and especially the strengthening of partisan loyalties.

"THIS KIND OF IMPACT"

Trump's challenges had political costs for him beyond what was visible in polling. Beginning immediately after his inauguration, the United States saw large and sustained protests in opposition to his presidency and agenda. This included the largest single-day protest in U.S. history up to that point, the Women's March on January 21, 2017, which included somewhere between 3.3 million and 5.2 million people across the country. In June 2018 there were about 1,081 protests of Trump's immigration agenda, including 738 protests on June 30, when approximately half a million Americans took to the streets on "Families Belong Together" mobilization day. There were many other examples.[12]

In turn, those protests gave rise to sustained local organizing. Some of this came from national organizations, including the Women's March and Indivisible. There were at least 4,600 groups associated with Indivisible as of January 2019. In other cases, local groups organized themselves, involving many people who had not been previously active in politics but were spurred to action by their opposition to Trump. These groups formed in all kinds of communities, but especially in closely contested congressional districts. Candidates running for political office were able to draw on these groups to enlist volunteers willing to do the spadework of electioneering, such as voter registration, phone-banking, and door-to-door canvassing.[13]

There is no way to quantify exactly how much that organizing paid off. But the midterm election provided vindication for Democrats. They gained forty-one seats and a 235–199 majority in the U.S. House; they gained 308 seats in state legislatures and took majority control in six state legislative chambers; and they regained the governor's mansion in seven states, including in key presidential battlegrounds like Michigan and Wisconsin. Only the U.S. Senate proved a disappointment for Democrats, with Republicans gaining two seats.

It is, of course, customary for the president's party to lose seats in the midterm. But the size of those seat losses is related to the popularity of the president. Midterm elections are, in large part, referenda on the incumbent president, especially given growing partisan polarization and the nationalization of local elections. Trump's unpopularity, combined with the substantial number of seats his party had to defend, meant that the GOP was forecast to lose almost exactly the number of House seats that they lost. Trump invited exactly this outcome when he stumped for Republican candidates and said, "Pretend I'm on the ballot."[14]

Trump appeared to hurt his party's chances in other ways. Making the repeal of the Affordable Care Act central to his first-term agenda was one example. In 2018, Democrats seized on the unpopularity of the repeal effort and made it the top issue in televised campaign advertising. Research found that House Republicans who voted to repeal the Affordable Care Act were less likely to win their race than Republicans who did not vote this way. Another example was Trump's treatment of women and his statements about racial and ethnic minority groups. Compared to 2016, House Republicans lost support in the midterm among voters who expressed less sexist attitudes toward women and were more willing to acknowledge the existence of racism—exactly the people likely to find Trump's history of mistreating women and his bigoted comments wrong and offensive. Trump also lost votes among people who were more favorable to immigration, a group that had been growing since his presidential campaign. Trump may have had particular responsibility here. Although many Republicans wanted Trump to focus on the growing economy during the midterm campaign, he chose instead to spend the weeks before the election fomenting fear of a caravan of immigrants who were traveling northward through Mexico toward the U.S. border.[15]

Trump did not accept any blame. Three weeks before the election, he took no responsibility for potential GOP losses and insisted that he was "helping people." He said, "I don't believe anybody's had this kind of impact."[16] For Trump, however, the true impact of the midterm backlash was serious. The election cost Trump and the GOP unified control of government and put House Democrats in a much stronger position from which to oppose—and impeach—Trump.

"A COMPLETE CONNECTION"?

To many people, and particularly Trump's critics, Trump's challenges—a majority's disapproving of him, protests against him, Republican seat losses in 2018—did not seem like enough punishment, somehow. To them, the question was why Trump was not even *more* unpopular. It seemed mysterious that Trump could have so many controversies and yet a relatively stable approval rating. Trump, of course, reveled in this, declaring before his election, "I could stand in the middle of Fifth Avenue and shoot somebody and I wouldn't lose voters."[17]

What stabilized Trump's approval ratings and enabled him to survive this stream of transgressions was one thing: Republican loyalty. Party polarization in presidential approval ratings had been increasing for some time. Trump's approval rating among Republicans hovered between 80 and 90 percent. If his overall approval rating were to fall below its typical range in the low 40s, at least some of these Republicans needed to sour on Trump enough to register their disapproval in polls. But throughout Trump's first three years, they did not.

This connection between Trump and Republican voters was sometimes described in almost mystical terms. In late 2019, Republican representative Patrick McHenry of North Carolina said that Trump "has a complete connection with the average Republican voter and that's given him political power here. Trump has touched the nerve of my conservative base like no person in my lifetime."[18]

This perspective seemed borne out by the experiences of Republican senators Jeff Flake and Lindsey Graham, who were critics of Trump during his 2016 campaign. But after Trump's election, Graham pivoted to support him, while Flake did not. Flake's net approval rating among Arizona Republicans dropped from about +30 points in 2014 to −19 in 2016, and to −49 in 2018 before he stepped down. Graham's criticism earned him a similar drop in approval among Republicans between 2014 and 2016. But after Graham became one of Trump's leading defenders, his net approval rating among South Carolina Republicans shot up to +64 in 2018. Graham put it plainly: "He's very popular in my state. When I help him, it helps me back home."[19]

Liking Trump versus Loving Trump

The notion that Trump's connection with Republican voters was "complete," however, is an exaggeration. Although a subset of Republicans was clearly enthusiastic about Trump, there were many whose views were favorable but not exactly rapturous. Moreover, just as among GOP leaders, a stubborn fraction of Republicans objected to his behavior or his policies. But, like Republican members of Congress, these Republican voters largely set aside their reservations and objections. Republicans who opposed aspects of Trump's agenda largely did not prioritize those issues as much as Republicans who supported Trump's agenda.

One way to characterize the connection between Trump and Republican voters is to take account of the intensity of Republicans' feelings about Trump. A simple statistic like the percent approving of Trump conceals variation in intensity, such as who "strongly approved" of Trump versus who just "approved" of him. There were many Republicans who supported Trump but not strongly. In weekly YouGov polls conducted from 2017 to 2019, an average of 54 percent of Republicans strongly approved of Trump while 30 percent approved and the rest disapproved or did not have an opinion. A similar fraction of Republicans (61%) reported having a "very favorable" view of Trump during this period, as opposed to a "somewhat favorable" or unfavorable view. The intensity of GOP support for Trump was a bit higher than Democratic support for Obama in the first three years of his presidency: on average, 42 percent of Democrats strongly approved of Obama and 56 percent had a very favorable view of him. But Trump's overall support among Republicans still depended on a mixture of more intense and less intense feelings. This is one reason why, in a November 2017 survey, the political scientist Larry Bartels found that when Republican voters were asked to rate Trump on a scale of 1 to 10, where 10 was the most favorable, the average was a 7. This was higher than the average for any other prominent Republican, like Mitch McConnell or Mitt Romney, but an average of 7 suggests that some Republicans felt favorably toward Trump without feeling rapture.[20]

This same pattern shows up when you track Republican voters over time. The Views of the Electorate Research (VOTER) Survey did so by tracking over 3,000 Americans from December 2016 until December 2019, interviewing them once each year and four times in all. One test of Trump's connection is how many Republicans maintained a favorable view or a strongly favorable view of him throughout this time period. In total, 75 percent had a consistently favorable view—meaning that roughly a quarter of Republicans had an unfavorable view of Trump, or did not express any view, at some point over this three-year period. However, only 38 percent had a consistently strongly favorable view, demonstrating again that Trump's popularity among Republicans depended on voters with positive but not overwhelmingly positive views of him. Most Republicans may have approved of Trump's job performance, but that does not mean they were deeply enthusiastic about him.

Trump's support also depended on the willingness of some Republican voters to set aside their personal disapproval or dislike of Trump's actions and personality. When it came to views of Trump as a leader and person, substantial fractions of Republicans actually had negative views. In a June 2018 Gallup poll, 38 percent did not think he "has chosen mostly good advisers and cabinet officers"; 38 percent did not find him "likable"; 33 percent said he was not a "person you admire"; 30 percent said he was not "honest and trustworthy"; and 21 percent said he did not "put the country's interests ahead of his own personal interests." On its face, those statistics suggest a fairly sizable reservoir of discontent within the party. But in June 2018, Trump's overall job approval among Republicans was about 89 percent, meaning that substantial numbers of these ostensibly discontented Republicans approved of a president whom they did not find likable, admirable, honest, and so on. They supported Trump as a president even though they believed he was a flawed person. They would undoubtedly have found like-minded Republicans in the U.S. Senate.[21]

Political Priorities

The idea that Trump had a "complete connection" with Republican voters suggested that it was Trump's unique personality that ensured their support. But equally if not more important may have been their political priorities.

How Republican voters responded to Trump's policy agenda also helped ensure their support for him. When Trump campaigned for the Republican nomination for president, he demonstrated that a candidate could build a winning coalition—at least in the large and fractured 2016 field—with a combination of aggressive anti-immigration policies and surprisingly liberal economic policies, such as raising taxes on the wealthy. There had always been Republican voters who were willing to go further to limit immigration than many Republican leaders were. And there had always been Republican voters who had not bought into the party's conservative economics. The question was how Republican voters would respond to Trump's governing agenda.

It is instructive to focus on three of the biggest issues from Trump's first three years: tax cuts, the border wall, and family separation. As we discussed in chapter 2, these were central to his governing agenda. These issues also reveal important features of Republican voters—and particularly whether they prioritize economics or identity issues.

As we have noted, the tax bill that Trump signed largely abandoned the populist rhetoric of his campaign and gave most of its benefits to the wealthy. Just as in 2016, this appeared to be at odds with what substantial numbers of Republicans wanted. In Nationscape surveys conducted throughout the latter half of 2019, 38 percent of Republicans wanted to *raise* taxes on people making $250,000 per year or more and 52 percent wanted to raise taxes on those making $600,000 or more—that is, the opposite of what the Trump plan did. This may help explain why about 20–25 percent of Republicans did not support the tax plan itself, according to Gallup polls.[22]

With immigration, Trump's aggressive agenda proved popular with Republicans in some respects but not others. The border wall was fairly popular. When asked in 2019 Nationscape surveys whether they supported a border wall, 71 percent of Republicans expressed support while 17 did not, and 12 percent were unsure. Among Republicans who did have an opinion, 81 percent favored the wall. Its popularity stemmed in part from Trump's continued push for it: in Pew Research Center surveys, the percentage of Republicans who supported the wall increased about 8 points between his inauguration and January 2019.

But family separation was not nearly as popular: a plurality of Republicans (43%) opposed it, while only 35 percent supported it and 22 percent were unsure. Moreover, 36 percent of Republicans supported a path to citizenship for undocumented immigrants, even though Trump balked at pursuing it.[23]

Divisions within a party on policy issues are nothing new, of course. For years, political science research has shown that most partisans are not orthodox ideologues and that many hold a mix of views. Many partisans have views that are crosswise to those of their party. Those people could be called "cross-positioned." But the question is how much that matters. Sometimes voters who are out of step with their party or their party's president on certain issues are not just "cross-positioned" but genuinely "cross-pressured." Cross-pressures arise when they consider issues on which they are cross-positioned to be important and therefore face the challenge of reconciling their beliefs with what their party or president thinks. For this reason, cross-pressured voters are at higher risk of defecting from their party, such as by supporting the opposing party's candidates in elections. Democrats learned this the hard way in 2016, when a substantial fraction of white Obama voters with conservative attitudes about immigration and race defected to Donald Trump.[24]

But Republicans who were out of step with Trump did not appear to feel much pressure. They supported Trump even when they disagreed with him. One simple way to see this is to divide Republicans based on their views of tax increases on the wealthy and the border wall. Ignoring for the moment those who did not have an opinion on one or both issues, Republicans can be divided into four groups (the left side of table 3.1). The largest (50%) took consistently conservative positions: favoring the border wall and opposing a tax increase on incomes over $250,000. But a sizable plurality (32%) wanted the border wall and tax increases. The remainder opposed the border wall, and these voters were evenly divided in their view of the tax increase.

What is striking, however, is that views of taxing the wealthy had almost no relationship to approval of Trump (the right side of table 3.1). Republicans who supported the border wall overwhelming approved of Trump, no matter whether they supported or opposed tax increases for the wealthy. Only the 18 percent of Republicans who opposed the border wall were less likely to approve of Trump—and among this group, views of taxes mattered much less.

The same finding emerges from examining Republicans' views on both immigration issues: the border wall and family separation (table 3.2).

TABLE 3.1. GOP Views on Taxes and the Border Wall and Their Relationship to Trump's Job Approval

Border wall	Percent of GOP in each group			Percent of GOP approving of Trump	
	Raise taxes on wealthy			Raise taxes on wealthy	
	Support	Oppose	Border wall	Support	Oppose
Support	32	50	Support	90	95
Oppose	8	10	Oppose	42	53

Source: 2019 Democracy Fund + UCLA Nationscape surveys.

TABLE 3.2. GOP Views on the Border Wall and Family Separation and Their Relationship to Trump's Job Approval

Border wall	Percent of GOP in each group			Percent of GOP approving of Trump	
	Family separation			Family separation	
	Support	Oppose	Border wall	Support	Oppose
Support	45	35	Support	96	89
Oppose	3	17	Oppose	66	40

Source: 2019 Democracy Fund + UCLA Nationscape surveys.

Excluding respondents with no opinion, just under half (45%) of Republicans supported both policies. A substantial fraction (35%) supported the border wall but not family separation. Most of the rest (17%) opposed both. However, Republicans who opposed family separation did not penalize Trump. As long as they supported the border wall, they were almost as likely to approve of Trump overall as were Republicans who supported both elements of Trump's immigration agenda.

A similar finding emerges in the "revealed importance" experiments that we introduced in chapter 1. These experiments show that large numbers of Republicans, and especially those who supported more restrictive immigration policies, prioritized immigration over other issues, including the economic issues identified as potential elements of a more populist approach for the GOP.

Figure 3.3 shows the revealed importance of issues for Republicans interviewed in 2019 Nationscape surveys. First, this figure shows the revealed importance—how much more likely people are to choose a set of policies when the set includes that particular issue—among both Republicans who took the liberal position on that issue and Republicans who took the conservative position. Second, it shows the percentage of Republicans who took the conservative position as opposed to taking the liberal position or not expressing an opinion on that issue. The issues are sorted based on the revealed importance to Republicans with conservative positions.

At the top of the figure are several issues where large majorities take conservative positions and consider the issue to be important. The most important overall was impeachment: 79 percent of Republicans said that Trump should not be impeached, and for these Republicans the issue ranked highest in revealed importance, even before Trump's first impeachment trial began. For the few who did not oppose impeachment, the issue was not as important. The same pattern held for banning guns, slave reparations, late-term abortion, and the border wall. The question about banning all abortions attracted less support from Republicans (only 29% supported it), but for those Republicans the issue also ranks as very important. Of course, policies like banning all abortions, all guns, or instituting reparations were hardly likely in 2019. Republicans were reacting more to the threat of policies that they found highly objectionable.

This makes it all the more striking that the border wall was prioritized as much as these issues. Republicans who supported the border wall considered it almost as important as preventing a gun ban. And crucially, among the minority of Republicans who opposed the border wall, the issue was much less important. The same pattern characterized a blanket policy of deporting undocumented immigrants. About 57 percent of Republicans supported this, and for them the revealed importance of the issue was lower than that of the border wall but higher than many other issues. Here again, the 25 percent of Republicans who opposed the policy considered it a lower priority. They were cross-positioned, but not very cross-pressured. When asked about "banning people from predominantly Muslim countries from entering the United States," Republicans were more divided, but again, those who supported the ban prioritized the issue more than those who did not. Likewise, even though a large number of Republicans supported a path to citizenship for Dreamers (59% vs. 26% who opposed it), the issue did not stand out as particularly important for them. It was certainly far less important to them than the border wall was to its supporters.

The only Trump immigration policy that *opponents* of the policy prioritized more than *supporters* of it was family separation. Republican opponents of family separation, however, prioritized it less than Republican supporters of the border wall prioritized the wall. This helps explain why Republicans who supported the border wall but not family separation approved of Trump at a rate similar to those who supported both the border wall and family separation. The border wall was a higher priority.

The experiments also showed why Trump suffered no apparent drop in approval for his failure to follow through on populist economics. For example, among the 49 percent of Republicans who wanted higher taxes for people making over $600,000, the revealed importance of the issue was lower than the revealed importance of the border wall to its supporters. This helps explain why the vast majority of Republicans who supported the border wall but wanted to increase taxes on the wealthy approved of Trump anyway. Republicans who wanted populist economics did not particularly care when Trump opted for conservative economics. Again, they appear cross-positioned but not really cross-pressured.

In sum, Trump's stable approval ratings in the face of perpetual scandals can be traced to his support among Republican voters, and this

---

Figure 3.3.
Support and Revealed Importance of Policies among Republicans in 2019. Republicans include respondents who identified with or leaned toward the Republican Party. Percent with a conservative view is calculated among all respondents, including those who did not have an opinion. The conservative position on trade is defined here as opposition to limiting trade. The conservative position on cutting taxes on families making under $100,000 is defined as favoring tax cuts. *Source*: Democracy Fund + UCLA Nationscape surveys (July–December 2019).

	Revealed importance	Percent with conservative view
	Liberal views / Conservative views	
Impeach Trump		79
Ban guns		84
Slave reparations		76
Allow late term abortion		73
Ban abortion		29
Build border wall		72
Green New Deal		44
No military support for Israel		57
Ban assault rifles		45
Reduce size of military		77
Allow limited abortion		40
Medicare for all		53
Mass deportation		57
Muslim travel ban		33
Ten Commandments in public bldgs		74
Public guns registry		40
Allow transgender in military		41
Debt free state college		44
Legalize marijuana		38
Federal health insurance		53
Broad path to citizenship		46
$15 minimum wage		47
Limit gun magazines		43
Citizenship for wire transfers		68
Require abortion waiting period		62
Abortion coverage optional		55
Dreamer path to citizenship		26
Cut taxes under $100,000		70
Universal jobs guarantee		36
Right to work law		45
Cap carbon emissions		30
Eliminate estate tax		62
More oil and gas drilling		49
Raise taxes over $250,000		49
Separate immigrant children		35
Provide school vouchers		38
12 weeks maternity leave		28
Low income health subsidy		28
Merit-based immigration		47
Big environmental program		25
Health care public option		31
Raise taxes over $600,000		34
Limit trade		32
Universal gun background checks		9

0   .1   .2   .3   .4   .5   0%   50%   100%

reinforced his support among Republican leaders wary of being on the wrong side of their voters. Voters and leaders alike were willing to overlook reservations about Trump's personal behavior. Republican leaders could take comfort in Trump's embrace of the party's traditional stance on many issues and in the knowledge that, when Trump pushed heterodox positions, they could often defeat him in Congress. For GOP voters, heterodox positions are not uncommon—and especially support for some progressive economic policies. Trump had wooed those voters to win the primary. But when his administration's big tax bill went in the opposite direction, there was little price to pay among these voters, who may have wanted a different tax bill but did not care about taxes as much as they cared about other things Trump promoted. Trump's election had spawned a long debate about what was most responsible for his support—identity politics or economics. Three years into his presidency, identity politics took precedence for Republican voters.

Thus, Trump, unlike other recent presidents who were relatively unpopular heading into their election year, did not face even a serious primary threat. Jimmy Carter faced Senator Ted Kennedy, who won 38 percent of the votes cast in the 1980 Democratic primary. George H. W. Bush faced Patrick Buchanan, who won 23 percent of the votes cast in the 1992 GOP primary. Neither Kennedy nor Buchanan succeeded, but both provided a tougher test than any of the major Republican candidates who challenged Trump in the primary: businessman Rocky De La Fuente, former Massachusetts governor William Weld, former representative Joe Walsh, and former representative Mark Sanford (who lost his congressional primary after his ambivalence about Trump provoked Trump to endorse his opponent). Together, these candidates won barely 4 percent of the votes cast in the 2020 primary. Their chances were not helped by the decision of several state Republican parties to cancel their state's primary outright and bind their state's delegates to Trump.

Even if many in the party had reservations, the GOP cast its lot with Trump again, for better or worse.

A PRECARIOUS REELECTION BID

On February 4, 2020, Donald Trump walked into the chamber of the House of Representatives to deliver the annual State of the Union address. As he came to the rostrum, Speaker of the House Nancy Pelosi, who had only weeks before presided over Trump's first impeachment, extended her hand to him for the customary greeting. Trump ignored her. Pelosi then omitted the traditional phrase "I have the high privilege and distinct honor" from her introduction of Trump.[25]

In his address, Trump framed the state of the country as "a great American comeback" with "incredible results." He said "jobs are booming" and "incomes are soaring" and "confidence is surging" and "our country is thriving." He said "our economy is the best it has ever been." He described a "vision" of "the world's most prosperous and inclusive society—one where every citizen can join in America's unparalleled success and where every community can take part in America's extraordinary rise."

This was, in a nutshell, Trump's pitch for reelection. It was certainly received that way by the Republican members of Congress, who set aside any concerns about Trump and turned the moment into a campaign rally by chanting "Four more years!" In the year leading up to his address, many political reporters and analysts saw the economy as Trump's best argument—"the strongest card in his reelection deck," strong enough even to put him "on track for a 2020 landslide." And when Trump was acquitted by the Senate the day after this speech, it appeared to put him even more on track to overcome his many challenges and controversies and win a second term. As one former administration official said, "The 'oh, shit' feeling . . . is gone."[26]

At the beginning of the election year, the reality for Trump was actually somewhere between "landslide" and "oh, shit." Simple forecasts of the 2020 election showed that neither Trump nor his Democratic opponent was strongly favored to win. The reason, once again, was Trump's unusual unpopularity.

A simple forecast for presidential elections can be built off a few key factors: the state of the economy, the president's popularity, whether the incumbent candidate is running for reelection, and how long the president's party has held the White House. The party of the incumbent president tends to win a larger share of the vote when the economy is growing, the incumbent is popular, the incumbent is running for reelection, and the party has held the White House for only one term rather than two or more in a row. Moreover, the relationships between presidential election outcomes and economic growth and presidential approval tend to be somewhat stronger when the president is running for reelection. Taken together, these factors certainly do not capture all the influences on election outcomes. But they provide a useful baseline.[27]

When 2020 began, Trump had the benefit of solid economic growth. Over the previous two quarters, the nonannualized growth in gross domestic product was 1.2 percent. Trump's approval rating, however, averaged only 41 percent in December 2019. This number—and the fact that Trump's approval remained low despite the growing economy—was his central challenge. A statistical model based on only those two factors suggested that Trump would win 49.7 percent of the major-party popular vote—a margin only slightly smaller than when he lost the national popular vote to Clinton in 2016.[28] A model that includes incumbency, and that also allows the apparent effect of economic growth and presidential popularity to vary depending on whether the incumbent is running, forecast a more evenly divided election: according to this model, Trump would win almost exactly 50 percent of the vote. A more favorable model for Trump was one that factored in economic growth, presidential approval, and also the time the GOP had controlled the White House. Since incumbent parties tend to do worse the longer their "tenure," Trump benefited accordingly, and was forecast to win 52 percent of the popular vote by this model. The upshot of these various models, however, was anything but a guaranteed reelection. (Details of these models appear in the appendix to this chapter.)

When Trump was out on the campaign trail in the fall of 2019, he said to an audience in Manchester, New Hampshire, "Whether you love me or hate me, you have got to vote for me."[29] Trump's problem, however, was that the people who loved him were less than half the electorate. Despite a growing economy, Trump was not a clear favorite in 2020.

But because Trump's popularity never plummeted, he was not a massive underdog either. In fact, Trump had won before when he was no more popular than he was when he embarked on his reelection campaign. To do it again, he needed at least one of two things. One was for the good economy to continue. The other was a Democratic opponent almost as unpopular as he was.

He got neither.

4

A House United

We have one moral imperative, and that's to beat Donald Trump.

—JAMES CARVILLE, DEMOCRATIC CAMPAIGN
STRATEGIST, FEBRUARY 4, 2020

ON SEPTEMBER 12, 2019, ten of the Democratic candidates for president gathered for a debate at Texas Southern University in Houston. Up front, the candidates leading the national polls stood in the middle: Joe Biden, the former vice president and Delaware senator, now running his third presidential campaign; Bernie Sanders, the Vermont senator and 2016 presidential candidate; and Massachusetts senator Elizabeth Warren. The ideological differences within the party—the moderate Biden, the progressives Sanders and Warren—were center stage.

Those differences emerged not long into the debate when the candidates discussed health care. Biden criticized Warren and Sanders for proposing "Medicare for All," a system of government-provided health insurance that would replace private insurance plans. Biden said it would be too expensive and proposed instead to expand the Affordable Care Act, which was enacted when Biden was vice president.[1] Warren defended her plan, saying it could be paid for by increasing taxes on the wealthy and corporations, and Sanders said that his plan would actually be cheaper than the status quo and criticized pharmaceutical and insurance companies for profiteering. Biden referred to Sanders as a "socialist."

Things got testier in an exchange between Biden and former Obama cabinet secretary Julián Castro, who accused Biden of giving contradictory accounts of whether Americans would have to opt in to an insurance plan or be automatically enrolled. In what was perceived as a shot at Biden's mental competence, Castro asked, "Are you forgetting what you said two minutes ago?"

Castro and Biden went back and forth until other candidates put an end to it. The entrepreneur Andrew Yang chided them, saying, "Come on, guys!" South Bend mayor Pete Buttigieg said, "This is why presidential debates are becoming unwatchable." Minnesota senator Amy Klobuchar put it this way: "A house divided cannot stand. And that is not how we are going to win this."

The scene in Houston illustrated the challenges the Democratic Party faced in the 2020 primary. There were a lot of candidates. There was no dominant front-runner. And there were plenty of disagreements about health care and other issues. Political commentators anticipated a "battle royale" and "a bitter fight between liberals and leftists."[2]

A fight certainly seemed to be brewing in 2019 and early 2020 during the "invisible primary," the period before the actual voting begins in primaries and caucuses. Neither Democratic leaders nor donors coordinated on a front runner, leaving the race unsettled. Biden did win the most support among the few party leaders who endorsed a candidate, but he struggled to raise money, generate positive news coverage, and otherwise establish himself as the likely nominee. Probably the best news for Biden during the invisible primary was that no other candidate emerged as a clear alternative. The candidates who leveraged media attention to break out of the pack, such as Buttigieg and Warren, eventually saw their poll numbers decline as they experienced the scrutiny that comes with being the surging candidate.

The drama continued once the voting began. Biden's early stumbles in the Iowa caucus and New Hampshire primary appeared to put his candidacy in real jeopardy and raised the prospect—worrying to many Democrats—of a Sanders nomination. But then two things happened to help Biden win. First, the electoral power of his more racially diverse coalition became manifest in the South Carolina primary and the states that voted on Super Tuesday. Second, party leaders, including Sanders, finally rallied around him. This is how Democrats not only avoided the "house divided" that Klobuchar warned about but coalesced so quickly around Biden.

Despite what seemed historic and unusual about 2020—the acrimony within the party dating back to 2016, the sheer number of Democratic candidates, a topsy-turvy invisible primary—the 2020 result was remarkable for its similarity to past primaries and especially the 2016 contest between Hillary Clinton and Bernie Sanders. Biden won by building a coalition much like Clinton's—one that leaned on African American voters, older voters, and committed Democrats. And as with Clinton, Biden's support among African Americans appeared to derive in part from his association with Obama. Both Biden's and Clinton's victories show that in an increasingly multiracial Democratic Party, the candidate who can build a multiracial coalition has the best chance of winning. And building that coalition is about not just the candidate's race, but also their record and experience.

The 2020 primary resembled past Democratic primaries in another respect: the ideological "battle royale" ultimately fizzled. It is easy to imagine that the policy differences on display in the Houston debate were widely known to Democratic voters and reflected in deep divides within the Democratic electorate. But although some Democrats voted for the candidate whom they perceived as the best match ideologically, many Democratic voters did not know where the candidates stood ideologically or see differences between them. Most strikingly, the growing homogeneity within the Democratic Party, which we discussed in chapter 1, produced liberal majorities on many issues and only modest differences among the supporters of the different candidates.

Finally, Democrats were able to unify because their biggest political priorities were the issues on which they mostly agreed. In chapter 3, we showed how Republicans' priorities largely dovetailed with Trump's own agenda, helping them support him despite their occasional reservations. Among Democrats, the same issues were also their top priorities, although of course their views on those issues reflected their opposition to Trump. In short, the priorities of Democrats were much more the issues on which they disagreed with Trump than the issues on which they disagreed with each other.

At the same time, Biden's victory did raise uncomfortable questions for the party about the prospects of candidates who were not white men. Many asked whether sexism hindered Elizabeth Warren's candidacy and whether the party's focus on electability—choosing a candidate who could beat Trump—benefited white male candidates like Biden. But despite uncomfortable questions and even the occasional unwatchable debate, the Democratic Party emerged from the primary far more unified than many observers had expected when phrases like "bitter fight" and even "toxic distrust" were being thrown around.[3] Indeed, Democratic primary voters were actually less divided in their views of the candidates than in the 2016 or 2008 primaries. This put Biden in a stronger position to accomplish the party's ultimate goal: beating Trump.

THE TRAUMA OF 2016

It is always difficult to lose an election, but for Democrats Trump's victory in 2016 was a particularly terrible shock. Not only was Clinton widely expected to win based on preelection polls, but it seemed impossible that someone like Trump, whom Democrats believed was fundamentally unfit for the office, could win. Democrats were "traumatized," said one Iowa political activist. And angry. One Democratic donor said, "I'm not putting another fucking dime in until someone tells me what just happened."[4] Hillary Clinton tried to oblige, penning an election postmortem actually called *What Happened*. But this did little to settle the debate. Democrats continued to question why they lost, but struggled to settle on any clear answer.

Indeed, what is striking about the Democratic Party after 2016 is just how many answers there were. The political scientist Seth Masket interviewed dozens of Democratic activists in 2017 and heard many different explanations. About half of the activists blamed Clinton herself. Some blamed her lack of campaign effort—for instance, that she never made an appearance in Wisconsin, which she lost narrowly; others blamed her campaign message. Others, including Biden, said that she was just not a good candidate.[5] About 30 percent of activists blamed "identity politics"—the idea that Clinton and the party focused too much on African Americans, Latinos, the LGBT community, and women, and not enough on other groups and especially the "white working class."

Another explanation for Clinton's loss focused on her primary opponent, Bernie Sanders. Some blamed him for tying Clinton up in a long and divisive primary. By May 2016, nearly 60 percent of Sanders supporters rated Clinton unfavorably, and at the Democratic National Convention in July, Sanders's supporters booed and protested the proceedings. Yet despite these divisions, about 80 percent of Democratic primary voters who reported voting for Sanders ultimately reported voting for Clinton in November. But at the end of the 2016 campaign, the dynamic between Sanders and Clinton—and thus between his supporters and the broader Democratic Party—was much more like détente than rapprochement.[6]

After 2016, the Sanders-aligned faction of the party seemed ascendant. Two Sanders-aligned candidates—Alexandria Ocasio-Cortez and Ayanna Pressley—successfully challenged longtime Democratic incumbents Joseph Crowley and Michael Capuano, respectively, in the 2018 congressional primaries. Ocasio-Cortez's popularity on social media made her an instant star within the party. She, Pressley, and two other first-term progressive representatives—Michigan's Rashida Tlaib and Minnesota's Ilhan Omar—became known as "The Squad" and soon clashed not only with Donald Trump but also with Democratic leaders, including House Speaker Nancy Pelosi.

Commentators quickly jumped on the idea that the Democratic Party was facing its own version of the Tea Party, a conservative faction that emerged within the Republican Party after Obama's election. To be sure, this characterization was exaggerated. In 2018, there was no spike in primary challengers to Democratic incumbents. In fact, Crowley and Capuano were the only Democratic incumbents to lose in primary elections. And there was little evidence of the GOP's mode of factional politics, where outside groups motivated by ideology spent money to knock out moderate incumbents in primaries.[7]

Nevertheless, the intraparty conflict was significant enough to affect the 2020 presidential nomination process itself. After the 2016 election the Democratic National Committee established a "Unity and Reform Commission" to consider changes to that process, motivated largely by complaints from Sanders supporters. One of the leading complaints was about superdelegates, Democratic leaders who make up about 15 percent of the delegates at the national convention and whose votes, unlike "pledged delegates," are not determined by primary or caucus outcomes in their state. Superdelegates can conceivably steer the nomination to a different candidate than the one who has won the most pledged delegates, although this has not happened since superdelegates were created after Jimmy Carter's loss in 1980, including in 2016, when Clinton won the majority of both superdelegates and pledged delegates. Sanders wanted to eliminate them entirely, but as a compromise, the commission forbade them from taking part in the initial floor vote at the convention. This compromise favored Sanders because it meant party leaders could not swing the outcome away from him on the first round of balloting. It also helped ensure that the primary would not devolve into a divisive fight over process.

SOMETHING "BIGGER AND BETTER" THAN BIDEN?

With Donald Trump's reelection prospects so uncertain, it is no surprise that there were lots of Democrats wanting to run against him. But the sheer number of Democratic candidates was unheard of: there were twenty-eight who had held a significant elective office or would receive significant media coverage during the primaries. This exceeded even the 2016 Republican primary, which featured seventeen candidates.

The large field made it harder for Democratic elites to do what a political party usually tries to do during the invisible primary: coordinate on a front-runner. When that is successful, influential actors within the party identify a candidate who has two qualities: they are satisfactory to the party in their credentials and policy positions, and they have a good chance of winning the general election.[8] But in 2020, the party's success in identifying a front-runner was partial, at best. Biden emerged from the invisible primary with some backing within the party but not enough to put him in a dominant position.

Biden was an experienced politician. He was first elected a U.S. senator in 1972 and represented Delaware until 2009, when he became vice president under Barack Obama. His 2020 campaign was his third for president. He ran in a crowded 1988 Democratic field but withdrew early after news coverage identified instances in which he cribbed passages from other politicians' speeches and exaggerated his own biography. In the 2008 Democratic presidential primary, his poll numbers languished in the single digits and he withdrew after finishing fifth in the Iowa caucus. As Obama's vice president, he would have been a natural successor, but as the 2016 primary campaign was getting underway, Biden was dealing with the illness of his son Beau, who died of cancer in May 2015. When Biden began seriously considering a run several months later, Hillary Clinton had locked up the support of most leaders in the party. Even Obama was reportedly against Biden's entering the race. Ultimately, Biden stayed out.[9]

Biden declared his candidacy for the 2020 contest on April 25, 2019. In his speech that day, he attacked Trump for his response to the 2017 white supremacist rally in Charlottesville, Virginia, and for his "embrace of dictators and oligarchs." He repeated his common refrain that "we are in a battle for the soul of this nation." One *New York Times* story said that Biden "presented himself as a steely leader for a country wracked by political conflict" and "believes voters will embrace him as a figure of stability and maturity." But the story went on to detail the potential challenges Biden would face: in short, he was an older white man with a reputation as a moderate. As the story put it, Biden would have to appeal to "Democratic voters who tend to prize youth, diversity, and unapologetic liberalism."[10]

If Democrats wanted an alternative to Biden on virtually any dimension, that person could be found in this large field. Senator Cory Booker was African American; Kamala Harris was the daughter of parents from Jamaica and India; Julián Castro was Hispanic American. The field also included prominent women officeholders, most notably Harris, Warren, Klobuchar, and New York senator Kirsten Gillibrand. Buttigieg was the first openly gay candidate to run for the party's nomination.

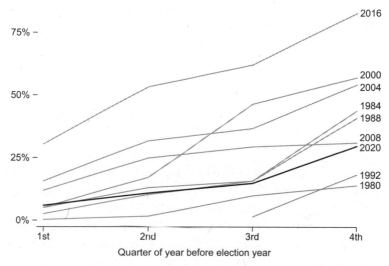

Figure 4.1.
Percentage of Democratic Officeholders Endorsing a Presidential Candidate before the
Iowa Caucus. *Note*: Officeholders include Democratic governors, senators, and U.S.
House members. Endorsements prior to the year before the election are included in the
first quarter. Endorsements in an election year but before the Iowa caucus are included
in the fourth quarter. *Source*: Cohen et al., *The Party Decides*; FiveThirtyEight.

The difficulty the party had in identifying a consensus nominee was
visible in candidate endorsements by party leaders during the invisible
primary. These endorsements are useful signals because they are public
and they come before any caucuses or primaries.[11] But in 2020, most
party leaders sat on the sidelines: by the Iowa caucus, only 30 percent
of Democratic governors, senators, and U.S. House members had endorsed any candidate (figure 4.1). This was fewer than in most other
Democratic primaries since 1980. Even though the large 2020 field gave
Democratic leaders many candidates to choose from, most leaders did
not choose any of them.

Among those who did endorse, Biden earned more than any other candidate. In total, almost 16 percent of leading Democratic officeholders endorsed him, equaling 53 percent of all the endorsements made before the Iowa caucus. This was similar to Clinton in 2008, who won the endorsements of 16 percent of these Democratic leaders and 52 percent of all the endorsements made in that year's invisible primary.[12] The challenge facing Biden was rooted in the same intraparty divisions visible since 2016. For example, many prominent progressive Democrats, including "The Squad," endorsed Sanders or Warren. And although Biden won more endorsements from African American members of Congress than did the other presidential candidates, he was not endorsed by Black leaders like Rev. Al Sharpton and Stacey Abrams. Even Obama was reportedly not enthusiastic about Biden's candidacy in 2020, much as he had not been in 2016.[13]

Thus, the party found itself in a place it had been before, especially in 2004 and, to some extent, 2008. In those primaries, there was no clear heir apparent, as there had been in 2000 (Vice President Al Gore) or 2016 (Hillary Clinton). It was harder for party leaders to coordinate on a consensus favorite and easier instead to worry about the liabilities of any particular candidate. Was Biden too old? Were Sanders and Warren too liberal? Was Buttigieg too inexperienced? Would Warren, Harris, and other women or people of color potentially be hurt by their gender or race or both? And so on.

But in 2020, the situation was made even more challenging by the evolution of the campaign finance system, which can be summarized in two words: easy money. Compared to earlier years, more candidates are now able to raise more money in presidential primaries, even without much support from party leaders.[14] That was true in the 2016 primary, when Sanders won almost no endorsements from party leaders but leveraged his support among small donors to raise over $235 million. This was true in 2019 as well: a number of candidates raised credible amounts of money, and once again there was no dominant front-runner (figure 4.2). Two wealthy candidates, Michael Bloomberg and Tom Steyer, each spent more than $200 million of their own money to fund their campaigns. Many others raised at least enough to mount a campaign.

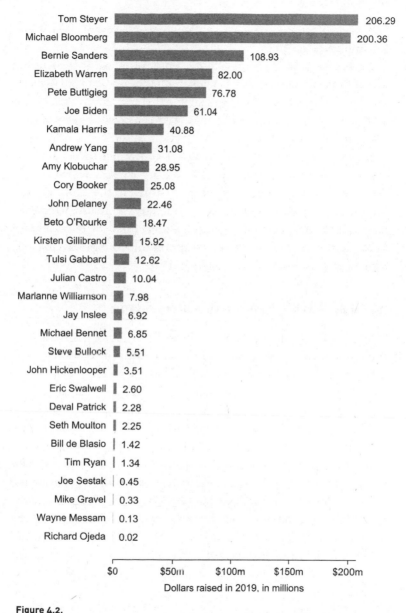

Candidate	Amount (millions)
Tom Steyer	206.29
Michael Bloomberg	200.36
Bernie Sanders	108.93
Elizabeth Warren	82.00
Pete Buttigieg	76.78
Joe Biden	61.04
Kamala Harris	40.88
Andrew Yang	31.08
Amy Klobuchar	28.95
Cory Booker	25.08
John Delaney	22.46
Beto O'Rourke	18.47
Kirsten Gillibrand	15.92
Tulsi Gabbard	12.62
Julian Castro	10.04
Marianne Williamson	7.98
Jay Inslee	6.92
Michael Bennet	6.85
Steve Bullock	5.51
John Hickenlooper	3.51
Eric Swalwell	2.60
Deval Patrick	2.28
Seth Moulton	2.25
Bill de Blasio	1.42
Tim Ryan	1.34
Joe Sestak	0.45
Mike Gravel	0.33
Wayne Messam	0.13
Richard Ojeda	0.02

Dollars raised in 2019, in millions

Figure 4.2.
Total Money Raised by Democratic Presidential Candidates in 2019. *Note*: For Bloomberg and Steyer, the figures include the personal wealth that they spent. *Source*: Federal Elections Commission.

Fifteen candidates raised at least $10 million, and eleven raised at least $20 million.

By contrast, in 2007 only four Democratic candidates raised $20 million or more: Obama, Clinton, John Edwards, and Bill Richardson. Biden himself raised just $8.4 million that year. In 2019, the author Marianne Williamson raised about that much, even though she had never held elective office.[15]

Biden's slower pace of fund-raising was concerning to his campaign and a recurrent story in the news media. One headline from October 2019 was "Why Biden Is Getting Crushed in the All-Important Money Race." Indeed, one major Democratic fund raiser, who even donated to Biden out of "loyalty," said, "I don't think Joe Biden is going to be the nominee. I think there's a thirst for something down the road taking us towards something bigger and better."[16]

THE PROMISE AND PERIL OF PRIMARY NEWS COVERAGE

With a large field and no clear consensus choice among party leaders and donors, the question was whether one of the candidates could rise to the top by leveraging news coverage to raise their visibility and standing within the field. There are presidential primary candidates who have pulled off this feat, even without much preexisting support in the party. In some cases, the increasing media coverage of the invisible primary has fueled media-driven candidacies even before the voting starts. For example, in 2016, both Donald Trump and Bernie Sanders saw their media coverage and poll numbers increase substantially during the invisible primary. In other cases, candidates have garnered media coverage because of a better-than-expected showing in early caucuses or primaries and sought to use the newfound attention to win later contests. In 2004, John Kerry's unexpected victory in the Iowa caucus gave him enough momentum to win the nomination. The same happened to Obama in 2008.[17]

But presidential primaries also show the limits of relying on news coverage to jump-start a campaign. For many candidates, media attention is only temporary and follows a cycle of "discovery, scrutiny, and decline." An event deemed newsworthy vaults the candidate into the headlines ("discovery"), usually producing positive coverage. But the candidate's newfound prominence also invites media to delve into their biography and record, often uncovering inconsistencies and controversies. It was exactly this sort of scrutiny that helped sink Biden's 1988 campaign. Since then, any number of candidates have seen the media spotlight turn harsh. The resulting decline in their poll numbers sometimes means the de facto end of their bid, even if they stay in the race.[18]

In 2019 and 2020, the Democratic primary did not see a candidate leverage news attention to achieve durable success. Instead, the breakout moments of discovery fueled temporary rises in the polls before media scrutiny focused attention on the candidates' limitations.

Using transcripts of cable network coverage to capture media attention, we identified three candidates who experienced discovery, scrutiny, and decline: Harris, Buttigieg, and Warren.[19] Harris experienced two moments of "discovery"—when she announced her candidacy and held her kickoff rally in Oakland, and when she criticized Biden at the June 27 candidate debate for having opposed a school busing program in Delaware (figure 4.3). In both moments, news coverage of Harris spiked and her poll numbers increased. But in each case, discovery was followed by scrutiny. There was scrutiny of trivial things, like whether Harris had listened to the rappers Tupac Shakur and Snoop Dogg in college (their albums did not debut until after she graduated), as she apparently claimed. There was also scrutiny of substantive things, like whether her record as the district attorney of San Francisco and the state attorney general of California was out of step with some Democrats' distrust of the criminal justice system. For example, a February 11 *New York Times* story said she faced "a chorus of skepticism, especially from the left." In the weeks and months after the June debate, Harris garnered less and less coverage, and her poll numbers slid. A late-November *New York Times* story described her campaign as riven with tensions and quoted a senior staff member who said that she had never seen a presidential campaign "treat its staff so poorly." Harris dropped out on December 3.[20]

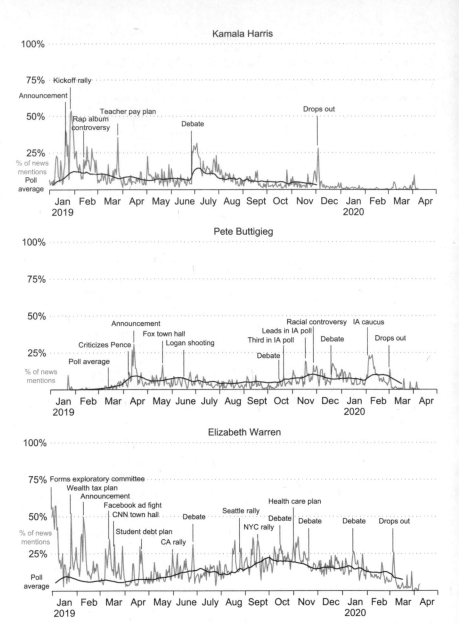

Figure 4.3.

Harris, Buttigieg, and Warren News Coverage and National Poll Average. Percentage of news mentions is the candidate's share of all mentions of the Democratic presidential candidates on cable networks. Poll average is the smoothed average of the candidate's standing in national primary polls. *Source*: Internet Archive; FiveThirtyEight.

Pete Buttigieg also experienced several cycles of discovery, scrutiny, and decline that were visible in both news coverage and polls (figure 4.3). He drew early news attention for criticizing Vice President Mike Pence's record on LGBT rights, for the announcement of his candidacy, and for a well-received appearance on Fox News. Typical of this discovery phase, the news coverage was generally positive. A *Los Angeles Times* piece published that day called him the "hottest thing in politics." But after a fifty-four-year-old African American man, Eric Logan, was shot and killed by a South Bend police officer on June 16, Buttigieg faced significant criticism. News accounts delved into Buttigieg's rocky relationship with the African American community in South Bend. Rep. Marcia Fudge of Ohio, the former chairwoman of the Congressional Black Caucus, said "Pete has a Black problem."[21]

A similar cycle repeated in the fall. After Buttigieg garnered positive news coverage for his performance in the October 15 debate ("Pete Buttigieg wins the night" was the headline in the *Boston Globe*) and for improving poll numbers in Iowa, controversy about Buttigieg's record on race arrested any momentum. This time, it stemmed from a caustic essay, "Pete Buttigieg Is a Lying MF," that criticized Buttigieg for 2011 comments in which he blamed a lack of role models for the challenges facing poor Black children in schools. This was more fodder for stories about Buttigieg's weak standing with African American voters.[22]

Even though Buttigieg's poll numbers slipped after this controversy, both nationally and in Iowa, Buttigieg outperformed his Iowa poll numbers and narrowly beat Sanders in the February 3 Iowa caucus. Although Buttigieg's victory took three days to confirm because of delays in vote counting, he did see a spike in news coverage and his poll numbers and then finished second in the New Hampshire primary on February 11, just behind Sanders. This was consistent with previous patterns: performance in the Iowa caucus as well as the subsequent bump in media attention are positively associated with performance in New Hampshire.[23] But Buttigieg could not sustain this momentum when the race shifted to Nevada and South Carolina. In South Carolina, Buttigieg's lack of support among African American voters cost him: he came in fourth with only 8 percent of the vote. He dropped out the next day and endorsed Biden right before the Super Tuesday primaries.

Elizabeth Warren experienced a long and gradual increase in news attention and poll numbers rather than the quicker ups and downs that Harris and Buttigieg experienced (figure 4.3). Compared to them, she received more news coverage and more support from Democrats in polls for most of 2019. The rollout of Warren's campaign generated large spikes in news coverage—ones larger than either Harris or Buttigieg received. She generated coverage after Facebook deleted and then restored her digital ads that criticized the company and for the rollouts of plans to deal with student loan debt and opioids. "I have a plan for that" became her catchphrase, and news coverage said she was "forcing her rivals to play catch-up and stake out their own positions." Coverage of her campaign events was also positive, including her March 18 appearance at a CNN town hall ("policy-fluent," "energetic") and a May 31 rally in Oakland ("show of force").[24]

Warren's ascent took a page from Bernie Sanders's 2016 campaign and threatened his 2020 campaign. Like Sanders, she was a progressive who could raise funds without relying on big-money donors. As Sanders did in 2016, she made news for her big rallies in liberal-leaning cities—including even larger ones in Seattle in August (15,000 attendees) and New York City in September (20,000 attendees). Commentators talked about how her "massive crowds" signaled her campaign's "organic energy." Her poll numbers continued to climb. By the end of September, she was in second place behind Biden. Several Iowa polls had her tied or leading the field. Altogether, Warren's rise from April to the end of September—a shift of about 16 points in national polls—matched Sanders's rise during the same period in 2015, when his poll numbers increased from 7 points to 23.[25]

But eventually, Warren faced significant scrutiny of the very thing that made her stand out: her detailed policy plans. At the October 15 candidate debate, Warren came under attack again for her embrace of Medicare for All. As Biden did at the September debate, Buttigieg and Amy Klobuchar pushed Warren on how she would pay for Medicare for All and specifically whether middle-class Americans would need to pay higher taxes. But unlike in September, postdebate news coverage centered on these attacks, with headlines like "Warren takes punches" and "Warren draws fire from all sides." The scrutiny of Warren only intensified after she became the only candidate to release a plan to pay for Medicare for All on November 1. Biden's campaign spokesperson said Warren was using "mathematical gymnastics" and that "it's impossible to pay for Medicare for All without middle class tax increases." Reporters quoted experts skeptical of the plan's "big assumptions." One *Washington Post* column was headlined, "Elizabeth Warren's Biggest Political Decision May Be Her Worst." Meanwhile, Sanders received little scrutiny for brushing off questions about how he would pay for Medicare for All.[26]

This scrutiny appeared to cost Warren. Her poll numbers began to decline and never recovered. She came in third in the Iowa caucus behind Buttigieg and Sanders and fourth in New Hampshire, where she won only 8 percent of the vote and did not meet the 15 percent threshold needed to win any delegates. She did not win delegates in the Nevada caucus or South Carolina primary either. Two days after Super Tuesday, she ended her campaign.

Joe Biden and Bernie Sanders experienced a different trajectory than Harris, Warren, or Buttigieg. Biden and Sanders were better known when the campaign started, and so there was less to discover about them. During the invisible primary, they experienced fewer surges in positive news coverage and thus their poll numbers remained stable, putting them in first or second place for much of 2019. In this way, their campaigns resembled that of Mitt Romney in 2012 or Hillary Clinton in 2016. What changed this static pattern were the early caucuses and primaries. Sanders's successes in Iowa, New Hampshire, and Nevada—combined with very poor showings by Biden—vaulted Sanders into the lead. It appeared to many as if Sanders would win. But Biden's victories in South Carolina and many states whose primaries were held on Super Tuesday brought his campaign back to life.

For Sanders, some spikes in his news coverage occurred after the usual types of events—his kickoff rally, the release of a student debt plan, an October rally featuring Alexandria Ocasio-Cortez, and reports of record-breaking fund-raising (figure 4.4). But intermingled with this positive coverage was more scrutiny than he received in 2015, when he was the most favorably covered candidate—Democrat or Republican—according to a systematic analysis of news coverage of that year's invisible primary. For example, when Sanders released his tax returns in April 2019, reporting over $500,000 in income, news coverage called him "part of the 1%." A June 12 speech defending democratic socialism led to news coverage about how Sanders's views "complicate" his campaign. Sanders's hospitalization after a heart attack in early October was framed as "casting uncertainty over a candidacy already struggling to win new voters."[27] Overall, Sanders received more coverage in his head-to-head race with Hillary Clinton than he did in 2020, when he was less novel of a political figure and when he had to compete with a larger number of candidates. Between June 1 and December 31, 2019, he received an average of 13 percent of mentions of the candidates, compared to 24 percent in 2015. His poll standing was lower, too: an average of 16 percent in 2019, compared to 25 percent in 2015.

But Sanders hung in because Biden was not winning any additional support as the invisible primary went on (figure 4.4). Except for a brief polling spike when he announced his candidacy, Biden's poll numbers were remarkably stable, averaging just over 25 percent for much of the summer and fall. Part of the reason was that even though Biden frequently got the most news coverage of any candidate—between June and December 2019, Biden's average daily share of candidate mentions was 38 percent, well above Warren (17%) and Sanders (13%)—much of that coverage was unfavorable.

Even before he announced his candidacy, Biden faced allegations that he had inappropriately kissed and touched a former Nevada legislator, Lucy Flores. In the wake of Flores's allegation, there were complaints

---

Figure 4.4.
Sanders and Biden News Coverage and National Poll Average. Percentage of news mentions is the candidate's share of all mentions of the Democratic presidential candidates on cable networks. Poll average is the smoothed average of the candidate's standing in national primary polls. *Source*: Internet Archive; FiveThirtyEight.

Bernie Sanders

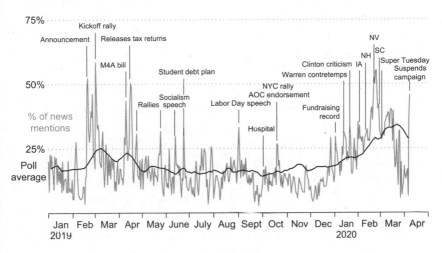

100% ···

75% ···
- Announcement
- Kickoff rally
- Releases tax returns
- M4A bill
- Student debt plan
- Rallies
- Socialism speech
- Labor Day speech
- NYC rally
- AOC endorsement
- Hospital
- Warren contretemps
- Clinton criticism IA
- Fundraising record
- NH
- NV
- SC
- Super Tuesday Suspends campaign

% of news mentions

50% ···

25% ···

Poll average

Jan 2019 Feb Mar Apr May June July Aug Sept Oct Nov Dec Jan 2020 Feb Mar Apr

Joe Biden

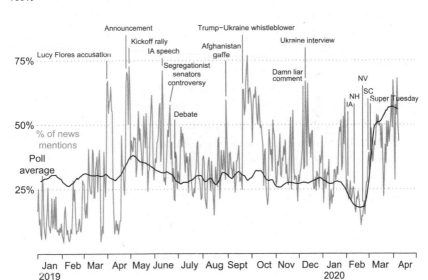

100% ···

75% ···
- Lucy Flores accusation
- Announcement
- Kickoff rally
- IA speech
- Segregationist senators controversy
- Afghanistan gaffe
- Trump–Ukraine whistleblower
- Ukraine interview
- Damn liar comment
- Debate
- NV
- NH
- IA
- SC
- Super Tuesday

% of news mentions

Poll average

50% ···

25% ···

Jan 2019 Feb Mar Apr May June July Aug Sept Oct Nov Dec Jan 2020 Feb Mar Apr from other women as well. In response, Biden could only manage what one news report called a "convoluted apology." Then, in the early weeks of his official campaign, he generated coverage not only for an Iowa speech criticizing Trump but also for a controversial remark about his positive working relationship with segregationist senators in the 1970s. A *Washington Post* headline from that time: "Joe Biden Picked a Bad Week to Have a Bad Week."[28]

There were other bad weeks. On August 30, Biden made news for telling a false story about a visit to Afghanistan when he was vice president. CNN snarked: "If the day ends in a 'y' it's a good bet that Joe Biden has stumbled into yet another campaign trail gaffe." Even the extensive coverage of Trump's attempt to pressure Ukraine to investigate the Bidens did not necessarily generate sympathetic coverage of Biden. For example, one September news story noted that Trump's accusations were "unfounded" but still said that Biden was "at the center of a massive political scandal" that could hurt his campaign. When Biden called a retired Iowa farmer a "damn liar" for confronting him about Hunter Biden's role, he was judged as showing "authenticity, emotion, and a readiness for a fight" but also acting "undisciplined." After an Axios interview in which Biden pledged that as president he would not let family members benefit from their connections to him, Axios asked: "Will Biden move away from a posture of defending his son's honor to acknowledge and address legitimate concerns about his own judgment among some Democrats and swing voters?" A *New York* magazine headline was even more blunt: "Joe Biden Still Can't Answer Basic Questions about Hunter and Burisma." Biden's struggles reportedly led Hillary Clinton to seriously consider entering the primary race.[29]

Despite this negative coverage, Biden still led in national polls, although Sanders gained some ground as Warren's poll numbers declined. Biden and Sanders were nearly tied in Iowa caucus polls as well. But when the primary season began, in Iowa on February 3, Biden struggled. His 14 percent vote share put him behind Buttigieg, Sanders, and Warren. This underwhelming performance was an eerie echo of the concerns that kept him out of the race in 2016. Then, one of Obama's advisers, David Plouffe, had urged him not to run, saying, "Mr. Vice

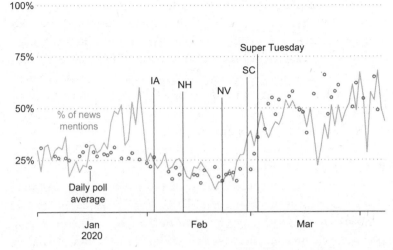

Figure 4.5.
Joe Biden's Share of News Coverage and National Poll Average, January 1–April 8, 2020. Percentage of news mentions is the candidate's share of all mentions of the Democratic presidential candidates on cable networks. Daily average is the raw average of the candidate's standing in national primary polls. *Source:* Internet Archive; FiveThirtyEight.

President, you have had a remarkable career, and it would be wrong to see it end in some hotel room in Iowa with you finishing third behind Bernie Sanders." In 2020, it turns out, Biden's career was threatened by a fourth-place finish.[30]

In the wake of this disappointment, Biden reshuffled his campaign team as his poll numbers began to slide and his campaign began to run short of cash. Figure 4.5, focusing on the period beginning January 1, 2020, shows this trend in the polls clearly. At the same time, Biden's chances of winning the nomination dropped in both forecasting models and prediction markets. Biden then did even worse in the New Hampshire primary—coming in fifth with 8 percent of the vote and winning no convention delegates. Biden did manage a second-place finish in the Nevada caucus, but he was far behind Sanders.[31]

Biden's unexpectedly large losses in the first three primaries hurt him badly in the polls. Prior to Iowa his polling had hovered at around

27 percent. After Nevada his number plummeted to below 16 percent. At that point, bettors in the prediction market PredictIt gave him only a 13 percent chance of winning the nomination, down from 31 percent on February 1. Meanwhile, this market gave Sanders a 65 percent chance as of the day after the Nevada caucus. Many Democratic party leaders and activists were horrified at the prospect of a Sanders nomination. "I've never seen this level of doom," said one. Some began to look to Michael Bloomberg as an alternative.[32]

The South Carolina primary, on February 29, changed Biden's fortunes virtually overnight. Biden had called the state his campaign's "firewall" a month earlier.[33] He was not wrong. Drawing on support within the African American community, Biden won 49 percent of the vote compared to Sanders's 20 percent. One news report called this a "decisive victory" and said it made Biden "the clear alternative" to Sanders. Many observers credited Biden's victory to the February 26 endorsement of South Carolina representative James Clyburn, a very prominent leader in the African American community. It was, indeed, a remarkable turnaround, as Clyburn had suggested in 2018 that Biden should not even get in the race. Now, according to one news report, "James Clyburn changed everything for Joe Biden's campaign."[34]

It is hard to know how much the Clyburn endorsement mattered. To some, the fact that Biden outperformed his poll numbers in South Carolina suggested that Clyburn's endorsement gave him a boost. On the other hand, it is clear that Biden was gaining ground before the endorsement, and perhaps his performance on Election Day was just a continuation of that trend.[35] Moreover, there was one survey in the field in South Carolina when Clyburn announced his endorsement, and it showed no difference in African American support for Biden in the days before and after the endorsement.[36] Biden's victory in South Carolina appeared to depend more on his long-standing support among African American primary voters, which we explore below, than on this one endorsement. (See the appendix for more details.)

The impact of Biden's win in South Carolina was visible almost immediately in national polls (figure 4.5). In a Morning Consult poll conducted right before the South Carolina primary, 21 percent supported

Biden. The day after the primary, this increased to 26 percent. A few days later, this increased again to 36 percent. Meanwhile, Sanders's poll numbers slid from 33 percent to 28 percent.

Biden's victory pushed Democratic leaders to do what many had hesitated to do: rally to his side. Barack Obama began making calls, including to other Democratic candidates.[37] Both Buttigieg and Klobuchar dropped out and endorsed Biden, as did fourteen Democratic governors, senators, and members of the House in the three days after the South Carolina primary. Suddenly, the party leaders who had been reticent to endorse any Democratic candidate got behind Biden.

In the March 3 Super Tuesday primaries, Biden won in ten states. This blew open his lead in the polls: in a March 5–8 Morning Consult poll, 56 percent supported Biden while only 38 percent supported Sanders. Biden's standing had increased by about 35 points in barely more than a week. And more Democratic leaders came aboard. Sixty-seven more governors and members of Congress endorsed Biden in the ensuing month.

The subsequent primaries only expanded Biden's lead. With his victory all but assured, the only remaining question was whether Sanders would continue to battle for as long as he did in 2016. Leading Democrats put pressure on him to end his campaign. On April 8, right after Wisconsin primary voters went to the polls and before the results could be announced, Sanders dropped out. "I cannot in good conscience continue to mount a campaign that cannot win and which would interfere with the important work required of all of us in this difficult hour," Sanders said, alluding to the party's ultimate goal of beating Trump. The following week, Sanders endorsed Biden. The race was over.[38]

BIDEN'S WINNING COALITION

News accounts framed Biden's surge and the "short, orderly primary" that resulted as "the biggest surprise of 2020."[39] But even if Biden's victory was hardly preordained, its roots were there all along. Those roots were grounded in demographics of Democratic voters and the groups of primary voters to whom Biden had particular appeal: older voters, loyal Democrats, African Americans, and voters whose ideological orientation was centrist or center-left rather than strongly progressive. In November 2019, a senior Biden strategist had said that "our strength is the fact that we have a broad and diverse coalition."[40] He was right. That this coalition could bring Biden victory was unsurprising—a similar coalition had helped Hillary Clinton win the nomination in 2016.

Initially, the large field of candidates in 2020 meant that the 2016 coalitions were fractured. Surveys of the same Democratic primary voters in both 2016 and then in 2019–20 found that, for example, about 37 to 40 percent of Clinton 2016 voters supported Biden in the months immediately before the first caucuses and primaries. Sanders's 2016 voters were also divided. As of December 2019, Sanders was winning only 20 percent of his 2016 voters; the largest share (32%) intended to vote for Warren. The later dynamics of the primary—Biden's surge after South Carolina, the exit of other candidates—helped sort out these fractured coalitions. Ultimately, the majority of Clinton 2016 voters reported voting for Biden (62%). Biden also won about a fifth (22%) of Sanders's 2016 voters, although most reported voting for Sanders or Warren.

To see how the demographic building blocks of Biden's coalition resembled those of Clinton's coalition, consider the role of three factors: age, race, and partisanship (figure 4.6). In 2016, Clinton did significantly better among older voters, while Sanders did best among the youngest age cohort. This reflects the typical attraction of younger voters to candidates with a message of change, which drew them not only to Sanders in 2016 but also to Gary Hart in 1984 and Barack Obama in 2008. Clinton also did better than Sanders among Black Americans and Hispanic Americans, while white voters were relatively split between the two candidates. In part, this reflected Clinton's service in the Obama administration, which helped boost her standing among Black Americans. Finally, Clinton did better among primary voters who explicitly identified as Democrats rather than independents, while Sanders did better among independents. This reflects both her historic association with the Democratic Party and Sanders's rejection of it.[41] The left-hand

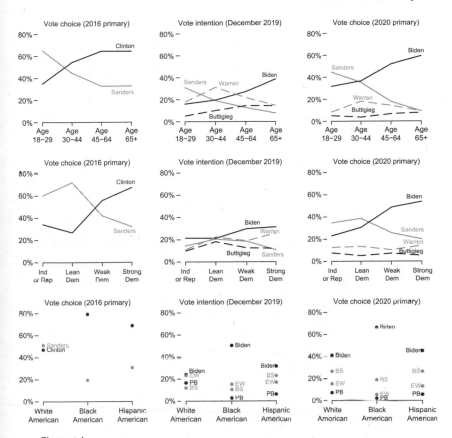

Figure 4.6.
The Relationship between Age, Partisanship, and Race and Voting in the 2016 and 2020 Primaries. *Source*: VOTER Survey.

panels in figure 4.6 show these relationships in 2016, drawing on Views of the Electorate Research (VOTER) Survey data.

In the 2020 primary, these patterns were somewhat evident by the end of 2019, but the crowded field and lack of a dominant front-runner muted them. The middle column of figure 4.6 shows that, relative to younger voters, older voters were more likely to favor Biden, Bloomberg, or Buttigieg. Sanders led among the youngest voters, as he did in 2016, although Warren polled well with those aged 30–44. As in 2016, Sanders also polled a bit better among independents leaning Democratic than among Democrats with a stronger partisan identity, while the reverse was true for Biden. (Notably, Warren polled better among strong Democrats than Sanders did, showing that she appealed to voters solidly in the party as well as those more on its periphery.) But the relationship between partisanship and vote intentions was much weaker at that point than in 2016. The same was true for race. White voters were divided among different candidates while both Black and Hispanic voters favored Biden, just as they had favored Clinton in 2016. But Biden's lead among Black and Hispanic voters was at that point smaller than Clinton's was when the 2016 primaries concluded, which reflected the more fractured field of candidates in 2020.

However, by the end of the primary season, Biden's surge and the withdrawal of the other candidates helped Biden gain support among various groups, but especially among Democratic primary voters who actually identified as Democrats (right-hand column of figure 4.6). This fits a familiar pattern of "activation" in primary elections, whereby characteristics of voters that predispose them to support a candidate become stronger predictors of their choices as the campaign goes on.[42] The result of this activation was that Biden's coalition came to resemble Clinton's even more closely. Sanders still performed the best among the groups who were his strongest supporters in 2016—independents, younger voters—although the fractured field and shorter contest in 2020 meant that he won fewer votes overall. At one point before Sanders entered the race, his pollster had argued that he could win in a crowded field if he relied on his hard-core supporters and won a steady 25–30 percent of the vote in each state.[43] The 2020 results showed the challenge inherent in this approach, which, as his team knew then, would not work if the race narrowed to Sanders and one other candidate.

Part of the reason Biden's coalition helped him win is simple math: the demographic groups that tended to support him make up a big chunk of the party. The very large samples in the Nationscape survey project illuminate the demographics of Democratic voters overall and in key states (table 4.1). For example, older voters are more numerous

TABLE 4.1. Demographics of Democratic Primary Voters (Percent)

	All states	Iowa and NH	Nevada	South Carolina	Super Tuesday states
Race/ethnicity					
White	54	80	45	46	48
Black	19	4	18	44	17
Asian	7	3	11	1	9
Latino	18	10	23	8	24
Age					
18–29	20	20	22	16	21
30–44	25	22	27	20	26
45–64	32	34	31	36	32
65+	23	24	20	28	21
Party identification					
Strong Democrat	54	52	56	57	53
Weak Democrat	26	19	27	18	26
Leaning Democrat	11	19	10	14	12
Independent	3	6	3	4	4
Republican	5	5	5	7	5
Ideological identification					
Very liberal	18	20	24	18	18
Liberal	30	32	30	27	30
Moderate	38	38	33	39	38
Conservative	10	7	10	12	10
White subgroups					
White college graduate	25	34	17	20	24
White noncollege	29	46	29	27	24
White liberal	28	42	26	23	26
Sample size	182,097	2,300	2,173	2,679	63,702

Source: Democracy Fund + UCLA Nationscape surveys, July 2019–January 2021. The table combines respondents who intended to vote or reported voting in a Democratic caucus or primary.

than the youngest voters. Strong Democrats are more numerous than independents. Black Americans are numerous in the primary electorates in key states like South Carolina but not in Iowa and New Hampshire.

Across all states, several key facts stand out: barely more than half of Democratic primary voters are white (54%), only a fifth are under the age of 30, most identify as Democrats and not independents, and only 18 percent identify as "very liberal." White college graduates and white liberals, who appear prominently in accounts of Democratic Party politics, each constitute barely one-quarter of the party's likely primary voters. The challenge facing candidates like Sanders and Warren was clear: the types of groups that they appealed most to—younger voters, white college graduates, liberal voters—are not large enough to constitute a winning coalition by themselves. This is particularly true when the primary shifts from Iowa and New Hampshire to South Carolina.

Thus, although Biden's prospects seemed grim when he limped out of New Hampshire, this was because he had yet to compete on the territory most favorable to him. Once the race moved to more racially diverse states, the electoral power of Biden's coalition became apparent. To be sure, doing well among the groups central to Biden's coalition, or Hillary Clinton's, is no guarantee of winning the Democratic presidential nomination. But in a year where many people thought the Democratic Party wanted someone new or "bigger and better," it is striking how much the winning coalition was not so new at all.

WHY THE IDEOLOGICAL BATTLE FIZZLED

To some, Biden's victory was a surprise because he seemed out of step with ideological trends in the party, in particular its "unapologetic liberalism." But despite the party's shift to the left and the growing strength of progressive voices in the party, a relative moderate won the nomination. The pitched ideological battle that was expected never came. Exploring why helps explain not only Biden's success but also the nature of voter decision-making in primary elections.

In some ways, primary elections offer promising conditions for ideological or policy-oriented voting. Voters cannot simply rely on their
party identification, which is an efficient shortcut for voting in general
elections and appears to limit any effects of ideology and policy.[44] Thus,
when primary candidates take differing stands on policy issues and
make their differences visible, voters' views on those issues can help
them choose a favored candidate. For example, in the 2016 Republican
primary Donald Trump was, relative to his rivals, more critical of immigration and more supportive of liberal economic policies, like raising
taxes on the wealthy and protecting entitlement programs like Social
Security and Medicare. And, indeed, surveys showed that Republicans
with more conservative views on immigration as well as more liberal
views on economic policy were more likely to support Trump than the
other Republican candidates.[45]

However, in some previous Democratic primaries, the role of ideology
and policy was limited. In 1984, for example, Democratic primary voters
did not really perceive ideological differences between the ostensible
moderate, Walter Mondale, and the more liberal Gary Hart; Democratic
primary voters who identified as liberal actually had more favorable views
of both candidates than voters who did not. In 2008, voters' views on a
wide range of issues did not predict support for Obama in the primary. In
2016, although Democratic primary voters who identified as strong liberals were more likely to support Sanders than Clinton, voters' views on
actual policy issues were not much associated with their choice of Sanders
or Clinton—including their views on the issues that appeared to divide
the two candidates, such as the government's role in health care. Sanders's
voters were more likely to call themselves liberals but were not necessarily
more liberal in their views on the issues salient in the primary.[46]

In 2020, the Democratic primary seemed even more ideologically
fractious than in 2016, given the proliferation of candidates and the presence of both Sanders and Warren in addition to Biden, Buttigieg, and
other candidates considered more moderate. But the ideological con-
tours of the field were not always well understood by voters. In several Nationscape surveys conducted in March and early April 2020,

respondents were asked to place themselves as well as Biden, Sanders, other Democratic candidates, and Donald Trump on a five-point scale ranging from "very liberal" to "very conservative." At this point, after a year or more of the primary campaign, relatively few Democratic primary voters, including those who had already voted as well as those who intended to vote in a primary, did not know where to place Biden (14%) and Sanders (13%). But anywhere from a fifth to a third did not know where to place other Democratic candidates, even though primary voters are, politically, a fairly attentive group. For example, 22 percent could not place Warren at all, 30 percent could not place Buttigieg, and 37 percent could not place Klobuchar.

Moreover, even among voters who could place the candidates on this scale, they did not always perceive an ideological difference between the candidates, and, if they did, their perceptions did not necessarily accord with what most political observers perceived. For example, most observers considered Sanders more liberal than Biden. But among Democratic primary voters, only about half (52%) placed Sanders to the left of Biden on this scale. Among the rest, 21 percent did not see any difference between them, 10 percent put Biden to Sanders's left, and the rest could not place one or both candidates. The same thing was true when comparing Biden to Warren. Fewer Democratic primary voters put Warren to Biden's left (38%), while 28 percent could not place one or both, 23 percent saw no difference, and 11 percent put Biden to the left.

Among the Democratic primary voters who could place one or more candidates, their perceptions looked sensible in the aggregate (figure 4.7). On average, voters placed Biden more toward the center left, Warren and Sanders further left, and Trump well to the right. Notably, the average Democratic primary voter was closer to Biden than Warren or especially Sanders. Overall, 40 percent of Democratic primary voters placed themselves and Biden at exactly the same spot on this 5-point spectrum. Fewer saw themselves as identical to Warren (34%) or Sanders (28%). This is the logical outcome for a party in which, despite its leftward shift, more primary voters identified as moderate than very liberal.

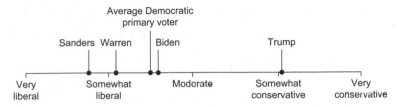

Figure 4.7.
Democratic Primary Voters' Average Ideological Placement of Themselves and the ·
Candidates. *Source*: Democracy Fund + UCLA Nationscape surveys, March 5–April 2,
2020.

These perceptions of the candidates mattered for how much Democratic voters' ideological identification was correlated with their choice of a candidate. The expected correlation—self-identified liberals were more likely to support Sanders than Biden—emerged most clearly among those who placed Sanders to Biden's left. The correlation was weaker among those who placed the candidates at the same point or could not place one or both candidates. In short, ideological identification appeared to affect Democratic primary voting, but any effect was far from automatic. It depended a great deal on how voters perceived the candidates.[47]

Of course, ideological identification does not necessarily capture the nuances of people's views on policy. And much of the primary was centered on policy issues, such as taxes and health care. But even here, two things kept the primary from resembling a "battle royale." For one, the policy differences among the supporters of various Democratic candidates were not that large, especially when compared to the differences between Democrats and Republicans. For another, the relationship between policy views and support for the leading candidates, Biden and Sanders, was muted.

Drawing on large battery of policy questions in the 2019 Nationscape surveys, table 4.2 presents the percentage supporting a subset of these policies among Biden, Sanders, and Warren supporters as well as Republicans.[48] The remaining respondents either opposed the policy or

TABLE 4.2. Policy Attitudes among Likely Democratic Primary Voters versus Republicans

	Percent who agree with the policy			
	Warren supporters	Sanders supporters	Biden supporters	Republicans
Abortion				
Permit abortion in cases other than rape, incest, or when the woman's life is in danger	82	72	72	44
Require a waiting period and ultrasound before an abortion can be obtained	21	30	31	52
Permit late-term abortion	42	36	29	13
Immigration				
Build a wall on the southern border	9	11	13	72
Create a path to citizenship for all undocumented immigrants	77	74	68	36
Ban people from predominantly Muslim countries from entering the United States	8	11	14	33
Charge immigrants who enter the United States illegally with a federal crime	18	21	24	64
Healthcare				
Provide government-run health insurance to all Americans	76	80	64	30
Provide the option to purchase government-run insurance to all Americans	81	73	75	48
Enact Medicare for All	73	80	59	29
Abolish private health insurance and replace with government-run health insurance	48	53	30	16
Guns				
Ban assault rifles	86	69	81	43
Limit gun magazines to ten bullets	77	61	72	38
Environment				
Cap carbon emissions to combat climate change	89	78	79	44
Enact a Green New Deal	69	59	50	20

TABLE 4.2. (*continued*)

	Percent who agree with the policy			
	Warren supporters	Sanders supporters	Biden supporters	Republicans
Taxes				
Raise taxes on families making over $600,000	86	78	79	49
Raise taxes on families making over $250,000	64	61	59	33
Labor				
Raise the minimum wage to $15/hour	85	82	78	39
Guarantee jobs for all Americans	67	77	70	48
Civil Rights/Liberties				
Legalize marijuana	74	77	61	48
Grant reparations payments to the descendants of slaves	42	42	36	10
Education				
Ensure that all students can graduate from state colleges debt free	79	86	72	40
Foreign Policy				
Impose trade tariffs on Chinese goods	24	25	28	56
Reduce the size of the U.S. military	37	37	20	10

Source: Democracy Fund + UCLA Nationscape surveys, July December 2019.

did not express an opinion. (A table with all policies is in table A4.4. The appendix also presents a more direct test of the relationship between policy attitudes and voting in the primaries.)

What stands out is how similar Biden, Sanders, and Warren supporters were. Compared to Biden supporters, only slightly larger fractions of Warren and Sanders supporters had liberal issue positions. For example, a large majority of Warren voters (86%) supported raising taxes on families making at least $650,000 per year, but so did 79 percent of

Biden voters. And as one might expect, most Sanders voters and War-ren voters favored Medicare for All when it was presented without any further information, the option to purchase government health insur-ance (a "public option" or "Medicare for all who want it"), and provid-ing government health insurance for everyone (something closer to Sanders's or Warren's ultimate vision of a single-payer system). Most Biden supporters favored these things too, but with smaller majorities. There were larger differences among Warren, Sanders, and Biden sup-porters when a government insurance plan was described as abolish-ing private insurance—one consequence of a pure single-payer system—but when framed in this fashion, the program was not very popular, period. Even among Sanders supporters, only about half sup-ported it.

The same pattern holds for most of these issues: majorities of Demo-cratic primary voters take the liberal position, and those liberal majori-ties are a little larger among Sanders or Warren supporters than Biden supporters. One exception is gun control, where Sanders voters were actually less liberal than Biden or Warren supporters. But overall, the differences do not suggest any yawning ideological divides within the Democratic electorate. They appear to reflect a party that has actually become less divided, not more so—the natural consequence of the tec-tonic shifts we have described.

There was a final reason that policy issues proved less divisive than many assumed, and it had to do with the issues that Democratic voters cared most about. Throughout 2019, the Nationscape experiments on re-vealed importance showed that as the party prepared to vote on a nominee, Democrats' highest priorities had much more to do with Trump than the issues being debated among the Democratic candidates (figure 4.8).

Figure 4.8.

The Policy Priorities of Democrats. Democrats include respondents who identified with or leaned toward the Democratic Party. Percentage with a liberal view is calculated among all respondents, including those who did not have an opinion. The liberal position on trade is defined here as limiting trade. The liberal position on cutting taxes on families making under $100,000 is defined as not cutting taxes. *Source*: Democracy Fund + UCLA Nationscape surveys, July–December 2019.

	Revealed importance		Percent with liberal view
	Conservative views	Liberal views	
Separate immigrant children			84
Impeach Trump			74
Ban abortion			75
Mass deportation			66
Build border wall			75
Muslim travel ban			72
Ban assault rifles			76
Universal gun background checks			93
Allow limited abortion			72
Dreamer path to citizenship			84
Debt free state college			76
$15 minimum wage			78
Medicare for all			66
Broad path to citizenship			69
Allow transgender in military			77
Cap carbon emissions			78
Big environmental program			76
Universal jobs guarantee			68
Federal health insurance			69
Legalize marijuana			67
Low income health subsidy			79
Raise taxes over $600,000			77
Ban guns			29
Ten Commandments in public bldgs			41
12 weeks maternity leave			00
Limit gun magazines			66
Abortion coverage optional			59
Raise taxes over $250,000			56
Green New Deal			53
Public guns registry			72
Require abortion waiting period			48
Slave reparations			35
Health care public option			76
More oil and gas drilling			46
Allow late term abortion			32
Limit trade			59
Reduce size of military			27
Provide school vouchers			45
No military support for Israel			29
Citizenship for wire transfers			39
Right to work law			31
Merit-based immigration			32
Eliminate estate tax			27
Cut taxes under $100,000			10

-.1   0   .1   .2   .3   .4   0%   50%   100%

Several of the most important issues concerned impeachment and Trump immigration policies, along with abortion and gun control. Many of these policies were also important to Republicans, as we discussed in chapter 3. But, of course, Democrats were on the opposite side: substantial majorities of Democrats took the liberal position or the anti-Trump position.

By contrast, many of the policies related to health care and taxes—two issues frequently debated among the Democratic candidates—ranked as less important. The revealed importance of supporters of Democrats' biggest priorities (impeaching Trump and preventing family separation at the border) was over 0.40. This suggests that when a set of policies contained the respondents' position on one of these two issues (whether for or against) 40 percent more people chose that set. For supporters of raising taxes on those making at least $600,000, enacting Medicare for All, or raising the minimum wage to $15 an hour, the revealed importance was closer to 0.30—not unimportant, of course, but clearly less important. Thus, not only were supporters of the Democratic candidates not that divided in their policy views, but Democrats' biggest policy priorities were ones that helped pull the party together.

For progressive leaders who cared deeply about issues like health care and taxes, many of whom backed Sanders or Warren, the primary was a keen disappointment. Alexandria Ocasio-Cortez said that progressives needed to learn "political lessons" from the outcome. For some journalists, the primary was a puzzle. How was it, one wondered, that progressive policies, such as Medicare for All, were more popular among Democratic voters than were the candidates championing those ideas?[49] One key reason is that those were not the issues most central to Democrats.

To say that the 2020 Democratic primary fell short of a "bitter fight" is not to say that there were no disagreements within the Democratic Party. It is simply to say that rank-and-file Democratic voters, many of whom were not necessarily following the party's debates, agreed far more often on policy than they disagreed—and any disagreements about policy did not always map cleanly onto the choices voters made in presidential primaries.

BIDEN'S APPEAL AMONG AFRICAN AMERICAN VOTERS

If the Democratic primary disappointed some progressives, it disappointed many fewer African American voters. Indeed, the primary once again demonstrated their importance to the party's coalition—and the coalition of any presidential candidate who wants to lead the party. Three factors appeared central to Biden's appeal to this group: characteristics of African American voters, such as age and partisanship; Biden's association with Obama; and the lesser appeal of the progressive politics of a candidate like Sanders.

On its face, Biden did not seem like a candidate who would be the clear front-runner among African Americans. In his long political career, he had taken positions on racial issues that were increasingly considered controversial as the party shifted on these issues. One was the opposition to school busing that had elicited criticism from Harris. Another was support for the Violent Crime Control and Law Enforcement Act of 1994, which critics blamed for furthering the criminal justice system's punitive treatment of African Americans. In his 2008 campaign, Biden had taken credit for this bill, calling it the "Biden crime law."[50] Beyond these positions, there were Biden's racially insensitive gaffes, such as his warm reminiscences about working with segregationist senators. Coupled with Biden's poor record was a Democratic field that contained many other candidates, including prominent people of color, who could potentially appeal to Black voters. Indeed, when Harris entered the race, her initial strategy was exactly what ended up helping Biden win: do well enough in the diverse South Carolina electorate to vault her into contention on Super Tuesday.[51]

But the experiences of African American candidates in prior Democratic primaries show that a shared racial identity is not always enough to attract the support of Black voters. In 1984 and 1988, Jesse Jackson's success in winning Black voters' support depended on the circumstances of the contest. In 1984, for example, he won the support of most Black voters (77%) but did not do as well among older Black voters, who were more skeptical about his chances of winning the nomination and believed the leading candidate, Walter Mondale, was also supportive of Black interests. In 1988, when the field was more fractured and there was no clear alternative like Mondale, Jackson did much better, winning the support of almost all Black voters (92%).[52] In 2008, Barack Obama was not the leading candidate among African American voters until after his surprising victory in the Iowa caucus. By the end of January, after Obama won the January 26 South Carolina primary, he had the support of two-thirds of African Americans. It took the momentum from these early victories to establish Obama as a viable candidate, even in the eyes of Black voters.[53]

Thus, when a candidate like Harris did not develop much momentum, she failed to win much support among African American voters. In July, which was about the high-water mark for Harris in national polls, the Nationscape surveyed showed that only 13 percent of likely African American primary voters favored her, compared to 7 percent of white voters. Harris did better among African American women (16%) than men (9%), but even among African American women, far more (33%) supported Joe Biden at that point in time.[54] And as Harris's poll numbers began to drop, they did so among African American voters as much as whites. In the Nationscape survey conducted right before Harris dropped out, only 6 percent of Black voters and 3 percent of white ones supported her.

Biden's advantage among African American voters stemmed from their demographics as well. Compared to other Democratic primary voters, African American voters had "more" of the characteristics that were associated with Biden support. There is evidence for this in Nationscape surveys, which have large enough samples to provide reliable estimates for Democratic primary voters of different racial and ethnic backgrounds (see table A4.8). Compared to other racial or ethnic groups, a larger fraction of Black Democratic primary voters identified as "strong" Democrats, which fits with the long-standing social norm within the African American community of supporting the Democratic Party.[55] A larger fraction of African American primary voters identified as moderate or conservative, compared to primary voters who were white, Hispanic, or some other race. African American primary voters were also a

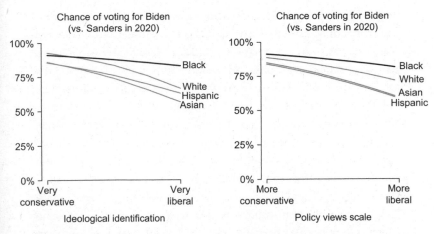

Figure 4.9.
How the Role of Ideology and Party Identification in Democratic Primary Voting Varies across Racial and Ethnic Groups. Findings are based on statistical models that also account for partisanship, age, race or ethnicity, and gender. Full results are in table A4.9. *Source*: Democracy Fund + UCLA Nationscape surveys, July 2020–January 2021.

bit less liberal on the scale of policy liberalism, relative to every other racial or ethnic group except Hispanic primary voters.

Biden was also helped by this fact: even Black voters whose political beliefs might have attracted them to candidates like Sanders or Warren remained loyal to Biden. Part of the reason is that factors like political ideology traditionally have had less effect on the voting behavior of African Americans in general elections.[56] This was true in the 2020 primary as well: African Americans' self-identified political ideology and their views on specific policy issues were also less strongly associated with their candidate choices (figure 4.9). Liberal Black primary voters were hardly any more likely to back Sanders than were moderate or conservative Black voters.

Another crucial component of Biden's appeal to African Americans was his association with Barack Obama. During Obama's presidency, the voters most favorable to Obama, including African Americans, became much more favorable to white politicians in Obama's administration, including both Biden and Hillary Clinton. As a result, surveys showed that African Americans liked Biden more than they did previous vice presidents in Democratic administrations, including Al Gore and Walter Mondale. Moreover, African Americans with the most favorable views of Obama also had more favorable views of Biden, relative to the minority of African Americans with unfavorable views of Obama.

Thus, Biden, like Clinton in 2016, was able to tap into his association with Obama to shore up support within the Black community. He certainly did his best to strengthen that association during the campaign—for example, by saying "I'm with Barack" when defending the Affordable Care Act in the September primary debate. Sanders lost on this count, as he had long been a critic of Obama and even considered running a primary campaign against him in 2012.[57]

Joe Biden began his campaign as an older white man who seemed to many observers somewhat out of step with the modern Democratic Party. Indeed, in early April 2020, right after Sanders dropped out, a Pew Research Center poll found that a substantial number of Democrats (41%) said that it "bothered" them that "the likely Democratic nominee is a white man in his 70s." But only 28 percent of Black Democrats said it bothered them. His primary campaign, and Clinton's in 2016, showed how older white candidates could build and sustain support in the African American community—and turn that support into a presidential nomination.[58]

GENDER, SEXISM, AND ELECTABILITY

For many Democratic primary voters, what bothered them about nominating an older white man was not just his race but his gender. As the Democratic field was winnowed to male front-runners and then a male nominee, it raised again the question of whether women candidates, and especially Warren, faced barriers in the primary. This concern was certainly on Democrats' minds even before the primary: in a June 2018 poll, 64 percent of Democrats said that gender discrimination was a major reason that there were not more women in political office.[59] In 2020, the concern about gender discrimination took on an added dimension: whether the party's desire for "electability"—that is, a candidate who could beat Trump—put women candidates at a disadvantage.

The evidence suggests that Warren's experience mirrored Hillary Clinton's from 2016. First, she gained relatively little in terms of additional support from women voters. Second, she did poorly among the minority of Democratic voters with sexist attitudes and better among Democratic voters with progressive attitudes about gender. In Warren's case, however, this support from progressive Democrats was not enough to make her competitive with Biden.

But on the question of electability—one that lingered long after Clinton's defeat—it is not clear how much perceptions of electability hurt Warren or helped Biden. The evidence is murky in part because these perceptions proved so malleable throughout the campaign.

In 2016, Hillary Clinton embraced gender in her campaign. Clinton said in one 2015 debate that "fathers will be able to say to their daughters, 'You too can grow up to be president.'" But she did only slightly better among women in 2016 than she did in her 2008 primary campaign, when she largely avoided discussing her gender. She also did worse among Democratic primary voters, and particularly men, who expressed more sexist attitudes, although those losses were mitigated because there were relatively few such voters in the Democratic primary electorate.

In 2020, the Democratic Party had shifted even further to the left on gender issues as part of the growing alignment between partisan politics and identity politics that we described in chapter 1. This was one reason why Lucy Flores's allegation about Biden was so concerning to his campaign. Biden also faced criticism for how he had handled the sexual harassment accusations brought by Anita Hill against Clarence Thomas when Thomas was nominated for the Supreme Court in 1991 and Biden was the chair of the Senate Judiciary Committee. Sanders had reason for concern as well after a number of staffers from his 2016 campaign came forward in 2018 to describe its hostile climate toward women. On top of that, Warren said in January 2020 that Sanders had told her in 2018 that a woman could not beat Donald Trump. Sanders denied this, but in the ensuing controversy Hillary Clinton criticized him too, saying "it's part of a pattern" for Sanders.[60]

But Warren's experience was largely a repeat of Clinton's. Like Clinton, Warren emphasized her gender by, for example, taking and publicizing selfies with little girls at her campaign stops.[61] Yet like Clinton, she did not garner extraordinary support from women voters. Throughout the summer and fall of 2019, weekly Nationscape surveys showed that women were only about 2 to 6 points more likely to support her than men were. At the end of the primaries, when the Nationscape and VOTER Survey projects asked how people had voted, Warren did only 2 points better among women than men.

A different way of thinking about gender focuses not on a voter's or a candidate's gender itself but instead on how people think about gender. One useful framework for measuring gender attitudes seeks to capture subtle biases against women by asking people the questions noted in chapter 1, such as whether there is discrimination against women or whether women get undeserved special favors. This measure of gender attitudes was shown to be distinctively important to how people voted in the 2016 general election and to a host of political attitudes after Trump's election.[62]

Gender attitudes were also distinctively important in the 2020 Democratic primary compared to 2016, based on statistical models of vote choice that also include factors such as partisanship, ideological identification, economic policy views, and demographic characteristics (figure 4.10; further details are in the appendix). In 2016, Democratic primary voters who expressed more progressive gender attitudes on this scale were a bit more likely to support Clinton than Sanders, compared to those who expressed less progressive gender attitudes. But given that most Democratic primary voters expressed progressive views—about 75 percent are in the lowest quarter of the scale—the fact that all 2016 voters did not hold progressive gender views may not have cost Clinton many votes.

In 2020, by contrast, the relationship between gender attitudes and voting for Warren was steeper. This is true when comparing Warren

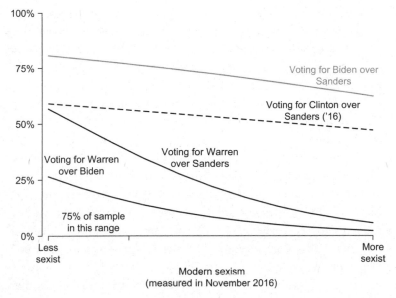

Figure 4.10.
Gender Attitudes and Voting in the 2016 and 2020 Democratic Primaries. Findings are based on statistical models that also account for economic policy views, ideological identification, partisanship, age, race or ethnicity, and gender. Full results are in table A4.10. *Source:* VOTER Survey.

voters to Biden voters and especially to Sanders voters. By comparison, gender attitudes did not distinguish Sanders from Biden voters, once other factors were taken into account. One implication is that Warren would have benefited more than Biden or Sanders if everyone in the electorate had held progressive views on gender. Of course, we cannot be sure that it was Warren's gender that produced these differences, although we have at least tried to account for factors, like ideology and economic policy views, that could also have distinguished Warren from the other candidates in voters' minds. If Warren's gender is the precipitating factor, then her presence as a woman candidate "activated" those attitudes, making them a stronger correlate of how people voted in the Democratic primary and perhaps helping her win support among voters with progressive attitudes on gender.[63]

At the same time, there were clearly limits to how much progressive gender attitudes appeared to help Warren. Among the most progressive primary voters, Warren did almost as well against Sanders as Clinton did. But she ran well behind Biden even among these progressive voters. Regardless of whether gender is defined in terms of people's identity or their attitudes about issues like sexual harassment, it does not appear to be a strong enough force on its own to propel a woman candidate into strong contention.

This brings us to the question of electability. Throughout the primary, this question—which candidate or candidates could beat Trump—was central to the Democratic Party's deliberations. In a May 2019 poll, 97 percent of Democrats said that it was very or extremely important to beat Trump. Democrats also prioritized electability more in 2020 than in recent elections. In a June 2019 YouGov poll, 58 percent of likely Democratic primary voters said they wanted "a nominee who can win the general election in November" as opposed to "a nominee who agrees with your position on most issues." That 58 percent figure was higher than in similar polls before the 2004, 2008, and 2016 primaries (where the same percentage was 26%, 25%, and 36%, respectively).[64]

What made electability a fraught topic was gender. It was clear that some Democrats, perhaps thinking of Hillary Clinton's experience in 2016, were unsure that a woman candidate could beat Trump in 2020. This was a central theme in early reporting about the primary and Warren's candidacy in particular. For example, a July 2019 *New York Times* story said that "the party finds itself grappling with the strangely enduring question of the electability of women." An August 2019 *New York Times* story about Warren said, "Even as she demonstrates why she is a leading candidate for the party's nomination, Ms. Warren is facing persistent questions and doubts about whether she would be able to defeat President Trump in the general election."[65]

Electability is hard to assess, and polls took different approaches to measuring it. Several polls sought to measure electability indirectly, through what was sometimes called the "magic wand" question.

Democratic primary voters were first asked who they intended to vote for and then asked who they would choose if they could use a magic wand to automatically make that person president without needing to win the general election first. If people gave a different answer to the magic wand question, this was presumed to measure their "true" preference without taking electability into account.

Across four such polls in 2019, Biden did worse on the magic wand question than the standard vote intention question by an average of 8 points. Warren did better by an average of 3 points and Buttigieg by 3 points. Sanders did the same in both questions. This suggests that perceptions of electability boosted Biden's poll standing, and that concerns about electability placed Warren and others in the field at some disadvantage.

A more direct way to measure electability was to ask whether a candidate could beat Donald Trump. There were two versions of this type of question: rating and ranking. Rating questions asked respondents to evaluate the electability of each candidate separately, while ranking questions asked respondents to choose the candidate most likely to beat Trump. Responses to both types of questions showed that electability was not an immutable characteristic of candidates. Instead, perceptions of electability changed over the campaign, driven by the same events that affected the candidates' standing in the polls.

For both Harris and Warren, campaign events that raised their profile and support also led people to update perceptions of their electability. As a result, perceptions of electability were likely a *consequence* as much as a cause of whether people supported a candidate and intended to vote for them. These patterns also mirror research on earlier presidential primaries, which found that people may change their perceptions of electability to accord with how they feel about the candidates: if they like a candidate, then they will say that the candidate is electable.[66]

For example, when Harris peaked in polls in late June, 50 percent of YouGov respondents said that she would beat Trump and only 20 percent said he would beat her—a difference of 30 points (see the top panel of figure 4.11). At that point, Harris was rated more electable

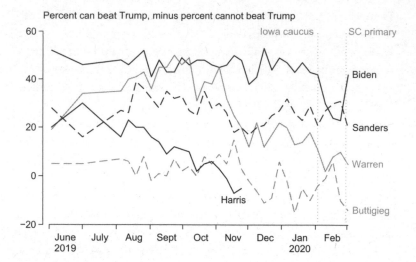

Percent can beat Trump, minus percent cannot beat Trump

Iowa caucus SC primary

Biden

Sanders

Warren

Harris

Buttigieg

June 2019 — July — Aug — Sept — Oct — Nov — Dec — Jan 2020 — Feb

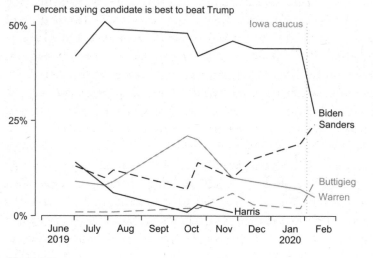

Percent saying candidate is best to beat Trump

Iowa caucus

Biden
Sanders

Buttigieg
Warren

Harris

June 2019 — July — Aug — Sept — Oct — Nov — Dec — Jan 2020 — Feb

Figure 4.11.
Trends in Perceptions of Electability of Major Democratic Candidates. *Source*: YouGov polls (top panel); Quinnipiac polls (bottom panel).

than Buttigieg or Sanders. But as Harris's poll numbers slid, so did perceptions of her electability.

Elizabeth Warren's rise in the polls also coincided with an increase in her electability rating (top panel of figure 4.11). By September, she was tied or even ahead of Biden and further ahead of Sanders and especially Buttigieg. For example, in the September 22–24, 2019, poll, 65 percent of likely Democratic primary voters said that Warren would beat Trump and only 15 percent said she would lose. The comparable numbers for Biden were 62 percent and 19 percent. In the ranking question, Warren also gained substantially: in July, 9 percent said she was the best candidate to beat Trump, and by September, that had increased to 21 percent (bottom panel of figure 4.11).[67]

For Biden, the dynamics were different. Perceptions of Biden's electability remained stable through the summer and fall. Those perceptions changed because there was direct evidence of whether Biden could, in fact, win elections. His poor showing in the Iowa and New Hampshire contests led to a drop in people's belief that he could beat Trump as well as a drop in his poll numbers. Perceptions of Sanders's and Buttigieg's electability changed in response to these contests as well. Indeed, at one point Sanders was rated more electable and nearly tied with Biden on the ranking question. But this all changed again immediately after the South Carolina primary, when ratings of Biden's electability shot up and his poll numbers rebounded.[68]

One interpretation is that Biden's poll numbers were sustained, at least in part, by the view that he was electable. When new information suggested that Biden might in fact be a weak candidate, Democratic primary voters downgraded his electability and then shifted away from Biden to other candidates. Thus, perceptions of electability were a plausible cause of why at least some Democrats backed Biden.

Of course, this data does not permit rigorous tests of whether people's perceptions of electability were driving their views of the Democratic candidates, or whether the reverse was true and people simply said that the candidate they favored for other reasons was electable. Nevertheless, there is a suggestive pattern here. Candidates other than Biden had to "prove" their electability by generating favorable news coverage and attracting support from primary voters. If they did that, then voters saw them as more electable.

But Biden started the race with most voters already seeing him as electable—a fact that could reflect his race and gender as well as his political experience and more moderate policy views. Electability then buoyed his poll standing as long as his performance in the primaries suggested that he was a strong candidate. This was another reason why Biden's South Carolina victory was so crucial. It put him back on a path to winning the nomination—and reassured Democrats that he could compete with Trump in November.

UNITY

On March 17, 2020, after winning primaries in Florida and Illinois, Biden gave a speech that signaled his status as the party's eventual nominee and sought to win over supporters of other candidates. He said, "Our goal as a campaign, and my goal as a candidate for president, is to unify this party and then to unify the nation."[69] It seemed remarkable to imagine the Democratic Party being unified given the acrimony after Clinton's loss in 2016, the divisions in the party's "Unity and Reform Commission," and the battle among its many presidential candidates. But the 2020 primary ended up being shorter and less divisive than those of 2008 and 2016. For Democrats, the fight in 2020 was against Trump more than against each other.

This greater unity was visible in public opinion data. Throughout the primary, weekly Nationscape surveys showed that Democratic primary voters' views of the leading candidates were favorable overall. As of the week of Biden's speech, for example, 77 percent of Democrats had a favorable view of Biden, 72 percent had a favorable view of Sanders, and 67 percent had a favorable view of Warren. There had been ups and downs in those percentages in the preceding months, but any shifts were modest. Thus, even as Democrats had to make choices among these candidates, they tended to like most of them.[70]

Moreover, the more they liked one of the candidates, the more they liked many others. The more favorable someone's view of Biden, the

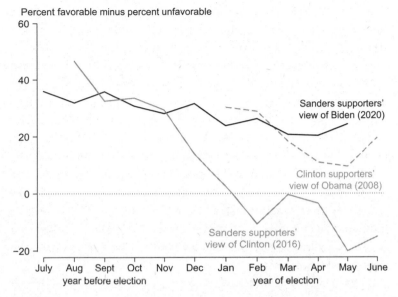

Percent favorable minus percent unfavorable

Figure 4.12.
Views of Democratic Presidential Nominees among Supporters of Their Main Primary
Opponent (Hillary Clinton Supporters in 2008, Bernie Sanders Supporters in 2016
and 2020). Source: National Annenberg Election Study, January–June 2008; YouGov/
Economist polls, August 2015–June 2016; and Democracy Fund + UCLA Nationscape
surveys, July 2019–May 2020.

more favorable their view of Warren and Sanders; and the more favorable someone's view of Sanders, the more favorable their view of Biden
and Warren. Views of Warren and Sanders were more tightly linked than
they were with views of Biden, perhaps reflecting Warren and Sanders's
similarities as fellow progressives. But nevertheless, all of these correlations were positive. By comparison, at the end of the 2008 primary
views of Clinton were slightly *negatively* correlated with their views of
Obama. At the end of the 2016 primary, views of Clinton were even more
negatively correlated with views of Sanders. In other words, the more
Democratic primary voters liked Sanders in 2016, the *less* they liked Clinton. The more they liked Sanders in 2020, the *more* they liked Biden.[71]

The contrast among the 2008, 2016, and 2020 Democratic primaries is
also visible in how the losing candidate's supporters felt about the winning
candidate (figure 4.12).[72] In 2008, Clinton supporters' views of Obama

dropped steeply from January to May before rebounding somewhat at the end of the primary season, when Obama became the de facto nominee. Throughout the 2016 primary campaign, Sanders supporters' views of Clinton took an even sharper nosedive. By June 2016, only 42 percent had a favorable view of her while 57 percent had an unfavorable view—a net favorability rating of −15. But 2020 was different. By May, most Sanders supporters (59%) had a *favorable* view of Biden—or about the same fraction as had the opposite view of Clinton at that point in 2016.

Thus, Biden was right to feel confident in his ability to unify the party, especially in an era of calcified politics and strong party loyalty. But one thing about his speech was off: the setting. Biden did not speak in front of a cheering crowd, but instead from the basement of his home in Wilmington, Delaware. He stood at a makeshift podium flanked by a pair of American flags. The video feed was not as crisp as usual. The sound quality was mediocre.

The COVID-19 pandemic was beginning to change the presidential campaign, just as it would change the country. "Tackling this pandemic is a national emergency akin to fighting a war," Biden said from his basement. At that point, few knew how costly that war would be.

5

"Deadly Stuff"

Chinese Identify New Virus Causing Pneumonialike Illness: The
New Coronavirus Doesn't Appear to Be Readily Spread by Humans,
but Researchers Caution That More Study Is Needed.

—*NEW YORK TIMES,* JANUARY 8, 2020

THE OUTBREAK OF THE NOVEL CORONAVIRUS—SARS-CoV-2,
a "severe acute respiratory syndrome coronavirus"—and the disease it
produced, COVID-19, dramatically altered the day-to-day lives of
Americans. Early optimism about the virus turned out to be wrong: it
spread easily among people in close contact, often produced severe
symptoms requiring hospitalization, and killed over 350,000 Americans
in 2020 and even more in 2021.[1]

Within weeks of the end of the Democratic nominating contest, the
United States was transformed by the disease. Travel and recreation
dwindled. Many schools and businesses shut their doors. Friends and
family went months without seeing each other face to face. In places that
were hit especially hard, elected officials and medical professionals had
to improvise to diagnose and treat infected people—and to house the
bodies of those who died. Just north of Central Park in New York City,
pews in one of the largest churches in the country were replaced by
makeshift beds. Around the country, parking lots and city streets were
transformed into temporary morgues, lined with refrigerated trucks or
tractor trailers for the bodies of COVID-19 victims. Approximately one
million Americans have died of the virus, along with millions of others
across the world. There were millions more "excess" deaths—deaths above
what typical mortality trends would predict—that were due to undiagnosed

cases of COVID-19 as well as deaths from other causes that were magnified by the pandemic's chaos.

National crises provide leaders with the opportunity to tackle big problems and take decisive action. Crises are also moments that can unify a divided country and give the president extraordinary political support. This was an opportunity that Trump, a chronically unpopular leader, really needed.

For a brief moment, it was an opportunity that Trump almost seized. In March 2020, he declared a national emergency, producing a rare moment of relative unity in public opinion about the coronavirus and a rare increase in his own approval rating. In a politically divided country, a bipartisan consensus is hard to find, but at that point roughly equal numbers of Democrats and Republicans were concerned about the virus and willing to back demanding countermeasures. Americans were already reducing their own travel and staying in their homes, even before some state and local governments put restrictions in place.

But within weeks, Trump changed course. He downplayed the mounting crisis, called for a "reopening" of the country, and sharply criticized leaders who did not follow suit. Trump treated the pandemic as an opportunity not to unify but to continue his divisive style of politics, in which every issue could be framed as "us versus them."

Trump's change produced an immediate effect: Republican concern about the virus dropped, as did their support for countermeasures such as limits on large gatherings. Thus, Americans' attitudes about COVID-19 became increasingly polarized along partisan lines, just like their attitudes toward so many other political issues.

To some, the divisions among Americans were the result of a libertarian culture, one that would not tolerate limitations on freedom even to fight a pandemic. But a static culture cannot explain the ebb and flow of these divisions. The real cause was political leaders like Trump. The pandemic showed that there could have been a meaningful consensus on how to respond to the pandemic. The pandemic also showed that political leaders can produce division on a novel issue like COVID-19, just as they produced the larger tectonic shifts and "identity shocks" we discussed in chapter 1.

The consequence of these divisions was apparent in how the country struggled to manage the pandemic. Many Republican state lawmakers took their cue from Trump, and thus the response to the pandemic became a "partisan patchwork," with different mitigation measures in different states and cities that depended on which political party was in charge.[2]

The consequence of Trump's divisiveness was visible for Trump himself. His approval ratings dropped after he pushed to reopen the country, even as many world leaders and governors of U.S. states saw their approval ratings increase and remain elevated. By the end of the presidential campaign, Trump's approval rating recovered a bit, but only to its pre-pandemic level. Just as Trump appeared to gain little support because of the economic growth during his first three years in office, as we noted in chapter 3, he lost little support because of the economic downturn and associated costs of the pandemic. This showed, once again, what a calcified politics looks like. At the same time, the small shifts that are possible even in calcified politics are important. Even a small uptick in Trump's approval rating would have been helpful in an election year.

In short, all the struggles that characterized Trump's first three years in office—the failure to seize on policy solutions that were already popular, the penchant for creating new controversies, the focus on divisive attacks—were no less visible in his response to the pandemic. Once again, Trump's actions endangered his own chance of reelection.

FROM SHUTDOWNS TO SURGES

The political narrative of the pandemic, and especially Trump's response, can be divided into roughly three periods. After the first confirmed cases of COVID-19 emerged in the United States in late January 2020, the Trump administration responded with public denials and insufficient countermeasures, even as they acknowledged the threat privately. This produced a "lost February." But as the outbreak worsened, there came a second short period—a "March moment"—when Trump declared a national emergency, announced his support for new restrictions, and talked about the virus in grave terms. This lasted only a few weeks, however. During the third period, beginning in April, Trump backtracked, began to downplay the virus again, lobbied for reopening the country, and attacked political leaders who disagreed.

Understanding this chronology is crucial because, as we will see, the changes in the Trump administration's posture—and Trump's own statements—had important effects on public opinion, initially helping build a consensus behind stronger countermeasures but then helping to undo that consensus and create partisan divisions.

A Lost February

The first infections from COVID-19 emerged in December 2019 in Wuhan, China. Within a month there were almost 8,000 confirmed cases across nineteen countries, and the World Health Organization (WHO) declared the COVID-19 outbreak a "Public Health Emergency of International Concern."[3] The first confirmed case in the United States was reported on January 20. These early days of the pandemic were crucial. When viral infections can be easily transmitted from person to person, the number of infections can increase exponentially because one infected person may infect multiple other people. Without early and decisive actions, a virus can spread so rapidly that it becomes difficult to contain.

A striking fact about the Trump administration's early response was the gap between what they believed privately and what they said publicly. In private, Trump advisers, and even Trump himself, knew that the outbreak could become a serious problem. On January 28, Trump was told by his national security adviser, Robert C. O'Brien, that the coronavirus outbreak "will be the biggest national security threat you face in your presidency. This is going to be the roughest thing you face." In a February 7 phone call with *Washington Post* reporter Bob Woodward— which Woodward did not report publicly until September 2020— Trump accurately described how the virus is transmitted and clearly stated that it posed a major threat to public health: "You can just breathe the air and that's how it's passed. And so that's a very tricky one. That's a very delicate one. It's also more deadly than even your strenuous flus. This is deadly stuff."[4]

But publicly Trump minimized the virus and was angry when others in his administration did not echo this assessment. He was reportedly furious when Nancy Messionnier, the director of the Centers for Disease Control's Center for Immunization and Respiratory Disease, warned a group of reporters on February 24 that "the disruption to everyday life might be severe" and the Dow Jones average dropped 1,000 points in response. Two days later, Trump sounded a far more upbeat note and directly contradicted what he had told Woodward barely two weeks before: "It's a little like the regular flu that we have flu shots for. And we'll essentially have a flu shot for this in a fairly quick manner." Messionnier and other CDC officials found themselves sidelined.[5]

Moreover, the steps that the Trump administration took did not work. Trump had closed U.S. borders to travelers from China on January 31, but almost 40,000 travelers entered the United States on flights from China after the closure and were subject to minimal, if any, health screening. Moreover, many U.S. cases came from travelers from Europe, not China. Meanwhile, the CDC's new COVID test had major defects and, as U.S. scientists developed their own tests, the federal government was slow to approve them. Trump pretended otherwise, saying on March 6 that "anybody that wants a test can get a test." But a senior CDC official would later say, "We missed the game." The first confirmed U.S. death from COVID-19 came on February 29.[6]

A March Moment

In March, however, Trump did an about-face as the virus continued to spread. On March 13, two days after the World Health Organization declared that COVID-19 was a pandemic, Trump declared a national emergency. He committed $50 billion in government spending to fight the virus and called on states to set up operations centers and hospitals to implement emergency preparedness plans. He empowered Secretary of Health and Human Services Alex Azar to waive regulations that impeded the fight against the disease. He pledged to accelerate testing capacity. This was a remarkable turnaround, considering that only three days before Trump had said, "Just stay calm. It will go away." On March 16, the Trump administration issued new guidelines recommending that states shut down bars, restaurants, and similar establishments and that Americans avoid large gatherings. Trump said that his son, Barron, had asked, "How bad is this?"—the outbreak—and Trump had told him, "It's bad. It's bad." Trump said that the outbreak could last until July or August and it "could be longer than that." Two weeks later, on March 31, Trump said that "this could be a hell of a bad two weeks" and that the virus was "vicious."[7]

Trump's new message was echoed by his conservative allies, who had previously been downplaying the virus as well. For example, on March 9 the Fox News personality Trish Regan said that the virus was just something that Trump's opponents were using in "yet another attempt to impeach the president." On March 13, when Trump declared the national emergency, she said, "We must test for the virus in order to stop the spread of it" and warned of "what could be a very great recession . . . even a depression." On March 10, Sean Hannity downplayed the virus, saying, "Healthy people, generally, 99 percent recover very fast, even if they contract it." On March 13, Hannity called Trump's move "a massive paradigm shift in the future of disease control and prevention" and "a bold, new precedent."[8]

Trump's move shifted policy in the states too, especially those where Trump was popular and a Republican governor was in office. Republican governors had taken longer to declare an emergency or enact social distancing policies in early 2020 than did Democratic governors. But after Trump's declaration, Republican governors got the political cover they appeared to need. This is why Trump's stance was so important: it helped shape not only federal policymaking but also policymaking in the states, which were the entities fully empowered to take steps like closing businesses.[9]

Along with Trump's belated acknowledgment of the outbreak's seriousness was an attempt to cast blame, especially on China. Throughout January and February, Trump had actually praised China's leader, Xi Jinping, on multiple occasions, saying things like "I think President Xi is working very, very hard. I spoke to him. He's working very hard. I think he's doing a very good job." But Trump and his allies soon began calling the coronavirus "the Chinese virus" or "the Wuhan virus." Trump himself said "Chinese virus" more than twenty times between March 16 and March 30, by one count. Before a March 19 briefing, he even crossed out "corona" in "coronavirus" on the text of his prepared remarks and wrote "Chinese."[10]

In the remaining weeks of March, the toll of the virus became clearer. More school systems canceled in-person instruction. Large gatherings—concerts, sporting events, religious services—were canceled too. Americans traveled less and spent more time in their homes. Signs of an economic contraction emerged. Consumer spending fell and the unemployment rate increased as people were laid off or lost their jobs when businesses reduced their operations or closed. Meanwhile, the number of infections continued to surge, straining hospitals, medical staff, and even morgues. Doctors and nurses described the extraordinary stress and heartbreak they experienced, especially when they were the only people who could be with COVID-19 patients as they suffered and died. One New York City nurse said, "This morning I looked up and the doctor resident was bawling, crying in his mask, and I started crying and the other nurse started crying. We're all human, you know, there's only so much we can take."[11]

The country desperately needed a "paradigm shift" in fighting the pandemic. But one did not come.

A Spring Decline, Subsequent Surges

A successful fight against the pandemic required at least five important elements: adequate medical supplies for hospitals; infrastructure for widespread testing; public use of masks and social distancing; an effective vaccine; and a solution to the economic crisis that was affecting millions of Americans.

On the latter two counts, there was rapid progress. On March 27, Trump signed the Coronavirus Aid, Relief, and Economic Security (CARES) Act, which was supported by large bipartisan majorities in

Congress and provided an unprecedented $2.2 trillion in economic stimulus, including cash payments to individual Americans, increased unemployment benefits, loans to small businesses and larger corporations, and aid to state and local governments. This bill was extraordinarily popular, unlike much of what Trump had pushed for by that point his term. In the March 19–26 Nationscape survey, 80 percent of Americans favored increased spending on unemployment insurance and 80 percent wanted the federal government to make cash payments to Americans. The CARES Act also included funding for Operation Warp Speed, which helped pharmaceutical companies develop and test coronavirus vaccines. These vaccines would be available to Americans within a year.[12]

But on the other counts—medical equipment, testing, masks, and local restrictions—there were problems. As a result, initial progress against the virus was reversed by larger surges in cases in the summer and fall (figure 5.1). Throughout this period, Trump, despite having signaled determination to fight the virus, backed away. Moreover, Trump undermined the very steps that he proposed in his emergency declaration. The surge in cases during the summer and fall thus represented a failure of Trump's own apparent goals and served to ensure the pandemic remained an obstacle to his reelection.

One problem was that the Trump administration delegated the responsibility for obtaining medical supplies to states. In a conference call with governors the day he declared a national emergency, Trump initially said, "We're backing you 100%" but then said the opposite: "Also, though, respirators, ventilators, all the equipment—try getting that yourselves." Governor Jay Inslee of Washington expressed disbelief that Trump was not going to mobilize the federal government's resources. He said, "That would be equivalent to Franklin Delano Roosevelt, on December 8, 1941, saying, 'Good luck, Connecticut, you go build the battleships.'" Trump said, "We're just the backup."[13]

As a consequence, states ended up in bidding wars for protective equipment for health care workers, sometimes even competing with the federal government for these products. Governor Charlie Baker of Massachusetts, a Republican, secured 3 million masks, only to have the

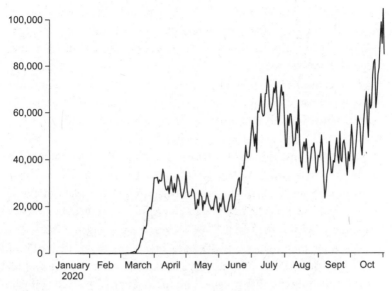

Figure 5.1.
Daily Number of Confirmed Cases of COVID-19 in the United States, January 1–
November 2, 2020. *Source*: Our World in Data.

federal government take them when they arrived in the United States.
Baker ended up shipping supplies on the private plane of the New
England Patriots owner Robert Kraft to avoid federal scrutiny. When
asked about the bidding war among states, Trump said that the states
"have to work that out."[14]

There were similar problems with COVID-19 testing, despite widespread agreement that the country needed more testing, especially after
the faulty CDC test. The Trump administration again put the onus on
the states, with the federal government only to "act as a supplier of last
resort." Some in the White House opposed a larger role for the federal
government because they believed the virus would mostly affect Democratic states and thus the White House could blame those governors.
Trump himself suggested that the country needed fewer tests because
he wanted there to be fewer confirmed cases. In June Trump said, "When
you do testing to that extent, you're gonna find more people, you're

gonna find more cases. So I said to my people, 'slow the testing down, please.'" In July, the administration opposed new federal spending for testing.[15] The inability of people to discover whether they had the virus helped it continue to spread.

An even more polarizing issue was face masks. Within a few months of the outbreak, it became clear that the virus was transmitted via airborne particles and that an ordinary cloth mask could reduce transmission. Two studies found that places in which the governor or mayor mandated that individuals wear masks in public settings experienced slower growth in confirmed COVID-19 cases than other places.[16]

Trump, however, did not consistently endorse this guidance or wear a mask in his own public appearances. In April he suggested that there was some downside to masks: "They've learned about face masks—the good and the bad, by the way. It's not a one-sided thing, believe it or not." Unsurprisingly, Trump usually appeared without a mask and refused to recommend that people wear them. Instead, he said, "This is voluntary. I don't think I'm going to be doing it." Trump also belittled Biden for wearing a mask. Trump's stance contradicted not only health professionals but also many in his own party who supported wearing masks, including Ohio governor Mike DeWine, Texas senator John Cornyn, Florida senator Marco Rubio, and Senate Republican leader Mitch McConnell. In June, Steve Doocy of Fox News said, "I think if the president wore one, it would just set a good example." Trump did not wear a mask in public until a visit to Walter Reed Hospital on July 11.[17]

Trump's stance toward other COVID-19 measures, particularly state and local restrictions, became less equivocal and more hostile. Although the Trump administration's own guidelines recommended that states shut down certain businesses and that Americans avoid large gatherings, Trump would not commit to them. Within a week after those guidelines were released, Trump began walking back his somber remarks. On March 23, he said: "So I think Easter Sunday, and you'll have packed churches all over our country." On March 29: "We can expect that, by June 1, we will be well on our way to recovery." On April 3: "I said it was going away, and it is going away." On April 5: "We're starting to see the light at the end of the tunnel."[18]

Trump's concern was that the restrictions on businesses and gatherings were hurting the economy. As he put it in a tweet, "WE CANNOT LET THE CURE BE WORSE THAN THE PROBLEM ITSELF!" Certainly, the economy *was* hurting. The unemployment rate spiked to 14.7 percent in April—higher than in the harshest recessions of the previous decades. In the second quarter of 2020, the U.S. gross domestic product (GDP) dropped a remarkable 9 percentage points compared to the first quarter, which was already down 1.3 points from the last quarter of 2019. There had been no quarter even remotely as bad in the history of the official GDP measure, which dates to 1947.[19]

Trump seemed to believe that the economic downturn was due to the restrictions on businesses and commerce and thus that reopening the country would restore the economy to its pre-pandemic state. But research showed that the slowdown in economic activity occurred mostly before states and localities implemented these restrictions, suggesting that the downturn stemmed from people's desire to avoid the virus. Consequently, the key to restoring economic growth was not reopening the country amid large numbers of viral infections but fighting the virus first. One study of the 1918–19 flu pandemic found that U.S. cities with more stringent restrictions did somewhat *better* economically in the years after the pandemic than did other cities. In short, there was no zero-sum trade-off between helping the economy and preventing COVID-19 infections and deaths. The bigger risk was ending the restrictions too soon.[20]

Moreover, the restrictions were helping. There was good reason to expect this. Studies of the 1918–19 flu pandemic showed that similar restrictions were correlated with lower viral transmission and fewer deaths. In the spring of 2020, several studies documented that COVID-19 cases and fatalities had declined sharply in the places that enacted restrictions. The decline in the number of cases (figure 5.1) documents the progress made.[21]

Nevertheless, on April 16, only a month after Trump had called for closing businesses and limiting large gatherings and when the nation's caseload was barely below its peak to that point, Trump said that governors could begin to relax restrictions. The next day, Trump escalated his rhetoric and backed protestors who had challenged state restrictions, tweeting "LIBERATE MICHIGAN!" and "LIBERATE MINNESOTA!" and "LIBERATE VIRGINIA!"

The protests began to escalate. On April 30, protestors in Michigan brandished signs comparing Democratic governor Gretchen Whitmer to Adolf Hitler and saying, "Tyrants Get the Rope." Armed men entered the state capitol and some stood in the State Senate gallery holding assault rifles. Trump, who had already tangled with Whitmer about the pandemic response (he called her the "failing Michigan governor"), backed the protestors, tweeting, "The Governor of Michigan should give a little, and put out the fire. These are very good people, but they are angry. They want their lives back again, safely! See them, talk to them, make a deal." Several months later, the FBI arrested fourteen men affiliated with a Michigan militia group for plotting to kidnap Whitmer and overthrow the state government.[22]

Republican governors faced challenges too. In Ohio, DeWine, whose pandemic response was described in a March 2020 news article as "ahead of the curve," found himself under fire from members of his own party. In August, three Republicans in the Ohio House of Representatives drafted articles of impeachment because they thought DeWine's coronavirus orders were unconstitutional. Texas governor Greg Abbott followed Trump by reopening the state on May 1, but found himself dealing with a spike in cases later in the summer. After he issued a statewide mask order in July, Republican groups in eight different counties censured him.[23]

As the number of COVID-19 cases increased in June and July, Trump simply denied this reality. On June 17, Trump told Sean Hannity that the virus was "fading away." Vice President Mike Pence wrote an op-ed arguing that the "panic" about a second wave of infections was "overblown" and that "we are winning the fight against the invisible enemy." A few days later, Trump held his first campaign rally of the pandemic in Tulsa. Rallygoers had to sign an agreement waiving their right to sue the campaign if they got sick. Right before the event the Trump campaign disclosed that six staff members who had been working on the rally, along with two Secret Service agents, had tested positive for the virus. City officials had pleaded with Trump to cancel the rally, to no avail. In an interview, one Trump supporter who attended the rally said that the outbreak was "all fake. They're just making the numbers up."[24]

Such a statement was the logical consequence of the Trump administration's mixed messages about the pandemic's seriousness and the inconsistent guidance about how to mitigate it. One former CDC official, Richard Besser, said that "without that daily reinforcement, you have what is happening around the country—people not believing the pandemic is real, cases rising in some places and the possibility that some communities' health care systems will get overwhelmed." A mixed message from leaders set the stage for an increasingly polarized public.[25]

FOLLOW THE LEADER

Throughout 2020, ordinary Americans' opinions and behavior were strongly shaped by the politics of the pandemic as much as by the pandemic itself. The messages that people heard from political leaders affected whether they were concerned about the virus, whether they approved of political leaders, and whether they would support restrictions on their lives. This connection between what voters hear from political leaders and what voters believe themselves is a long-standing finding in academic research on public opinion.

Central to the story was Trump, and how Republican voters responded to him. When he took the pandemic seriously, so did Republican voters. When he advocated for restrictions on businesses and gatherings, so did Republican voters. This was visible in Trump's "March moment," which produced an unusual bipartisan consensus in otherwise polarized times. This is the sort of consensus Trump could have leveraged to fight the virus. Indeed, taking the virus seriously appeared to help Trump politically. He became *more* popular in March. For a brief moment, the pandemic looked as if it might provide Trump with an opportunity to remedy his chronic unpopularity.

But when Trump pushed to reopen the country and began again to downplay the pandemic, his opposition to restrictions on businesses and gatherings led many Republican voters to oppose them as well. And so the country's unity proved fleeting. Party polarization reemerged and deepened. The consequence was not just a growing gap between Democrats and Republicans, but also a divide among Republicans that mirrored the one among Republican leaders like DeWine and the officials who wanted to impeach him.

This polarization both hampered the country's response to the pandemic and hurt Trump politically. His overall popularity dropped and approval of his handling of the pandemic fell even lower. This singular opportunity for Trump to improve his own political fortunes passed.

Public Concern about Viral Outbreaks

The effect of Trump's stance—as well as the general importance of political messages in viral outbreaks—is visible first in overall public concern about outbreaks. Here, it is helpful to compare the coronavirus outbreak to the earlier U.S. outbreaks of the Ebola virus in 2014 and the Zika virus in 2016. In each case, the polling firm YouGov asked a simple question: "How concerned are you about an [Ebola, Zika, coronavirus] epidemic here in the United States?" Comparing responses shows just how much politics mattered, and much more so than the nature of the outbreaks themselves.

The Ebola outbreak in 2014 was quite limited in the United States. There were only four confirmed cases and one death. Nevertheless, the virus gained significant attention, particularly from Republican lawmakers who sought to use the outbreak as a cudgel to criticize the Obama administration in the run-up to the midterm election. Republican members of Congress were much more likely to talk about Ebola than Democratic members and, naturally, more likely to criticize Obama. As one of Senator Ted Cruz's staff members tweeted, "Before Obamacare there had never been a confirmed case of Ebola in the United States." Trump himself sent many tweets raising concerns about Ebola and criticizing Obama, including for playing golf during the outbreak. Unsurprisingly, then, Republican concern outpaced Democratic concern in the fall of 2014 (figure 5.2), although concern among both groups declined as the threat of the virus receded. During this period, an average of 74 percent

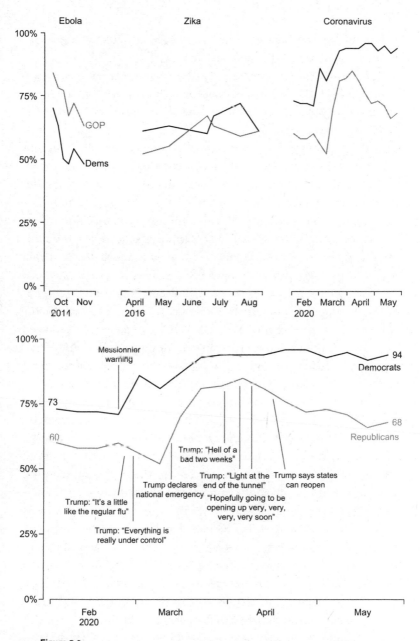

Figure 5.2.
Partisan Trends in Concern about U.S. Viral Outbreaks. The figure shows the percent who are somewhat or very concerned about each outbreak. *Source*: YouGov/*Economist* polls.

of Republican were very or somewhat concerned about an Ebola epidemic, compared to 56 percent of Democrats.[26]

The Zika epidemic was more widespread than Ebola, with 5,826 cases in the United States but no deaths. In general, it attracted less political attention, lower levels of concern, and only modest and inconsistent partisan differences in concern.

At the beginning of the coronavirus outbreak, partisan differences in concern were opposite to what happened during the Ebola outbreak. Now, Republicans were less concerned than Democrats. When the question about concern was first fielded in a February 2–4 YouGov/ *Economist* poll, 60 percent of Republicans were "somewhat" or "very concerned" compared to 73 percent of Democrats (figure 5.1). In February, the gap between the two parties only grew. In the March 8–10 poll, 81 percent of Democrats were concerned about a coronavirus epidemic, compared to 52 percent of Republicans. Indeed, concern among Republicans had dropped 8 points in two weeks as Trump pushed back against Messionnier's warning and likened COVID-19 to the flu. This showed just how much Trump's message mattered. Throughout this period, concern among Republicans was also much lower than their concern about Ebola in 2014, which again shows the difference partisan cues make.[27]

When Trump started taking the pandemic seriously, Republicans responded to that, too. In the poll conducted on March 15–17, immediately after Trump's declaration of a national emergency, the percentage of Republicans who were concerned increased 18 points, to 70 percent. The following week, it was 81 percent. In the poll conducted on April 4–6, which came after Trump's "hell of a bad two weeks" comment, 85 percent of Republicans were concerned, as were 90 percent of Democrats. There were still differences between the parties in exactly how concerned they were—in the April 4–6 poll, 70 percent of Democrats were "very concerned" as opposed to 44 percent of Republicans— but nevertheless there was an increasing, and increasingly bipartisan, feeling that the virus was serious. At that point, Republican concern about the virus finally matched their concern about Ebola.

But Republican concern faded as Trump began to downplay the virus again, with optimistic comments in early April followed by his formal announcement that the states could reopen. Of course, those comments alone did not make most Republicans unconcerned about the virus. By the end of May, when YouGov stopped asking this question, 68 percent expressed at least some concern. Nevertheless, Trump's shift was clearly mirrored among his party's voters. And this partisan divergence would persist throughout the summer. In Nationscape surveys, despite some increase in Republican concern as the caseload increased in June, Democrats remained more concerned than Republicans.[28]

Views of Trump

Trump faced a real risk: running for reelection in the midst of a national crisis and a plummeting economy. But polling from the beginning of the crisis showed how he could do that successfully: take the virus seriously and show that his administration was doing something about it.

At the outset of the year, Trump's overall approval rating was hovering in the low 40s, as usual (figure 5.3). In the initial polls about his handling of COVID, he polled several points better. However, approval of his handling of COVID dropped in late February and into early March, when Trump dismissed concerns about the virus. But especially after he announced the national emergency, approval of how he was handling COVID increased about 5 points, to nearly 50 percent. His overall approval rating, typically so stable, increased by almost the same amount, peaking around 46 percent. Such figures hardly indicated widespread popularity, but they were a welcome change for a chronically unpopular president. Notably, these higher approval ratings did not come just from Republicans, but from independents and even Democrats, too. At the end of March, about 20 percent of Democrats actually approved of Trump's handling of COVID—an unusually high number for a polarizing president in polarized times.

Had Trump sustained this increase in support, or even managed to stabilize his support at this level, that would have been a serious boon to his political fortunes. But during the spring and summer, both types of approval rating fell. By the end of July, only 40 percent approved of the job he was doing, and now a smaller, rather than a larger, number

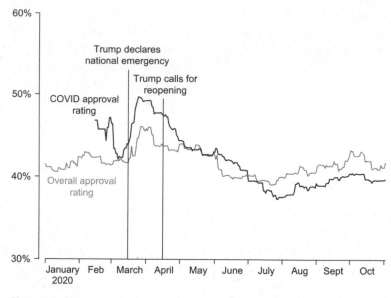

Figure 5.3.
Percentage of Americans Who Approve of Trump's Handling of COVID-19 and His Overall Job Performance. *Source:* FiveThirtyEight daily averages from public polls.

approved of how he was handling the pandemic—38 percent, down from nearly 50 percent. The fairly steady drop in Trump's COVID-19 approval suggests that it did not depend on the number of cases, which fell and then increased from April to July. More likely is that at least some Americans were judging Trump for his specific actions and those of his administration. The start of the fall presidential campaign brought an increase in the approval ratings, with Trump's overall approval recovering and his COVID-19 rating edging upward. But Trump's overall approval rating ended up about where it was before the pandemic started, and still below its level in late March.

The trajectory of Trump's approval stands out even more when compared to net approval of other world leaders (figure 5.4). Some leaders saw their approval rating increase around the same time as Trump's, and by a much larger amount, but experienced no or little decline. Australia's Scott Morrison, Germany's Angela Merkel, and, to some degree, Canada's

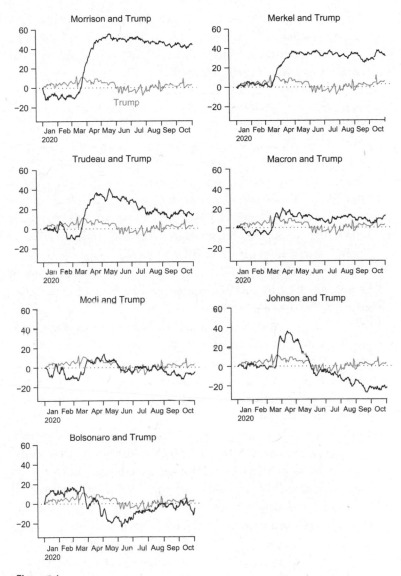

Figure 5.4.

Shift in Net Approval Rating of World Leaders Compared to Trump (Net Approval on January 1, 2020 = 0). *Source*: Morning Consult polls. For world leaders, these are seven-day moving averages calculated by Morning Consult. For Trump polls, these are plotted individually at the midpoint of their field periods with missing data linearly interpolated.

Justin Trudeau illustrate this most clearly. France's Emanuel Macron and India's Narendra Modi also saw their ratings increase by a smaller amount. Prime Minster Boris Johnson of England, a Trump ally, saw his approval rating rise in March, and then again when Johnson had a difficult bout with COVID-19 himself in early April. But in May, Johnson began pushing to relax COVID restrictions, emphasizing the economic cost of business shutdowns and changing the country's slogan to "Stay Alert" instead of "Stay at Home." Within a couple weeks, there was what news reports called a "growing revolt" against Johnson's efforts. Meanwhile, his approval rating fell, similarly to Trump's. Brazil's Jair Bolsonaro—who, like Trump, frequently downplayed the pandemic's seriousness—saw his approval drop during the spring and summer. It rebounded somewhat later, but never to its pre-pandemic level.[29]

Trump also fared poorly compared to many U.S. governors (figure 5.5). Between January and October 2020, the net approval ratings of governors increased by 4 points, on average, even though Trump's was almost exactly the same in October as it was in January. But just like world leaders, governors benefited politically from the pandemic only when they appeared to take it seriously and did not rush to reopen their states in response to Trump's urging. This was apparent in the different experiences of Democratic and Republican governors: on average, Democratic governors had net approval ratings 15 points higher in October than January.[30]

By contrast, Republican governors lost 9 points of approval over these months, on average. Many of the Republican governors who saw the largest drops in their approval ratings had resisted issuing stay-at-home orders, as in Iowa, or pushed to reopen earlier, as in Florida. Indeed, seven of the eight governors to lose more than 10 points in net approval were Republicans, including Ron DeSantis in Florida, Doug Ducey in Arizona, Kim Reynolds in Iowa, Greg Abbott in Texas, and Brian Kemp in Georgia. Their fates seem analogous to a world leader like Bolsonaro or Boris Johnson. However, not all Republican governors saw their approval ratings decline. Indeed, Mike DeWine's net approval was 25 points higher in October than January. The same was true for Republican governors like Charlie Baker in Massachusetts or Larry

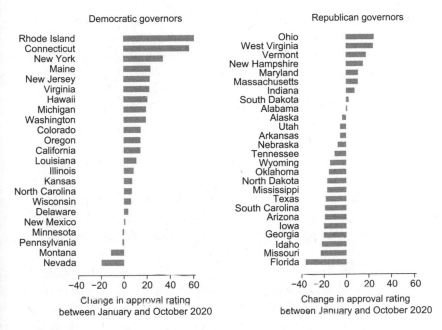

Figure 5.6.
Change in Net Approval Rating of U.S. Governors, January–October 2020. *Source:*
Morning Consult polls of registered voters, aggregated to the month.

Hogan in Maryland, who, like DeWine, were more assertive in responding to the virus.

In sum, many world and state leaders benefited politically from the pandemic. This occurred even in places, like Italy or New York, that were very hard hit by the virus. But that benefit was predicated on taking the virus seriously rather than pushing to ease restrictions amid significant numbers of COVID-19 infections and deaths.

Personal Behavior

At the outset of the pandemic, relatively few people reported that they had had the coronavirus or knew someone who had. Nevertheless, the vast majority of Americans reported important changes to their personal lives to reduce the threat of infection (figure 5.6). Notably, there were only modest differences between Democrats and Republicans.

As the pandemic continued, increasing and similar fractions of Democrats and Republicans reported a case of COVID-19 themselves or for someone they knew. Roughly similar fractions reported taking steps to avoid being infected or spreading infection. In Nationscape surveys from March to May, large majorities said that they had canceled travel plans, stopped visiting family and friends, and stayed at home for prolonged periods. In the summer and fall, majorities continued to take precautions. Most Americans reported that they had worn a mask in public. Just over half reported socializing while social distancing. Many fewer said that they were socializing but without distancing. An increasing number did report travel for nonessential reasons but this was hardly universal.[31]

Of course, "roughly similar" does not mean identical. On balance, Democrats were a bit more likely to take these actions to mitigate the virus or avoid actions that could spread it. Partisan differences were also clearer in how *frequently* people took steps to mitigate viral transmission. One example was the frequency of wearing masks. Nationscape surveys asked only whether you had "worn a mask when going out in public," with yes and no options. In surveys that asked about frequency, there were larger differences between Democrats and Republicans. For example, in a May 14–16 Huffington Post/YouGov poll—conducted while Trump was equivocating on the value of masks—71 percent of Democrats said that they "always" wore a mask "when you are in public and near other people." Only 48 percent of Republicans said that they wore a mask that frequently. Republicans were more likely than Democrats to say "most of the time" or "once in a while." Several weeks later, a late June Gallup poll revealed larger differences: 61 percent of Democrats said that they "always wore a mask outside" and 33 percent said they did so "very often." Among Republicans, the comparable numbers were 24 percent and 22 percent. Over a quarter of Republicans (27%) said they never wore a mask.[32]

Republicans also appeared less likely to engage in social distancing as measured by their actual behavior, not just by responses to surveys. For

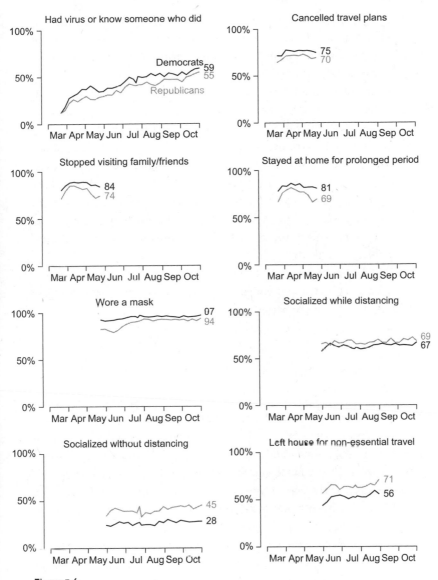

Figure 5.6.

Percentage Reporting Personal Experiences and Behaviors Related to COVID-19.

Source: Democracy Fund + UCLA Nationscape surveys.

example, cell phone location data showed that compared to Democratic-leaning counties, Republican-leaning counties had more people visiting places outside of their home, including shops, restaurants, and other public locations. These differences in behavior were not simply due to other factors. It was not the case, for example, that Republican-leaning counties saw more trips outside the home because they had fewer COVID infections. Instead, the apparent willingness of some Republicans to disregard warnings about nonessential travel may have stemmed in part from their media diet: localities with higher Fox News viewership were less likely to engage in social distancing. By contrast, one factor that appeared to encourage Republicans to stay home was a cue from a Republican leader: people in Republican-leaning counties appeared more likely to comply with stay-at-home orders in states with a Republican governor.[33]

But despite these relative differences between Democrats and Republicans, by and large members of both parties were prepared to make significant sacrifices to reduce the virus. The bigger question was whether they would be asked to.

Views of COVID-19 Restrictions

People's willingness to take steps to mitigate the virus depended not only on their own motivations but also on the formal restrictions in their community and the guidance they got from trusted leaders. However, the ability of state and local leaders to impose and maintain restrictions became harder in the face of public opposition—and that opposition was directly due to the statements of Trump and others who advocated for removing restrictions and reopening. Initially, most Americans backed these restrictions. But that changed when Trump decided to oppose the restrictions rather than explain to Americans why, despite the sacrifices entailed, business closures and stay-at-home orders would help fight the pandemic. Trump's opposition then kindled opposition among Republicans. As a result, the relative unity that could have helped Trump end the pandemic faded, complicating the work of state and local policymakers.

The initial consensus on state and local COVID policies was visible in Nationscape surveys, which began asking these questions the week of March 18–24, 2020. This was just after Trump had declared a national emergency and recommended that states shut down certain businesses and that people avoid large gatherings. The survey battery began with this preamble: "As you may know, some state and local governments have taken certain actions in response to the coronavirus and are considering other actions. Do you support or oppose the following actions?" In the list were these actions:

- "Cancel all meetings or gatherings of more than 10 people, like sports events, concerts, conferences, etc."
- "Close certain businesses where larger numbers of people gather, like theaters, bars, restaurants, etc."
- "Close schools and universities"
- "Require people who can work from home to work from home"
- "Restrict travel by plane, train, or bus"
- "Restrict all non-essential travel outside the home"
- "Encourage people to stay in their homes and avoid socializing with others"

In the first few weeks of surveys, there was widespread support for these measures among Democrats and Republicans alike (figure 5.7). Trump's personal support for restrictions likely encouraged Republicans to support them too, just as his declaration of a national emergency encouraged more Republicans to express concern about the virus (figure 5.2). Bipartisan support for these restrictions helped state and local leaders to implement them, which in turn helped reduce the number of COVID-19 cases and deaths. At this moment, the pandemic was a unifying event.

This made Trump's turn against these restrictions all the more puzzling. He was taking positions opposite to what the vast majority of Americans, and even a large majority of Republicans, believed. Trump had always been willing to side with narrow subsets of his party, but it is worth noting just how narrow that subset was. When he announced on April 16 that states could reopen, and then on April 17 sent the

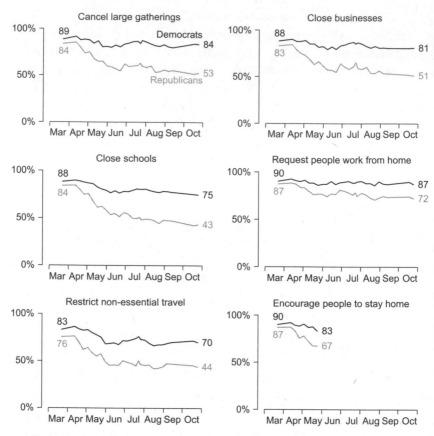

Figure 5.7.

Percentage Supporting State and Local COVID Restrictions. *Source*: Democracy Fund + UCLA Nationscape surveys.

"LIBERATE" tweets, only 12 percent of Republicans opposed canceling gatherings and 13 percent opposed closing certain businesses, based on the Nationscape survey from April 9 to 15. This meant that opponents of these restrictions were a very small group even within the GOP. The people willing to show up and protest these restrictions in states like Michigan were a smaller group still.

Indeed, these protests often attracted very modest crowds. In April, for example, the Crowd Counting Consortium identified 203 separate protests against the closing of businesses or other COVID-19 restrictions. Of the 161 protests in which news reports supplied an estimate of the maximum crowd size, the average was only about 240 people. Half of these protest attracted 100 or fewer people, and only twelve attracted 1,000 or more. But what these protests did attract was news coverage. In fact, these small anti-lockdown protests attracted far more media attention than 2019 protests that attracted thousands more participants, including protests against the Trump administration's immigration policies and protests in favor of Trump's impeachment. Trump's support for the anti-lockdown protests likely contributed to this level of news attention.[34]

Trump's shift to downplaying the virus and opposing these restrictions led a substantial number of Republicans to follow suit. Beginning in mid-April, the percentage of Republicans who supported restrictions on large gatherings dropped 30 points—from 86 percent in the April 9–15 survey to 56 percent in the June 18–24 survey, where it stayed for the rest of the campaign. There were similar drops in Republican support for closing businesses like bars and restaurants, closing schools and universities, and restricting nonessential travel. There were much smaller decreases among Democrats.

These trends in attitudes, as well as the growing distance between Democrats and Republicans, did not depend much on the trajectory of the pandemic in local communities. There were similar trends in all types of places, including those with an early spike in cases (like New York City), those with later increases in cases, and places that, as of the summer, had not yet experienced a significant outbreak. Overall, local rates of COVID infections and deaths explain relatively little about Americans' COVID attitudes. National politics, and particularly the messages from leaders like Trump, played a much larger role.[35]

Further evidence of the importance of political messages comes from examining how Democratic and Republican attitudes depended on the amount of attention people were paying to politics. Public opinion research, most notably that of the political scientist John Zaller, has long shown that people who pay closer attention to politics are more likely to receive and understand messages from political leaders. If leaders are largely in agreement on an issue, including both Democratic and

Republican leaders, then politically attentive people will best reflect that consensus. Zaller calls this the "one-message model." If leaders disagree—typically, this is along partisan lines—then politically attentive people will best reflect that debate and look the most polarized. This is the "two-message model." The spring and summer of 2020 show evidence of both models because of Trump's shift, which ensured that two messages would replace one.[36]

In the earliest Nationscape surveys, when both Democratic leaders and Trump backed restrictions on activity, the most supportive Americans were politically attentive people in either party (figure 5.8). For example, 94 percent of politically attentive Democrats backed closing businesses, as did 90 percent of Republicans. Support was still high, but not quite as high, among less attentive Democrats (82%) and Republicans (76%). There were similar patterns in support for canceling larger gatherings and restricting nonessential travel. Thus, when political leaders were largely united behind these restrictions, politically attentive people were the most supportive of that consensus.[37]

This relative consensus is especially remarkable because politically attentive Republicans were more likely to identify as conservative and more likely to favor "smaller government with fewer services" compared to Republicans who pay less attention to politics. In other words, politically attentive Republicans seemed the least likely to countenance intrusive government, even in a pandemic. But politically attentive Republicans also had one other quality: they were even more strongly supportive of Donald Trump.

Thus, it was no surprise that as Trump began to oppose state and local restrictions, politically attentive Republican followed readily. Between March and the end of July, politically attentive Republicans' support for these restrictions fell farther and faster than any other group. For example, their support for closing businesses fell from 90 percent to 56 percent. Among less attentive Republicans, the decline was much more modest—from 75 percent to 60 percent. Politically attentive Democrats, by contrast, were the group most supportive of restrictions throughout this period. This likely reflected the more consistent support among Democratic leaders.

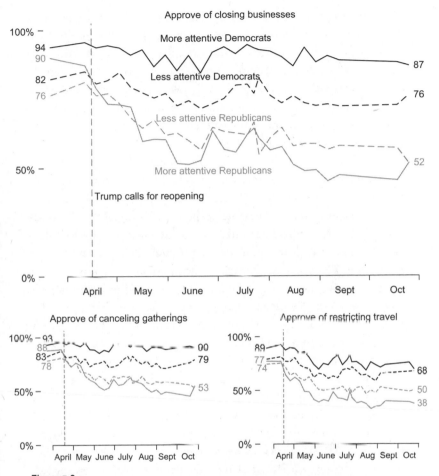

Figure 5.8.
Support for COVID Restrictions by Party and Level of Political Attentiveness, March–October 2020. *Source*: Democracy Fund + UCLA Nationscape surveys.

Despite these increasing partisan divisions, most Americans continued to support COVID restrictions. Even among Republicans, the decline in support created a divided party, not overwhelming opposition. Americans' support extended to other types of restrictions, too. For example, in a June *Huffington Post*/YouGov poll, 62 percent favored a government rule requiring people to wear masks in public when they were around other people. And 69 percent favored local stores requiring people to wear masks when shopping. Most Americans also favored restrictions on church services, despite Trump's wish for packed churches on Easter.[38]

This substantial support for COVID restrictions—even in the face of pushback from Trump—contradicts one of the prevailing narratives about public opinion during the pandemic. Commentators frequently portrayed the public as instinctively opposed to those restrictions. One claim was that "the public will uniformly push for more opening." And thus, public health professionals advocating these restrictions were told that they did not understand "the real world of politics." Another claim was that Americans would not tolerate policies that sought to rigorously identify infected individuals and their contacts. Maybe, the argument went, countries with an "authoritarian residue" could pull this off. But in the United States, "many Americans do not share this faith in government or willingness to limit individual freedom and privacy for population benefit." The Republican Party in particular was characterized as possessed by a "folk-libertarianism" or a "reflexive individualism disconnected from the common good."[39]

But these characterizations were inaccurate in two respects. One was that they simply underestimated the public's willingness to accept COVID restrictions—visible in both their opinions about state and local policies and in their behavior, which reflected an ongoing reticence to return to previous levels of activity. Majorities of Americans supported COVID restrictions even when surveys explicitly juxtaposed those restrictions with libertarian ideals. For example, 78 percent supported a mask mandate even when the alternative was framed as "respect for personal freedom."[40]

Secondly, these characterizations implied that any public opposition to COVID restrictions, especially among Republicans, was just some latent libertarianism come to life. But that fails to capture the real source of that opposition: political leaders like Trump. It was these leaders whose messages pushed some Americans to the view that "LIBERATION" was more important than wearing a mask or avoiding crowded gatherings. Thus, the challenge to mask mandates or stay-at-home orders did not bubble up from freedom-loving citizens. It arose because leaders started to criticize these policies, and some citizens who were aligned with those leaders changed their minds.

CONCLUSION

The year before the pandemic, the Centers for Disease Control published its *Field Epidemiology Manual*. Its chapter on "Communicating during an Outbreak or Public Health Investigation" states that "it is particularly important to determine who has primary responsibility and authority for communicating each aspect of the investigation" and that it is important to have a "primary message point" or "Single Overriding Health Communication Objective." In other words, there needs to be a single prevailing message at any point in time, delivered by a single primary authority.[41]

This is not how the Trump administration managed the pandemic. Trump himself could not settle on any "overriding objective" in the first months of the pandemic. He vacillated between denying and acknowledging the threat of the virus. He vacillated between trying to lead the nation's response and outsourcing responsibility to governors. When those governors took the reins, he vacillated between supporting and criticizing their policies. Eventually, he settled on a message out of step with the reality of the pandemic: to assert that the virus was going away and it was time to reopen the country. This persuaded some Republicans to join his opposition to COVID restrictions, but it was the wrong idea if the goal was fighting the pandemic. Trump could not even muster much empathy for the people dying of COVID-19. In early August, he told an interviewer, "They are dying. That's true. It is what it is."[42]

The pandemic offered Trump an opportunity that might have been politically advantageous: to show Americans that he could lead through a crisis. Many other leaders did just that and saw their popularity soar. True to form, however, Trump could not bring himself to promote (and ultimately benefit from) unity. Instead, he doubled down on division.

And in late May, when another national crisis began on the streets of Minneapolis, Trump did the same thing.

6

George Floyd

with Michael Tesler

Gone are the days when a protest could remain independent from the partisan arena, and speak simply to injustice or wrongdoing.

—DANIEL GILLION, *THE LOUD MINORITY*

ON MAY 25, 2020, George Perry Floyd Jr. was killed on the corner of Chicago Avenue and Thirty-Eighth Street in Minneapolis, Minnesota. Floyd, a forty-six-year-old African American man, had been handcuffed and pinned to the ground by four police officers responding to a call from an employee of a convenience store, who reported that Floyd had used a counterfeit $20 bill to buy a pack of cigarettes. One of the officers, Derek Chauvin, who was white, put his knee onto Floyd's neck. Floyd pleaded for his life, begged for his mother, and told the officer, "I can't breathe." Chauvin did not remove his knee. He restrained Floyd for more than nine minutes, ignoring the pleas of bystanders and continuing to kneel on Floyd's neck even after he lost consciousness and paramedics arrived. The three other officers at the scene did not intervene to stop Chauvin. Bystanders filmed the episode on their cell phones and this footage was circulated immediately.

In the days that followed, protestors against police violence took to the streets of Minneapolis and then to cities across the country. The murder of George Floyd ultimately led to the largest mass protest event in the nation's history. According to the Crowd Counting Consortium, there were about 4,700 separate demonstrations protesting police violence between May 25 and the end of June.[1]

Floyd's murder and these protests produced a broader reckoning with the history of racial prejudice and exclusion. Corporations, universities, and other institutions issued statements and took action to demonstrate their commitment to antiracism. NASCAR banned the display of Confederate flags at races. Quaker Oats dropped the brand name "Aunt Jemima" from its pancake and syrup products, acknowledging the racial stereotype behind the name. Even prominent Republicans, many of whom had not spoken out after other high-profile police killings of African Americans, expressed sorrow about Floyd's death and a desire to address racial inequalities in the criminal justice system. One headline captured what seemed like a watershed moment: "The Politics of Race Are Shifting."[2]

But Donald Trump was not shifting. After initially saying that Floyd's death was "very sad and tragic," Trump quickly seized on episodes of violence and looting that occurred during the protests. The president called the protestors "THUGS" and tweeted, "When the looting starts, the shooting starts," a phrase that segregationists long used to threaten Black civil rights protestors with violence. The next day he attacked Minneapolis mayor Jacob Frey as "the very weak Radical Left Mayor" and said he would "send in the National Guard & get the job done right." These comments were consistent with Trump's longtime affection for repressing protests. In 1990, for example, he had praised China's crackdown on protestors in Tiananmen Square, saying, "They were vicious, they were horrible, but they put it down with strength. That shows you the power of strength."[3]

In fact, of those eventually charged with federal crimes because of their actions during the protests, more than half were white and almost none were residents of Minneapolis. They appeared to have a range of motives; two were not even protesting racism but actually members of a far-right group.[4] In the moment, none of this was known, but that did not stop Trump from reacting with racially coded epithets, attacks on Democratic politicians, and threats of violence.

In Washington, DC, Trump took more direct action. Like many cities, Washington was experiencing extensive protests, including around the White House. At one point on May 29, after some protestors breached security fencing near the White House and attacked Secret Service officers, the Secret Service had Trump and his family moved to an underground bunker for their safety. Trump was angry with the perception that he was hiding in the bunker and wanted to do something to change that impression. On June 1, Trump decided to give a speech in the Rose Garden condemning the protests and then do a photo op at nearby St. John's Episcopal Church. Getting to the church required Trump to walk through Lafayette Square, just north of the White House, which had been the site of protests and was at that moment occupied by peaceful protestors. The Trump administration took extraordinary action to clear a path for the president, directing federal law enforcement to use tear gas, flash-bang explosions, and rubber bullets on those gathered in the square. Clergy and other church volunteers were pushed off the patio of the church. Trump and a group of administration officials, including the secretary of defense and the chair of the Joint Chiefs of Staff, then walked to the church, where Trump posed for pictures holding a Bible.[5]

The administration's actions were widely condemned. Bishop Mariann E. Budde, the leader of the Episcopal Diocese of Washington, said, "We need a president who can unify and heal. He has done the opposite of that, and we are left to pick up the pieces." Even some Republican leaders criticized Trump. Said Senator Ben Sasse: "I'm against clearing out a peaceful protest for a photo op that treats the Word of God as a political prop." Most Americans agreed. Polling in June consistently showed that majorities disapproved of Trump's response to the protests.[6]

It appeared that public opinion was shifting away from Trump in other ways as well. Immediately after Floyd's murder, prominent Democrats and Republicans alike condemned Chauvin's actions. Americans of all partisan stripes came to have less favorable views of the police and more concern about racial discrimination.

But the moment proved temporary. As the political scientist Daniel Gillion argues, protests in modern American politics are quickly subsumed by partisan politics, and the racial justice protests of 2020 were no different.[7] The consensus among Democratic and Republican leaders quickly broke down as Trump and other Republicans began criticizing the protestors. As a consequence, Democrat and Republican voters began to polarize as well. The consequence was *larger* partisan divisions on racial issues—larger than they had been even after the "identity shocks" of the divisive 2016 campaign. These growing divisions were directly tied to views of Trump himself: the more people disliked Trump, the more their racial attitudes shifted to be favorable to African Americans and less favorable to the police.

The biggest change was within the Democratic Party. Just as Democrats shifted away from Trump's anti-immigration stance toward an embrace of immigration (see chapter 1), they shifted toward a more liberal position on racial issues. Those shifts were underway before May 25, 2020, and were accelerated by many aspects of Trump's racial politics. But Floyd's murder, and Trump's reaction to it, only helped to push Democrats further to the left.

The same partisan politics played out on police reform, which was the central policy debate after Floyd's murder. Although there was some partisan accord on banning choke holds, this was really a priority only for Democrats. Republicans placed far more importance on opposing any effort to "defund" the police or decrease its size. Once again, the priorities of Democrats and Republicans only helped to reinforce their disagreements.

In many respects, then, the political impact of George Floyd's murder mirrored that of the pandemic. Both events had the potential to create unified political action, which was visible in initial moments of consensus among political leaders. But in neither case did any consensus last long, and a key factor was Trump himself. The result was not a watershed that transformed America's racial politics. It was a continuation and even intensification of the partisan polarization underway before Floyd's murder.

LESS THAN A RECKONING

In the wake of Floyd's murder, it was no surprise that many Democratic leaders would harshly condemn the actions of Derek Chauvin and connect Floyd's death not only to prominent police killings of other African

Americans but to broader issues of systemic racism in the criminal justice system as well. These issues had been gaining visibility in the party for some time, due especially to ongoing activism by the Black Lives Matter (BLM) movement. The fruits of that activism were visible in 2016, when Hillary Clinton's first major speech as a presidential candidate focused on the treatment of African Americans by police.[8]

What was notable about Floyd's murder, however, was that it engendered a sympathetic reaction among many Republican and conservative leaders, including those who had never been sympathetic to BLM and often defended the police after the deaths of African Americans. One was Senator Mitch McConnell, then the majority leader. On June 7, he said, "When Black Americans tell us they do not feel safe in their own communities, we need to listen. When citizens lack faith in our justice system, we need to respond. And when the equal protection of the law feels to some Americans like a contingency of demographics, we need to act." Two days later, at the Senate Republicans' lunch, Arkansas senator Tom Cotton said, "Young black men have a very different experience with law enforcement in this nation than white people and that's their impression and experience and we need to be sensitive to that and do all we can to change it."[9] Even on conservative talk radio, there were expressions of sympathy. On June 6, Rush Limbaugh said: "There is not a single person in this country, regardless of race or political affiliation, who did not think that the nine minutes of video of a policeman's knee on the neck of George Floyd was absolutely horrifying."

As we noted in chapter 5, when leaders of both parties express some consensus on a political issue, that helps create consensus among Democrats and Republicans in the mass public. That is exactly what happened in May and June 2020. For example, in a May 28–29, 2020, YouGov poll, there was bipartisan support for arresting Chauvin: 90 percent of Democrats and 68 percent of Republicans agreed. In a June 7–9, 2020, YouGov poll, 89 percent of Democrats and 72 percent of Republicans approved of "non-violent protests in response to George Floyd's death." There were still partisan differences, but they were far more muted than is often true on racial issues in general and on police

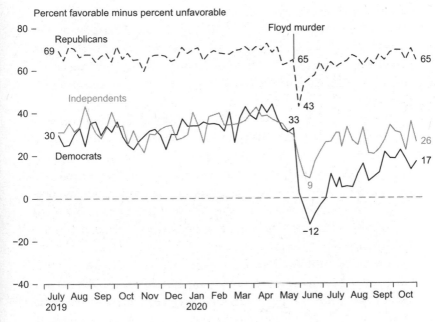

Percent favorable minus percent unfavorable

Figure 6.1.
Trend in Views of the Police. *Source:* Democracy Fund + UCLA Nationscape surveys.

killings of Black Americans in particular. Indeed, Floyd's murder led some commentators to wonder whether, as one *Politico* article put it, "a punitive brand of conservatism embraced by Trump and some GOP hardliners is rapidly falling out of step with public opinion."[10]

The initial shifts in public opinion were rapid and dramatic. For one, views of the police became much more critical. In Nationscape surveys conducted weekly starting in July 2019, views of the police were measured on a four-category scale ranging from "very favorable" to "very unfavorable." Prior to the Floyd murder, more people had a favorable view of the police than an unfavorable view —especially Republicans but also Democrats to a lesser extent (figure 6.1).

That changed immediately after Floyd's murder. The net favorability rating of the police became much less positive among all partisan groups, with drops among Democrats (+33 to −12), independents (+28 to +9), and Republicans (+65 to +43). Among Americans overall, views of the police fell 24 points, from +44 to +20. This was the largest one-week change in the net favorability of any social, political, or religious group measured in the Nationscape survey between July 2019 and January 2021.[11]

However, trends between different partisan groups began to diverge by the beginning of June. Republican attitudes bounced back almost immediately, and by the beginning of August, Republican attitudes about police had largely recovered to their pre-Floyd levels. Democrats' favorability toward the police increased more slowly over the remainder of the year but did not return to their previous levels by the end of the presidential campaign. This left the parties further apart than they had been before Floyd's death.

These trends in attitudes toward the police occurred in communities that experienced racial justice protests as well as those that did not (see table A6.2). There was not a clear localized effect of the protests on attitudes, as some previous research on civil rights protests has found. For example, research on protests during the civil rights movement, after the 1992 acquittal of the Los Angeles police officers who beat Rodney King, and during the first wave of BLM protests in 2014 found that people living near these protests developed more liberal attitudes, compared to those living further away.[12] But the protests in 2020 were far more widespread and accompanied by extensive national media coverage of Floyd's murder, including the infamous video footage. This helped expose Americans to news about Chauvin's actions regardless of whether local protests themselves drew attention to Floyd's death and the broader issues that it raised. Thus, attitude changes after Floyd's murder paralleled what we found about attitudes toward COVID-19 in chapter 5: changes in COVID attitudes reflected national influences, and especially messages from leaders like Trump, much more than local circumstances such as the number of COVID-19 deaths or infections in the community. Attitudes about the police were similarly "nationalized" in 2020.

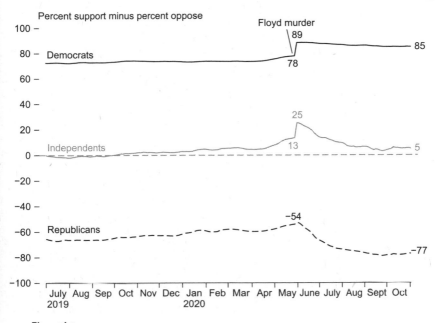

Figure 6.2.
Trends in Views of Black Lives Matter. *Source*: Civiqs surveys.

The liberal shifts in racial attitudes also encompassed opinions about the BLM movement. After Floyd's murder, support for BLM increased immediately, peaking at around 52 percent in polling by the firm Civiqs. At that point, only 29 percent opposed the movement, 17 percent said they did not support or oppose it, and the rest did not have an opinion. This increase in support was driven mainly by Democrats and independents (figure 6.2).

But as the summer progressed, support for BLM declined. This was true among all types of partisans and racial and ethnic groups, including African Americans. But the decline was particularly notable among Republicans. They never experienced a bump in support for BLM and instead more and more of them came to oppose it.[13]

A similar pattern was visible in Americans' perceptions of how much discrimination Black Americans face (figure 6.3). Among all Americans,

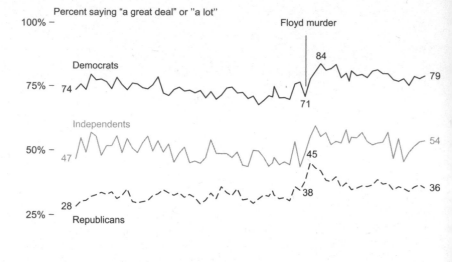

Figure 6.3.
Views of Discrimination against Black Americans. *Source*: Democracy Fund + UCLA
Nationscape surveys.

the percent saying that Black Americans faced "a great deal" or "a lot" of
discrimination increased from 55 percent to 63 percent within two
weeks. Similar shifts occurred among all partisan and racial groups. But
again, these changes faded with time.

Immediately after Floyd's murder, Americans also came to express more
sympathetic views of African Americans. In Nationscape surveys, an increasing percentage agreed that slavery and discrimination have created
economic hurdles for Black people and disagreed that Black people should
overcome prejudice without favors. The short-term shifts on these two
questions were once again driven disproportionately by changes among
Democrats. Over the summer and fall, some of these changes ebbed, although responses to the question about overcoming prejudice continued
to be more divided by party than they were before Floyd's death.[14]

Taken together, the public opinion trends show that Americans' racial attitudes shifted immediately after George Floyd's murder but ebbed in the months that followed. The lack of a durable shift among Americans overall, however, concealed a more lasting pattern of growing partisan polarization.

Two things help explain the overall trends in public opinion as well as the increase in partisan polarization: first, the drop in protests and resulting news coverage, and second, rhetoric from Trump and other Republicans that sought to shift attention away from Floyd's murder and to the protests themselves.

The BLM movement and the broader issue of systemic racism received an extraordinary amount of coverage after Floyd's murder. But the news attention was temporary, following a typical pattern called the "issue-attention cycle": a dramatic event or series of events creates a sharp spike in news coverage of those events and related issues, but the coverage eventually moves on to other topics. This cycle characterizes news coverage of many political issues. One example is high-profile mass shootings, which often get fleeting news coverage and thus have ephemeral effects on public opinion about guns and gun control. Another reason for the decline in news attention was the decline in protests. As research on the civil rights movement has shown, protests frequently serve to focus the news media's attention on racial injustice. As the protests after Floyd's murder dwindled, so did the volume of news stories about his murder as well as broader issues like racism.[15]

To show this cycle in news coverage and its relationship to protest activity, we rely on two data sources. The first is closed captioning data of cable news broadcasts from the TV News Archive to identify the number of clips that mentioned "George Floyd," "racism," or "Black Lives Matter." The second is a daily count of protests maintained by the Crowd Counting Consortium, which uses news accounts and crowdsourcing to identify episodes of protest activity in the United States, including when and where they occurred as well as their major concerns or goals. We included any protests that focused on police

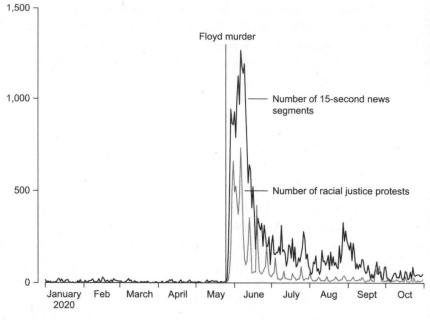

Figure 6.4.

Trends in the Number of Racial Justice Protests and Cable News Coverage of George Floyd, Black Lives Matter, and Racism, January 1–November 2, 2020. Protest trend is the number of protests coded as supporting police brutality, police accountability, racial justice, antiracism, George Floyd, or Black Lives Matter. News coverage trend is the number of fifteen-second blocks of cable news coverage (CNN, Fox News, and MSNBC) that mentioned "George Floyd," "Black Lives Matter," or "racism." *Sources*: Crowd Counting Consortium and Internet Archive TV News Archive.

brutality, police accountability, racial justice, antiracism, George Floyd, or BLM.[16]

The spikes in protests and coverage were immediately apparent (figure 6.4). In the two weeks following Floyd's death, there were hundreds of protests nearly every day in cities and towns across the country.[17] There were also thousands of cable news mentions of Floyd, BLM, and racism. But beginning around June 10, news coverage of these issues began to decline. This reflects the drop in protest activity. By the end of June, there were only a handful of protests happening daily.[18]

As the story faded from the news, opinions began to revert to their previous levels. This was true across demographic and political groups, including both Democrats and Republicans. It was true not only in Nationscape polling but in other polls as well. For example, Gallup polls found a drop in the percent of Americans who said that race relations or racism was the most important problem facing the country. This pattern illustrates how sustained activism and media attention were necessary if the Floyd protests were to have a persistent effect on public opinion.

The second factor in opinion change was an emerging conservative counternarrative, which supplanted the original message from Republican leaders, such as McConnell and Cotton, that was sympathetic to Floyd. In the counternarrative, the bigger threat was not racial injustice but rather the effort to fight it. Trump and his allies seized on the rare instances of violence at the protests and criticized calls by some activists to "defund the police." Trump railed against "angry mobs" and "agitators" and "looters" and "violent mayhem." Fox News was much more likely to cover events related to "defund" and "Portland" (the site of ongoing protests and some violent demonstrations) in the summer months of 2020 than were CNN and MSNBC.[19]

These partisan differences were further magnified by divergent reactions to a Kenosha, Wisconsin, police officer's shooting of a Black man, Jacob Blake, on August 23. On the political left, the Blake shooting sparked protests in Kenosha that extended to boycotts by NBA and WNBA athletes. But unlike after Chauvin's murder of Floyd, conservative politicians and media figures closed ranks around the Kenosha police. Attorney General William Barr, for example, contrasted the two incidents by stating, "Floyd was already subdued, incapacitated in handcuffs and was not armed. . . . In the Jacob [Blake] case, he was in the midst of committing a felony, and he was armed. So, that's a big difference." Barr's description of the Blake shooting was highly contested— Blake was shot in the back seven times—but it was prominent on the right and helped polarize public opinion: only 13 percent of Trump voters thought that the Blake shooting was unjustified, compared to 81 percent of Biden voters.[20]

The impact of this counternarrative is visible in the public opinion data. Although the shifts in attitudes were somewhat parallel across Democrats and Republicans, there were key differences. In terms of their support of the police, for example, Republican attitudes did not drop as precipitously as Democratic attitudes. Moreover, Republican attitudes recovered more quickly and to their level before Floyd's murder. Democratic attitudes also recovered but to a far lesser extent; even in early 2021, Democrats were still less favorable to the police than they had been before Floyd's murder. The counternarrative's effect is also visible in views of the BLM movement. After Floyd's murder, Republicans became far more opposed to BLM, even as Democrats shifted in the opposite direction.[21]

Part of the reason this counternarrative may have been so successful is that the Floyd murder did little to change Republican attitudes on broader issues related to race and policing. In one poll conducted very soon after Floyd's murder, when majorities of both Republicans and Democrats agreed that the police's use of force against Floyd was unjustified, Republicans were still far less likely than Democrats to believe that "police killings of African Americans are signs of a broader problem" or that "the criminal justice system treats whites better than Blacks." No more than a third of Republicans agreed with those ideas. Thus, most Republicans were skeptical of the central ideas motivating the racial justice protests and thus ready to believe Trump's attacks.[22]

LONG DIVISION

These diverging attitudes of Democrats and Republicans belied the initial optimism that Floyd's murder would create a broad-based change in public attitudes that in turn would help racial justice and civil rights causes. The impact of Floyd's murder on public attitudes is better seen not as a singular dramatic change but rather as an important element in the ongoing changes already underway, which led to more liberal attitudes among Democrats in particular. This "identity shock," as we have called it, is not just a generically partisan phenomenon. It is deeply connected to Donald Trump himself. Trump's brand of identity politics, which was visible well before Floyd's murder, helped push Democrats in the opposite direction in the years leading up to 2020, both before Floyd's murder and in its aftermath.

That attitudes about racial issues would change so dramatically was hardly preordained. In the 1990s and 2000s, attitudes about systemic racism and Black Americans did not shift much in the aggregate—a pattern that the political scientists Christopher DeSante and Candis Watts Smith have called "racial stasis." This was particularly evident in the aforementioned survey questions that capture how much people attribute racial inequality to structural forces, like slavery and discrimination, as opposed to individual-level factors like whether African Americans "try hard enough." The questions ask respondents whether they agree or disagree with four statements:

- "Over the past few years, Black people have gotten less than they deserve."
- "Irish, Italian, Jewish, and many other minorities overcame prejudice and worked their way up. Black people should do the same without any special favors."
- "It's really a matter of some people not trying hard enough; if Black people would only try harder they could be just as well off as white people."
- "Generations of slavery and discrimination have created conditions that make it difficult for Black people to work their way out of the lower class."[23]

But since 2011, there have been remarkable changes in these attitudes. This is visible in the Views of the Electorate Research (VOTER) Survey. Between 2011 and 2020, Americans overall have liberalized. For example, the percent of Americans who agreed that "over the last few years, Black people have gotten less than they deserve" rose from 20 percent to 45 percent over this decade. The number who agreed that discrimination and slavery prevent Black people from making economic progress increased from 35 percent to 48 percent. In addition, more Americans disagreed that Black people should overcome prejudice without special

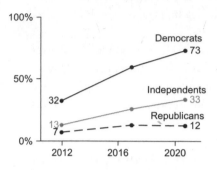

Over the past few years, Black people have gotten less than they deserve (percent agree)

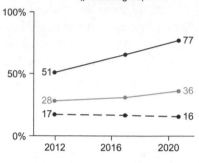

Slavery and discrimination make it difficult for Black people to work their way out of the lower class (percent agree)

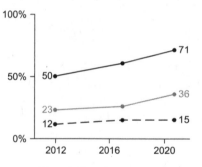

If Black people would only try harder they could be just as well off as white people (percent disagree)

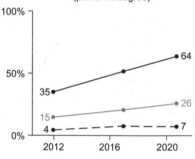

Other minorities overcame prejudice. Black people should do the same without any special favors (percent disagree)

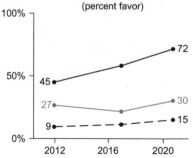

View of affirmative action programs for women and racial minorities (percent favor)

Figure 6.5.

Trends in Views of Racial Inequality and Affirmative Action, 2011–20. *Source*: VOTER Survey.

favors (20% vs. 37%) and that Black people could be "just as well off as white people" if they tried harder (31% vs. 45%).

In large part, these shifts were driven by Democrats and independents (figure 6.5). This was already evident in 2016, but the trends continued between 2016 and 2020.[24] Compared to 2011, Democrats in 2020 were far more likely to agree that Black people have gotten less than they deserve (32% vs. 73%) and to agree that discrimination makes it difficult for Black people to make economic progress (51% vs. 77%). Democrats were also more likely to disagree that Black people should overcome prejudice without favors and to disagree that Black people could be as well off as white people if they tried harder. Independents showed smaller but similar changes. Between 2011 and 2020, the number of Republicans who agreed or disagreed with these statements did not change substantially. Prior research has shown that partisan polarization on these measures began before 2011 but has clearly accelerated since.[25] Notably, these shifts were evident among white, Black, and Latino Democrats alike, although most of the change came from white Democrats. These movements largely closed the historic gap between white and Black Democrats.

On one issue, affirmative action, support for the policy has shifted in ways that parallel views about the origins of racial inequality (figure 6.5). Between 2011 and 2020, the percentage of Americans who said they favored affirmative action programs for women and racial minorities increased from 29 percent to 44 percent. These shifts were driven primarily by Democrats. Independents and Republicans shifted in the same direction, but by much less. Among Democrats, the shift was also driven primarily by whites. Their support for affirmative action increased 24 points between 2011 and 2020—almost completely closing the gap between white Democrats and Black and Latino Democrats.[26]

These changes are mostly *not* because of partisan sorting, with more racially liberal Americans switching into the Democratic Party and more racially conservative Americans switching out. Instead, these changes are driven by partisans who changed their attitudes about race. To see this, we can focus on VOTER Survey respondents who were interviewed in both 2011 and 2020 and identified as Democrats in both

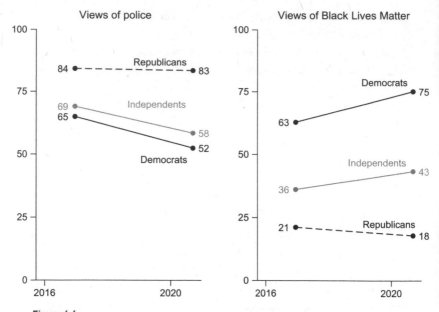

Figure 6.6.
Shifts in Views of Black Lives Matter and the Police. Views are measured on a 0–100 scale where 100 is the most positive rating. *Source*: VOTER Survey.

2011 and 2020. Among these consistent Democrats, there were similar trends in attitudes. For example, the percentage who agreed that Black people have gotten less than they deserve increased from 38 percent to 73 percent and the percentage who disagreed that Black people could be as well off as white people if they tried harder increased from 59 percent to 72 percent.[27] This means that within the party, people changed their attitudes in increasingly liberal directions.

These growing partisan differences were also visible in views of the police and BLM. In the VOTER Survey's interviews with respondents after the 2016 and 2020 elections, views of the police and BLM were measured with the same 0–100 feeling thermometer. Views of the police were net positive in both years but clearly lower in 2020 than 2016—an average of 65 versus 74 (figure 6.6). Favorability toward BLM shifted in the opposite direction: an increase in average thermometer ratings among all Americans from 41 to 50.

Both shifts were driven primarily by changes among Democrats and independents. Among Democrats, average thermometer ratings of police dropped from 66 to 53. Among independents, they dropped from 70 to 59. Republican views were stable (an average of 85 in 2016 and 84 in 2020). Similarly, Democrats' average rating of BLM rose 12 points while Republican attitudes did not change.

Among Democrats, changes in attitudes toward the police between 2016 and 2020 were similar among different races and ethnicities. Positive feelings toward police among white (68 vs. 54), Black (59 vs. 46), and Latino (70 vs. 55) respondents dropped similar amounts over this four-year period. Changes in Democratic attitudes toward BLM occurred mainly among white and Latino Democrats. While white (59 vs. 74) and Latino (60 vs. 70) ratings of BLM rose at least 10 points, changes among Black Democrats—already higher than other Democrats—were smaller (80 vs. 84).

THE "TRUMPIFICATION" OF RACIAL ATTITUDES

Taken together, the trends in all of these attitudes demonstrate that the partisan differences so evident in the 2016 election year have only intensified during Trump's presidency. In fact, a big part of the reason for these shifts, especially among Democrats, is Trump himself. His hostile statements about racial, ethnic, and religious minorities marked an important departure from the behavior of previous Republican candidates and helped push Democrats toward more liberal positions.

For a long time, the Republican Party's incentive has been to appeal to racially conservative voters without turning off other potential supporters by being overtly racist. This led to a racially coded dog-whistle politics that was often discernible only to people following politics closely. For example, in 1980, Ronald Reagan launched his general election campaign by giving a speech supporting "states' rights"—an argument frequently used by opponents of civil rights—at a county fair near Philadelphia, Mississippi, where three civil rights activists had been murdered in 1964. He also repeatedly invoked the racially stereotyped anecdote of "welfare queens" riding around in Cadillacs. The legal scholar Ian Hanley-Lopez writes, "Reagan always denied any racism and emphasized that he never mentioned race. He didn't need to because he was blowing a dog whistle." Another racial dog whistle came during the 1988 presidential campaign, in which Massachusetts governor and Democratic candidate Michael Dukakis was attacked as "soft on crime" in television ads that featured images of a Black inmate and focused on one, William Horton, who was convicted of violent crimes while on a temporary furlough from a Massachusetts prison.[28]

Those dog whistles became bullhorns during Trump's presidency. He said refugees coming to America were from "shithole" countries. He described some of the neo-Nazis at the violent rally in Charlottesville, Virginia, as "very fine people." He echoed white supremacist language to stoke fears of an "invasion" from Mexico. One of his 2018 television commercials on immigration was deemed so racist that NBC and even Fox News chose to stop airing it. In June 2020, Trump tweeted a video in which a man shouted "white power" at a group of racial justice protestors, a tweet that Trump later deleted but never disavowed.[29]

These types of messages matter for public opinion. Americans often develop their opinions via signals from those they perceive as political allies and enemies. In fact, cues from enemies can be more important than cues from allies. When a politician takes a strong position, it often leads members of the other party to take opposing positions.[30] Even before he became president, Trump's rhetoric and policies had this backfire effect. During his presidential campaign, Trump's constant push for a U.S.-Mexico border wall appeared to make it less popular among Democrats, as we noted in Chapter 2. His positions on race, immigration, and Islam created an incongruity for Democrats who disliked Trump but were otherwise more moderate or conservative on these issues. The easiest way for these Democrats to resolve this incongruity was to shift their positions away from Trump's.

This is precisely what happened among white Americans. Even more so than partisan identification, changes in their racial attitudes from 2016 to 2020 were correlated with their feelings about Trump. Using data from the VOTER Survey as well as the American National Election

Study panel, we found that white Americans' feelings about Trump in 2016 were strongly associated with subsequent changes in their responses to the same four questions about racial inequality as well as their feelings about the BLM movement and police. In particular, the less favorably white Americans felt toward Trump in 2016, the more their attitudes shifted in a liberal direction between 2016 and 2020 (see the appendix for more detail).

Of course, Democrats and Republicans had been moving apart on racial attitudes prior to Trump. But Trump's candidacy and then presidency helped accelerate the trend and put racial issues at the center of U.S. politics. The political scientist E. E. Schattschneider famously argued that politics is about organizing the "scope of conflict"—that is, which issues are fundamental to debates between contending sides. For a long time, a divided Democratic Party, subtler racial dog-whistling within the Republican Party, and a public characterized by racial stasis meant that racial issues were not always central to U.S. party politics. But then a Republican presidential candidate and president explicitly targeted racial, ethnic, and religious minorities. The resulting identity shock pushed the Democratic Party to liberalize on racial issues. Thus, the "scope of conflict" visible in American political parties increasingly includes questions about civil rights and racial justice.

THE DEBATE ABOUT POLICING

In the wake of George Floyd's murder, a distinct set of civil rights issues became central to this conflict. These issues concerned how to reform police departments and procedures to prevent unnecessary violence caused by police officers, which all too often injured or killed African Americans in particular because they are disproportionately stopped by police.[31] For advocates of police reform, the question was how to build the coalition necessary to effect change. For both the Democratic and Republican parties, there was a further concern: how to navigate these issues in a way that did not divide their party and, given the ongoing presidential campaign, hurt the party's chances of winning.

The reforms being debated included changes to police tactics, such as a ban on choke holds or neck restraints, that raise the risk of asphyxiation, as in Floyd's death. There were more ambitious reforms as well. One was to end or limit "qualified immunity," or protections from civil lawsuits that police officers have for actions taken in the line of duty. Another was to reduce the scope of police activity, such as by shifting traffic enforcement to other municipal employees or by investing in health workers who could handle situations involving mentally ill people.

The final, and most controversial, proposal was to reduce funding for police departments. This is what the slogan "defund the police" meant in most cases, although there were more radical proposals that would dissolve existing police departments and replace them with something different. In Minneapolis, for example, there would eventually be a proposal to replace the police department with a new Department of Public Safety, eliminate the requirement that the city have a certain number of police officers per capita, and replace some officers with social workers and mental health professionals. The issue of police defunding took on outsized attention in news coverage. On the major cable news networks, for example, there were four times as many mentions of defunding the police than mentions of choke holds between Floyd's murder and Election Day.[32]

The partisan politics of these reform proposals differed dramatically. This was true both in how many Democrats and Republicans supported these proposals and in the importance they attached to them. In July 2020, the Nationscape project fielded a special wave of its survey that measured attitudes toward several police reforms along with other issues, some of which had been part of previous surveys and others of which were new to this July survey. The police reforms were banning choke holds, eliminating qualified immunity, decreasing the size of the police force and the scope of its work, and "defunding the police."

By far the most popular was banning choke holds, with 66 percent of respondents supporting this, 19 percent opposing, and 15 percent not expressing an opinion. A plurality of respondents (45%) supported ending qualified immunity while 34 percent opposed it. Both proposals to scale back policing were much less popular, including decreasing the

size of the police (26% support vs. 55% oppose) and "defunding" the
police (21% vs. 60%).

Banning choke holds was the only one of these policies to attract
majority support across a range of demographic and political groups.
For example, 81 percent of Democrats and 52 percent of Republicans
supported it. Ending qualified immunity attracted support from a majority
of Democrats (57%) but only about a third of Republicans. Neither decreasing the size of police forces nor defunding the police attracted
majority support among Democrats or Republicans, but notably these
issues divided Democrats more than Republicans. For example, Democrats were nearly evenly split on decreasing the size of police forces
(39% in support vs. 41% opposed). By contrast, only 15 percent of Republicans supported this and 75 percent opposed it.

The parties disagreed even more on which of these reforms was a
priority. Based on the revealed importance experiment in this survey,
the most important issue for Democrats was banning choke holds (figure 6.7). In fact, this was not only the most important police reform
proposal but also one of the most important issues to Democrats of any
included in this survey, ranking alongside guaranteed housing and several
policies related to immigration and gun control. By contrast, Democrats
attached much less importance to the other police reforms, even to ending qualified immunity, which a majority of the party also favored.

The priorities of Republicans were starkly different. For them, the
most important policing issues were defunding the police and decreasing the scope of its work, both of which most Republicans opposed
(figure 6.8). These issues were about as important as two other policies
anathema to Republicans: a ban on guns and legal abortion under any
circumstances. Unlike Democrats, Republicans attached much less importance to banning choke holds, even though a majority favored it.

These results echo the earlier revealed importance experiments (see
chapters 3 and 4). Republicans tended to care more about issues on
which most Republicans took the conservative position and Democrats
tended to care more about issues on which most Democrats took the
liberal position. Even when there was overlap between the parties, such

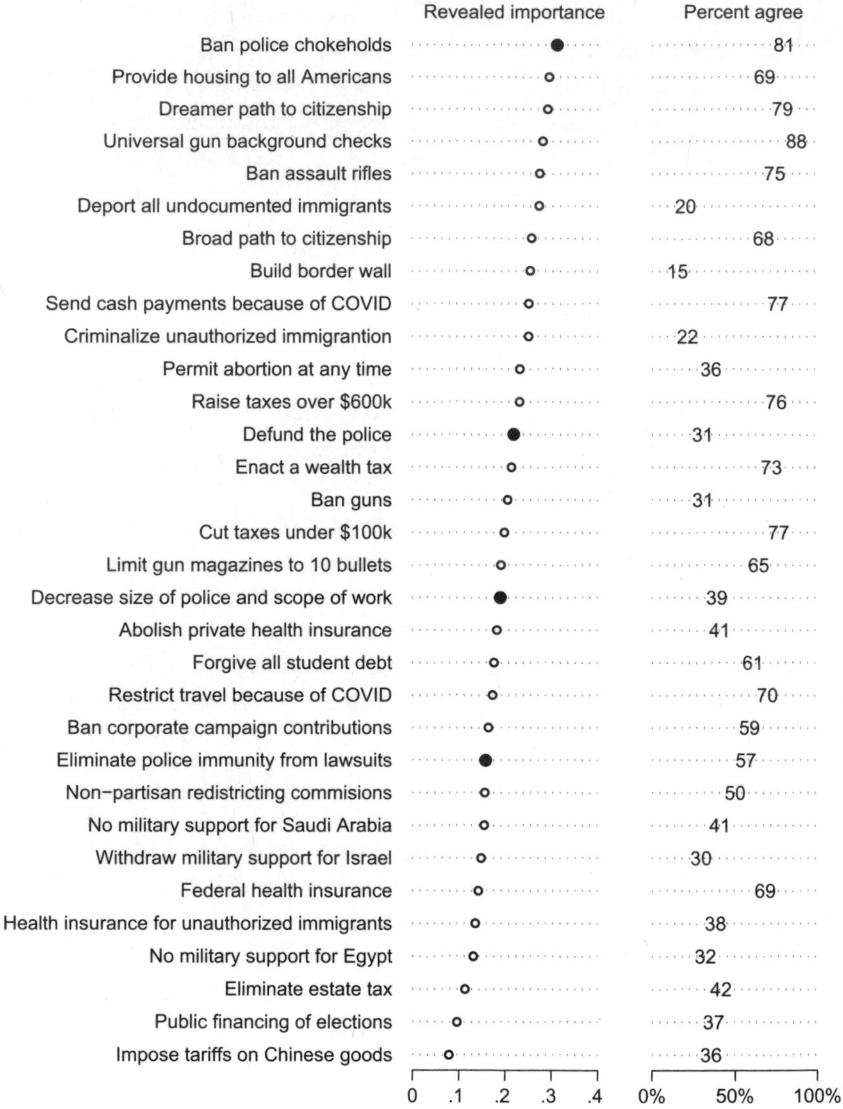

Figure 6.7 — Revealed Importance and Support for Policies among Democrats, July 2020.

Policy	Revealed importance	Percent agree
Ban police chokeholds		81
Provide housing to all Americans		69
Dreamer path to citizenship		79
Universal gun background checks		88
Ban assault rifles		75
Deport all undocumented immigrants		20
Broad path to citizenship		68
Build border wall		15
Send cash payments because of COVID		77
Criminalize unauthorized immigrantion		22
Permit abortion at any time		36
Raise taxes over $600k		76
Defund the police		31
Enact a wealth tax		73
Ban guns		31
Cut taxes under $100k		77
Limit gun magazines to 10 bullets		65
Decrease size of police and scope of work		39
Abolish private health insurance		41
Forgive all student debt		61
Restrict travel because of COVID		70
Ban corporate campaign contributions		59
Eliminate police immunity from lawsuits		57
Non–partisan redistricting commisions		50
No military support for Saudi Arabia		41
Withdraw military support for Israel		30
Federal health insurance		69
Health insurance for unauthorized immigrants		38
No military support for Egypt		32
Eliminate estate tax		42
Public financing of elections		37
Impose tariffs on Chinese goods		36

Scale: Revealed importance 0 | .1 | .2 | .3 | .4   Percent agree 0% | 50% | 100%

Figure 6.7.
Revealed Importance and Support for Policies among Democrats, July 2020. *Source*: July 2020 Democracy Fund + UCLA Nationscape survey.

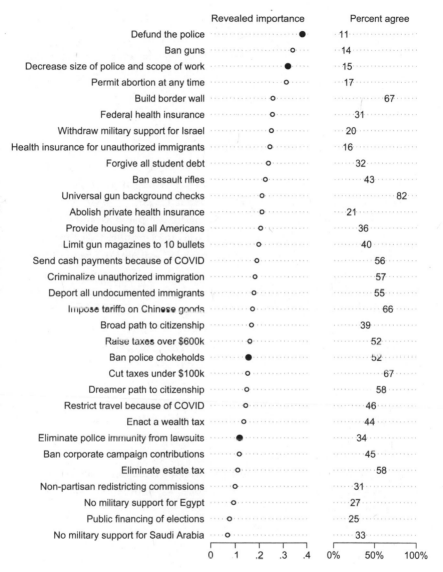

Figure 6.8.
Revealed Importance and Support for Policies among Republicans, July 2020. *Source*:
July 2020 Democracy Fund + UCLA Nationscape survey.

as on banning choke holds and opposition to defunding the police, the two parties did not agree about how important the issue was. Once again, the policy priorities of the parties were far more conducive to division than consensus.

CONCLUSION

After Lafayette Square was cleared so that Trump could stage the photo opportunity at St. John's Episcopal Church, Joe Biden said, "Donald Trump has turned this country into a battlefield driven by old resentments and fresh fears. He thinks division helps him."[33]

That was the question looming for the fall campaign: would division help Trump? At least since Richard Nixon's 1968 presidential campaign, race had been considered an effective wedge issue for the Republican Party—one that could splinter the Democratic coalition of nonwhite voters, racially liberal white voters, and racially conservative white voters.[34] Trump arguably used this strategy successfully in his 2016 campaign, winning enough racially conservative white Obama voters to thread a narrow path through the Electoral College.

After Floyd's murder, Trump appeared ready to follow a similar strategy, this time with a focus on violent protestors and efforts to "defund the police." This strategy has many historical analogs. Republican candidates have often tried to pry racially conservative voters away from the Democratic Party by shifting the focus from broadly accepted principles of racial equality, such as the wrongness of segregation or discrimination, to the more controversial policies that addressed racial issues. In this sense, "defunding the police" was another in a long line of unpopular racialized policies, including school busing and affirmative action, that became campaign fodder.

At the same time, Trump was confronting—and Biden was leading—a transformed Democratic Party. Between 2012 and 2020, racially conservative Democrats mostly defected to the Republican Party or, more often, shifted their racial attitudes to be more liberal. In short, there were fewer cross-positioned or cross-pressured voters for Trump to win over with racialized wedge issues. Perhaps ironically, Trump himself was responsible for this change, given that the liberal shift was a direct response to his brand of identity politics. In turn, this shift enabled and encouraged Democratic politicians like Biden to take stronger positions on racial equality than their counterparts in years past. The question was whether this transformed Democratic Party would hang together when confronted with an issue, like defunding police, that divided the party.

If Trump was successful, the election could turn on something other than the pandemic, especially given the summer surge in COVID-19 cases and the struggling economy. He soon found, however, that changing the subject would not be so easy.

7

The Death Star and the Basement

Joe Biden and the Democrat Socialists will kill your jobs, dismantle your police departments, dissolve your borders, release criminal aliens, raise your taxes, confiscate your guns, end fracking, destroy your suburbs, and drive God from the public square.

—DONALD TRUMP, OCTOBER 15, 2020

Anyone responsible for that many deaths should not remain as the president of the United States.

—JOE BIDEN, OCTOBER 22, 2020

ON AUGUST 17, 2020, the first night of the Democratic National Convention, a woman named Kristin Urquiza spoke. She was not a politician and she was not a celebrity. She was a daughter, mourning the death of her father, Mark. He had died of COVID-19 six weeks earlier, alone in an Arizona intensive care unit. Kristin Urquiza had received national attention for the obituary she wrote in the *Arizona Republic*, in which she said:

> Mark, like so many others, should not have died from COVID-19. His death is due to the carelessness of the politicians who continue to jeopardize the health of brown bodies through a clear lack of leadership, refusal to acknowledge the severity of this crisis, and inability and unwillingness to give clear and decisive direction on how to minimize risk. Mark's daughter Kristin Danielle and daughter-in-law Christine are channeling our sadness and rage into building an awareness campaign so fewer families are forced to endure this. We honor

Mark's life by continuing this fight for others, even in these darkest moments.

At the convention, Urquiza singled out one politician in particular: Donald Trump, whom her father had voted for. She said, "My dad was a healthy 65-year-old. His only pre-existing condition was trusting Donald Trump. And for that he paid with his life."[1]

A week later, on the first night of the Republican National Convention, two other ordinary Americans appeared on-screen, sitting on a sofa in a wood-paneled room. "Good evening America," the man said. "We are Mark and Patty McCloskey. We're speaking to you tonight from St. Louis, Missouri, where just weeks ago you may have seen us defending our home as a mob of protesters descended on our neighborhood." His wife joined in, saying, "America is such a great country . . . you have the right to own a gun and use it to defend yourself. What you saw happen to us could just as easily happen to any of you who are watching from quiet neighborhoods around our country." The McCloskeys were describing a June 28 incident in which a group of Black Lives Matter (BLM) protestors walked down the private street where the McCloskeys lived. In response, the McCloskeys emerged from their home, yelled at the protestors to leave, and, during the resulting verbal exchange, pointed guns at them. Photos of the event went viral, and the McCloskeys were charged with unlawful use of a weapon.

The settings and speakers at the party conventions were a microcosm of the general election campaign. Like the election overall, both conventions were disrupted by the pandemic. Democrats opted for an entirely virtual event. Republicans were initially set to hold their convention in North Carolina, then moved it to Jacksonville, Florida, because of COVID-19 restrictions in North Carolina, and then moved it to Washington, DC, for similar reasons. The resulting convention combined remote and in-person events, despite the pandemic, and, even more controversially, used the White House as the backdrop for this purely political spectacle.

The messages at the two conventions also signaled what was ahead in the fall. For Biden, the pandemic and the ensuing economic fallout became central to his case for replacing Trump. Alongside Biden was his running mate, Senator Kamala Harris, the first woman of color to be named to a major party presidential ticket. She represented the party's commitment to inclusivity, and Biden would amplify that commitment in the way he talked about issues of racial justice.

Despite a few moments of inclusivity during the GOP convention, such as a swearing-in ceremony for five new American citizens, Trump's campaign mainly featured the us-versus-them rhetoric evident after George Floyd's death. He spoke repeatedly of the threat posed by BLM protestors and by Biden himself. This was encapsulated in Trump's claim that Democrats would "dismantle your police departments." Patricia McCloskey amplified this idea at the convention, saying that Democrats wanted to "bring crime, lawlessness, and low-quality apartments into thriving suburban neighborhoods."

Biden and Trump broadcast these messages during the most expensive presidential campaign in modern history. Biden surprised many people by spending more money than Trump, but despite all of the spending, and despite a series of dramatic events during the campaign that culminated in Trump's own COVID-19 diagnosis, there was remarkable stability in the horse-race polls. This is the logical consequence of a more calcified politics, in which few voters are truly up for grabs and most will stick with their party's presidential candidate no matter what happens.

But in an era of partisan parity, when presidential elections can be decided by slim margins in a few states, small shifts among those relatively few swing voters can make a difference. In the 2020 campaign, those shifts seemed to help Biden more than Trump. Early on, Biden was already more popular than Trump and leading him in head-to-head polls. Then, in May and June, Trump became even less popular and Biden's polling lead widened. The timing corresponded to Trump's decision to downplay the pandemic and push to reopen the country, followed by his attack on the racial justice protests.

By the end of the campaign, Biden was in a stronger position than he had been when the election year began. Trump had mostly himself to blame.

PANDEMIC POLITICKING

Despite Joe Biden's convincing victory in the Democratic primary, many people were far from convinced that he was ready for the general election. His attempts to campaign safely given the COVID-19 pandemic—for example, by speaking from his home and communicating via social media—gave rise to questions and hand-wringing. A May 3 headline: "The Biden Campaign Faces a Mind-Boggling Challenge: How to Make Joe Go Viral." A May 13 headline: "COVID-19 Has Made the 2020 Campaign Virtual. That's a Disaster for Biden." To these political observers, Biden's virtual events were boring and his online presence weaker than Trump's. Trump took to criticizing Biden for campaigning from his "basement."[2]

Meanwhile, Trump's campaign seemed poised to dominate. As the incumbent president, Trump had a huge advantage: he could start fundraising much earlier. On top of that, Trump could husband his resources while Biden fought a competitive primary. The last time an incumbent president ran for reelection, Barack Obama raised $722 million while the challenger, Mitt Romney, raised $450 million, about a third of which he spent during the Republican primary. Romney needed fund-raising by the Republican Party and conservative super PACs to keep the general election money chase close.

It was no surprise, then, that Trump pulled in $204 million in 2019, compared to Biden's $60 million. In May 2020, a month after Biden clinched the nomination, Trump still had more than twice as much cash on hand as Biden. According to the *New York Times*, Democrats were "expressing anxiety about Mr. Biden's visibility and the campaign's agility, heading into a general election in which Mr. Trump has an enormous cash advantage and the bully pulpit of the presidency." At about this time, Trump's campaign manager, Brad Parscale, bragged that the campaign was just getting started, tweeting, "For nearly three years we have been building a juggernaut campaign (Death Star). It is firing on all cylinders. Data, Digital, TV, Political, Surrogates, Coalitions, etc. In a few days we start pressing FIRE for the first time." Included in the tweet was a GIF of the Death Star shooting its famous laser.[3]

But as a careful viewer of *Star Wars* may remember, the Death Star proved just a bit vulnerable. Soon, Trump's early fund-raising lead evaporated. From August until the end of the campaign, Biden outraised Trump by a substantial margin. Altogether Biden's campaign committee raised $1.04 billion to Trump's $774 million. Biden-aligned super PACs also outspent Trump's equivalents. To put Trump's fund-raising in historical perspective, his campaign committee raised less in inflation-adjusted dollars than did Obama's in both 2012 and 2008.[4]

Within the Trump campaign, there was plenty of blame to go around. News reports noted the sums spent on early ads (including during the Super Bowl), regular payments to Trump family and surrogates, payments to Trump properties, and chartered planes. Parscale, who had his own car and driver paid for by the campaign, was criticized for the campaign's profligacy and was ultimately replaced by a new campaign manager, Bill Stepien. Accountability within the campaign was not helped by the fact that a huge portion of the campaign's budget went to a limited liability company whose owners were not publicly known. By the fall, Stepien could say only that Trump had enough money to win—a far cry from any Death Star. Trump had lost the typical fund-raising advantage of incumbents.[5]

Losing the money chase to Biden did not mean that Trump trailed Biden in every form of electioneering. Because Trump took policies aimed at mitigating the pandemic less seriously than Biden, he held more in-person rallies, even in states where large gatherings were prohibited by state or local officials. The Trump campaign defended those events and accused critics of having a "double standard" whereby racial justice protests were okay but Trump rallies were not. Rallies not only appealed to Trump himself but also were seen by his campaign as a way to generate donations, local news coverage, and information about attendees for the campaign's database. By contrast, Biden typically had fewer, smaller, socially distanced campaign events that were designed to portray him as a responsible leader. Between June 20, the day of Trump's rally in Tulsa, and Election Day, Trump held 109 rallies and Biden held seventy-three. A week before Election Day, Trump bragged about this, telling an audience in Lansing, Michigan, that "Our rallies are bigger than they've ever been. I gotta say, I'm working my ass off here! Sleepy Joe, the guy goes to his basement."[6]

The Trump campaign also invested more in a traditional "ground game" while the Biden campaign was initially averse to tactics, like face-to-face voter contact, that posed a greater risk of viral infection. By one count, the Trump campaign opened 307 field offices in twenty-two states, far more than the 165 he had opened in 2016 though far fewer than Hillary Clinton had in 2016 or Barack Obama had in 2012. Biden opened none. Only in October did the Biden campaign begin door-to-door canvassing and open "supply centers" with materials like lawn signs for canvassers to distribute. The Biden campaign did contact voters through other means, such as phone calls, which can be almost as effective as door-to-door canvassing if those calls are made by trained volunteers who speak with potential voters in a warm and personal fashion. So even with Trump's larger investment, it is difficult to assess whether the Trump or Biden campaign's ground game was superior.[7]

In another category, however, Trump lagged far behind Biden: television advertising. The lion's share of a presidential campaign's budget goes to advertising, and Biden's fund-raising enabled him to air more advertisements than Trump during the fall of the election year (figure 7.1), which is the period when research shows that advertising can influence election outcomes.[8] From September 1 until Election Day, about 553,000 ads supporting Biden aired on broadcast television, compared to 249,000 supporting Trump. Biden's advantage from September 1 onward was visible in every media market in Arizona, Florida, Michigan, Pennsylvania, and Wisconsin, although Trump led Biden in Georgia.[9] By the end of the campaign, Trump aired fewer ads between September 1 and Election Day than Clinton had aired during the same period in 2016 (271,000). This shows how much the Trump campaign struggled, despite the advantages of incumbency.

Even in digital advertising, which was a much-ballyhooed part of Trump's 2016 campaign, Biden was competitive. This was a contrast to Hillary Clinton in 2016; in that election, Trump spent $84 million on digital media and Clinton spent only $20 million. In 2020, a study of spending on Facebook and Google (the two most prominent outlets for

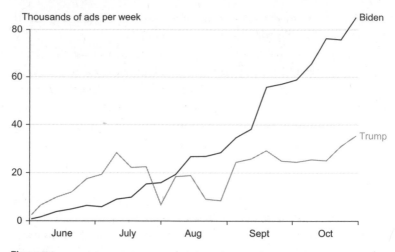

Figure 7.1.

Trends in the Volume of Broadcast Television Advertising. The Biden and Trump totals include all ads by the candidates as well as party committees and allied outside groups. *Source*: Kantar/CMAG data analyzed by authors.

campaign digital media) found that Trump spent $276 million to Biden's $213 million—much closer to parity than 2016's 4:1 ratio. What is more, any advantage for Trump was, as with his television advertising, concentrated in 2019 and early 2020, not closer to the election. Trump's digital ads were also more likely to contain fund-raising appeals than Biden's were, suggesting that Trump used digital media less to persuade people to vote for him and more to generate cash and, eventually, address his cash shortfalls.[10]

Ultimately, Trump's Death Star was not the battle station he had planned, and Biden's campaign amassed more firepower than many thought possible. But it was uncertain how much electoral campaigning would end up mattering. The effects of campaign activity in presidential general elections are almost always small, particularly in the modern era of strong party loyalty. Moreover, the pandemic complicated the situation, affecting not only how the candidates campaigned but also when and how citizens voted. Throughout the fall, a record number of citizens took advantage of relaxed rules governing absentee and mail voting to vote well in advance of Election Day itself. In battleground states, this meant that a significant amount of the electioneering would occur after many people had already voted—making the millions spent in the closing weeks of the campaign potentially less consequential.

BACKBONE

In the years leading up to the 2020 election, Joe Biden framed his opposition to Trump's presidency as a "battle for the soul of America." When Biden first said this in 2017, he was reacting to Trump's unwillingness to condemn unequivocally the white nationalists who rallied in Charlottesville, Virginia. But it was not clear how the idea could animate his entire presidential campaign. Even his own team was unsure. At one point, after Biden's early primary struggles in Iowa and New Hampshire, his pollster, John Anzalone, said, "No one knows what this 'soul of America' bullshit means."[11] Nor was it clear how this idea could help Biden beat an incumbent president who, as of early 2020, had presided over consistent economic growth and was planning to campaign for months on that record.

Then the pandemic, the economic downturn, and the protests after George Floyd's murder changed how both Biden and Trump thought about their campaign's central message. The pandemic and recession provided Biden a new justification for his candidacy and a new issue agenda—one centered on job losses, COVID deaths, and Trump's struggle to handle these crises. Trump was now in the position Biden had been before: trying to construct an argument for election under unfavorable conditions. This would have been challenging for any incumbent and it was no different for Trump, who simultaneously tried to defend his record, even at the risk of reminding voters of the country's travails, and to change the subject by launching a series of attacks on Biden, including on Social Security, taxes, and crime and policing.

In deciding on a message, Biden and Trump were confronting choices that all presidential candidates have to make.[12] The first choice is how to engage with the state of the economy and the country. When the economy is healthy, it is usually the central theme for the campaign of the incumbent president or, if that person is not running, the candidate from the incumbent's party. If the economy is poor, then the challenger will usually emphasize the issue and criticize the incumbent or the incumbent's party. In either case, the task is to remind voters of the conditions in the country and urge them to reward or punish the incumbent accordingly.

If the economy does not benefit a candidate's campaign, then they face a bigger challenge. They need to find an issue with two characteristics: their position is more popular than their opponent's, and their opponent is tied to that less popular position and cannot easily change it. For example, in 1960 John F. Kennedy argued that the United States lagged behind the Soviet Union, especially in the nuclear arms race. Kennedy talked not only about this "missile gap" but also about gaps in education, the arts, and science—all of which, according to Kennedy, meant that the Soviets were winning the race to the "new frontier." Kennedy linked Nixon to America's allegedly lackluster performance because, as Eisenhower's vice president, he was part of the administration that presided over the decline. This was something Nixon could not easily counter, especially because accurate information about nuclear arms, which would have shown Kennedy's claims to be exaggerated, was classified.

Of course, not every presidential candidate follows this template. Both candidates may choose to talk about the economy, presenting different viewpoints. In 2012, for example, Obama, the incumbent, sought to remind voters of the economic growth since the Great Recession and the financial crisis of 2008. Romney argued that any economic recovery had left too many people behind—one ad featured testimonials from "middle-class workers" describing their precarious circumstances—and thus that Obama had failed.[13]

The strategy of the Biden campaign and its allies followed this template. Biden focused on the country's dire circumstances and criticized Trump for his response to the pandemic. To see this strategy play out, consider the issues mentioned in the televised campaign advertising supporting Biden (figure 7.2). The most prevalent issues were the COVID-19

Figure 7.2.

Trends in the Issues Mentioned in Campaign Television Advertising. The data is daily counts of ad airings in thousands, aggregated to the week and plotted by the middle day of the week. The data includes ads aired by the two candidates as well as ads aired on their behalf by the parties and independent groups. *Source:* Kantar/CMAG.

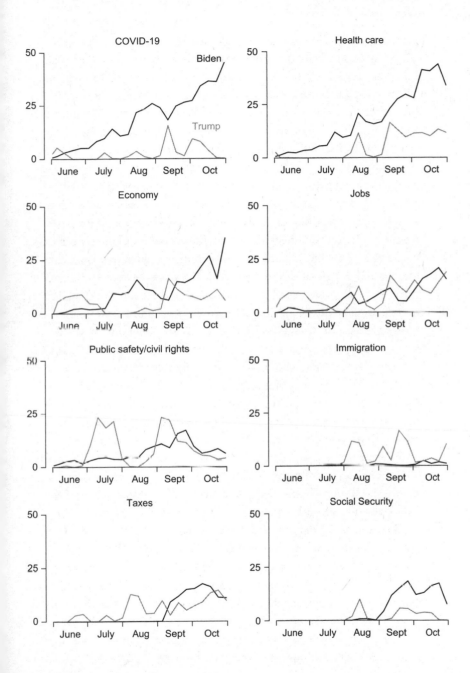

pandemic and health care. In one ad, called "Dignity," Biden focused on senior citizens and said that "their health and safety will be my responsibility" and promised "the best medical experts and scientists to advise on our response" to the pandemic. In another ad, "Personal," Biden described his tragic family story—the death of his first wife and infant daughter in a car crash, the death of his son from cancer—and criticized Trump for attempting to dismantle the Affordable Care Act. The people depicted in these ads were often wearing masks, reminding viewers of the pandemic even if the ads did not use the words "COVID" or "coronavirus."[14]

Ads supporting Biden frequently talked about the economy and jobs as well. In these ads, Biden's message was exactly what you would expect from a challenger running in a weak economy: point out the economic challenges, blame the incumbent, and promise to do better. For example, the Biden ad "Backbone" opened with images of Scranton, Pennsylvania, where Biden was born, and contrasted Biden's working-class roots and life of public service with Trump, who "ran for president for himself and for his friends on Wall Street." The "backbone" in the ad's title referred to the types of people who are the "backbone of the country" and thus the ones whom Biden would fight for.[15]

The tone of ads supporting Biden was remarkably positive, at least by the standard of some recent presidential elections. Biden and his allies ran very few purely attack ads; in most weeks of the fall campaign, attack ads made up about 10 percent of the total volume of his ad airings. Most of the ads emphasized the contrast between Trump and Biden, like the "Backbone" ad, or only promoted Biden and did not mention Trump at all, like the "Dignity" ad. In the closing week of the campaign, more than half of ads supporting Biden were purely positive.[16]

Biden's focus on the pandemic certainly put him on the right side of public opinion overall. By the fall of 2020, about two-thirds of Americans were somewhat or very concerned about the coronavirus (see chapter 5). More Americans trusted Biden than Trump to handle the pandemic: in an October 2020 poll, 52 percent of Americans chose Biden but only 40 percent chose Trump.[17]

Biden's emphasis on the economy also made sense in some ways. In the first part of 2020 there was a large drop in gross domestic product

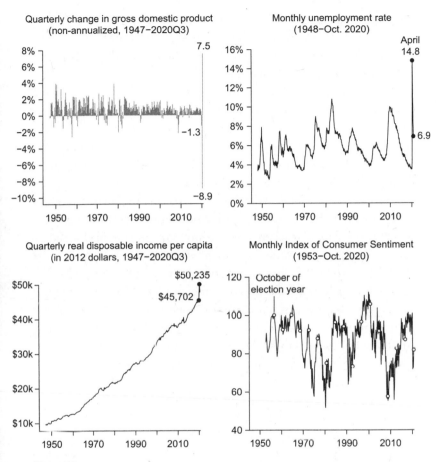

Figure 7.3.
Trends in Economic Indicators. *Sources*: St. Louis Federal Reserve FRED Database; University of Michigan.

(GDP) and a sharp spike in unemployment, both of which were extraordinary when compared with the historical trend (figure 7.3). Although both indicators bounced back somewhat in the summer and fall of 2020, both GDP and unemployment were still worse than before the pandemic and the economy remained in a recession. In Nationscape surveys, the percentage of Americans who said the economy was worse than a year ago increased from 20 percent in January 2020 to 75 percent in June, before declining slightly to about 65 percent by the end of October. In this respect, the concerns that Biden was articulating in his ads were shared by most Americans.

From another vantage point, however, the economic story was more complex. Because of the stimulus package passed in March 2020, people's incomes actually increased (figure 7.3). The increase was immediate and large by historical standards. Moreover, when people's views of the economy were measured with the larger set of questions in the Index of Consumer Sentiment (which we introduced in chapter 2), those views were not as dismal as the Nationscape question might suggest. The index had clearly shifted downward but it was nowhere near the lows it had reached in several previous recessions. Indeed, as of October 2020, consumer sentiment was about at the same level as October 2012, right before the incumbent president—Obama, in this case—was reelected. Consumer sentiment may not have dropped further in 2020 because it is based on survey questions about both current and future economic conditions, and some Americans may have had a more optimistic view of future conditions given the positive trends in the economy in the fall. Another challenge facing Biden was that Americans were more evenly divided on whom they trusted to handle the economy than they were on the pandemic. Neither Biden nor Trump had a clear advantage on this issue.[18]

Trump's messaging strategy was very different than Biden's. For one, the ads supporting Trump were much more negative. From mid-September through the end of the campaign, the percentage of ad airings that were purely attacks on Biden increased from 20 percent to nearly 60 percent. Most of the rest were ads contrasting Biden and Trump and very few were purely positive ads promoting Trump. Trump's tweets and other statements where no different. He shifted from just calling Biden "Sleepy Joe" to portraying him as mentally incompetent, with digital ads by Trump saying that "geriatric health is no laughing matter." As early as May 2020, Trump's scorched-earth tactics "rattled even some supportive Republicans" who worried that it would hurt not only Trump but other Republican candidates down the ballot. An internal Republican National Committee poll in May found that attacking Biden's mental competence was ineffective, but Trump persisted in it anyway.[19]

Trump also engaged with subjects like the economy and the pandemic (see figure 7.2), which an incumbent running in such conditions might not be expected to do. He and his allies aired ads about the pandemic and especially the economy tens of thousands of times. Trump's approach to the pandemic was to portray it as largely over, saying at a September rally that the United States had "rounded the final turn."[20]

He talked about the economy even more—indeed, "jobs" was the issue mentioned most often in the Trump campaign committee's ads— and in a similar way. One Trump ad, "Great American Comeback," flashed the statistics "1.37 million jobs created in August" and said "the greatest economy the world has ever seen is coming back to life." The ad then pivoted to attacking Biden, saying he wanted to "kill countless American businesses, jobs, and our economic future." This was Trump's strategy on the economy in a nutshell: set aside the economic shocks of the pandemic, which were the worst in April 2020, and focus instead on trends since that point, even though those trends had not returned the economy to its pre-pandemic health. Then accuse Biden of wanting to wreck the economy entirely. Trump was betting that voters would ignore the recession and focus instead on who could best lead the recovery.[21]

Trump attacked Biden on other grounds as well. Trump said that Biden favored "higher taxes and regulation" and wanted to cut Social Security and Medicare. At times, Trump paired accusations on issues like the economy and Social Security with references to immigration. For example, Trump claimed that Biden wanted to cut Social Security in order to "give your benefits to illegal immigrants." In another ad, Trump said that Biden's support for a path to citizenship for undocumented immigrants meant "11 million illegal immigrants competing for American jobs" and "eligible for free healthcare, Social Security, and Medicare." This was, of course, Trump's typical brand of identity politics—suggesting that undeserving people of color were taking things from "Americans."[22]

Trump's identity politics were even more visible on another issue: public safety. This topic represented Trump's most concerted attempt to do what Kennedy had done in 1960: focus the public's attention on something other than the economy and the pandemic. Trump's initial advertising on this issue came in July (figure 7.2). One ad, "Abolish," imagined a world in which someone calls 911 but hears a message saying, "Due to defunding of the police department, we're sorry but no one is here to take your call." The ad had footage of a burning building, looters, and protestors with "Defund the Police" signs. The ad said, "Joe Biden's supporters are fighting to defund police departments. Violent crime has exploded. You won't be safe in Joe Biden's America." Other Trump ads on this theme stated that "violent crime has exploded." The McCloskeys' appearance at the GOP convention amplified this message, as did Trump in his own tweets and public comments. At one point in July, Trump warned Americans in the suburbs that Biden "will destroy your neighborhood and your American dream" by allowing low-income housing that would lower home prices and raising crime. The racial connotations of this attack were obvious.[23]

By focusing on public safety and social order, Trump had several things working in his favor. The first was the fact that the murder rate in many cities around the country had been increasing in 2020. Although the rate of some other types of violent crime and property crime was actually decreasing, the salience of the murder rate meant that an increasing majority of Americans believed that there was more crime in the United States than a year ago: in an October 2020 Gallup poll, 78 percent believed there was more crime, up from 64 percent in October 2019.[24] Second, as we have documented, the sympathetic response to Floyd, including increasingly negative views of the police and positive views of the BLM movement, had ebbed by the fall of 2020. Third, a variety of polls made clear that "defunding the police" was unpopular. Trump's opposition to this idea put him on the same side as most Americans and, as we noted in chapter 6, the issue divided Democrats in particular. All of these facts could have made this strategy attractive to Trump. Trump's gambit was that he was on the popular side of an issue on which Biden was constrained because he could not disavow the racial justice protests and the fight for equality without alienating many Democrats.

But just because Trump had won in 2016 after using race as a wedge issue did not mean it would work in 2020. Just as Biden confronted a complex landscape when discussing the economy, Trump faced several complicating factors in his attempt to derive political benefits from a message about public safety. First, even if more Americans thought that crime was increasing in the country, they did not appear to feel personally threatened. In the same October 2020 Gallup poll, the percentage who said there was more crime in their local area was *lower* than a year before (38% vs. 43%). And *fewer* Americans said there was an area near them where they would be afraid to walk alone at night (29% vs. 37% the year before).

Second, Trump's position on "defunding the police" was no different than Biden's. Biden made this clear soon after Floyd's murder. In a June 10 op-ed in *USA Today*, Biden wrote, "I do not support defunding the police." Instead, he advocated the opposite: $300 million in new federal funding for community policing. Biden did call for various policing reforms: making federal funding contingent on police departments' record on civil rights; more widespread use of body cameras; and investments in mental health and drug treatment services so that people other than police officers could respond to some situations. Those measures were popular as long as the idea of investing in mental health and other services was not framed as a reduction in the police force. Biden also produced an ad in early September 2 in which he decried the violence that had occurred at a small number of the Floyd protests, saying, "Rioting is not protesting. Looting is not protesting. It's lawlessness, plain and simple." The ad then pivoted to calling Trump "weak" and "divisive" for fomenting violence and trying to "instill fear in America." The ad concluded with the biblical quotation "Be not afraid." Biden was not as constrained on this issue as Trump needed him to be.[25]

Of course, Biden did talk plainly about systemic racism and expressed sympathy for Black Americans who had experienced police violence and brutality. One news report described Biden as "walking a cautious line as he opposes defunding the police." And that was undoubtedly true. Nevertheless, "defund the police" was not clearly an issue where

Trump's position was more popular *and* where Biden was wedded to the unpopular position. Trump and his allies were left either to try to tar Biden by association by linking him to "defunding" advocates, as Trump did in the "Abolish" ad, or to resort to the false claim that Biden wanted to defund the police.[26]

A third factor that created a challenge for Trump was this: a larger fraction of Americans trusted Biden, not Trump, to handle the issues of public safety, crime, and law and order. In a June 2020 Pew Research Center poll, 46 percent were confident that Biden can "effectively handle law enforcement and criminal justice issues," compared to 43 percent who were confident in Trump. In an August 2020 Morning Consult poll, 47 percent trusted Biden to handle public safety, compared to 39 percent who trusted Trump. In the October *New York Times/Siena College* poll, 50 percent trusted Biden to "maintain law and order," compared to 44 percent who trusted Trump.[27] Of course, most people's answers to these survey questions were predictably partisan: Democrats trusted Biden, and Republicans trusted Trump. But these questions also showed that public safety and crime were not distinctively strong issues for Trump, especially compared to the economy, where he was tied with or even ahead of Biden in terms of the public's trust and confidence.

Finally, it was entirely possible that Trump's law and order campaign could actually work to his detriment. If voters saw the unrest as just another indication of how poorly the country was doing, then it would be the incumbent, not the challenger, who faced greater political risk. In this scenario, the unrest, like the pandemic and the recession, was just another bad thing happening on Trump's watch. Of course, Democrats made exactly this argument. The Democratic National Committee produced an ad with multiple scenes of violence—cars on fire, police chasing protestors, tear gas, the far-right protestors in Charlottesville—and called it "Donald Trump's America."[28]

Trump may have realized some of these weaknesses in using safety as a strategic focus. Despite a blitz of public safety ads in July and another in early September, they were mostly gone from the airwaves by October. News reports suggested that GOP strategists saw a key limitation to the strategy, which was also the limitation of Trump's style of politics generally: it appealed to the conservative party base but not so much to moderates or others.[29] This may explain why over the last month Trump focused more on jobs, health care, and taxes than on public safety. Thus, the Trump campaign never fully settled on a closing argument. Biden's campaign, by contrast, kept the focus on the pandemic and the economy to the end.

SUPER SPREADER

If Trump's goal was to convince Americans that the pandemic was nearly over and change the subject to something else, he had to confront another challenge: his own battle with COVID-19 in October 2020. His illness thrust the issue back to the forefront of news coverage and reshaped the information environment for the rest of the campaign.

The story of Trump's illness began with the death of Supreme Court Justice Ruth Bader Ginsburg on September 18 and Trump's announcement on September 26 that he would nominate Amy Coney Barrett to succeed her. To make the announcement, Trump held a Rose Garden ceremony as well as indoor receptions that were later linked to COVID-19 infections among attendees and White House staff. Trump officially tested positive on October 1 and was hospitalized on October 2, when his illness took a serious turn.

In late 2021, Trump's chief of staff, Mark Meadows, would reveal that Trump had actually tested positive on September 26 immediately after the Barrett reception, when he was about to get on Air Force One to go to a rally in Pennsylvania.[30] Trump then tested negative using a second rapid COVID test but never took a more reliable PCR test and instead continued with his schedule. This included the Pennsylvania rally, a White House reception for military families, and the September 29 debate with Biden. At the debate, Trump and his entourage arrived too late to be tested and several members of his party, including his wife, Melania, did not wear masks while sitting in the audience. From the debate, Trump went to a fund raiser and rally in Minnesota. Immediately afterward his close aide Hope Hicks tested positive and Trump himself did not feel well. Nevertheless, the next day he went to an indoor fund raiser of about 200 people at his New Jersey golf club. That night, he announced a positive test on Twitter.

The next day, October 2, Trump's blood oxygen levels plummeted, leading doctors to give him two experimental COVID treatments and then hospitalize him in case his condition deteriorated further. On October 3, he experienced another drop in blood oxygen and was given a powerful steroid. That day, the White House gave conflicting reports of Trump's health. His personal physician said he was "doing very well," but Meadows told reporters that the president's condition was "very concerning" and "we're still not on a clear path to recovery." Trump was reportedly angry with Meadows for being honest about his condition.[31]

On October 4, Trump felt better and insisted on being driven around the hospital grounds so that he could wave at supporters. On the evening of October 5, he returned to the White House even though he was still being treated with steroids and antiviral medication. He walked across the grounds and up to the White House balcony, where he removed his mask and, still breathing heavily, stood for a photo shoot. He then returned to stage the balcony appearance a second time with a camera crew in tow.

Within an hour, Trump tried to recast his ongoing struggle with COVID-19 as evidence of his heroism. He released a video that showed his White House return while dramatic music played. In a separate video message, he praised himself and downplayed COVID-19: "I stood out front. I led. Nobody that's a leader would not do what I did. And I know there's a risk, there's a danger, but that's OK. And now I'm better and maybe I'm immune, I don't know. But don't let it dominate your lives." Meanwhile, the Trump campaign superimposed Trump's head on a football player's body and tweeted a meme where he scores over a player whose head was the coronavirus molecule. The Trump campaign tried to use Trump's diagnosis as a talking point, saying, "He has experience now fighting the coronavirus as an individual. Joe Biden doesn't have that."[32]

Trump's COVID diagnosis led to a huge spike in news attention to the pandemic. This is visible in mentions of the word "coronavirus" or "COVID" on cable news outlets (figure 7.4). There was an initial spike

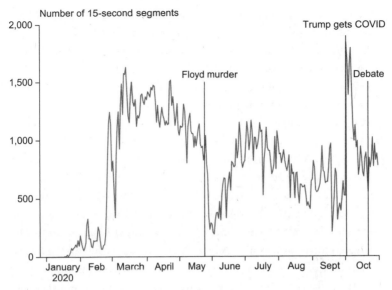

Figure 7.4.

Trends in the Volume of News Coverage of COVID-19, January 1–October 31, 2020. The figure presents the number of fifteen-second segments that included the words "COVID" or "coronavirus" in transcripts from CNN, Fox News, and MSNBC. *Source:* Internet Archive Television News Archive.

in the volume of coverage as viral infections spread throughout the United States in March 2020. The murder of George Floyd drove COVID out of the news for a brief period, but by July it returned to its previous level. Then, as the summer surge in cases began to abate, the volume of pandemic news coverage decreased as well. But when Trump was diagnosed, the number of stories increased by about 350 percent. Stories about Trump's COVID infection dwarfed other issues, including George Floyd's murder and policing. Even on Fox News there were more stories about COVID-19 in the week after Trump's diagnosis than stories about topics like BLM or Antifa, both of which had been central to the conservative news media's framing of the Floyd protests. Although the volume of COVID news dropped after Trump's recovery, it remained higher than it had been in August and September. In part, this was because the pandemic figured prominently in the final candidate debate, where Biden pushed his same line of attack, saying it would be a "dark winter" and that Trump "had no clear plan." Trump continued to strike the same optimistic note and emphasized how the country was "opening up."[33]

Despite Trump's optimism, the tenor of October's pandemic coverage was often unfavorable to Trump. New stories focused on the lax safety protocols leading up to the September outbreak and Trump's diagnosis. Just as he did in public, Trump had dismissed the need for masks in the White House, so few officials wore them and those who did were mocked. Other news stories noted that Trump's behavior during the White House outbreak could have endangered others, including Joe Biden at the first debate, attendees at fund raisers after the debate, the Secret Service agents who drove him to wave at supporters during his hospital stay, and White House staff once he left the hospital. The lack of information and conflicting information about Trump's condition and the extent of the White House outbreak only added to the uncertainty.[34]

At least some Trump administration officials hoped that his bout with COVID-19 would make him take the pandemic more seriously. Robert Redfield, Trump's director of the Centers for Disease Control, later said that he prayed that Trump would "show some humility" and "remind people that anyone could be susceptible to the coronavirus." But Trump's dismissiveness—"don't be afraid of it," "don't let it dominate your lives"—signaled that he would not change.[35]

Nevertheless, the pandemic continued to dominate the public's thinking. A polling project by CNN, the University of Michigan, and Georgetown University regularly asked Americans what they had heard, read, or seen about Trump or Biden in the past few days. The pandemic had almost always been the most frequent topic mentioned about Trump, and after Trump's COVID-19 diagnosis, it was even more frequently cited. The pandemic was also among the public's most important priorities for the country. In a *Huffington Post*/YouGov poll conducted two weeks before Election Day, respondents could select up to three issues that were most important to them. Among all voters, the three biggest were the economy (cited by 47%), health care (46%), and the coronavirus outbreak (31%). Only 22 percent cited immigration and only 9 percent cited crime. Trump's focus on identity politics did not elevate those issues above the economy and the pandemic.[36]

Trump wanted to portray a country on the upswing, but his own bout with the virus told a different story: the pandemic was far from over.

THE HORSE RACE

With so many dramatic events in the election year, it seemed logical that the horse race between Biden and Trump would be full of twists and turns. But what stood out more in the polling was the stability that is characteristic of calcified politics. As we argued in chapter 1, calcification means less willingness to defect from your party to the other party. New information about the candidates is more likely to strengthen people's partisan inclinations than change their minds.

Throughout 2020, this calcification posed the bigger challenge for Trump. He was viewed less favorably than Biden and always trailed him in trial heat polls that asked how people intended to vote. Moreover, what small shifts did occur tended to help Biden—and any such shifts can prove consequential given the relative parity between the two parties and the competitiveness of presidential elections.

Figure 7.5 tracks how favorably people viewed Trump and Biden throughout 2020 and how people intended to vote in a Trump-Biden election. Trump's challenge was clear: his net favorability was always negative, meaning that more Americans disliked him than liked him. Biden's net favorability was almost always positive. This was quite different than in 2016, when Trump's historic unpopularity was nearly matched by Hillary Clinton's.

Biden's advantage in terms of overall favorability was mirrored in other assessments. As of the summer of 2020, Biden led Trump in whether he was honest, cared about the needs of ordinary people, was a good role model, and was even tempered. The candidates were tied in who was courageous. Trump led only in who was energetic.[37] As the campaign went on, at least some assessments of Biden became even more positive. In Nationscape surveys, the percentage who said that

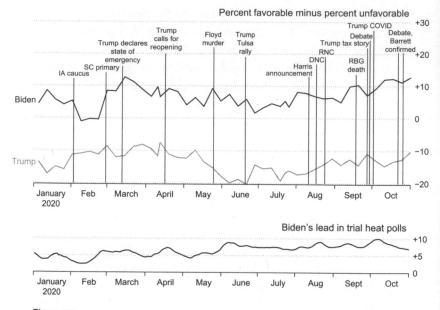

Figure 7.5.

Trends in Candidate Favorability and Trial Heat Polls. The trial heat trend is a smoothed average of public polls of likely or registered voters. *Source*: The favorability data is from weekly Democracy Fund + UCLA Nationscape surveys.

Biden "told the truth more than most other people in public life" increased by 10 points between June and Election Day. By the end of the campaign, only 31 percent said he told the truth less than others. By contrast, 52 percent said Trump was less truthful than others, and this fraction did not change during the campaign.

Unsurprisingly, then, Biden always led Trump in an average of pre-election polls. Of course, Democrats had seen Hillary Clinton lead Trump throughout the 2016 campaign and then go on to lose. In that race, she finished the campaign with a 4-point lead in the national polling averages but ended up winning the national popular vote by only 2 points and losing the Electoral College.[38] If the polls were also overestimating Biden's lead, then the size of that lead would matter even more.

Despite the overall stability in the race, both Biden and Trump did see small shifts in their standing. Biden's favorability rating and his lead in head-to-head matchups against Trump dropped as he struggled in the early primary contests but rebounded after the South Carolina primary. Biden's favorability then dropped somewhat between March and July, mainly because Republicans came to see him less favorably. Biden's net favorability rating among Republicans dropped from the −40s in March to almost −60 by the end of July. This was the natural consequence of Biden's becoming the de facto nominee. Because few Republicans intended to vote for Biden in the first place, this drop in Biden's favorability did not decrease his lead over Trump. Biden's favorability increased between July and Election Day because of the opposite pattern: growing support among Democrats. During these months, Biden's net favorability increased from +60 to +75 points among Democrats. Partisan rallies are one of the most predictable consequences of a presidential campaign, and 2020 was no different.[39]

For Trump, the most consequential period occurred in roughly the ten weeks between mid-April and early June. During this period, Trump began pushing to reopen the country and, once again, minimized the seriousness of the pandemic. We showed in chapter 5 that this shift coincided with a drop in his approval rating overall and his approval rating for the pandemic. Figure 7.3 shows that Trump's net favorability also dropped 10 points throughout this period.[40] Notably, the drop continued in the immediate aftermath of Floyd's murder as well. Crucially, Trump also lost ground to Biden in trial heat polls. Between early May and early June, Biden's lead over Trump increased from about 5 points to 8 points at the end of June.

There is no conclusive evidence for what caused these drops in Trump support. But they did coincide with Trump's dismissal of the pandemic and his attacks on the racial justice protests. In both cases, Trump chose to play to his base, or even its most hard-line contingent, and in both cases Trump's move proved unpopular with Americans generally.

The race remained mostly static for the rest of the campaign. Trump's favorability rating did improve, mainly due to a partisan rally among

Republicans, whose net favorability toward Trump increased from +54 to +67 between July and Election Day. But this increase in his favorability only brought Trump back to where he was at the beginning of March, and his favorability rating still lagged Biden's. Vote intentions, by contrast, did not shift much after June. The polling average on November 1—a 7-point lead for Biden—was nearly identical to the average on June 1.

CONCLUSION

In April 2016, *New York Times* columnist Maureen Dowd asked Donald Trump why he campaigned the way he did—with belligerence, nastiness, and so many insults. Trump replied, "I guess because of the fact that I immediately went to No. 1 and I said, 'Why don't I just keep the same thing going?'"

Four years later, Trump was still keeping the same thing going. Just as he had done in 2016, he appeared to endorse violence against his opponents. At a campaign rally on November 1, Donald Trump talked about hitting Joe Biden: "Those legs. Those legs have gotten very thin. Not a lot of base. You wouldn't have to close—you wouldn't have to close the fist." When a caravan of Trump supporters, some armed, surrounded a Biden campaign bus on a Texas highway and attempted to drive it off the road, Trump applauded them, saying, "These patriots did nothing wrong."[41]

And just as in 2016, he was ready to delegitimize the election outcome. He did this after he won in 2016, blaming his loss in the national popular vote on millions of votes from ineligible voters like undocumented immigrants. During the 2020 campaign, he raged against mail balloting, which states had increasingly employed as an alternative to in-person voting because of the risks of COVID-19. He leveled unsubstantiated allegations that Democrats were "rigging" the election or somehow stealing it from him. He floated the idea of postponing the election outright.[42]

Then, two days before the election, he said that he would simply declare victory on Election Night if he were leading, regardless of how many ballots remained to be counted. It was clear that many Republican leaders found his statements deeply troubling. A Senate GOP aide told two reporters that Trump's behavior was "despicable and un-American." But this person would not identify him- or herself. And other Republicans would not comment at all: senators Ben Sasse, Josh Hawley, and Lindsey Graham ignored inquiries.[43]

In short, Trump had not changed, and neither had the party's willingness to tolerate him, even his attacks on the electoral process itself. It was a harbinger of how far the GOP would go to win, no matter the cost.

8

Change (and More of the Same)

IT WAS NOVEMBER 7, a Saturday morning, when Joe Biden won the
2020 presidential election. After the ballots had finally been counted in
Pennsylvania, Biden's home state, he had a 306–232 advantage in the
Electoral College, almost identical to Donald Trump's 304–227 margin
in 2016.[1] After two unsuccessful presidential campaigns, in 1988 and
2008, and a difficult decision not to run in 2016, Biden would finally
occupy the office he had sought on and off for over thirty years. In a
speech that day, Biden said he was "honored and humbled." Elated
Biden supporters celebrated in the streets of Philadelphia, New York,
San Francisco, Washington, DC, and other cities.[2]

In many ways, Biden's was an unusual victory. Across the history of
presidential elections, incumbent presidents have won two-thirds of
their races.[3] It is especially rare for incumbents to lose after their party
has held the White House for only one term. Indeed, since the Twenty-
Second Amendment has limited the number of terms a president can
serve, Jimmy Carter and Trump are the only two incumbents to lose in
this circumstance.

But to many in the Democratic Party, it did not feel like a victory.
They had hoped that strong voter turnout would produce a complete
repudiation of Trump and the GOP up and down the ballot. Preelection

polls seemed to suggest a blowout was coming: Biden led by over 8 points in national polling averages and Democrats seemed poised to expand their House majority and reclaim the Senate majority.[4]

Instead, the election delivered much less. Biden's victory was excruciatingly narrow. Despite his 4.4-point margin in the national popular vote, Biden won by very small margins in the key battleground states (49.2%–48.9% in Arizona, 49.5%–48.8% in Wisconsin, and 49.9%–48.7% in Pennsylvania). Indeed, the Democratic Party's disadvantage in the Electoral College—how much it underperformed in key swing states compared to the national popular vote—was actually larger in 2020 than in 2016.[5]

Moreover, the Democrats barely eked out a Senate majority, needing victories in two runoff elections in Georgia to get to fifty seats and having to count on Vice President Kamala Harris to break ties. In the House, Democrats ended up controlling thirteen fewer seats than they had after the 2018 midterm election, leaving them with a slim, nine-seat majority. Biden would take office with unified Democratic control of Congress, but with very few votes to spare as he pursued an ambitious agenda. The morning after Election Day, Politico's influential "Playbook" newsletter called the election "an abject disaster for Democrats in Washington."[6]

Explaining the election's outcome requires an account of two things: why Biden won, but also why the election was so close. Of course, there are myriad reasons why the election turned out as it did. What we seek to do is place 2020 within the framework of factors that shape a typical presidential election, and to address some prominent claims about "what mattered."

Any explanation of Biden's victory must start with Trump's chronically low approval rating. Indeed, Trump's 4-point loss was consistent with the historical relationship between presidential approval and presidential election outcomes. This fact throws into sharp relief the consequence of decisions by Trump that appeared to cost him even a few points of approval. Had Trump been able to maintain the short-lived bump in approval he received because of the pandemic, he likely could have won the election.

The closeness of the election stemmed from the ideological and affective polarization between the two parties that has helped create an increasing calcification of people's political choices. That calcification would characterize the 2020 outcome was arguably unexpected. After all, the surge in turnout gave Biden over 15 million more votes than Clinton received, while Trump won about 11 million more than he had in 2016. And yet, between 2016 and 2020 there were only small shifts in outcomes in both states and counties as well as among individual voters. Indeed, within U.S. counties, the shifts between 2016 and 2020 were the smallest in the past seventy years of presidential elections.

Polarization was visible in how the public perceived the candidates: Trump was perceived as more conservative than in 2016, and Biden was perceived as more liberal than Hillary Clinton. Unsurprisingly, voting behavior was also more polarized: Trump gained votes among conservatives and Biden gained votes among liberals. This helped explain surprising aspects of the election, such as Trump's stronger performance among Latino voters: Trump's gains among moderate and conservative Latinos exceeded his losses among liberal Latinos. Polarization also meant that the changes in the candidates' coalitions largely offset each other, making it difficult for Biden to build a dominant coalition and thus a landslide victory.

A final consequence of calcification is that the election year's important events did not appear to affect the outcome very much. Local voting patterns did not depend much on Biden's advantage in televised campaign advertising. There was also little local impact of the rate of COVID infections or deaths in communities across the country. Even the racial justice protests and ensuing debate about criminal justice had an ambiguous impact at best, despite the prevailing concern after the election that they hurt Biden.

On its face, it might seem obvious that the 2020 election was characterized by partisanship and polarization. But that was hardly a certainty as the campaign was coming to a close. For some, it looked not like a year of electoral calcification, but the exact opposite. In October 2020, one political writer, George Packer of *The Atlantic*, saw the potential for a different kind of moment, one in which "an ossified social order suddenly turns pliable" and "prolonged stasis gives way to motion." Quoting the philosopher Gershom Scholem, Packer said the moment was a "plastic hour."[7]

But when all the votes were counted, the "plastic hour" had not come. True, a new president had won. But American politics seemed as set in stone as ever.

THE ECONOMY AND TRUMP'S APPROVAL RATING

To understand the 2020 election, a useful beginning is the basic factors that have long structured presidential election outcomes. Chief among them are the state of the economy and the incumbent president's public standing. In chapter 3, we showed that as of early 2020, those factors forecast a close election, with Trump losing narrowly because his unpopularity outweighed the economic growth during his first three years. Although the economy then went into a recession, we showed in chapter 7 that this pandemic economy had an unusual ambiguity: although the country's economic output shrank and Americans lost jobs, their incomes actually increased because of the federal government's stimulus package. As a result, Americans' evaluations of the economy were not nearly as negative as during previous recessions. But once again, Trump's approval rating moved little in response to these events, declining a few percentage points in the spring of 2021 and then rebounding in the fall—but only to his previous level of unpopularity (chapter 5).

How well, then, did the 2020 election fit the historical patterns between the fundamentals and previous presidential election outcomes? Figure 8.1 compares the incumbent party's major-party vote share to presidential approval and to three economic indicators that captured the ambiguity: changes in the size of the economy (measured with the gross domestic product, or GDP), changes in people's incomes, and evaluations of the economy. Major-party vote share refers to the incumbent party's share of the vote that goes to the Democratic and Republican candidates, excluding third-party or independent candidates. In

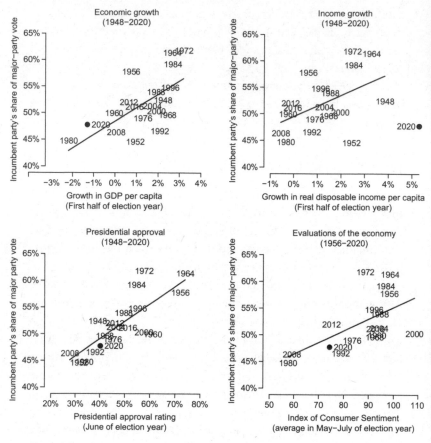

Figure 8.1.

How Economic Indicators and Presidential Approval Relate to Presidential Election
Outcomes. All economic growth rates are nonannualized. Presidential approval is an
average of all polls conducted in June of the election year. The diagonal fit lines are
estimated excluding the 2020 election year. *Sources*: US Election Atlas; St. Louis Federal
Reserve FRED Database; University of Michigan.

2020, Trump won 47.7 percent and Biden 52.3 percent. In each panel in
figure 8.1, the diagonal line captures the relationships between election
outcomes and these factors prior to 2020, thus showing how the 2020
outcome compares to these historical patterns.

Three findings stand out. First, the 2020 election outcome was more consistent with a shrinking economy than with the growth in incomes. Trump's share of the vote was somewhat higher than the change in GDP would have predicted, but far lower than what income growth would have predicted. In other words, the election was closer than both of these economic measures predicted. Second, the outcome was mostly in line with people's subjective economic evaluations, which did forecast a narrow defeat for Trump.

Third, the outcome in 2020 was very much in line with what Trump's approval rating predicted. Figure 8.1 depicts approval ratings as of June of the election year, simply to see how well election outcomes can be forecast from the political environment several months before Election Day. As of June, the historical pattern suggested that Trump's average approval rating (40%) would translate into a major-party vote share of 49 percent. This was only about 1 point more than Trump actually received.

One implication of these relationships between these fundamental factors and presidential election outcomes is that the 2020 outcome was not that hard to forecast. Of course, there is no way to know the exact "right" combination of factors to forecast a presidential election. But one summary of ten models found that the average prediction was a Trump two-party vote share of 47.3 percent, or almost exactly what he eventually won.[8] Even if the polls suggested Biden could run away with it, forecasts that built in other factors—or ignored polls entirely—showed that, although Trump was in trouble, the election would not be a Democratic landslide.

A second implication is that even a small increase in Trump's popularity could have swung the election in his favor. Before 2020, the historical relationship between presidential approval in June of the election year and major-party vote share suggested that each 1-point increase in approval leads to a 0.33-point increase in vote share. Assume, for example, that Trump's approval had stayed at 46 percent, where it was at the end of March 2020, when he began to take the coronavirus outbreak more seriously and then received a small bump in his approval rating. That would have left his approval rating 6 points higher than it actually was as of June 2020, after Trump's push to reopen the economy and his angry reaction to the George Floyd protests. That 6-point difference could have translated into 2 additional points of vote share, other things being equal. That means Trump would have received 49.7 percent of the major-party vote instead of 47.7 percent, turning the national popular vote into a toss-up. Given the Electoral College bias in the GOP's favor, a national popular vote margin of only 1 point in favor of the Democrats implies a Trump victory.

Of course, such a scenario is a conjecture at best. But it is a plausible one. Had Trump taken the pandemic more seriously—as did the many other governors and world leaders who experienced durable increases in their approval rating—he could have won. The 2020 election illustrated just how much small shifts can matter when the parties are so narrowly divided.

THE POWER OF PARTISANSHIP

There was another fundamental factor at work in 2020: partisanship. Well before Trump took office, growing differences between Democrats and Republicans helped make Americans' party loyalties a stronger force in their political thinking and voting behavior (chapter 1). During Trump's presidency, strong partisanship helped stabilize Trump's approval ratings, driven both by the resolute antipathy of Democrats and the continued support of Republicans (chapter 3). All of this contributed to a more calcified politics before the election year began. And then the dramatic events of that year—the pandemic, massive protests for racial justice—failed to fundamentally rearrange the political alignments that years of polarization and calcification had created. The 2020 election would only cement those alignments further.

The power of partisanship is visible in the *stability* of people's choices in 2020 compared to 2016. There are three places where that stability was evident: states, counties, and individual voters. The state-level results are depicted in figure 8.2 by comparing the presidential vote in pairs of adjacent elections: 2008 and 2012, 2012 and 2016, and 2016 and 2020. In all three cases, there is a strong relationship between how a state votes in one election and how it votes in another. But there is variation in the extent of the stability and the pattern of any changes.

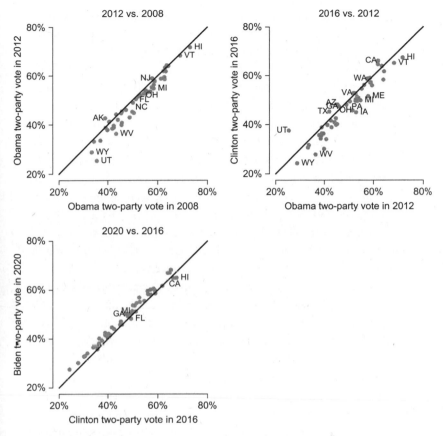

Figure 8.2.

Changes in Presidential Vote in the States, 2008–20. *Source*: US Election Atlas, https://uselectionatlas.org/.

Between 2008 and 2012, the main change was a shift to a smaller margin for Barack Obama than he had in 2008. This pattern, whereby most states shifted in a uniform direction, resulted from changes in the political environment. In 2008, Obama was running against the incumbent party in the midst of a punishing recession. In 2012, he was the incumbent running amid a modest economic recovery, conditions that were favorable to his reelection but not as favorable as the conditions that led to his initial victory. Any exceptions to this pattern were due to id-iosyncratic factors. For example, Alaska was an outlier because its governor, Sarah Palin, was on the Republican ticket in 2008 but not in 2012.

Between 2012 and 2016, by contrast, the state-level shifts were larger in absolute magnitude and not in a uniform direction. In absolute value, the average shift from 2012 to 2016 was 3.3 points, compared to 2.5 points from 2008 to 2012. Some shifts were in the pro-Democratic direction: Hillary Clinton did better than Obama in Arizona, California, Texas, and Virginia. She did worse in other states, especially Michigan, Ohio, Pennsylvania, and Wisconsin. These countervailing shifts stemmed from how the 2016 campaign helped to create a changing alignment sometimes called the "diploma divide": states with a larger fraction of white voters with college degrees shifted to Clinton and states with a larger fraction of white voters without college degrees shifted to Trump. In turn, this diploma divide can be traced to issues related to race and immigration: education is strongly related to people's views on those issues, and the 2016 campaign made those issues much more salient than had the 2012 campaign. This was the "identity shock" described in chapter 1.[9]

The shifts between 2016 and 2020 told a different story, however. First of all, those shifts were much smaller than between 2012 and 2016 or between 2008 and 2012, averaging only 2 points in absolute value. Second, unlike between 2012 and 2016, those shifts were much more uniform. Biden did better in almost every state than Clinton did in 2020. Thus, the altered alignment that 2016 created largely remained intact in 2020. What made the difference for Biden was that these shifts were just large enough to give him the lead in key swing states, which in turn gave him the victory in the Electoral College that eluded Clinton. This shows, once again, how much small shifts matter in an era of partisan parity.

The small size of the shifts between 2016 and 2020 was also apparent at the county level (figure 8.3). As we noted in chapter 1, the shift or "swing" between one election year and the next has been declining for some time. But the shifts between 2016 and 2020 stand out as particularly small. On average, counties shifted about 1.9 points in absolute

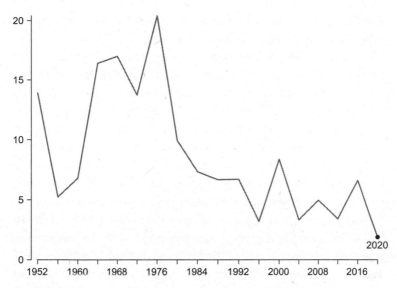

Figure 8.3.
Trends in the Magnitude of Election-to-Election Swings in Presidential Voting at the County Level. The figure depicts the average absolute value of county-level shifts in the Democratic candidate's percent of the major-party vote.

value, compared to 6.6 points between 2012 and 2016. Despite all of the twists and turns of the Trump presidency, the pandemic, George Floyd's murder and the ensuing protests, and the substitution of Joe Biden for Hillary Clinton, one could predict county outcomes in the 2020 election very well simply by knowing the outcomes in 2016.

Finally, there was also a very high level of stability at the individual level among people who voted in 2012, 2016, and 2020 (see table A8.1). This is visible in the Views of the Electorate Research (VOTER) Survey, which interviewed the same respondents in 2012, 2016, and 2020. Among respondents who voted in both 2012 and 2016, most voted for the same party: 81 percent of Obama voters reported voting for Clinton and 84 percent of Romney voters reported voting for Trump. But that stability was even greater from 2016 to 2020, when about 95 percent of both Clinton and Trump voters reported voting for their party's candidate.

Switching between parties—most famously exemplified by the "Obama-Trump" voters of 2016—was far less common.

One reason why the stability between 2016 and 2020 was greater than between 2012 and 2016 was that people who switched parties between 2012 and 2016 remained loyal to the party they supported in 2016. In the VOTER Survey, the vast majority of the Obama-Trump voters (87%) reported voting for Trump in 2020. Similarly, most of the Romney-Clinton voters (83%) supported Biden. That both groups stuck with the party they supported in 2016 helps explain why the 2016–20 county-level shifts were smaller than the shifts between 2012 and 2016. In short, most of 2016's swing voters looked like reliable partisans by 2020.

Another illustration of partisanship's power was visible in the Democratic Party specifically. A competitive presidential primary always raises the question of whether the party will unite around the nominee. That was no different after Biden emerged as the presumptive nominee. For example, an April 8, 2020, *New York Times* story noted Biden's "stunning political comeback" but warned "the challenge of uniting the party around him is just beginning." The headline of the story was "Now Comes the Hard Part for Joe Biden."[10]

However, we showed in chapter 4 that Biden actually emerged from the primary with relatively favorable feelings among the supporters of his chief opponent, Bernie Sanders. That translated into more support in the general election as well. To be sure, most Sanders supporters reported voting for Hillary Clinton in 2016—about 79 percent, according to VOTER Survey interviews conducted after the primaries and after the general election in 2016.[11] But in 2020, that fraction was even larger. In VOTER Survey interviews, 87 percent of Sanders supporters reported voting for Biden.[12] Of course, Biden also went to considerable lengths to woo Sanders supporters, including establishing teams that included more progressive or Sanders-aligned Democrats and were tasked with formulating proposals in various policy areas. There is no way to know exactly how much Biden's efforts mattered, but the upshot is clear: the partisanship visible in the general election results stemmed in part from the willingness of Democratic primary voters to get behind Biden.

PERPETUAL POLARIZATION

Even if differences in overall outcomes between 2016 and 2020 were small, the differences that did exist were consequential. In particular, the overall stability across counties and individuals concealed changes in the candidates' coalitions, including Biden's stronger performance among white voters with college degrees as well as Trump's stronger performance among Black and Latino voters. By one estimate, Trump did 3 percentage points better among Black voters and 8 percentage points better among Latino voters than he did in 2016. The fact that Trump could do better with these voters after four years of hard-line policies on immigration and civil rights surprised many observers. The difference among Latino voters was particularly striking and seemed to hurt Democratic candidates in many places, from south Florida to the Rio Grande Valley. To be sure, voters of color still favored Democrats by a substantial margin and they were integral to Biden's coalition and thus his victory. But few expected Biden to do worse than Clinton. One *New York Times* headline summed it up: "Liberals Envisioned a Multiracial Coalition. Voters of Color Had Other Ideas."[13]

What helps explain these changes in the candidates' coalitions is the same polarization that has been ongoing in American politics for decades but intensified between 2016 and 2020. Americans perceived even more ideological polarization between the two parties and became more polarized themselves. Their own political ideology and issue positions became even more strongly related to their vote in 2020 than in 2016. This was true across a range of racial and ethnic groups. In fact, as we will show, this ideological polarization helps account for Trump's surprisingly stronger performance among Latino voters, many of whom are conservative.

Changing perceptions of the political parties are visible first in how Americans' perceptions of Donald Trump's politics changed. Throughout his presidency, many more Americans came to see him as conservative. This is the logical consequence of how he governed. As we discussed in chapter 2, Trump's ideologically ambiguous campaign, where he flirted with ideas like taxing the wealthy, gave way to a conservative agenda as president.

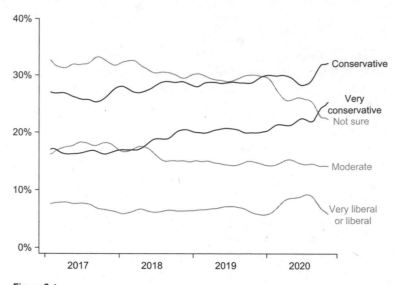

Figure 8.4.
Trends in Perceptions of Donald Trump's Ideology. *Source*: YouGov/*Economist* polls.

In YouGov/*Economist* polls conducted throughout Trump's presidency, the percentage of Americans who said Trump was "conservative" increased from about 27 percent to 32 percent between January 2017 and Election Day 2020 (figure 8.4).[14] The percentage who said he was "very conservative" increased from 17 percent to 25 percent. Meanwhile, the percent who said they were not sure or said he was "moderate" declined. In other words, more Americans came to have an opinion about Trump's ideology and most of them believed, arguably correctly, that he was conservative. This was true among different demographic groups as well. For example, the percentage of Latino voters who said Trump was conservative or very conservative increased from 34 percent to 49 percent.

Americans not only believed that Trump had moved to the right, but also tended to believe that Biden was to the left of Clinton. This was evident in the American National Election Study, which interviewed the same people in the fall of 2016 and the fall of 2020 and asked them how

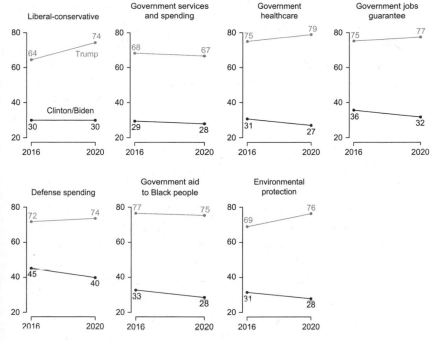

Figure 8.5.
Perceptions of the Issue Positions of the 2016 and 2020 Presidential Candidates. The graph shows average placements of Trump and Clinton (2016) and Trump and Biden (2020) on 7-point scales recoded to range from liberal (0) to conservative (100). *Source*: 2016–20 panel interviews from the American National Election Study (N=2,509).

they perceived the ideology of the presidential candidates as well as their positions on various issues.[15]

Here again, there was a notable shift in perceptions of Trump's ideology, from 64 to 74 on a 100-point scale (figure 8.5). Moreover, on almost all of the issues on which people placed the candidates—the role of government in various domains, spending on national defense, environmental regulation—their perceptions of the candidates were more polarized in 2020 than in 2016. In 2020, Americans tended to place Trump further to the right or Biden further to the left (or both), compared to where they placed Trump and Clinton in 2016.[16]

The fact that they perceived Biden as more liberal than Clinton is interesting, given that Biden sometimes tried to distance himself from the more liberal wing of the party—for example, on issues like policing. The perception may reflect the longer-term liberal shift within the Democratic Party and the fact that, although Biden and Clinton may be relative moderates within the party, they are themselves moving to the left along with the party. Certainly, Biden took positions on health care and the environment that were more liberal than Clinton's. For example, compared to Clinton, Biden proposed to allow even more Americans to buy into a government insurance plan and proposed a more ambitious, and expensive, plan to reduce carbon emissions.[17]

If the two parties are further apart ideologically and if Americans perceive those differences, then one consequence should be a stronger association between people's own ideological predispositions and their voting behavior. That is exactly what transpired in 2020 compared to 2016. On balance, Trump gained support among conservative-leaning voters and Biden gained support among liberal-leaning voters. These gains came from some combination of voters who voted in both 2016 and 2020 as well as voters who did not vote in 2016 but did vote in 2020 as part of the surge in turnout. The result was more ideological polarization in voting behavior.

One survey project, the Cooperative Election Study (CES), demonstrates this polarization. In 2016 and 2020, the survey interviewed separate samples of over 60,000 Americans. Because the CES includes data from administrative turnout records in each state, we also know whether voters actually voted in 2016 and 2020. In both years, the CES asked respondents the same questions about their ideological identification on the liberal-conservative spectrum, their attitudes about gun control and abortion, and their perception of the extent of racism in the United States. For illustration, we divided Americans into three groups (conservatives, moderates, and liberals) on each issue and calculated how Biden and Trump performed among that group, relative to Clinton and Trump in 2016. For ideological identification, these three groups reflect the terms that people used to describe themselves. For the other issues, the three groups are derived from building

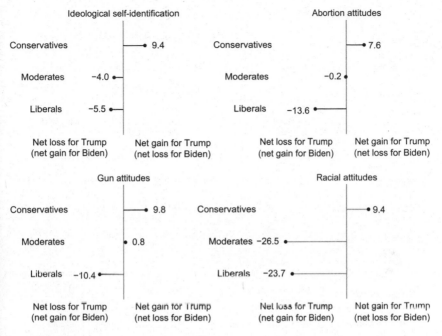

Figure 8.6.
Ideological Polarization in 2020 Voting Behavior (Percentage Point Gains or Losses for Biden and Trump vs. 2016). *Source:* 2016 and 2020 Cooperative Election Surveys.

scales based on responses to several questions about the issue. We then divided the sample roughly into thirds based on issue positions, meaning that labels like "conservative" or "liberal" reflect relative differences on these scales, not discrete groups.[18]

Figure 8.6 presents the differences in voting behavior between the two elections. For example, among all 2020 voters who identified as conservative or very conservative, Trump did 9.4 percentage points better than he did among conservatives who voted in 2016. Meanwhile, Biden performed 5.5 points better with voters who identified as liberal or very liberal, compared to how Clinton did among 2016 voters. This increased polarization, as Trump's performance among conservatives and Biden's performance among liberals made Americans' ideological identification a stronger predictor of how they voted in 2020 than in 2016.

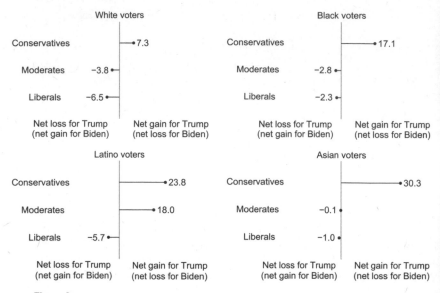

Figure 8.7.
Ideological Polarization in 2020 Voting Behavior among Racial and Ethnic Groups (Percentage Point Gains or Losses for Biden and Trump vs. 2016). Ideology is defined as respondents' self-identification as conservative, moderate, or liberal. *Source*: 2016 and 2020 Cooperative Election Surveys.

That was true of other issues as well. In 2020, Trump did better among people with conservative views on abortion and on gun control. He did better among people with conservative views on race—in this case, people who tended to see racism as a less important problem. Biden did better among liberals on these issues. The magnitude of these gains or losses varied with the issue, but the broad pattern was clear: not only did voters perceive larger ideological differences between the candidates in 2020, but their own ideological beliefs were more strongly related to their choice between Biden and Trump than they were to their choice between Clinton and Trump.

This pattern occurred among all major racial and ethnic groups (figure 8.7). Trump improved his performance among self-identified conservatives who identified as white, Black, Latino, or Asian American. For example, in 2016 Trump won Latino conservatives by a margin of 59 percent to 33 percent; in 2020 he won them by a margin of 74 percent to 24 percent. Biden improved his performance among self-identified liberals in every racial group. Ideological polarization was a widespread phenomenon, not something confined to certain racial groups.

This polarization helped explain Trump's surprising performance among a group like Latinos. Although Biden gained vote share among the 34 percent of Latino voters who identified as liberal in 2020, this was more than offset by the vote share he lost among the 38 percent who identified as moderate and the 28 percent who identified as conservative. Biden's weaker performance among these latter two groups ended up costing him among Latinos overall.

THE SOURCES OF POLARIZATION

This growing ideological polarization in voting behavior could come from different sources. One is turnout: new voters in 2020 may have voted in a polarized fashion. Another is shifts in candidate choice among the consistent voters who voted in both elections. If Trump gained votes among conservative Clinton voters, or Biden gained votes among liberal Trump voters, then this would have created more ideological polarization. Certainly there was evidence for this in 2016, when Trump won over some white Obama voters who had conservative attitudes on racial issues and immigration.[19]

But in 2020 there were many fewer voters who switched to the other party's candidate. This means that the ideological polarization in voting behavior was more likely to come from a third source: voters changed their issue positions in ways that aligned with their partisanship. For example, if Clinton voters moved left between 2016 and 2020, while Trump voters moved right, then voting in 2020 would look more ideologically polarized even if every Clinton voter voted for Biden and every Trump voter stuck with Trump. There was some precedent for this in 2016 as well: Democrats and Republicans appeared to shift their views on issues like race and immigration during the 2016 campaign itself, with Democrats moving left and Republicans moving right.[20]

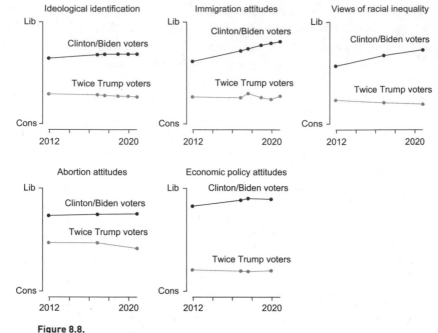

Figure 8.8.

Ideological Polarization among Consistent Democratic and Republican Voters. The figure presents trends in averages on different issue scales where higher values indicate more liberal positions and lower values more conservative positions. *Source*: Views of the Electorate Research Survey.

Between 2016 and 2020, partisans did continue to polarize in their views on a range of issues. One way to see this is to isolate consistent Democratic and Republican voters—those who reported voting for Clinton in 2016 and Biden in 2020, and those who reported voting for Trump in both elections. The VOTER Survey, which interviewed the same people several times between 2011 and 2020, allows that (figure 8.8). Consistent Democratic voters shifted to the left in how they identified themselves ideologically.[21] For example, in late 2011, 49 percent of consistent Democrats called themselves liberal or very liberal. By late 2020, that had increased to 56 percent. The percentage of consistent Trump voters who called themselves conservative or very conservative increased from 67 percent to 73 percent. Consistent Democrats moved even more rapidly toward a liberal view of racial inequality (as we showed in chapter 6) and especially immigration (as we showed in chapter 1). If anything, loyal Trump voters became more likely to have a conservative view of racial inequality. Loyal Trump voters also moved right on abortion, while loyal Democratic voters moved to the left on economic policies.

The same pattern of polarization emerged in other surveys, too. The American National Election Studies also interviewed the same respondents in both 2016 and 2020, and consistent Democratic and Republican voters were further apart in their views of the same issues on which they also perceived the candidates as more polarized.

Undoubtedly, ideological polarization does not explain all of the differences in voting behavior between 2016 and 2020. But polarization does provide a simple and general explanation, in the style of Occam's razor, as opposed to a series of boutique explanations for the behavior of specific groups. For example, after the election, prominent news stories said that Biden lost votes among Cuban and Venezuelan Americans in Florida because they disliked the socialist regimes in Cuba and Venezuela and were concerned that the Democratic Party had become too left-wing or "socialist," and he lost votes among Mexican Americans in the Rio Grande Valley because they feared losing oil-industry jobs under a Democratic president who wanted to wean the country from fossil fuels.[22] Perhaps those explanations were true for some voters. But since Biden lost votes among all kinds of Latino voters in all parts of the country, it is important to seek an explanation that can account for this broader pattern among Latinos and that can help understand differences in voting behavior among other groups as well. Ideological polarization helps to accomplish that.

THE LOCAL EFFECTS OF COVID-19 AND CAMPAIGN ADVERTISING

Focusing on ideological polarization to explain the differences between 2016 and 2020 might seem to ignore the distinctive events of the election year itself—and especially the pandemic and the historically expensive presidential campaign. In particular, it seems plausible that local election outcomes could depend on how hard different places were hit by the pandemic or by which candidate won the "air war" in televised campaign advertisements in different local media markets. Both factors seemed as if they could benefit Biden in particular. Trump was the incumbent in office as the country suffered thousands of COVID-19 deaths. And Biden vastly outspent Trump on the airwaves, as we described in chapter 7.

But there was little evidence that either of these things affected voting behavior at the local level. Biden did not win a larger share of the vote in counties with more COVID-19 deaths or where he had an advantage in ads. This was yet another reason the election was relatively close, despite conditions that seemed to favor Biden.

To be sure, there was clearly the potential for the pandemic to affect local election outcomes. The study of military casualties in war and presidential elections has shown that not only do overall casualties appear to hurt incumbent presidents or their parties at the national level, but casualties may also cost incumbents vote share in the communities where soldiers were from. One reason may be that military deaths get attention in local media, heightening any blame that local residents place on the incumbent party. A similar dynamic could have characterized deaths from COVID-19. Indeed, early research linking weekly Nationscape surveys to data on COVID deaths in survey respondents' county or state between March and August 2020 found that the number of COVID deaths at the state and county level was associated with a lower likelihood of intending to vote for Trump as well as Republican candidates in down-ballot races.[23]

But this pattern did not emerge in the election outcome itself. After accounting for other factors, there was not a statistically significant relationship between the cumulative number of COVID infections per capita and Biden's share of the vote, compared to Clinton's (see table A8.2). That is, counties that experienced more COVID infections did not appear to shift toward Biden to a statistically discernible extent. Paradoxically, Biden actually did *worse* in counties that experienced more cumulative deaths from COVID-19 compared to counties that experienced fewer deaths. We suspect that this is not because COVID-19 deaths somehow created support for Trump or opposition to Biden; rather, there was likely another factor at play. Given that many conservatives took the pandemic less seriously (see chapter 5), it is possible that very conservative areas had more COVID deaths and particularly high support for Trump. Regardless, the results indicate that the electoral impact of deaths from COVID-19 was not like that of military casualties in the past. The current pandemic better resembled one of the last major pandemics, the Spanish flu pandemic of 1918, which also had little local impact on voting for either governors in 1918 or the president in 1920.[24] Thus, to the extent that the pandemic hurt Trump and helped Biden, it was at the national level more than the local level.

Previous research has also shown that televised campaign advertising affects local presidential election outcomes in the places where those advertisements are aired. The most comprehensive assessment, which examined how broadcast advertising data in the 2000 through 2016 presidential elections affected outcomes in U.S. counties, found that the side that aired more ads over the last two months of the campaign—combining candidate, party, and outside group ads in the presidential race—did win more vote share. The size of this relationship was modest, to be sure: for every 100 more ads a candidate aired relative to their opponent, they received 0.02 more points of vote share (that is, two-hundredths of a percentage point). Given that the average advantage in local broadcast advertising in counties was 400 airings, that would translate into 0.08 points.[25]

But as we demonstrated in chapter 7, Joe Biden's advantage in television advertising was much larger than usual for a presidential campaign. Combining local broadcast ads aired over the last two months, Biden's average advantage across U.S. counties was 1,100 ads. But his advantage was even larger because he also aired ads on national broadcast and cable television, which would have aired in every media market in every state. This means that over the last two months of the 2020 campaign, Biden's average advantage over Trump was closer to a whopping 13,000 ads.

However, it is not clear that this advantage ended up helping him. Among survey respondents interviewed weekly as part of the Nationscape

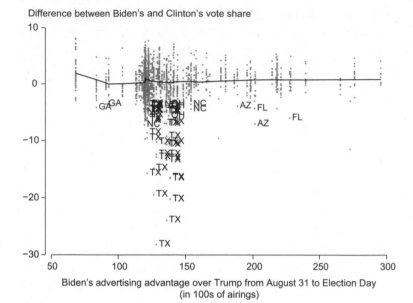

Figure 8.9.
The Relationship between Biden's Advertising Advantage and County Shifts in Vote Share from 2016 to 2020. Each dot represents a county, with certain outlying counties labeled with their state. *Source of advertising data*: Kantar Media.

project, there was no consistently meaningful relationship between the balance of advertising in their county and whom they intended to vote for. For example, respondents who were interviewed right after a period in which Biden's advertising greatly outpaced Trump's were not more likely to say they would vote for Biden, compared to respondents interviewed after a period in which Biden's advertising advantage was smaller (see table A8.4).

A similar finding emerged in the actual election results. Biden's advertising advantage in the last two months of the campaign was not associated with a higher vote share in U.S. counties, relative to Hillary Clinton's 2016 vote share (figure 8.9). The relationship was mostly flat. If anything, there could be a small negative relationship, which is what the statistical models also show (see table A8.2). That a historically large gap in advertising did not translate into additional votes may again reflect the stability between the 2016 and 2020 elections and the difficulty of moving many voters.

THE RACIAL JUSTICE PROTESTS AND "DEFUNDING THE POLICE"

To many observers, the most electorally consequential events of 2020 were the murder of George Floyd, the racial justice protests, and the debates about criminal justice policy. After the "abject disaster" of the election, many prominent Democrats blamed the party's unexpectedly poor performance on the unpopular idea of "defunding the police," which figured not only in Trump's advertising but in Republican advertising in congressional races as well. Two days after the election, there was a contentious conference call among Democratic members of Congress in which Rep. Abigail Spanberger, a moderate Democrat from Virginia, summed up the view of many, saying, "Don't say defund the police when that's not what we mean" and declaring, "If we are classifying Tuesday [the election] as a success . . . we will get fucking torn apart in 2022."[26]

Although racial justice and policing were frequently cited in explanations of the election's outcome, solid evidence was hard to come by. Part of the challenge is that many potentially important things happened in quick succession: Floyd's murder, the racial justice protests, Trump's criticisms of those protests, Trump's attacks on Biden on crime and criminal justice, the debate about "defunding the police" specifically, Biden's own statements and explicit opposition to defunding, and so on. It is difficult to disentangle them. Another part of the challenge is just the usual struggle to separate correlation from causation, especially when so much of voters' reaction to these events was driven by their own partisanship, as we showed in chapter 6. For this reason, people's views of the police or Black Lives Matter (BLM) may have been mostly a consequence of how they tend to vote, rather than a direct cause of how they voted in 2020.

Ultimately, we find that various dimensions of the racial justice protests and criminal justice debates did not hurt Biden and could possibly have helped him. Four different pieces of evidence speak to this.

National Trends

One initial piece of evidence comes from the national polling, which we described in chapter 7 but is worth noting again. Polling showed that in June and July—the period when there was the most news coverage of Floyd's murder and the racial justice protests—Biden actually gained support. He led Trump by about 5.5 points the week before Floyd's murder. This increased to nearly 9 points by mid-June before declining slightly to roughly 7 to 8 points, where it would stay for the rest of the campaign. If the protests or the issues they raised were politically damaging to him, it did not show up at precisely the moment when it should have.

Moreover, it was not clear that Biden suffered among groups within the electorate who were supposedly turned off by the protests or the idea of defunding the police. For example, some postelection reporting argued that Biden lost support among Latinos for this reason.[27] But weekly Nationscape surveys showed that Biden's margin among Latinos was declining well before Floyd's murder, and there was no clear punctuated drop afterward. Indeed, if anything, the rate of decline slowed down somewhat after Floyd's murder, instead of accelerating as it should have if the debate over policing and racial justice caused a sudden surge of Latino support for Trump.

Local Impact of Racial Justice Protests

Another piece of evidence comes from examining the local impact of the racial justice protests that took place in the spring and summer of 2020. Here, there was reason to think that these protests could influence the actual outcome of the election—just not any consensus on whether they would help Biden or Trump.

One scholarly account, the political scientist Daniel Gillion's book *The Loud Minority*, argues that protests aligned with liberal causes have tended to help Democrats. For example, liberal protest activity in congressional districts between 1960 and 1990 was associated with a higher vote share for Democratic candidates and a lower share for Republican candidates. Moreover, Gillion found that African American turnout in congressional districts that experienced BLM protests in 2016 increased relative to 2012, even as African American turnout dropped overall.[28]

But one question is whether all types of protest activity help Democrats and, in particular, whether protests that are accompanied by violence can actually elicit a backlash and help Republicans. One study of Black-led protests in the United States between 1960 and 1972 concluded exactly that. The study, by political scientist Omar Wasow, found that counties in which nonviolent protests occurred saw a 1–2 percentage point increase in Democratic vote share in the 1964, 1968, and 1972 elections. Counties in which violence occurred shifted in the opposite direction, with Republican candidates gaining about 2 percentage points. Wasow also found that the violent protests that occurred after the assassination of Martin Luther King Jr. in April 1968 may have had an even larger effect: counties where those protests occurred shifted approximately 5 points toward the Republican candidate, Richard Nixon. This was a large enough shift that the Democrat, Hubert Humphrey, would likely have won the election if those protests had not occurred.[29]

Wasow's research figured in a bigger debate in 2020 about whether the election year would become a replay of 1968. Some commentators feared that violence at racial justice protests after George Floyd's murder would help reelect Trump. Others noted key differences between 1968 and 2020. For one, nonviolence was by far the norm after Floyd's murder, and at times any violence was perpetrated by police against the protestors, rather than by the protesters themselves.[30] For another, Trump was the incumbent in 2020, while Nixon was the challenger in 1968. Any unrest or violence in the country might reflect poorly on the incumbent, much like an economic recession does. Complicating this debate was that the academic research does not consistently find that violence at racial justice protests has hurt the Democratic Party. One study of the riots after the 1992 Rodney King verdict in Los Angeles— when the police officers who beat King were acquitted—found that in areas proximate to the riots, more new voters (both white and Black) subsequently registered with the Democratic Party than with the Republican Party.[31]

To examine the potential impact of the racial justice protests in 2020, we again draw on data from the Crowd Counting Consortium, which recorded the incidence of these protests as well as various characteristics, including whether there were arrests, injuries to protestors, injuries to the police, or property damage. We then divided counties into three groups: the 57 percent that had no protests between May 25, when George Floyd was murdered, and Election Day; the 35 percent that had protests but did not have any arrests, injuries, or property damage; and the remaining 8 percent that had protests in which one or more of those things occurred. To be clear, in cases where there were arrests or injuries to protestors, it may not have been because protesters were violent. The arrests could have been for other reasons, such as staying out past a curfew. Moreover, in some cases injuries to protesters resulted from violent police actions. But this simple three-part categorization provides initial purchase on whether voters in counties where racial justice protests occurred voted differently than voters in counties without these protests.

One way to examine this question is to leverage the weekly Nationscape surveys conducted during the protests. This speaks to the question of whether people changed how they intended to vote based on whether a protest took place in their county. We found little evidence of any impact: people in counties with racial justice protests in the weeks immediately before their interview did not change their vote intention, compared to people in counties without protests (see table A8.3.)

Another way is to look at the county-level vote returns. Here, there were differences based on whether a county had experienced a racial justice protest—but the differences were not in the direction that many observers suspected. If anything, Biden did *better*, relative to Clinton in 2016, in counties where these protests occurred (figure 8.10). In counties with no protests, Biden's share of the major-party vote was nearly identical to Clinton's (an average shift of only −0.2 percentage points). In counties that had protests with no arrests, injuries, or property damage, Biden outperformed Clinton by 1.4 points. In counties with protests that had some combination of arrests, injuries, and property damage, Biden outperformed Clinton by 1.7 points.

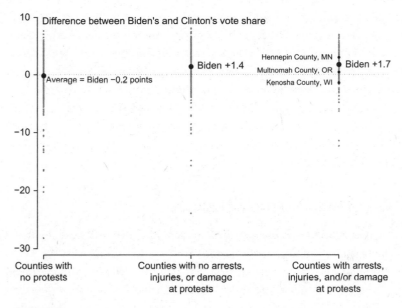

Figure 8.10.
County Shifts in Vote Share, 2016–20, Based on Presence and Circumstances of Racial Justice Protests. *Source for protest data:* Crowd Counting Consortium.

Figure 8.10 also makes clear that these average differences conceal substantial variation. For example, among counties that saw arrests, injuries, or damage, there were certainly places where Biden lost vote share. One was Kenosha County, Wisconsin, where there were protests and violence after the police shooting of Jacob Blake on August 25, 2020. The protests attracted counterprotesters, one of whom, Kyle Rittenhouse, shot and killed two men. In Kenosha County, Biden's share of the vote was 1.4 points lower than Clinton's.[32] But in other cities with substantial protests and violence—including Minneapolis itself (Hennepin County, MN) and Portland (Multnomah County, OR)—Biden's share of the vote was higher than Clinton's.

Of course, the places in which protests occurred were not a random set of counties. But even when we account for other county attributes—their racial composition, educational composition, median income, and population size—Biden still did approximately 1 point better than Clinton in counties with protests, regardless of whether those protests were accompanied by arrests, injuries, or property damage (see table A8.2).

There is, however, no way to determine from this evidence that the protests actually *caused* Biden to win more votes in the places where those protests occurred. But certainly the evidence does not suggest that Biden was hurt in those places. If that is true, then 2020 was different from 1968 after all.

Effect of Trump Ads on Crime and Public Safety

A third window into the electoral effects of Floyd's murder and its aftermath centers on the counternarrative of Donald Trump. After the election, there was much speculation that Trump's argument about crime, violence, and policing had hurt Biden and other Democrats, especially given how few Americans appeared to support defunding the police. One way to test this is to examine the impact of Trump's advertising on this topic. We showed in chapter 7 that issues related to "public safety" were a prominent theme in Trump's advertising, but there was variation over time in how frequently it was discussed. And of course, there was variation in where those ads aired as well.

The question is whether Trump gained support when and where those public safety ads were aired. By marrying the advertising data to the Nationscape surveys, we can speak to this. The answer is that there was *no* significant association between Trump's advertising on this issue and how people intended to vote. Specifically, the number of Trump ads about public safety in either the week or the month before people were interviewed did not appear to affect whether they intended to vote for Trump or Biden. In short, exposure to hundreds or even thousands of these ads in a short period of time did not change people's attitudes (see table A8.4).

This is perhaps unsurprising, given that television advertising overall did not appear significantly correlated with election outcomes in counties. Moreover, it is possible that Trump's public safety message failed to resonate because so many Americans disapproved of how he reacted to Floyd's murder, because more Americans appeared to trust Biden on issues related to public safety, and because Biden himself was clear in opposing "defund the police" (see chapters 6 and 7). In short, Trump may have thought he had a winning message, but that was ambiguous from the outset. Studying the effect of this message through the lens of his advertising cannot supply conclusive evidence, of course, but it does suggest again that Biden was not obviously damaged.

Feelings about the Police and Black Lives Matter

A final question is whether people's views about the police or the BLM movement actually influenced their vote. For example, perhaps Biden lost more votes among those who favored the police or opposed defunding than he gained from people who felt less favorably about the police and supported reforms like a ban on chokeholds. Unsurprisingly, it is easy to show correlations between people's views about the police, policing procedure, or BLM and how they feel about Biden or Trump. In chapter 6 we showed how there were significant and, in some cases, growing partisan divisions on this topic.

But people's views of the police or BLM may have been more a consequence of people's voting behavior than a cause. We have already seen evidence of growing division in political attitudes, even among people who did not change the party they voted for in 2016 and 2020 (figure 8.8). The same thing is true in how they viewed the police. For example, among Clinton/Biden voters, the overall rating of the police dropped from 67 to 58 on a 0–100 scale. Among voters who supported Trump in both elections, their ratings stayed about the same (87–88).

A more formal statistical analysis leverages these 2016 and 2020 interviews among the same respondents to examine whether people's views of the police and BLM affected their choice of candidates or whether people's choice of candidates affected their view of the police. That analysis shows much more evidence that people's view of the police or BLM changed, not their voting behavior (see table A8.5). This echoes the findings in chapter 6 and in other research: Americans are changing their attitudes on racially charged issues in ways that reinforce their partisanship.[33]

Again, this is not conclusive evidence. We lack the ability to do similar tests with views of criminal justice policy, separate from views of the police overall. But this evidence still raises an important cautionary note. In the Trump era, when an already polarized public often confronted even more polarizing messages from political leaders, people tended to take their cue from their party's leaders, changed their attitudes in ways that reinforce their partisanship, and rarely considered voting for the other party's leader. In 2020, this may have kept policing from being the wedge issue that Trump hoped it would be and that Democrats feared.

CONCLUSION

Biden's victory capped an election year that was both historic and horrifying. There were historic protests about racial justice. There was a historic surge in turnout. There were the horrifying deaths of George Floyd and many who fell ill during the pandemic.

In explaining Biden's victory, however, what stands out is something more mundane: an unpopular president lost his bid for reelection. Unpopularity did not doom Trump in 2016, when he was not the incumbent and faced a relatively unpopular opponent in Hillary Clinton. Four years later, however, Trump had different and arguably bigger challenges. He was the incumbent during major national crises, and the majority of Americans judged his performance unfavorably. At the same time, Americans viewed Biden more favorably than they had Clinton. Trump was in a weaker position and had to face a stronger opponent.

At the same time, the narrowness of Biden's victory testified to other familiar patterns in our politics. The polarization endemic in American politics for decades only continued. Democrats and Republicans were even further apart than they had been four years before. People's partisan predispositions were even more ossified, with few shifts since 2016. The remarkable events of 2020 did not necessarily sway many voters and, indeed, intensified these long-term trends toward greater polarization and calcification.

On November 7, Biden gave his victory speech in Wilmington, Delaware. Amid the many thank-yous—to his wife and family, to Kamala Harris, to his campaign team, to the voters who supported him—Biden tried to sound a very different note than what Americans typically heard from Donald Trump. Biden said, "I pledge to be a president who seeks not to divide but to unify, who doesn't see red states and blue states, only sees the United States." He said, "It's time to put away harsh rhetoric, lower the temperature, see each other again. Listen to each other again. And to make progress, we have to stop treating our opponents as enemies." He said, "This is the time to heal in America."[34]

But Biden was about to learn just how far Trump and his Republican allies would go to prevent Biden from having the chance. They would pose a challenge not only to Biden's presidency, but to American democracy itself.

9

Subversion

SPALDING COUNTY, GEORGIA, sits about forty miles south of Atlanta along Interstate 75. About 65,000 people live there. It has been safely Republican for many years, and Trump won about 60 percent of the vote there in 2020. It is not really a swing county.

But Georgia is a swing state. And after Biden's narrow victory in Georgia, combined with the election of two Democratic senators in runoff elections in early 2021, the Republican-led state legislature and the Republican governor, Brian Kemp, decided to make some changes. They passed a bill that allowed the state elections board, also controlled by Republicans, to assume control of any county election board after conducting a "performance review."

Spalding County was one of six counties whose election board was restructured. Under the old system in Spalding County, each party chose two members of the board and the fifth was chosen by a coin flip. Now the fifth member would be appointed by local judges, who tend to be conservative.

And that is how Vera McIntosh, a Black Democrat, was ousted from the election board and replaced by James Newland, who happened to be the vice chair of the Spalding County Republican Party. "They wanted control," McIntosh said afterward. "They got control."[1]

What happened in Spalding County was emblematic of the norm-shattering partisan politics that Joe Biden said he wanted to heal. But Biden soon discovered how difficult that would be. A new party in the White House changes many things—not least the direction of policy—but all presidents soon experience how much their fortunes are constrained by longer-term trends.

From the start of Biden's term, the tectonic shifts of partisan polarization affected his public stature. Even before he could establish a record as president, his approval rating was more polarized along party lines than any president in the history of modern polling. Nothing Biden did in his first months changed this.

Partisan polarization also affected Biden's ability to deal with the country's crises. Polarization on pandemic lockdowns and mask mandates carried over to COVID-19 vaccines, as large numbers of Republicans refused to be vaccinated. Partisan polarization on the racial justice protests and Black Lives Matter movement carried over to the trial of Minnesota police officer Derek Chauvin, as large numbers of Republicans disagreed with the guilty verdict. The identity shock that Trump helped to catalyze continued to reverberate.

As Biden took office, a different kind of crisis was also looming: a crisis for American democracy. Trump did not succeed in keeping Biden out of the Oval Office, but his attempted election subversion attracted the support of Republican lawmakers across the country: the majority of Republicans in the House, eighteen Republican state attorneys general, and countless state and local officials. Most Republican voters believed Trump's false claims too, and continued to doubt the election outcome and the legitimacy of Biden's presidency. The violence of the January 6 insurrection produced little accountability within the Republican Party for Trump or anyone else who had helped to incite it.

The crisis did not stop when Trump left the White House. If anything, it grew worse. What happened in Spalding County was playing out across the country: state and local Republican leaders loyal to Donald Trump were trying to gain control of how elections were run. They sought to change the rules and gain control of the political offices that had the power to certify elections. The Republican officeholders who refused to go along with Trump's attempt at subversion found themselves being challenged for reelection by Trump loyalists and, in the worst cases, subject to repeated death threats.

In an era of polarization, calcification, and close competition for control of the White House and Congress, there is a growing incentive for partisans to subvert elections if it helps them win. A faction of the Republican Party was clearly ready to do so in 2020. The challenge to American democracy is whether it will succeed in the future.

A POLARIZED PRESIDENCY

The idea of unity was central to Joe Biden's campaign. Unlike some of his Democratic rivals, Biden eschewed a politics of anger and campaigned as a "sober and conventional presence," as one news account put it. One Biden campaign ad said he intended to "lead," "unite," and "heal" America. When Trump left office, he famously said "We were not a regular administration." Biden appeared to promise a very regular administration.[2]

But the long-term tectonics of partisan polarization meant that Biden's message, however well meaning, was unlikely to resonate with his opponents. Democrats and Republicans increasingly differ in their views of presidents. Although it seemed as if Biden could reduce those differences, especially compared to a divisive figure like Trump, if anything the opposite occurred.

In fact, when Biden took office, Democrats and Republicans were more polarized in their views of him than of any president in seventy years, essentially since the beginning of modern polling. A Gallup poll conducted from January 21 to February 2, 2021, found that 98 percent of Democrats and 11 percent of Republicans approved of him—a gap of 87 points. This exceeded the partisan gap in approval when Trump took office, when there was a 76-point gap between Democrats and Republicans (14% vs. 90% approval, respectively). When Obama took office, the gap was 45 points (88% vs. 43%).[3] This meant that Biden took office with a relatively low approval rating of about 57 percent.

In his first weeks and months as president, Biden did seek to increase his popularity by promoting popular policies. This was a contrast with Trump, who, as we argued in chapter 2, focused his initial efforts on executive actions that were popular with Republicans but not Americans as a whole. But several of Biden's executive actions polled well overall and with significant numbers of Republicans: prohibiting workplace discrimination based on sexual orientation and gender identity (64% of Republicans favored this); requiring masks on federal property (54% of Republicans favored); continuing to suspend federal student loan repayments (46% of Republicans favored); and continuing a ban on evictions (49% of Republicans favored). Biden's signature legislative initiatives—a $1.9 trillion COVID relief package as well as an infrastructure plan—were also far more popular than Trump's, such as the 2017 tax cuts.[4]

Of course, Biden also did things that were popular with Americans overall but opposed by most Republicans. He restarted the Deferred Action for Childhood Arrivals program (opposed by 66% of Republicans). He rejoined the Paris climate agreement (opposed by 63%). He ended new wall construction at the U.S.-Mexico border (opposed by 80%). Thus, Biden's agenda was a mixture of broadly popular ideas and ideas that were mostly popular within his own party. But unlike Trump's, Biden's agenda was not as much dominated by purely partisan priorities.

Nevertheless, over Biden's first months in office, his approval rating dropped by about 10 points as he dealt with a series of crises and challenges: rising inflation, a chaotic withdrawal of U.S. troops from Afghanistan, and another surge in COVID-19 cases. But the partisan polarization in his approval rating persisted: in a November 2021 Gallup poll, 90 percent of Democrats and 6 percent of Republicans approved of the job he was doing—a gap of 84 points. Given how low his approval rating was at the start, the drop in Biden's approval took it to a level similar to Trump's at the same point in his presidency, despite Biden's attempts at a different style of leadership and efforts to enact some popular legislation.

After the election, some prominent Democrats argued that the best way for the party to move forward was to focus on policy proposals that polled well, an idea they called "popularism."[5] This would mean pushing ideas like COVID relief and abandoning ideas like "defund the police." That was probably reasonable advice, but it is not clear how much popularism affects a president's popularity in our current political environment. Just as Trump did not always become more unpopular when he did unpopular things, Biden did not become more popular when he did popular things. This is the logical consequence of both polarization and calcification for presidential approval ratings. It is not easy to change many people's view of the president.

THE VACCINE OR "YOUR FREEDOMS"

The new surge in COVID-19 cases that began in August 2021 showed that the pandemic would pose a challenge to Biden much as it had to Trump. But unlike Trump, Biden had a major new tool in the fight against the pandemic: the COVID-19 vaccines.

The vaccines arrived in December 2020 and were the culmination of Operation Warp Speed, the extraordinary effort to develop and produce COVID vaccines that the Trump administration had set in motion. It seemed, therefore, that vaccines offered a way out of the partisan polarization that characterized the pandemic. They were a way to fight COVID that Trump could take credit for and that avoided the restrictions on businesses and gatherings or the mask mandates that Trump and many Republicans opposed (see chapter 5).

But instead, the COVID vaccines became yet one more issue bound up with partisanship. This began, characteristically, with Trump himself. Initially, Trump did little to promote the vaccine. He was angry that it did not become available until after the election and he falsely accused the companies who made the vaccine and the Food and Drug Administration of purposely delaying it. And while Joe Biden and Kamala Harris received their vaccine shots on camera in December, Trump and his wife, Melania, did not disclose the fact that they were vaccinated before Trump left office. Only in March 2021 did this news become public, when a Trump adviser told CNN.[6]

Trump's public statements about the vaccine were equivocal, similar to his earlier statements about masks. At times, he spoke positively about the vaccine. In February 2021, he told attendees at the Conservative Political Action Conference "how unpainful that vaccine shot is, so everybody get your shot." In March, he said in a Fox News interview, "It's a great vaccine. It's a safe vaccine and it is something that works." In April, he told Fox's Sean Hannity, "I encourage people to take it, I do." In December, he said at a public event that he got a vaccine booster shot and said that the development of the vaccine was "historic."[7]

But in other public remarks, Trump sowed distrust in the vaccine or suggested that people had no obligation to get vaccinated. In a July 2021 statement, Trump criticized Biden's vaccine distribution and wrote that "people are refusing to take the Vaccine because they don't trust his Administration, they don't trust the Election results, and they certainly don't trust the Fake News, which is refusing to tell the truth." At an August 2021 rally in Alabama, Trump initially said, "I recommend take the vaccines. I did it. It's good. Take the vaccines." After some people booed, Trump then pivoted and said, "No, that's OK. That's all right. You got your freedoms. But I happened to take the vaccine. If it doesn't work, you'll be the first to know. OK? I'll call up Alabama, I'll say, hey you know what? But it is working. But you do have your freedoms you have to keep. You have to maintain that." Trump said the same thing in December, at almost the same time that he praised the vaccine in Dallas (where he was booed as well). In a separate interview, he said "Forget about the mandates, people have to have their freedoms."[8]

Trump's reticence about the vaccine encouraged his media allies to be skeptical. On Fox News, Laura Ingraham called Biden's plan to go door to door to promote the vaccine "creepy stuff." Tucker Carlson said that Biden wanted to "force people to take medicine they don't want or need." On a later episode, Carlson spoke out against university mandates that students get vaccinated: "They shouldn't get the shot. It's not good for them. There's a risk involved, much higher than that of COVID, but colleges are forcing them anyway."[9]

These messages from Trump and others mattered for public opinion. As we showed in chapter 5, citizens' views about the pandemic showed a "follow the leader" dynamic, whereby Democratic and Republican voters responded to what their party's leaders said about the risks of the virus and the measures needed to fight it.

Now, with Democratic leaders solidly supporting the vaccine but many Republican leaders equivocating or even spreading misinformation, there was a large partisan divide in whether people chose to get vaccinated. Almost a year after the vaccines became available, a December 12–14, 2021, YouGov/*Economist* poll found that 90 percent of Democrats said that they had gotten at least one shot of a COVID-19 vaccine but only 62 percent of Republicans said this. As of this writing, the majority of the unvaccinated population is Republican.[10]

Republican voters often echoed the claims about the vaccine that were promoted by conservative media figures and other skeptics. For example, a July 2021 YouGov poll asked which was the "greater risk," "possibly contracting COVID-19, or possibly having a bad reaction to the COVID-19 vaccine?" The vast majority of Democrats (74%) said contracting COVID. The majority of Republicans (54%) said that it was a reaction to the vaccine. When asked whether it was true that "the U.S. government is using the COVID-19 vaccine to microchip the population," 65 percent of Democrats but only 32 percent of Republicans said that this was "definitely false." Other polls found that far more Republicans than Democrats believed that pregnant women should not get the vaccines or that the vaccines would cause infertility.[11]

It was no surprise, then, that Republicans pushed back when Biden announced a policy that would require private businesses with at least 100 employees to vaccinate their employees or have employees take a weekly COVID test. In a September 2021 Morning Consult poll, only 33 percent of Republicans supported this move, compared to 80 percent of Democrats.[12] Ten Republican attorneys general filed suit to challenge the policy, and in January 2022 a majority of Supreme Court justices blocked this requirement.

Meanwhile, the need for a successful vaccination campaign became even more acute. New variants of the coronavirus continued to emerge, leading to successive waves of cases and deaths. And more and more, those deaths were occurring in Republican strongholds. The unwillingness of Trump, Fox News hosts, and some other party leaders to endorse vaccination wholeheartedly was not necessarily affecting these elites—after all, even Trump was vaccinated, as were 90 percent of Fox News employees. But ordinary Republicans who heard the equivocation and misinformation and then refused vaccination were paying the price, even with their lives.[13]

There was another ominous consequence to the Republican skepticism of COVID-19: their skepticism toward vaccines generally. In several states, Republican lawmakers sought to strike down vaccine mandates of any kind, including for routine polio and measles vaccines. Surveys showed growing gaps between Democrats and Republicans in their willingness to get a flu vaccine. And belief in perhaps the most pernicious vaccine myth of all—that they cause autism—was itself becoming more aligned with partisanship. Eight years earlier, when a July 2013 YouGov poll asked, "Do you think vaccines cause autism?" there was virtually no partisan difference: 11 percent of Democrats and 9 percent of Republicans said yes. But in July 2021, when a YouGov poll asked whether it was true or false that "vaccines have been shown to cause autism," the same small fraction of Democrats (11%) said it was "definitely" or "probably" true. But among Republicans, that fraction was significantly higher (27%).[14]

One insidious feature of partisan polarization in the United States is that it tends to metastasize. Issues that did not seem partisan at all suddenly become so, and specifically because party leaders promote diverging reactions among their voters. The Republican push against the COVID-19 vaccine risked making even routine public health guidance like the polio vaccine a battle between red and blue.

CRITICAL RACE

If there was another issue that needed Biden's pledge to unite and heal, it was race. This was the issue on which Trump's hard-line positions created extraordinary controversies. Consequently, this was the issue on which there was the most, and the most rapid, change among

Democrats, who shifted sharply to embrace more progressive positions on immigration and racial justice. Biden's own positions reflected the party's leftward shift, but at the same time he was more moderate than some in his party. This was visible in his rejection of certain progressive positions such as "defunding the police."

But even if Biden wanted greater unity, the growing differences between the parties on racial issues were not easily reversed. This was visible three months after Biden's inauguration at the trial of Derek Chauvin. On April 20, 2021, a unanimous jury convicted Chauvin of second-degree unintentional murder, third-degree murder, and second-degree manslaughter in the killing of George Floyd. But the broader reaction was anything but unanimous. In a CNN poll conducted after the verdict, almost all Democrats (97%) were satisfied with the verdict. Biden himself called it "a step forward." But only 53 percent of Republicans approved of the verdict. A number of Republican and conservative leaders sought to reprise the counternarrative in which the racial justice protesters were the threat. Florida governor Ron DeSantis said that "the jury is scared of what a mob may do." Tucker Carlson said the verdict was just the jury's way of saying, "Please don't hurt us."[15]

This response to the Chauvin verdict showed how issues related to race and criminal justice are increasingly divided along partisan lines, just like racial issues generally. It was not always this way. In 1992, after four Los Angeles police officers were acquitted in the beating of Rodney King, a May 1992 CBS/New York Times poll found that 71 percent of Republicans and 81 percent of Democrats disagreed with the verdict. But Republicans in particular have become much less sympathetic to claims of racial bias. For example, when George Zimmerman was acquitted of murder after killing an unarmed Black teenager, Trayvon Martin, in 2012, only 22 percent of Republicans were dissatisfied with the verdict, compared to 68 percent of Democrats.[16]

Other racial issues created political heat in the first months of Biden's presidency. One was how to teach about race and racism in schools. Conservatives targeted the 1619 Project, a 2019 New York Times series that emphasized the importance of slavery in the American founding (1619 was when the first enslaved Africans were brought to the thirteen colonies). The project attracted rebuttals from some historians, who argued that the series exaggerated the importance of slavery to those fighting for independence from Britain. Trump then created a 1776 Commission to support "patriotic education," whose January 2021 report attracted even broader criticism of its historical inaccuracies and political agenda. Conservatives also targeted the idea of critical race theory, a multifaceted body of academic work that grew out of legal studies in the 1970s and, generally speaking, argues that racism results not just from individual prejudice but also because it is embedded in U.S. institutions, laws, and culture. In 2021, states began to forbid the use of 1619 Project materials in public schools as well as the teaching of ideas linked to critical race theory.

Of course, it was hardly clear that any public school was teaching actual critical race theory. It was also unclear that many Americans were following these controversies closely. In a July 2021 Ipsos poll, only 16 percent of Americans said they were "very familiar" with critical race theory and 8 percent said they were very familiar with the 1619 Project (indeed, 58% said they had never heard of it.)

But Republicans and Democrats certainly differed on whether and how to teach about race. In this same poll, 85 percent of Democrats supported "teaching high school students about racism and its impact in the United States," compared to 58 percent of Republicans. The divide was even larger in terms of how many "strongly" supported this (66% of Democrats vs. 27% of Republicans). There was more support, and especially intense support, among Democrats.[17]

What underpins these debates about race—and what makes it so difficult to bridge partisan divides—is that Republicans and Democrats differ fundamentally in their beliefs about who experiences discrimination and thus how government should respond. This is evident in an April 2021 UCLA poll that asked people how much discrimination there was against a variety of racial, ethnic, religious, and gender groups in the United States (figure 9.1).

Democrats tended to perceive the most discrimination against Black Americans, Asian Americans, Muslim Americans, Latinos, women, and Jewish people. They believed that Christians, men, and white Americans

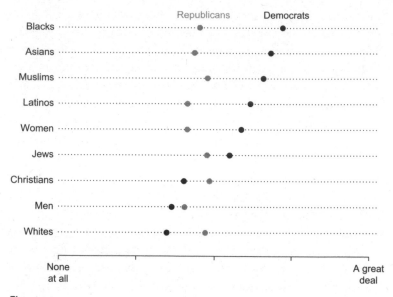

Figure 9.1.
Democratic and Republican Perceptions of Discrimination Experienced by Social Groups.
The dots represent the average on a five-point scale for Democrats and Republicans.
Source: UCLA COVID-19 Health and Politics Project, March 25–April 13, 2021.

experience relatively little discrimination. Republicans perceived things
much differently. Compared to Democrats, they perceived much less
discrimination against minority racial and ethnic groups and women.
Indeed, if anything, Republicans perceived a bit more discrimination
against white Americans than other racial groups, against Christians
than Muslims or Jews, and against men than women.

It is no surprise, then, that Democrats and Republicans disagree on
specific issues involving racial bias and racism, whether in policing, in
public school curricula, or elsewhere. Democrats tend to see a racial
order in which historically marginalized groups, like Black Americans,
continue to be marginalized. Republicans see a racial order in which
historically privileged groups, like white Americans, are now the real
victims.

When Biden gave his public remarks on the day of the Chauvin verdict, he talked about the work needed to mitigate racial disparities and

specifically "the work we do every day to change hearts and minds as well as laws and policies." But this work is difficult precisely because Americans' hearts and minds reflect fundamentally different conceptions of these disparities. To many Republicans, the problem Biden sought to address—racial discrimination against Black Americans—is not really a problem at all.

DENYING THE ELECTION, REWRITING THE INSURRECTION

After Biden's victory, it became all too clear that the country would continue to face many of the same national crises, especially the pandemic. But the 2020 election created a different kind of crisis as well: a crisis of democracy. The crisis involved a direct challenge to two bedrock principles of a functioning democracy: the willingness of the losers to respect the outcome of a fair election and to consent to a peaceful transfer of power.

Before Biden's victory, Trump said explicitly that he would challenge the election if he lost. He even refused to commit to a peaceful transfer of power, saying in September, "We're going to have to see what happens" because the mail-in ballots "are a disaster." Biden himself saw potential danger in Trump's comments, saying in August 2020 that he was worried about Trump screwing around with the election outcome. "When the hell have you heard a President say, 'I'm not sure I'll accept the outcome,'" Biden asked.[18]

Trump kept his promise. At 2:30 a.m. the morning after the election, Trump said, "This is a fraud on the American public." After Biden was declared the winner, Trump and his allies made a series of unsubstantiated claims alleging irregularities and voter fraud. They promoted baroque conspiracy theories such as "Italygate," in which Trump supporters alleged that a defense contractor in Rome had used satellites to switch votes from Trump to Biden. They filed dozens of lawsuits challenging voting procedures in multiple states. Virtually all of these were dismissed, often by Republican-appointed judges. One such judge, Matthew Brann, who presided over a case in U.S. District Court in Pennsylvania, described Trump's lawsuit as "strained legal arguments without merit and speculative accusations . . . unsupported by evidence."[19] A lawsuit brought by Texas attorney general Ken Paxson and seventeen other Republican attorneys general sought to overturn the electoral votes in four states and allow Trump to win. The Supreme Court refused to even hear it.

Trump and other administration officials also pressured the Department of Justice to investigate voter fraud. At one point, Trump chief of staff Mark Meadows unsuccessfully pushed the acting attorney general, Jeffrey Rosen, to investigate Italygate. Rosen was incredulous. Soon afterward, Trump threatened to replace him with a loyalist who would carry out his demands. Trump stood down after a dramatic Oval Office meeting in which DOJ and White House lawyers told Trump they would resign en masse if he did that.[20]

Trump pressured state lawmakers, too. He brought Michigan Republican officials to the White House. He called Brian Kemp, the governor of Georgia, and asked him to call a special session of the state legislature and override the results. He called Pennsylvania's speaker of the house. He called the Georgia secretary of state, Brad Raffensperger, and said, "I just want to find 11,780 votes," the number that would flip the state in Trump's favor. Trump allies held a conference call with Republican state legislators from Arizona, Michigan, Pennsylvania, and Wisconsin to argue that there was massive fraud and they should vote to decertify the results of the election in their states.[21]

Trump's inner circle also promoted the idea that that state legislatures had the constitutional authority to throw out slates of electors in states that Biden won and replace them with a pro-Trump slate. In this way, state legislatures would simply countermand the will of their state's electorate, again under the false idea that the outcome was tainted by fraud.[22]

Trump's pressure campaign continued all the way up until January 6, as his allies strategized about whether Mike Pence could change the result of the election, given his role in overseeing the certification of the election results in the Capitol that day. Trump told Pence, "You can either go down in history as a patriot, or you can go down in history as a pussy." Pence asked confidants, including former vice president Dan

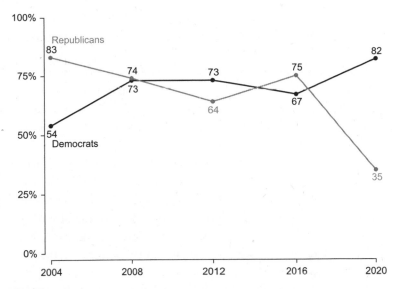

Figure 9.2.
Percent Confident That Their Vote Was Counted Accurately. *Source*: Pew polls compiled by Bowman and Goldstein, "Voices on the Vote."

Quayle, who was also from Indiana, if there was a way he could avoid certifying the results of the election. Quayle told him no. Pence ultimately did not accede to Trump's demands, unlike the many Republicans who voted not to certify the results. Pence also became the target of violent rhetoric at the insurrection, with some rioters chanting, "Hang Mike Pence!"[23]

The campaign to overturn the election created a persistent climate of distrust among Trump supporters. The week before the election, 62 percent of Trump voters were confident that the election would be conducted fairly and accurately, according to Nationscape surveys. That number fell to 29 percent the week after the election. This level of distrust was far greater than is typical for voters of the losing party. A survey conducted by the Pew Research Center found that only 35 percent of Trump voters were confident that their vote was counted—the lowest among voters of the losing party since 2004 (figure 9.2). Even a year later, a November 2021 Public Religion Research Institute poll found that 68 percent of Republicans agreed that the election had been stolen from Trump.[24]

Republicans' distrust of the election system was mirrored in their refusal to accept Biden as the legitimate president. In a December 2020 Suffolk University poll, 78 percent of Republicans said Biden was not the legitimate president. By contrast, immediately after the 2016 election, about 23 to 33 percent of Clinton voters said that Trump was not the legitimate president, depending on the poll. Even in 2004, when only a bare majority of Democrats said they were confident their vote had been counted accurately, 60 percent said he had "won fair and square," according to a Gallup poll.[25] In short, it is typical for voters in the losing party to have less confidence in the outcome and less support for the legitimacy of the winning candidate than do voters in that candidate's party. But the aftermath of 2020 was not typical.

Republican doubts about the election persisted well into Biden's first year in office. Even in November 2021, a Suffolk University poll found that 71 percent of Republicans still denied Biden's legitimacy. In a December 2021 University of Massachusetts poll, 74 percent of Republicans said that Biden's victory was "probably" or "definitely not legitimate." Among respondents who denied Biden's legitimacy, large majorities cited discredited claims about the election. For example, 83 percent said that fraudulent ballots had been counted and 81 percent said that absentee ballots from dead people had been counted.[26] All of this was the logical consequence of Trump's ongoing denials of and false claims about the election. By one count, lies about the election were the most prominent theme in Trump's public statements in the first half of 2021. Moreover, Trump-allied legislators in states such as Arizona and Wisconsin continued to "investigate" the 2020 election in search of fraud that they could not find.[27]

These investigations baffled even some local Republican leaders. In Wisconsin, one Republican legislator, Kathy Bernier, called the investigation, which was led by former Wisconsin Supreme Court justice Michael Gableman, "a charade." She also spoke ominously about the anger and potential violence that the investigation incited: "Mr. Gableman is coming to my county, and I will attend that meeting along with my concealed carry permit, to be perfectly honest. Because it keeps jazzing up the people who think they know what they're talking about—and they don't."[28]

The unwillingness of Trump and his allies to commit to a peaceful transfer of power was visible on January 6, both in their incitement of the crowd at the rally that preceded the insurrection and in Trump's reticence to call off the rioters that afternoon. Immediately afterward, it seemed like there might be a reckoning about the violence and the role of Trump and others in encouraging it. Trump's approval rating dropped sharply, by about 5 points, in the week following the riot. His support among Republicans weakened, too: in YouGov polls the percent of Republicans who "strongly" approved of him dropped from 64 percent to 47 percent. In a Civiqs poll, 90 percent of Republicans supported arresting the people who had breached the Capitol.[29]

But instead of a reckoning, there was appeasement and revisionism. Few Republican leaders supported any attempt to hold Trump accountable. When members of Congress moved quickly to a second impeachment proceeding against Trump—making him the first U.S. president to be impeached twice—many Republican elites stuck by Trump's side. Only ten House Republicans voted to impeach Trump and only seven Republican senators voted to convict him. This was a remarkable level of bipartisanship for an impeachment proceeding given historical precedents, but still, the vast majority of Republicans opposed it.

Soon afterward, Republicans deemed insufficiently loyal to Trump experienced consequences within the party. Both Mike Pence and Mitch McConnell—who had spoken out against Trump's attempt to subvert the election on the Senate floor right before the rioters broke in—saw their support among Republican voters plummet, even as Trump's did not.[30] House Republicans stripped Rep. Liz Cheney of Wyoming of her leadership position within the party because she was so critical of Trump's actions on January 6. She and other Republican critics also faced censure votes from the Republican Party organization in their states. The Wyoming Republican Party eventually voted not to recognize Cheney as a Republican at all.

There was also little GOP support for establishing a House committee to investigate the events of January 6. Only two Republicans—Cheney and Rep. Adam Kinzinger of Illinois—voted to create the committee. Almost no Republicans were interested in an investigation that might reveal even more damning details about their party's former president, or even their congressional colleagues.

Other Republican leaders sought to recast the events of that day entirely, arguing that the actions of the rioters were not serious. Republican representative Andrew Clyde of Georgia described the insurrection as "a normal tourist visit." On Fox News, Tucker Carlson echoed this sentiment, saying in September 2021 that the rioters "don't look like terrorists. They look like tourists." Carlson and others spread the false claim that the insurrection was the result of a government conspiracy to entrap Trump supporters. Other GOP leaders argued that the rioters should not face criminal sanction. Rep. Madison Cawthorn of North Carolina said that those who had been arrested were "political hostages." Donald Trump said that the rioters were "being persecuted so unfairly." In an October 2021 statement, Trump was even more direct: "The insurrection took place on November 3, Election Day. January 6 was the Protest!"[31]

The effects of these arguments were visible in public opinion. In a September 2021 Pew Research Center poll, the majority of Republicans (57%) said that too much attention had been paid to the January 6 riot (compared to 8% of Democrats). A July 2021 Civiqs poll found that the percentage of Republicans who supported arresting the rioters, which had been 90 percent in January, was now 55 percent. Unsurprisingly, there was a connection between denying Biden's victory and downplaying the insurrection. The Pew Research Center poll found that compared to Republicans who believed Biden won, Republicans who believed Trump had won the election were more likely to say that the rioters had been punished too severely.[32]

In one respect, it did not matter that fewer Republicans wanted to punish the rioters. For the rioters who were identified and arrested, their court proceedings continued, and many earned stiff sentences. The more serious possibility was that this attempt to rehabilitate the rioters and rewrite the history of the insurrection would only serve to justify attempts to overturn future elections, even violently. Indeed, between

October 2015 and December 2021, the percentage of Republicans who said that violent action against the government could be justified increased from 22 percent to 40 percent, even as there was no change among Democrats. And between 2017 and 2021, the percentage of Republicans who said that a military coup could be justified if there was a lot of corruption increased from 32 percent to 54 percent—a record level for either party. Of course, these survey questions are hypotheticals and do not tell us whether voters will support any real-life act of political violence. But what they do indicate is a substantial reservoir of potential support, especially among Republicans.[33]

THE CRISIS CONTINUES

When a political party loses a presidential election, there is typically hand-wringing and soul-searching. After the GOP loss in 2012, for example, the Republican National Committee commissioned a report called the "Growth and Opportunity Project" to diagnose the party's shortcomings.[34] In 2020, however, there was little soul-searching within the GOP. If anything, it was Democrats who were more concerned after a Biden landslide never materialized. The more prevalent response among Republican lawmakers was to pass new laws to address the things that Trump blamed for his defeat. In other words, Republicans were more interested in changing the rules than in changing how they played the game.

One part of this effort was passing new laws in many states that would restrict voting, and especially the mail-in balloting that Trump blamed for his loss. By one count, in the first six months of 2021 eighteen states passed thirty new laws that changed their voting regulations. Many laws imposed new limits on mail voting and early voting as well as new requirements for voter identification. Even more bills were introduced and pending. Perhaps the broadest and most restrictive bills were passed in the GOP-controlled battleground states of Arizona, Florida, and Georgia.[35]

There is no question that issues like voting by mail and voter identification at polling places were highly important not only for lawmakers but also for voters. From January 21 to February 3, 2021, we ran a separate "revealed importance" experiment to assess how Democrats and Republicans felt about these voting provisions alongside other issues, some of which were part of previous experiments (see, for example, chapters 3 and 6) and some of which were new to this survey.

The results showed that at this point in time, these voting provisions were important to people. Among Democrats, 80 percent supported voting by mail, and it was essentially tied for second in revealed importance along with several other issues. The only issue more important to Democrats at that point was impeaching Trump. Requiring proof of identification in order to vote, which 69 percent of Democrats also supported, ranked as significantly less important. Among Republicans, voting by mail and voter identification were both among the top issues, and most Republicans opposed voting by mail and favored voter identification. The importance of voting by mail to both parties shows once again that both parties tend to care a lot about the issues on which they disagree. (See the full results in figures A9.1 and A9.2.)

However, it was unclear how much changing these particular rules of the game would actually help Republican candidates win in the future. Studies of voter identification laws have not found consistent evidence that these laws keep people (of either party) from voting. A study of the expansion of mail balloting in 2020 did not find that it helped either party. In short, it is not obvious that changing election laws to make it easier to vote helps Democrats or hurts Republicans.[36]

More concerning to the preservation of democracy was the second part of the GOP effort to change the rules, which involved the sort of tactics visible in Spalding County. In a number of states, Republican lawmakers proposed or passed laws that sought to insert state legislatures into election administration at the expense of the executive branch or traditionally professional and nonpartisan administrators. For example, another part of Georgia's law removed the secretary of state from the state election board, a provision that targeted Brad Raffensperger for his refusal to back Trump's effort to "find" more votes. In three pivotal states—Arizona, Georgia, and Nevada—lawmakers introduced bills that would give the state legislature the final say over certifying election results. This again was targeted at incumbent Republican governors, such as Brian Kemp and Arizona's Doug Ducey, who, like Raffensperger, would not go along with Trump's campaign to overturn the results in their state. There were 148 bills along these lines introduced in thirty-six states, according to an April 2021 report by the group Protect Democracy.[37]

Supporters of Trump's election fraud claims also began running for political office. One initial count identified 163 Republicans running in 2022 who embraced Trump's claims, including candidates for governor, the U.S. Senate, and the U.S. House of Representatives, as well as offices like attorney general and secretary of state, which would give them significant authority over the state's election procedures if they won. The candidates for secretary of state included Rep. Jody Hice in Georgia, who voted not to certify Biden's election, and state representative Mark Finchem in Arizona, who attended a "Stop the Steal" rally before the insurrection. In fact, ten of the fifteen Republican candidates for secretary of state in Arizona, Georgia, Michigan, Nevada, and Wisconsin had said that the 2020 election was stolen or called for more investigation of their state's results, according to a systematic review by Reuters. Simultaneously, Trump supporters began to encourage like-minded people to be local election workers. Finchem said, "The only way you're going to see that this doesn't happen again is if you get involved. Become a precinct committeeman."[38]

State and local election administrators faced another threat after the 2020 election: violence. In April 2021, four months after Trump pushed Brad Raffensperger to find votes, Raffensperger's wife, Tricia, received text messages saying, "We plan for the death of you and your family every day" and "You and your family will be killed very slowly." These were just two examples of the threats they received. Brian Kemp received threats as well, as did Georgia elections director Chris Harvey, Georgia state legislators, and a number of local election officials and poll workers. For example, two Fulton County poll workers, Wandrea "Shaye" Moss and Ruby Freeman, who were targeted explicitly by Trump and his allies, reported multiple threats. One was awoken in December 2021 by loud banging at her door and had to call 911. The other changed her appearance and avoided going out in public. Trump supporters even threatened her teenage son. There were many stories like this across the country. Indeed, one survey of local election officials found that 17 percent had been threatened and 33 percent felt unsafe.[39]

Of course, it is not certain that these restrictive voting bills will pass, or that candidates who deny the legitimacy of the 2020 election will win, or that death threats will drive devoted public servants from their jobs. But these factors create the growing risk that a fraudulent effort like Trump's will succeed and actually steal a future election. In a close election, it would only take legislative majorities in a few states to overturn the outcome.

CONCLUSION

One of the U.S. Capitol Police officers on duty on January 6 was a man named Anton. Like many of the officers, he was traumatized by what he had experienced but remained on the job for several months after he and other officers had been violently attacked. He described driving to the Capitol with a sense of dread and trying to muster the strength to get out of his car and go to work. He would repeat a phrase his mother, a devout Christian, had taught him: "May we pass every test."[40]

The aftermath of the 2020 election was its own test—a test for American democracy. It is an open question whether the country passed. On the one hand, Trump's attempts to subvert the outcome failed. Members of the institutions designed to counter the unlawful use of executive power—including Congress, the courts, and state governments—pushed back. On the other hand, Trump's attempted subversion produced a durable belief in the illegitimacy of the election and, more importantly, a concerted effort to make subversion easier the next time by leveraging the same institutions, such as state governments, that served as a bulwark in 2020.[41]

There is a broader test for American democracy as well, and it will outlast Trump's own political career. The factors important to the story of 2020—the tectonic polarization of the parties, the identity shock that oriented partisan conflict around issues like immigration and civil rights, and the importance of those issues to both Democrats and

Republicans—only make democratic subversion more tempting. Polarization creates an incentive for partisans to countenance undemocratic behavior by the party they favor. The farther apart the parties are on issues that voters care about, the harder it becomes to envision life under the opposition. Moreover, divides on issues related to identity are particularly difficult to bridge as they touch on the very question of who deserves full membership in the national community.[42]

The calcified politics that results from these divides is difficult to change. It withstood the extraordinary events of 2020, including a global pandemic, a massive racial justice movement, and a direct attack on the U.S. Capitol. It derives in part from clear differences between what the Democratic and Republican parties stand for and from voters' increasing ability to perceive those differences and to know which side they prefer. It subsumes new issues—as it did with COVID-19—so that they fail to transcend partisanship and instead merely reinforce current divides.

What can change calcified patterns is losing elections. When one party suffers badly enough at the ballot box, it will often moderate on the issues that it blames for its losses. This can mitigate divides between the parties. In an era of partisan parity, however, neither party loses badly enough or for a long enough period of time to bring about this type of change. And if the next election offers the real promise of controlling Congress or the White House without changing course, there is little incentive for the losing side to do so. The Republican Party after the 2020 election is a case in point.[43]

But even so, election subversion is not inevitable. Political leaders can limit any zeal for overturning fair outcomes and for postelection violence. It was not that long ago that Mitt Romney and Hillary Clinton promptly conceded their defeats in presidential elections, after all. What candidates choose to do and say in defeat affects how voters react.[44] After the 2020 election, Trump's choice was clear, and plenty of people in his party were willing to follow along.

How well American democracy meets its current challenge depends on what leaders choose to do in the future. At this moment, the leaders who lose may be just as important as those who win.

May we pass this test.

APPENDIXES

APPENDIX TO CHAPTER 1

The Nationscape survey project was led by Lynn Vavreck and Chris Tausanovitch of the Department of Political Science at UCLA, in collaboration with the Democracy Fund Voter Study Group. Approximately 6,250 respondents were interviewed each week from July 10, 2019, until January 18, 2021, producing a total sample size of 494,796 American adults. In addition, three "parallel" surveys of 10,000 respondents, each containing some novel instrumentation, were conducted April 2–11, 2020, July 15–25, 2020, and January 21–February 3, 2021.

Nationscape samples were provided by Lucid, a market research platform that runs an online exchange for survey respondents. The Nationscape samples drawn from this exchange matched an initial set of demographic quotas on age, gender, ethnicity, region, income, and education. Respondents were then sent from Lucid directly to survey software operated by the Nationscape team. All respondents took the survey online and completed an attention check before taking the survey. The survey was conducted in English.

The survey data was then weighted to be representative of the American population. The weights were generated using a simple raking technique, as there is little benefit to more complicated approaches.[1] One set of weights was generated for each week's survey. The targets to which Nationscape was weighted were derived from the adult population of the 2017 American Community Survey of the U.S. Census Bureau. The one exception was the 2016 presidential vote, which was derived from the official election results released by the Federal Election Commission. The survey was weighted on the following factors: gender, the four major Census regions, race, Hispanic ethnicity, household income, education, age, language spoken at home, nativity (U.S.- or foreign-born), 2016 presidential vote, and the urban-rural mix of the respondent's ZIP code. The survey was also weighted on the following interactions: Hispanic ethnicity by language spoken at home, education by gender, gender by race, race by Hispanic origin, race by education, and Hispanic origin by education.

In an initial investigation of this methodology, we compared the results from a Nationscape pilot study to benchmarks from high-quality government surveys. In particular, we sought to determine whether Nationscape came as close to these benchmarks as online samples previously evaluated by the Pew Research Center, all of which also rely on nonprobability sampling combined with sample matching, quotas, and/or weighting to achieve representativeness. In addition, we compared Nationscape's performance to results from the Pew Research Center's American Trends Panel, which is recruited via probability sampling. The median absolute difference between Nationscape estimates and the set of government benchmarks was 3.5 percentage points, which was comparable to the performance of both the other nonprobability samples and the American Trends Panel.[2]

CONJOINT EXPERIMENT

Each survey contained an embedded experiment designed to measure the importance that respondents attach to various policies. Earlier in the survey, respondents were asked whether they agreed or disagreed with forty-four policies, such as "Cap carbon emissions to combat climate change." They were also asked their opinion on eight other considerations, such as whether to impeach Donald Trump and the importance of electing a woman or a gay man as president.

Later, respondents reached a section with the following prompt:

You are almost done! For the last exercise we are going to show you two sets of outcomes—we call them A and B. We want you to choose the one that you prefer.

We realize that neither set may perfectly reflect your preferences. If this happens just pick the set that comes closest to your views even if it isn't perfect. Assume the only difference between set A and B are the things listed on the page—everything else is the same.

This was followed by ten questions. In each question, respondents were presented with two sets and asked, "Given this choice, which one would you prefer?" The sets were composed of between two and four policies, randomly drawn from the policies asked previously. One set is chosen at random to contain the policy exactly as stated before, for example, "Cap carbon emissions to combat climate change." And the other one always contains its negation: "Do not cap carbon emissions to combat climate change." Because the policies are drawn at random from a list of that included the forty-four public policies and the eight other considerations, very few sets looked the same. Here is an example of a set with three policies:

Given this choice, which one would you prefer?

Set A	Set B
Do not cap carbon emissions to combat climate change	Cap carbon emissions to combat climate change
Do not deport all undocumented immigrants	Deport all undocumented immigrants
Do not allow the display of the Ten Commandments in public schools and courthouses	Allow the display of the Ten Commandments in public schools and courthouses

○ Set A

○ Set B

This experiment gives us purchase on how much people care about each of these policies. Imagine that a respondent agreed that carbon

TABLE A1.1. Revealed Importance of Issues in 2019

Issue	Revealed importance	Standard error
Impeach Donald Trump	0.326	0.005
Ban all guns	0.313	0.003
Ban assault rifles	0.302	0.003
Deport all undocumented immigrants	0.299	0.003
Build wall on southern US border	0.294	0.005
Never permit abortion	0.272	0.003
Create path to citizenship for undocumented immigrants brought here as children	0.270	0.003
Require background checks for all gun purchases	0.265	0.005
Separate children from their parents when parents can be prosecuted for illegal entry into the US	0.261	0.005
Create a path to citizenship for all undocumented immigrants	0.252	0.003
Ensure that all students can graduate from state colleges debt free	0.242	0.005
Permit abortion in cases other than rape, incest, or when the woman's life is in danger	0.240	0.003
Provide government-run health insurance to all Americans	0.238	0.003
Limit gun magazines to 10 bullets	0.232	0.003
Raise minimum wage to $15/hour	0.232	0.005
Grant reparations payments to the descendants of slaves	0.231	0.005
Legalize marijuana	0.226	0.005
Subsidize health insurance for lower income people not receiving Medicare or Medicaid	0.222	0.003
Ban people from predominantly Muslim countries from entering the United States	0.220	0.005
Allow transgender people to serve in military	0.213	0.005
Enact Medicare for All	0.207	0.005
Allow display of Ten Commandments in public schools and courthouses	0.205	0.005
Guarantee jobs for all Americans	0.197	0.005
Cap carbon emissions to combat climate change	0.196	0.005
Reduce the size of the US military	0.196	0.005
Raise taxes on families making over $600,000	0.195	0.003
Require companies to provide 12 weeks of paid maternity leave for employees	0.194	0.005

TABLE A1.1. (*continued*)

Issue	Revealed importance	Standard error
Provide the option to purchase government-run health insurance to all Americans	0.184	0.003
Cut taxes for families making less than $100,000 per year	0.183	0.003
Create a public government registry of gun ownership	0.180	0.005
Withdraw military support for the state of Israel	0.178	0.005
Make a large-scale investment in technology to protect the environment	0.178	0.005
Permit late term abortion	0.172	0.004
Enact a Green New Deal	0.172	0.005
Require a waiting period and ultrasound before an abortion can be obtained	0.160	0.005
Allow employers to decline coverage of abortions in insurance plans	0.157	0.005
Raise taxes on families making over $250,000	0.154	0.005
Require proof of citizenship or legal residence to wire money to another country from the US	0.145	0.005
Provide tax-funded vouchers to be used for private or religious schools	0.123	0.005
Remove barriers to domestic oil and gas drilling	0.120	0.005
Limit trade with other countries	0.110	0.005
Eliminate the estate tax	0.110	0.003
Allow people to work in unionized workplaces without paying union dues	0.109	0.005
Shift from a more family-based to a more merit-based immigration system	0.072	0.006

Source: Democracy Fund + UCLA Nationscape surveys (July–December 2019).

emissions should be capped and that display of the Ten Commandments should be allowed in schools and courthouses, but does not think that all undocumented immigrants should be deported. In this case, the respondent has a choice to make. Set A contains the respondent's position on deportation; set B contains the respondent's positions on carbon emissions and the Ten Commandments. The respondent's choice thus provides a sense of how much he or she prioritizes these policies. Across the roughly 500,000 respondents, each answering ten of these questions, there are over five million choices in total.

We can use this data to estimate how important each policy is to all respondents combined as well as to supporters and opponents of the policy. The "revealed importance" of each policy captures how much the inclusion of that policy in a set of policies increases the chance that respondents chose that set. Higher values mean that respondents attach more importance to that policy.

Table A1.1 presents the revealed importance of all issues in the 2019 surveys, averaging across all respondents, including both supporters and opponents. (A subset of these results is graphed in figure 1.4). The exact question wording is provided in the first column, along with estimates of revealed importance and their associated standard errors.

APPENDIX TO CHAPTER 2

To measure the productivity of Trump and the Republican Congress, we relied on data collected by political scientist Sarah Binder.[1] Binder measures productivity (versus gridlock) by first identifying issues on the public agenda. This is based on issues mentioned in unsigned *New York Times* editorials since 1947. These editorials are used to supply a consistent source for what issues are salient. In 2017–18, the size of the agenda (twenty-nine salient issues) was about the historical average, and many of the issues discussed in these editorials were what Trump was trying to address, such as immigration and infrastructure. Then the question is what percent of those issues saw successful legislative action (i.e., a bill passed and signed into law).

Based on this measure, 62 percent of these salient national issues saw no successful legislative action in 2017–18 (figure A2.1). A lack of success is not uncommon even under unified government, as earlier episodes make clear. But Trump and congressional Republicans struggled far more than average, and certainly more than did Obama and congressional Democrats in the first two years of Obama's presidency. Ultimately, when Republicans controlled the White House and Congress in 2017–18 they made relatively little progress addressing issues on the national agenda.

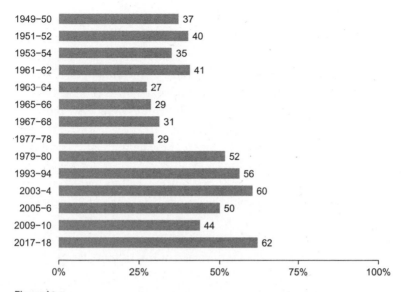

Figure A2.1.
Percent of Salient Public Agenda Issues without Successful Legislative Action in Periods of Unified Government. *Source*: Sarah Binder.

APPENDIX TO CHAPTER 3

FORECASTING MODELS OF THE PRESIDENTIAL ELECTION

The statistical models of presidential election outcomes are based on the eighteen elections between 1948 and 2016. For each election, we calculated the incumbent party's percent of the major-party vote—that is, the votes received by the Democratic and Republican candidates, leaving aside any third-party or independent candidates. The key factors in these models are:

- The change in gross domestic product between the first and third quarters of the election year. This is calculated as: $\ln(\text{GDP}_t) - \ln(\text{GDP}_{t-2})$. The GDP data was obtained from the St. Louis Federal Reserve's FRED database (the variable GDPC1).[1]

- The president's approval rating as of June of the election year. This data was originally collected by George Edwards and Gary Jacobson. We updated the data to include all polling on Barack Obama's approval rating, as compiled by the Huffington Post's Pollster, and Donald Trump's approval rating, as compiled by FiveThirtyEight. If there were multiple polls in June, we took the average.
- A dichotomous variable for whether the incumbent president was running for reelection (1948, 1956, 1964, 1972, 1976, 1980, 1984, 1992, 1996, 2004, and 2012). This variable is important mainly in interaction with the change in GDP and presidential approval.
- A dichotomous variable for whether the incumbent party had held the White House for one term or two or more terms ("incumbent tenure").[2]

In calculating a forecast for 2020, we used the estimate of GDP growth (1.2 percentage points of nonannualized growth from the first to the third quarters of 2020) and Trump's observed approval rating of 41 percent. We estimated each model using the Clarify statistical package, generating 1,000 simulated values of the coefficients, thereby taking into account their underlying uncertainty.[3] We also generated an estimate of the model's overall error, using the standard error of the regression multiplied by a random draw from a t-distribution with degrees of freedom equal to those in the model. Multiplying by this value from the t-distribution has the effect of adding uncertainty to the prediction because the t-distribution has greater dispersion than a standard normal distribution.

Using these values for the independent variables, coefficients, and errors, we generated 1,000 predicted outcomes and the associated 95 percent confidence interval. Table A3.1 shows the coefficients and standard errors from the models discussed in the text as well as the associated forecast.

TABLE A3.1. Aggregate Models of 1948–2016 Presidential Election Outcomes and Associated Forecasts

	Model 1	Model 2	Model 3
Presidential approval rating (June)	0.27* [0.06]	0.16 [0.08]	0.20* [0.05]
Growth in GDP (Q1–Q3)	1.57* [0.55]	1.08 [1.09]	1.74* [0.44]
Approval × incumbent running		0.14 [0.11]	
GDP × incumbent running		0.34 [1.24]	
Incumbent running		−4.83 [5.11]	
Incumbent tenure			−3.62* [1.15]
Constant	36.64* [2.62]	40.60* [3.95]	45.30* [3.45]
Adjusted R-squared	0.73	0.77	0.83
Forecasted share for incumbent party	49.7	50.1	51.9%
95% confidence interval for forecast	[44.6, 54.7]	[45.5, 54.8]	[47.7, 56.2]

Coefficients and standard errors are from least squares regression models. The dependent variable is the incumbent party's percent of the major party vote ($N = 18$). * $p < 0.05$.

Model 1 shows the well-established impact of both GDP growth and presidential approval on election outcomes. The associated forecast shows a very narrow loss in the national popular vote for the incumbent party (the Republicans), who are expected to win 49.7 percent of the major-party vote.

Model 2 shows that the impact of presidential approval and GDP appears larger when the incumbent is running. To be sure, these effects are not estimated very precisely, given the small sample of elections here, and this lack of precision of course adds uncertainty to any forecast. But the magnitude of the coefficients—especially for presidential approval—suggests that these two factors matter more when the actual incumbent is on the ballot. Because those factors pushed in opposite directions as of early 2020—the economy helping Trump, but his low approval rating hurting him—the forecasted vote share is very similar to the first model (50.1%).

Finally, the third model shows that incumbent tenure is associated with a lower vote share, as previous work has also found. This benefits a president who has served only one term and creates a more optimistic forecast for Trump (a 51.9% vote share).

APPENDIX TO CHAPTER 4

THE CLYBURN ENDORSEMENT AND BIDEN SUPPORT IN SOUTH CAROLINA

To estimate the apparent impact of Rep. James Clyburn's endorsement of Joe Biden, we leveraged a poll conducted by Data for Progress that was in the field for February 23–27, 2020. Clyburn's endorsement was public on the morning of February 26, so we consider anyone interviewed on February 26–27 to be interviewed after the endorsement was made ($N = 1,048$ were interviewed before and $N = 414$ were interviewed after).

For both white and Black respondents who intended to vote in the Democratic primary, we regressed their support for Biden (coded $1 =$ Biden and $0 =$ another candidate) on whether they were interviewed after the endorsement, whether they identified as a Democrat (versus Republican, independent, or something else), their age, their gender, and whether they had a college degree.

The results (table A4.1) show that Black respondents interviewed after Clyburn's endorsement were no more likely to support Biden. If anything, white respondents interviewed after the endorsement were a little less likely to support Biden. (As in other surveys and states, Biden does better among both white and Black respondents who are older or identify as a Democrat.) In a separate analysis (not shown), we also found no differences in Biden's favorability rating among Black respondents based on when they were interviewed.

TABLE A4.1. Models of Support for Biden among Likely South Carolina Democratic Primary Voters

	White voters	Black voters
Interviewed after Clyburn endorsement	−0.40	−0.003
	(0.23)	(0.26)
Democrat	0.70	0.63
	(0.20)	(0.25)
Age 30 to 39	4.49	0.83
	(2.87)	(0.58)
Age 40 to 49	3.65	0.55
	(2.90)	(0.55)
Age 50 to 59	5.05	1.40
	(2.86)	(0.52)
Age 60 to 69	5.59	1.31
	(2.85)	(0.51)
Age 70+	5.52	3.35
	(2.85)	(0.61)
Female	0.21	0.11
	(0.20)	(0.21)
College graduate	0.13	−0.30
	(0.22)	(0.20)
Constant	−8.66	−1.73
	(2.85)	(0.55)
N	1,023	218

Cell entries are logit coefficients with standard errors in parentheses. The dependent variables are coded 1 for those who intended to vote for Biden and 0 otherwise.

Source. Data for Progress poll conducted among likely Democratic primary voters in South Carolina, February 23–27, 2020.

STABILITY AND CHANGE IN DEMOCRATIC PRIMARY VOTING BEHAVIOR

Two different survey projects shed light on the candidates' coalitions in the 2016 and 2020 primaries. Both surveys interviewed the same respondents in both elections, allowing us to track changes between 2016 and 2020 with greater precision than if two separate groups of respondents had been interviewed.

The Views of the Electoral Research (VOTER) Survey asked people their vote in the 2016 primary in July of that year and then reinterviewed people in both December 2019 and September 2020 and asked about the 2020 primary. The December 2019 interview captured vote intentions among likely Democratic primary voters prior to the start of the caucuses and primaries. The September 2020 interview captured vote choice among people who reported voting in a caucus or primary.

The second survey, the University of Pennsylvania's Institute for the Study of Citizens and Politics (ISCAP) Survey, interviewed the same group of Democrats and independents who lean toward the Democratic Party in both January 2016 and January 2020. This survey shows how those who intended to vote for Sanders or Clinton in 2016 intended to vote at the start of the 2020 primaries.

Table A4.2 reports the relationship between 2016 primary vote choice and either pre-primary vote intentions or post-primary vote choice in the 2020 Democratic primary. These results show that the 2016 candidate coalitions were initially divided among the 2020 candidates as of pre-primary interviews in December 2019 or January 2020. After the primaries were over, the results show that most 2016 Clinton voters voted for Biden while 2016 Sanders voters were divided among the 2020 candidates.

One consequence of Biden's gains and the winnowing of the field is that some voters who had intended to vote for a different candidate as of late 2019 had to choose between Biden and Sanders. Many of them ended up voting for Biden. For example, Warren voters broke nearly evenly between the two: 26 percent of early Warren supporters ended up voting for Biden (versus 22% for Sanders). Biden did better with Buttigieg supporters, winning about a third of early Buttigieg supporters and 16 percent of early Sanders supporters.

Table A4.3 reports the relationship between vote intentions and vote choice in the Democratic primary. This is based on interviews with self-reported Democratic primary voters from November 22 to December 23, 2019, and from August 28 to September 28, 2020, that were conducted as part of the VOTER Survey. Panel A reports the results for all respondents and Panel B reports the results for respondents in states that held a primary or caucus before Bernie Sanders dropped out and Biden became the de facto nominee.

TABLE A4.2. Voting Behavior in the 2016 and 2020 Presidential Primaries

A. Vote Intention

	Dec. 2019 vote intention, VOTER Survey (Percent)				Jan. 2020 vote intention, ISCAP Survey (Percent)	
	Clinton 2016 voter	Sanders 2016 voter	Voted in 2016 GOP primary	Did not vote in 2016	Clinton Jan. 2016 supporter	Sanders Jan. 2016 supporter
Warren	14.5	32.0	1.1	5.6	23.4	14.0
Biden	36.5	7.3	1.7	12.5	39.9	14.8
Sanders	6.1	20.2	0.7	7.0	6.1	32.7
Buttigieg	9.7	11.7	1.1	4.1	6.6	9.8
Klobuchar	2.7	1.4	0.3	1.0	2.7	4.6
Bloomberg	3.2	2.4	0.7	0.9	9.0	11.3
Other candidate	14.0	8.1	4.2	6.0	11.7	12.3
Not sure	8.6	7.7	2.2	9.7		
Will not vote in a primary	1.7	4.8	6.5	33.0		
Will vote in GOP primary	3.1	4.5	81.6	20.3		
Sample size	907	688	1,438	1,163	252	149

B. Vote Choice (September 2020 Interview, VOTER Survey)

	Clinton 2016 voter	Sanders 2016 voter	Voted in GOP primary	Did not vote in a primary
Warren	9.7	18.0	0.2	3.1
Biden	61.8	22.0	3.2	13.1
Sanders	5.9	33.5	1.1	3.6
Buttigieg	8.5	5.0	0.6	1.6
Klobuchar	1.9	1.4	1.0	0.5
Bloomberg	2.3	1.1	0.9	0.8
Other candidate	1.6	2.3	0.5	0.5
Not sure	1.8	1.0	0.1	3.0
Did not vote in a primary	3.5	12.9	13.5	54.7
Voted in GOP primary	2.8	3.0	78.9	19.0
Sample size	812	619	1,276	991

Cell entries are column percentages (e.g., the percent of 2016 Clinton voters who voted for Biden). VOTER Survey questions were asked of all respondents. ISCAP survey questions were asked only of respondents who identified as Democrat or independent-leaning Democrat.

TABLE A4.3. Democratic Primary Voting Behavior, December 2019 versus September 2020

A. All Respondents

Dec. 2019 intention	2020 vote choice (Percent)								
	Warren	Biden	Sanders	Buttigieg	Klobuchar	Bloomberg	Other	Not sure	Did not vote
Warren	31.9	26.1	21.8	0.9	0.8	1.8	0.2	2.4	11.8
Biden	2.5	65.1	6.0	0.7	0.8	2.0	0.8	1.4	16.9
Sanders	6.2	15.7	54.8	0.1	0.4	0.6	0.0	2.8	18.7
Buttigieg	5.3	33.5	10.7	27.2	1.1	1.0	0.3	0.6	15.4
Klobuchar	8.0	32.0	7.5	1.7	23.0	2.1	1.9	0.9	10.4
Bloomberg	0.5	23.6	14.4	1.8	1.6	26.2	2.9	0.0	23.4
Other	6.5	28.8	9.1	2.8	3.4	4.2	5.8	2.1	26.1
Not sure	6.3	25.3	5.4	5.0	1.2	1.3	1.1	6.3	37.7
Wouldn't vote	1.4	4.9	4.0	0.7	0.6	1.2	0.1	1.5	72.8

B. Respondents in States That Held a Primary or Caucus before Sanders Dropped Out (April 8)

Dec. 2019 intention	2020 vote choice (Percent)								
	Warren	Biden	Sanders	Buttigieg	Klobuchar	Bloomberg	Other	Not sure	Did not vote
Warren	35.4	19.6	23.2	1.5	0.9	2.8	0.3	3.5	9.2
Biden	0.8	62.3	7.5	1.0	0.6	2.7	0.2	1.8	18.5
Sanders	8.7	14.1	55.0	0.0	0.5	0.9	0.0	2.4	17.6
Buttigieg	4.9	28.7	6.0	35.0	1.1	1.1	0.4	0.5	15.2
Klobuchar	5.3	28.1	9.6	1.1	20.3	2.7	2.4	1.1	13.3
Bloomberg	0.8	11.4	14.5	2.8	1.1	32.0	0.0	0.0	35.3
Other	7.5	24.2	9.6	2.7	4.1	5.9	6.3	2.4	25.9
Not sure	6.7	19.6	3.7	4.3	1.9	1.8	0.6	7.6	44.0
Wouldn't vote	1.3	4.3	3.8	0.0	1.0	0.5	0.0	1.0	71.4

Cell entries are row percentages.

Source: VOTER Survey.

These results show patterns of movement among the same set of respondents, and especially how Biden accrued support not only among those who initially intended to vote for him but also among supporters of many other candidates. For example, even when Sanders was still in the race, Biden won almost as many of Warren's initial supporters (19.6% of whom reported voting for Biden) as did Sanders (23.2% reported voting for Sanders).

POLICY ATTITUDES AMONG DEMOCRATIC PRIMARY VOTERS AND REPUBLICANS

Table A4.4 presents a list of all of the policy questions regularly included in the Nationscape surveys as well as the percent who agree with that policy among supporters of Elizabeth Warren, Bernie Sanders, and Joe Biden. Policy views among Republican respondents are provided as a contrast. The percent who agree is calculated as a percentage of those who agreed, disagreed, or had no opinion. In general, these results show a high degree of consensus among supporters of these Democratic candidates, especially when compared to Republicans.

MODELS OF DEMOCRATIC PRIMARY VOTING BEHAVIOR

To conduct a direct test of the relationship between policy differences and voting in the primaries, we draw on the Nationscape and VOTER Survey projects, each of which has its own strengths and weaknesses. The Nationscape data has the extensive set of policy questions, including on topics like Medicare for All, that were directly relevant to the 2020 primary. We combined these questions into an overall index of "policy liberalism."

However, Nationscape cannot address a perennial chicken-and-egg question: do voters' policy views lead them to choose a like-minded candidate, or do voters choose a candidate for other reasons and then adjust their policy views to match the candidate's? For example, a voter who had already decided to support Warren could then decide to support taxing the wealthy because they were persuaded by her plan for a

TABLE A4.4. Policy Attitudes among Warren, Sanders, and Biden Supporters and among Republicans

	Percent who agree with the policy			
	Warren supporters	Sanders supporters	Biden supporters	Republicans
Abortion				
Never permit abortion	8	13	12	29
Permit abortion in cases other than rape, incest, or when the woman's life is in danger	82	72	72	44
Require a waiting period and ultrasound before an abortion can be obtained	21	30	31	52
Allow employers to decline coverage of abortions in insurance plans	16	21	26	55
Permit late-term abortion	42	36	29	13
Permit abortion at any time	40	33	28	13
Immigration				
Deport all undocumented immigrants	13	17	19	57
Create a path to citizenship for undocumented immigrants brought here as children	90	85	84	59
Separate children from their parents when parents can be prosecuted for illegal entry into the United States	8	9	8	35
Build a wall on the southern border	9	11	13	72
Create a path to citizenship for all undocumented immigrants	77	74	68	36
Require proof of citizenship or legal residence to wire money to another country from the United States	33	37	44	68
Shift from a more family-based to a more merit-based immigration system	23	29	29	47
Ban people from predominantly Muslim countries from entering the United States	8	11	14	33
Charge immigrants who enter the United States illegally with a federal crime	18	21	24	64
Healthcare				
Subsidize health insurance for lower-income people not receiving Medicare or Medicaid	85	79	80	50
Provide government-run health insurance to all Americans	76	80	64	30

	Percent who agree with the policy			
	Warren supporters	Sanders supporters	Biden supporters	Republicans
Healthcare				
Provide the option to purchase government-run insurance to all Americans	81	73	75	48
Enact Medicare for All	73	80	59	29
Abolish private health insurance and replace with government-run health insurance	48	53	30	16
Guns				
Ban assault rifles	86	69	81	43
Require background checks for all gun purchases	95	92	94	86
Limit gun magazines to ten bullets	77	61	72	38
Ban all guns	31	29	30	10
Create a public government registry of gun ownership	77	72	75	42
Environment				
Cap carbon emissions to combat climate change	89	78	79	44
Make a large-scale investment in technology to protect the environment	86	77	77	48
Remove barriers to domestic oil and gas drilling	18	26	28	49
Enact a Green New Deal	69	59	50	20
Taxes				
Raise taxes on families making over $600,000	86	78	79	49
Cut taxes for families making less than $100,000	82	80	80	70
Raise taxes on families making over $250,000	64	61	59	33
Eliminate estate tax	37	40	47	62
Labor				
Raise the minimum wage to $15/hour	85	82	78	39
Require companies to provide twelve weeks of paid maternity leave for employees	85	85	78	56
Guarantee jobs for all Americans	67	77	70	48
Allow people to work in unionized workplaces without paying union dues	38	44	41	45

Continued on next page

	Percent who agree with the policy			
	Warren supporters	Sanders supporters	Biden supporters	Republicans
Civil Rights/Liberties				
Legalize marijuana	74	77	61	48
Allow transgender people to serve in the military	86	80	75	41
Allow the display of the Ten Commandments in public schools and courthouses	32	37	48	74
Grant reparations payments to the descendants of slaves	42	42	36	10
Education				
Ensure that all students can graduate from state colleges debt free	79	86	72	40
Provide tax-funded vouchers to be used for private or religious schools	21	30	32	38
Trump				
Impeach President Trump	83	79	79	11
Foreign Policy				
Withdraw military support for the state of Israel	35	35	27	18
Limit trade with other countries	15	19	18	32
Impose trade tariffs on Chinese goods	24	25	28	56
Reduce the size of the U.S. military	37	37	20	10

Cell entries are the percent who agree with the policy (versus opposing the policy or having no opinion). Warren, Sanders, and Biden supporters are likely Democratic primary voters who indicated a preference for the candidate. Republicans include independents who lean Republican.

Source: 2019 Democracy Fund + UCLA Nationscape surveys.

wealth tax. Because Nationscape surveys were all conducted in 2019 and 2020, the estimates of the effects of policy views could be inflated if voters changed their policy views to match those of their preferred candidate.[1]

One way to avoid this issue is to rely on measures of policy views that predate the 2020 campaign and cannot be affected by the campaign itself. The VOTER and ISCAP surveys allow this because both interviewed the same respondents several times over multiple years and thus have relevant measures of policy views from earlier interviews, as well as questions about voting in the 2016 and 2020 Democratic primaries. This allows for comparisons between the two primaries as well as a test of policy-driven voting that helps determine whether prior policy views actually affected primary voting. This helps deal with the chicken-and-egg problem, although it entails the additional assumption that people did not change their views since they were measured in the earlier interview. Both surveys' policy questions are more limited, however. In the VOTER Survey, we constructed an index of policy positions from 2011 on four issues: whether to expand Obamacare, raise taxes on the wealthy, provide government health insurance to all Americans, and have more or less government regulation of business (alpha = 0.89). In the ISCAP survey, we constructed an index of policy positions in October 2012 on two issues: a seven-point scale capturing whether respondents favored increasing or decreasing government services and spending, and a seven-point scale capturing whether respondents favored keeping or repealing the 2010 health care law (alpha = 0.70). These survey questions were certainly relevant to the Democratic primaries in 2016 and 2020 but did not speak to the details of every policy debate among the candidates.

First, we present results from the VOTER Survey (table A4.5). Each dependent variable is measured as a dichotomy (e.g., reported voting for Clinton versus Sanders). In the 2016 primary, the dependent variable is self-reported vote choice as of a July 2020 interview. In the 2020 primary, the dependent variables are (1) vote intentions among self-reported likely Democratic voters as of the November–December 2019 interview and (2) self-reported vote choice measured in the September 2020 interview.

TABLE A4.5. Models of 2019 Democratic Primary Vote Intention or 2020 Primary Vote Choice (VOTER Survey)

A. Models with Attitudinal Variables Measured in December 2011

	Clinton vs. Sanders	Biden vs. Sanders		Biden vs. Warren		Sanders vs. Warren	
		2019	2020	2019	2020	2019	2020
Economic policy views	−0.05	−0.80	−0.02	−1.92	−1.60	−1.02	−1.26
	(0.18)	(0.43)	(0.33)	(0.38)	(0.45)	(0.43)	(0.46)
Liberal identification	−0.77	−1.69	−0.78	−1.48	−1.00	0.22	−0.28
	(0.12)	(0.30)	(0.24)	(0.24)	(0.24)	(0.26)	(0.28)
Democratic partisanship	1.40	1.30	1.30	0.73	0.75	−0.55	−0.45
	(0.12)	(0.27)	(0.22)	(0.22)	(0.23)	(0.25)	(0.26)
Age	1.53	4.15	3.76	3.32	2.86	−0.57	−0.93
	(0.22)	(0.56)	(0.46)	(0.45)	(0.48)	(0.51)	(0.56)
Male	−0.12	0.01	−0.27	0.21	0.23	0.34	0.59
	(0.07)	(0.19)	(0.13)	(0.15)	(0.16)	(0.17)	(0.19)
African American	1.04	0.78	0.37	1.07	0.91	0.23	0.55
	(0.13)	(0.27)	(0.23)	(0.21)	(0.27)	(0.29)	(0.32)
Hispanic American	0.73	0.04	0.09	0.4	0.16	0.28	0.01
	(0.18)	(0.37)	(0.34)	(0.32)	(0.36)	(0.37)	(0.43)
Asian American	0.78	−0.92	−0.52	−0.23	−0.39	0.55	0.01
	(0.30)	(0.53)	(0.52)	(0.50)	(0.53)	(0.44)	(0.54)
Another race	0.24	−0.43	−0.48	0.12	−0.07	0.47	0.29
	(0.19)	(0.38)	(0.31)	(0.35)	(0.37)	(0.34)	(0.39)
Constant	−1.49	−1.23	−1.51	−0.49	0.55	0.46	1.73
	(0.20)	(0.44)	(0.35)	(0.38)	(0.43)	(0.42)	(0.46)
N	2,889	786	1,143	998	1,096	652	543

B. Models with Attitudinal Variables Measured in November 2016

	Clinton vs. Sanders	Biden vs. Sanders		Biden vs. Warren		Sanders vs. Warren	
		2019	2020	2019	2020	2019	2020
Economic policy views	0.23	−1.24	−0.21	−1.95	−2.43	−0.84	−1.51
	(0.20)	(0.47)	(0.35)	(0.41)	(0.52)	(0.47)	(0.52)
Liberal identification	−1.16	−1.77	−1.19	−1.62	−1.37	0.36	0.03
	(0.12)	(0.29)	(0.22)	(0.24)	(0.24)	(0.25)	(0.27)
Democratic partisanship	2.05	1.65	1.68	0.67	1.18	−1.22	−0.91
	(0.14)	(0.27)	(0.23)	(0.24)	(0.26)	(0.25)	(0.26)

TABLE A4.5. *(continued)*

B. Models with Attitudinal Variables Measured in November 2016

	Clinton vs. Sanders	Biden vs. Sanders		Biden vs. Warren		Sanders vs. Warren	
		2019	2020	2019	2020	2019	2020
Age	1.33	4.01	3.61	3.09	2.81	−0.51	−1.05
	(0.23)	(0.57)	(0.46)	(0.45)	(0.48)	(0.52)	(0.56)
Male	−0.13	−0.12	−0.28	0.13	0.16	0.31	0.53
	(0.07)	(0.19)	(0.13)	(0.15)	(0.16)	(0.18)	(0.18)
African American	1.03	0.73	0.29	1.14	0.89	0.35	0.63
	(0.13)	(0.27)	(0.23)	(0.21)	(0.27)	(0.30)	(0.32)
Hispanic American	0.70	−0.1	−0.01	0.35	0.02	0.29	0.2
	(0.19)	(0.38)	(0.35)	(0.32)	(0.37)	(0.38)	(0.44)
Asian American	0.90	−1.17	−0.51	−0.22	−0.37	0.67	0.1
	(0.31)	(0.54)	(0.53)	(0.52)	(0.55)	(0.45)	(0.55)
Another race	0.32	−0.36	−0.44	0.05	−0.11	0.36	0.25
	(0.20)	(0.39)	(0.32)	(0.36)	(0.37)	(0.35)	(0.39)
Constant	1.97	−0.89	−1.39	−0.15	1 18	0.72	2.27
	(0.22)	(0.47)	(0.38)	(0.41)	(0.50)	(0.47)	(0.55)
N	2,889	786	1,143	998	1,096	652	543

Cell entries are logit coefficients with standard errors in parentheses. Dependent variables are coded so that the first candidate is coded 1 and the second 0 (e.g., for "Clinton vs. Sanders," Clinton is 1 and Sanders is 0). In the 2019 models, the dependent variables are vote intentions among likely Democratic primary voters. In the 2020 models, the dependent variables are primary vote choices among those who reported voting in a Democratic primary.
Source: VOTER Survey.

The independent variables are coded in this fashion:

- Economic liberalism is a scale combining three questions: "Do you favor raising taxes on families with incomes over $200,000 per year?"; "Do you think it is the responsibility of the federal government to see to it that everyone has health care coverage?"; and "In general, do you think there is too much or too little regulation of business by the government?"
- Liberal identification is based on respondent's self-reported identification on a five-category scale ranging from very liberal to very conservative. This is coded 1 = very liberal, 0.5 = liberal, and 0 = moderate, conservative, or no opinion.

- Democratic partisanship is based on respondent's self-reported identification on a seven-category scale ranging from strong Democrat to strong Republican. It is coded 1 = strong Democrat, 0.67 = weak Democrat, 0.33 = independent-leaning Democrat, and 0 = independent, Republican, or something else.
- Age is based on respondents' self-reported birth year, subtracted from 2016 or 2020, and rescaled to the 0–1 interval.
- Male is coded 1 = male and 0 = female (the survey did not include codes for other gender identities).
- A series of dichotomous variables captures racial identification, where those who identified as white non-Hispanic are the excluded category in the regression model.

Panel A reports results using covariates measured in December 2011. In 2016, the 2011 policy index had no relationship to voting for Clinton versus Sanders. The same was true in 2020: primary voters' 2011 economic views had no relationship to voting for Biden versus Sanders. If anything, there was more evidence of a relationship between policy views and voting for Warren. Liberal primary voters were more likely to support Warren than Biden or Sanders.

Panel B reports results using covariates measured in December 2016. The results are similar in both sets of models, although generally the relationships between voting behavior and economic policy views, liberal identification, and Democratic partisanship are stronger using the 2016 covariates than the 2011 covariates. This makes sense given their closer proximity to the 2019 and 2020 survey interviews. Models using the ISCAP Survey panel produce similar results to models of the VOTER Survey data (table A4.6). In the ISCAP Survey models, the dependent variables are vote intention among self-reported Democrats in January 2016 and January 2020 interviews. Economic policy attitudes are not significantly associated with voting for Biden versus Sanders, but are for Biden versus Warren. The effect of these attitudes in the Sanders-versus-Warren model is also in the same direction—more liberal voters were more likely to vote for Warren than Sanders—but the effect is not estimated as precisely.

The third set of models presented are based on Nationscape surveys. These models were drawn on the surveys conducted from the pre-primary

TABLE A4.6. Models of 2020 Democratic Primary Vote Intention (ISCAP Survey)

	Clinton vs. Sanders	Biden vs. Sanders	Biden vs. Warren	Sanders vs. Warren
Economic policy views	−0.35	−0.82	−2.20	−1.17
	(0.45)	(0.85)	(0.89)	(0.92)
Liberal identification	−0.39	−1.09	−0.60	−0.02
	(0.28)	(0.54)	(0.52)	(0.59)
Democratic partisanship	1.50	0.79	0.94	0.23
	(0.31)	(0.55)	(0.52)	(0.63)
Age	0.01	0.04	0.02	−0.02
	(0.01)	(0.01)	(0.01)	(0.01)
Male	0.03	−0.09	−0.52	−0.71
	(0.17)	(0.31)	(0.30)	(0.36)
African American	0.92	1.29	0.98	−0.39
	(0.23)	(0.45)	(0.38)	(0.54)
Hispanic American	0.56	−0.17	0.08	0.22
	(0.27)	(0.43)	(0.43)	(0.49)
Another race	0.39	−0.89	−0.52	0.28
	(0.30)	(0.57)	(0.57)	(0.53)
Constant	−1.06	−0.80	0.84	1.75
	(0.39)	(0.67)	(0.73)	(0.77)
N	657	252	252	160

Cell entries are logit coefficients with standard errors in parentheses. Dependent variables are coded so that the first candidate is coded 1 and the second 0 (e.g., for "Clinton vs. Sanders," Clinton is 1 and Sanders is 0). The dependent variables are vote intentions among self-identified Democrats.

Source: ISCAP Survey.

period (July 2019–January 2020) to capture vote intention and the post-primary period (July 2020–January 2021) to capture self-reported vote choice. The models are similar to those estimated in the VOTER Survey, except that the policy liberalism measure encompasses more than economic policy. This measure was constructed from fifty policy questions from the main policy module included on the Nationscape survey. Twenty of these policy questions were asked to every respondent and the rest were asked at random. The scale is constructed using a standard item response model that treats ideology as a latent trait. We use a quadratic utility model that is estimated with expectation maximization (EM) as implemented by the R software package gpuideal.[2] Respondents were then sorted in order of their scale value and given a score

TABLE A4.7. Models of 2020 Primary Vote Choice (Nationscape Surveys)

	Biden vs. Sanders		Biden vs. Warren		Sanders vs. Warren	
	2019	2020	2019	2020	2019	2020
Policy liberalism	−1.23	−1.77	−1.77	−1.88	−0.50	0.04
	(0.05)	(0.05)	(0.06)	(0.08)	(0.06)	(0.08)
Ideological identification	−0.99	−1.50	−1.75	−1.94	−0.53	−0.22
	(0.05)	(0.05)	(0.06)	(0.07)	(0.06)	(0.08)
Democratic partisanship	0.75	1.40	0.24	0.87	−0.76	−0.70
	(0.03)	(0.03)	(0.04)	(0.05)	(0.04)	(0.05)
Age	4.19	2.74	1.12	0.89	−3.25	−2.17
	(0.06)	(0.06)	(0.06)	(0.08)	(0.07)	(0.09)
Male	−0.19	0.02	0.13	0.28	0.33	0.27
	(0.02)	(0.02)	(0.02)	(0.03)	(0.02)	(0.04)
Black American	0.37	0.57	0.86	0.80	0.42	0.18
	(0.03)	(0.03)	(0.03)	(0.05)	(0.04)	(0.06)
Hispanic American	−0.18	0.08	0.23	0.39	0.42	0.31
	(0.03)	(0.03)	(0.04)	(0.05)	(0.03)	(0.05)
Asian American	0.09	−0.05	0.07	0.02	−0.03	0.1
	(0.05)	(0.05)	(0.06)	(0.07)	(0.06)	(0.07)
Another race	−0.12	−0.15	0.26	0.14	0.42	0.34
	(0.06)	(0.06)	(0.08)	(0.09)	(0.07)	(0.10)
Constant	−0.20	1.39	2.14	3.51	2.39	2.07
	(0.05)	(0.05)	(0.06)	(0.08)	(0.06)	(0.08)
N	44,774	57,073	34,871	48,058	34,679	19,239

Cell entries are logit coefficients with standard errors in parentheses. Dependent variables are coded so that the first candidate is coded 1 and the second 0 (e.g., for "Biden vs. Sanders," Biden is 1 and Sanders is 0). In the 2019 models, the dependent variables are vote intentions among likely Democratic primary voters. In the 2020 models, the dependent variables are primary vote choices among those who reported voting in a Democratic primary.

Source: Democracy Fund + UCLA Nationscape surveys.

equal to their observed quantile of their ideal point in this sorted distribution of ideal points. The resulting scale is constructed to run from 0 (the most conservative respondent) to 1 (the most liberal).

This measure of policy liberalism was related to primary voting behavior in 2020, and in the predictable direction: more liberal policy attitudes were associated with a lower chance of voting for Biden (table A4.7). However, the magnitude of this relationship was modest. For example, a strong liberal, defined here as someone at the 95th percentile

TABLE A4.8 Attributes of Likely Democratic Primary Voters, by Race or Ethnicity (Percent)

	White	Black	Hispanic	Asian	Another race
Percent intending to vote for Biden	29	42	24	28	25
Average age	50.4	47.2	42.0	45.7	39.9
Party identification					
Strong Democrat	50	64	50	35	46
Weak Democrat	27	23	32	41	28
Leaning Democrat	13	8	10	15	17
Independent or GOP	10	5	8	9	10
Ideological identification					
Very liberal	19	14	18	11	20
Liberal	35	26	27	32	32
Moderate	35	40	38	43	36
Conservative	7	9	8	7	6
Very conservative	2	4	2	2	1
Unsure	3	8	7	4	5
Average policy view (0–1 scale where 1 = most liberal)	0.68	0.66	0.66	0.67	0.72
Sample size	38,445	13,077	12,080	3,088	1,260

Sample is limited to respondents who intended to vote in a Democratic presidential primary or caucus.
Source: 2019 Democracy Fund + UCLA Nationscape surveys.

on the scale among Democratic primary voters, was only about 10 points less likely to vote for Biden (vs. Sanders) than someone at the 50th percentile (i.e., the median Democratic primary voter).

RACIAL AND ETHNIC DIFFERENCES IN DEMOCRATIC PRIMARY VOTING BEHAVIOR

Table A4.8 presents the distribution of different demographic and political characteristics among Democratic primary voters of different races or ethnicities. These show that Black primary voters in particular tended to have the characteristics that were associated with voting for Biden.

Table A4.9 presents the models that underlie figure 4.9. These models are identical to the vote choice models in table A4.7, except that

TABLE A4.9. Models of 2020 Primary Vote Choice, by Racial or Ethnic Group

A. Models of Biden vs. Sanders Vote

	White	Black	Hispanic	Asian American
Policy views scale	−1.76	−1.34	−2.04	−1.98
	(0.07)	(0.12)	(0.10)	(0.20)
Ideological identification	−1.86	−0.74	−1.25	−1.55
	(0.07)	(0.12)	(0.10)	(0.22)
Democratic partisanship	1.66	1.24	0.99	1.04
	(0.04)	(0.08)	(0.07)	(0.14)
Age	2.81	2.75	2.59	2.78
	(0.07)	(0.16)	(0.16)	(0.26)
Male	0.05	−0.16	0.13	−0.16
	(0.03)	(0.06)	(0.05)	(0.09)
Constant	1.42	1.37	1.77	1.83
	(0.06)	(0.11)	(0.10)	(0.20)
N	32,194	10,702	9,755	2,845

B. Models of Biden vs. Warren Vote

	White	Black	Hispanic	Asian American
Policy views scale	−2.36	−1.10	−0.76	−1.77
	(0.10)	(0.21)	(0.17)	(0.31)
Ideological identification	−2.19	−0.75	−1.57	−1.99
	(0.10)	(0.19)	(0.18)	(0.33)
Democratic partisanship	0.86	1.07	1.11	0.52
	(0.06)	(0.14)	(0.11)	(0.22)
Age	1.17	0.85	−0.25	−0.08
	(0.10)	(0.24)	(0.24)	(0.34)
Male	0.37	0.11	−0.03	0.38
	(0.04)	(0.10)	(0.08)	(0.14)
Constant	3.92	2.89	3.08	3.96
	(0.10)	(0.19)	(0.17)	(0.32)
N	27,652	9,528	7,505	2,178

Cell entries are logit coefficients with standard errors in parentheses. Dependent variables are coded so that Biden vote choice is coded 1 and Sanders or Warren is coded 0.

Source: Democracy Fund + UCLA Nationscape surveys.

they are estimated separately for different racial or ethnic groups. Figure 4.9 presents the shift in the probability of a Biden vote associated with a shift between the 10th and 90th percentiles in the policy views scale and the minimum and maximum values of ideological identification.

THE ROLE OF SEXISM IN DEMOCRATIC PRIMARY VOTING BEHAVIOR

Figure 4.11 presents the relationship between a measure of gender attitudes called "modern sexism" and vote choice in the 2016 and 2020 Democratic primaries. This is based on models using the VOTER Survey data. The independent variables in these models are all measured in the 2016 wave and are constructed in the way described earlier (for table A4.5). These models also include an index of modern sexism that is based on agreement or disagreement with five statements (alpha = 0.78):

- "When women demand equality these days, they are actually seeking special favors."
- "Women often miss out on good jobs because of discrimination."
- "Women who complain about harassment cause more problems than they solve."
- "Sexual harassment against women in the workplace is no longer a problem in the United States."
- "Increased opportunities for women have significantly improved the quality of life in the United States."

Table A4.10 presents the results of the models. In Panel A, the measure of modern sexism is from the November 2016 wave, which allows us to compare its effect in both the 2016 and 2020 primaries. Panel B replicates these models for the 2020 primary, using a later measure of modern sexism in the November 2018 wave. Both sets of results suggest a larger correlation between sexism and voting for Biden or Sanders versus Warren, compared to Biden versus Sanders.

TABLE A4.10. Models of 2020 Primary Vote Choice, including a Sexism Measure

A. Models with Modern Sexism Measured in November 2016

	Clinton vs. Sanders	Biden vs. Warren	Biden vs. Sanders	Sanders vs. Warren
Modern sexism (2016)	−0.48	−2.75	−0.93	−3.07
	(0.26)	(0.62)	(0.43)	(0.67)
Policy liberalism	−0.12	0.96	−0.3	0.16
	(0.20)	(0.46)	(0.36)	(0.52)
Ideological identification	−0.82	0.83	−0.84	0.18
	(0.13)	(0.25)	(0.24)	(0.29)
Democratic partisanship	1.39	−0.73	1.35	0.48
	(0.12)	(0.24)	(0.22)	(0.27)
Age	1.61	−3.04	3.86	1.09
	(0.23)	(0.49)	(0.47)	(0.58)
Male	−0.24	−0.08	−0.26	−0.32
	(0.08)	(0.17)	(0.16)	(0.20)
Black American	1.02	−0.88	0.45	−0.45
	(0.13)	(0.27)	(0.23)	(0.33)
Hispanic American	0.69	−0.23	0.14	−0.16
	(0.19)	(0.38)	(0.36)	(0.46)
Asian American	0.83	0.44	−0.50	−0.03
	(0.30)	(0.54)	(0.53)	(0.56)
Another race	0.19	0.10	−0.44	−0.32
	(0.19)	(0.38)	(0.31)	(0.40)
Constant	−1.31	0.46	−1.20	−0.55
	(0.23)	(0.47)	(0.40)	(0.52)
N	2,837	1,072	1,119	535

B. Models with Modern Sexism Measured in November 2018

	Biden vs. Warren	Biden vs. Sanders	Sanders vs. Warren
Modern sexism (2018)	−2.06	−1.07	−2.64
	(0.63)	(0.44)	(0.66)
Policy liberalism	1.36	−0.26	0.60
	(0.48)	(0.36)	(0.52)
Ideological identification	0.81	−0.85	0.15
	(0.26)	(0.25)	(0.30)
Democratic partisanship	−0.79	1.29	0.39
	(0.25)	(0.23)	(0.28)

TABLE A4.10. (*continued*)

B. Models with Modern Sexism Measured in November 2018

	Biden vs. Warren	Biden vs. Sanders	Sanders vs. Warren
Age	−2.92	3.65	0.85
	(0.51)	(0.49)	(0.60)
Male	−0.14	−0.21	−0.36
	(0.17)	(0.16)	(0.20)
Black American	−0.82	0.44	−0.45
	(0.28)	(0.25)	(0.35)
Hispanic American	−0.11	0.19	0.09
	(0.37)	(0.37)	(0.46)
Asian American	0.32	−0.34	0.13
	(0.55)	(0.54)	(0.58)
Another race	0.02	−0.49	−0.42
	(0.41)	(0.32)	(0.42)
Constant	0.02	−1.08	0.79
	(0.50)	(0.41)	(0.54)
N	997	1,039	498

Cell entries are logit coefficients with standard errors in parentheses. Dependent variables are coded so that the first candidate is coded 1 and the second 0 (e.g., for "Clinton vs. Sanders," Clinton is 1 and Sanders is 0). The dependent variables are primary vote choices among those who reported voting in a Democratic primary.

Source: VOTER Survey.

APPENDIX TO CHAPTER 6

MODELS OF CHANGE IN RACIAL ATTITUDES, 2016–20

To examine the correlates of changing racial attitudes between 2016 and 2020, we draw on two data sets: the December 2016 and September 2020 waves of the Views of the Electoral Research (VOTER) Survey as well as the 2016 and 2020 waves of the American National Election Study (ANES) panel survey. In each survey, we calculated how much respondents who participated in both waves changed their attitudes on three dimensions: their views of racial inequality, their feelings toward Black Lives Matter, and their feelings toward police. Views of racial inequality were measured with the four questions noted in chapter 6. These were scaled into a single index range from 0 to 1, where higher values indicate a stronger belief that racial inequality is due to individual-level factors (like Black Americans not trying hard enough) as opposed to structural factors (like the legacy of slavery). Feelings toward Black Lives Matter and the police were measured with feeling thermometers that ranged from 0 to 100, where 0 equals very cool or unfavorable feelings and 100 equals very warm or favorable feelings. We rescaled those measures to range from 0 to 1 as well. Then we subtracted 2016 scores from 2020 to create measures of change that could range from −1 to +1.

We modeled those changes as a function of several characteristics measured in 2016: their favorability toward Donald Trump (a feeling thermometer in the ANES; a four-category favorability measure in the VOTER Survey), party identification, ideological identification, age, gender, and education level.

Table A6.1 presents these results, which show that the most consistent correlate of attitude change was feelings toward Trump. In particular, the less positively people felt toward Trump, the larger the shift toward a liberal position on racial inequality, a more favorable view of Black Lives Matter, and a less favorable view of police.

MODELS OF RACIAL ATTITUDES AND RACIAL JUSTICE PROTESTS

To examine the relationship between racial justice protests and racial attitudes, we merged the protest data from the Crowd Counting Consortium (see figure 6.4) with weekly Nationscape surveys. Specifically, we matched each respondent in the survey to the number of protests that took place in their county in each of the three weeks before and after their interview. Our analysis focuses on two questions in the Nationscape surveys: favorability to the police (measured with a four-category scale) and perceptions of discrimination against Black people (measured with a five-category scale ranging from "none" to "a great deal").

The models include a set of individual-level controls for age, education, race or ethnicity, gender, Hispanic identification, party identification, and the interaction between race and education. The models also

TABLE A6.1. Models of Changes in Racial Attitudes, 2016–20

	Views of racial inequality		Feelings toward Black Lives Matter		Feelings toward police	
	ANES	VOTER	ANES	VOTER	ANES	VOTER
Feelings toward Trump	0.075	0.070	−0.117	−0.129	0.053	0.085
	(0.019)	(0.011)	(0.025)	(0.017)	(0.020)	(0.013)
Party identification	−0.029	0.019	−0.02	−0.063	−0.008	−0.011
	(0.021)	(0.015)	(0.028)	(0.022)	(0.022)	(0.017)
Ideological identification	0.006	−0.021	0.001	−0.008	0.054	0.070
	(0.028)	(0.018)	(0.038)	(0.028)	(0.030)	(0.021)
Male	0.005	−0.018	−0.003	0.046	0.004	0.077
	(0.010)	(0.019)	(0.013)	(0.030)	(0.010)	(0.023)
Age in years	0.007	0.007	−0.073	0.011	0.054	0.004
	(0.020)	(0.006)	(0.027)	(0.010)	(0.021)	(0.008)
Education	−0.031	−0.027	0.009	−0.005	−0.012	−0.048
	(0.017)	(0.012)	(0.023)	(0.019)	(0.018)	(0.015)
Constant	−0.064	−0.041	0.120	0.097	−0.106	−0.124
	(0.017)	(0.016)	(0.022)	(0.024)	(0.017)	(0.019)
N	1,989	2,543	1,983	2,543	1,997	2,543

Cell entries are least squares regression coefficients with standard errors in parentheses. Dependent variables are the change in the dependent variable between the 2016 and 2020 waves of interviewing. Values of the dependent variables could range between −1 and +1. All independent variables are measured in the 2016 wave and range between 0 and 1.

Sources: 2016–20 American National Election Panel Survey and September 2020 VOTER Survey.

include fixed effects for respondents' county of residence and for the week of the respondent's interview (since each survey wave took place over a week). The first set of fixed effects account for characteristics of counties that may themselves be correlated with whether a racial justice protest took place at all. The second set of fixed effects accounts for the potential for attitudes to change over time, regardless of where respondents lived.

The results did not show clear evidence that respondents in counties that saw protest activity had different attitudes than those in counties that did not (table A6.2). In auxiliary models (not shown), we explored alternative ways of coding the protest variables, including using the number of protests in a county, rather than whether any protest took

TABLE A6.2. Models of the Effects of Local Social Justice Protests

	Favorability toward the police	Perceptions of discrimination against Black people
Protest 1–7 days before interview	3.246 (1.763)	0.004 (0.008)
Protest 8–14 days before interview	0.875 (1.786)	0.007 (0.008)
Protest 15–21 days before interview	−3.068 (1.778)	0.0004 (0.008)
Individual-level controls	Yes	Yes
County fixed effects	Yes	Yes
Survey wave fixed effects	Yes	Yes
N	458,764	459,569

Cell entries are least squares regression coefficients, with standard errors in parentheses. The dependent variables are coded so that higher values indicate more favorable views of the police and perceptions of greater discrimination against Black people.

Source: Crowd Counting Consortium and Democracy Fund + UCLA Nationscape surveys.

place, as well as coding protests by whether some combination of property damage or police injuries (or neither) took place. None of these alternative codings produced evidence of consistent correlations between protest activity and attitudes.

APPENDIX TO CHAPTER 8

INDIVIDUAL-LEVEL STABILITY AND CHANGE IN VOTE CHOICE, 2012–20

We use three surveys to compare how voting behavior in one election is correlated with voting behavior in the subsequent election. All three surveys interviewed the same respondents across two or more elections between 2012 and 2020. The central limitation is that these surveys rely on voters' reports of whether they voted, and some people likely reported voting when they did not. The surveys are thus not well suited to assess voter turnout, including the surge in turnout between 2016 and 2020. But the surveys' data does shed light on what fraction of the same

TABLE A8.1. Trends in Candidate Preferences

A. VOTER Survey (cell entries are row percentages)

	2016 vote			
	Hillary Clinton	Donald Trump	Other candidate	Did not vote
2012 vote				
Barack Obama	81%	9%	4%	6%
Mitt Romney	5	84	6	5
Other candidate	25	38	34	3
Did not vote	20	21	4	56

	2020 vote			
	Joe Biden	Donald Trump	Other candidate	Did not vote
2016 vote				
Hillary Clinton	95%	2%	1%	1%
Donald Trump	2	94	1	3
Other candidate	37	41	19	2
Did not vote	36	23	< 1	41

B. ISCAP Survey (cell entries are row percentages)

	2016 vote			
	Hillary Clinton	Donald Trump	Other candidate	Did not support anyone
2012 vote				
Barack Obama	78%	8%	8%	5%
Mitt Romney	7	76	12	5
Other candidate	28	20	36	16
Did not vote	25	29	9	37

	2020 vote intention			
	Joe Biden	Donald Trump	Other candidate	Would not vote
2016 vote				
Hillary Clinton	93%	2%	3%	2%
Donald Trump	8	91	0	1
Other candidate	19	46	17	17
Did not support anyone	18	35	3	44

Continued on next page

TABLE A8.1. (*continued*)

Panel C. ANES (cell entries are row percentages)

	2020 vote			
	Joe Biden	Donald Trump	Other candidate	Did not vote
2016 vote				
Hillary Clinton	82%	3%	2%	13%
Donald Trump	6	78	2	14
Other candidate	45	27	9	18
Did not vote	24	17	2	58

Note: VOTER Surveys were conducted in November 2012, November 29–December 29, 2016, and November 16–December 7, 2020, elections ($N = 8,005$ in both 2012 and 2016; $N = 3,343$ in both 2016 and 2020). ISCAP surveys were conducted in November 2012, November 11–December 15, 2016, and October 7–22, 2020 ($N = 1,043$ in both 2012 and 2016; $N = 794$ in both 2016 and 2020). The post-2016 ISCAP survey asked who you supported in the presidential election but not whether you voted. The 2020 ISCAP survey took place preelection and asked who you would support if the election were held today. The 2016 and 2020 ANES were conducted November 9, 2016–January 8, 2017, and November 8, 2020–January 4, 2021, respectively ($N = 2,670$ in both 2016 and 2020).

voters report voting consistently for one party's candidate as opposed to switching between candidates.

One such survey is the Views of the Electoral Research (VOTER) Survey. We use interviews conducted in the month or so after the 2012, 2016, and 2020 elections. These are the results reported in the text and they are presented in panel A of table A8.1.

Panel B of table A8.1 shows the trends from 2012 to 2016 and from 2016 to 2020 among respondents in the University of Pennsylvania's Institute for the Study of Citizens and Politics (ISCAP) survey (see the appendix to chapter 4). This survey differed from the VOTER Survey in two respects. First, it did not ask whether people voted but simply whom they supported, if anyone. Second, the 2020 interview occurred in October rather than after the election. Thus, we can only compare vote choice in 2016 to vote intentions in 2020. Despite those differences, the ISCAP data tells a similar story about stability: the number of respondents who stuck with the same party in two consecutive elections was much higher from 2016 to 2020 than from 2012 to 2016. However, the ISCAP survey does suggest that any switching benefited Biden more than Trump. About 8 percent of 2016 Trump voters reported voting for Biden, while only 2 percent of Clinton voters voted for Trump in 2020.[1]

Panel C of table A8.1 draws on the American National Election Study (ANES), which interviewed the same respondents after the 2016 and 2020 elections. The ANES employs a more elaborate question designed to elicit accurate reports of turnout, so it recorded higher percentages of nonvoters than the other two surveys. But as in the other two surveys, very few people reported switching between the Democratic and Republican candidates. And as in the ISCAP survey, a larger fraction of 2016 Trump voters in the ANES reported voting for Biden (6%) compared to Clinton voters who voted for Trump four years later (3%).

MODELS OF COUNTY ELECTION OUTCOMES

We estimate the effects of three factors on county-level presidential election outcomes:

- the cumulative number of per capita COVID deaths and infections a county experienced between the beginning of the pandemic and Election Day;
- the balance of television advertisements supporting Trump and Biden that were aired in that county in the two months before Election Day; and
- whether a racial justice protest took place in the county between May 25, 2020 (the date of George Floyd's murder), and Election Day.

We estimate the relationship between those factors and Biden's share of the major-party vote. These models also account for Clinton's vote share in each county in 2016, demographic attributes of these counties, and changes in those demographics between the two elections. The results indicate whether these three factors, net of the others, were correlated with changes in Biden's share of the vote compared to Clinton's in 2016. The full results from these models are presented in table A8.2.

TABLE A8.2. Models of County Election Outcomes

	Model 1	Model 2	Model 3	Model 4	Model 5	Model 6	Model 7
Racial justice protest		0.009* [0.002]					
Racial justice protest (arrests, injuries, damage)			0.010* [0.002]				
Racial justice protest (no arrests, injuries, damage)			0.009* [0.002]				
Racial justice protest (police injury, damage)				0.011* [0.003]			
Racial justice protest (no police injury, damage)				0.009* [0.002]			
COVID infections per capita (cumulative)					0.039 [0.065]		
COVID deaths per capita (cumulative)						-2.262* [1.011]	
Biden advertising advantage (last two months, in 1000s)							-0.0004* [0.0002]
Clinton vote share	0.950* [0.010]	0.944* [0.011]	0.944* [0.011]	0.944* [0.011]	0.950* [0.010]	0.950* [0.010]	0.950* [0.010]
Percent Black	0.014 [0.013]	0.019 [0.014]	0.019 [0.014]	0.019 [0.014]	0.014 [0.012]	0.018 [0.014]	0.014 [0.013]
Percent Latino	-0.102* [0.020]	-0.098* [0.019]	-0.098* [0.019]	-0.098* [0.019]	-0.101* [0.022]	-0.098* [0.019]	-0.102* [0.020]
Median income ($10,000s)	0.002 [0.001]	0.002* [0.001]	0.002* [0.001]	0.002* [0.001]	0.002 [0.001]	0.001 [0.001]	0.002 [0.001]

	(1)	(2)	(3)	(4)	(5)	(6)	(7)
Percent with a BA	0.143*	0.127*	0.124*	0.124*	0.152*	0.150*	0.141*
	[0.042]	[0.040]	[0.040]	[0.040]	[0.043]	[0.041]	[0.042]
Percent with HS degree	−0.099*	−0.081*	−0.080*	−0.080*	−0.093*	−0.095*	−0.100*
	[0.012]	[0.014]	[0.014]	[0.014]	[0.014]	[0.013]	[0.012]
Percent college-educated white	0.007	0.014	0.016	0.015	0.008	0.005	0.008
	[0.037]	[0.036]	[0.036]	[0.037]	[0.035]	[0.035]	[0.037]
Change in % Black	0.201*	0.178*	0.177*	0.178*	0.201*	0.197*	0.202*
	[0.051]	[0.050]	[0.050]	[0.050]	[0.049]	[0.050]	[0.050]
Change in % Latino	0.291*	0.273*	0.272*	0.272*	0.292*	0.291*	0.293*
	[0.045]	[0.046]	[0.045]	[0.046]	[0.047]	[0.047]	[0.045]
Change in median income	−0.002	−0.003*	−0.003*	−0.003*	−0.003	−0.003	−0.002
	[0.001]	[0.001]	[0.001]	[0.001]	[0.001]	[0.001]	[0.001]
Change in % BA	−0.011	−0.013	−0.012	−0.012	−0.014	−0.012	−0.01
	[0.047]	[0.047]	[0.047]	[0.047]	[0.049]	[0.047]	[0.047]
Change in % HS degree	0.076*	0.063*	0.063*	0.063*	0.075*	0.076*	0.076*
	[0.024]	[0.023]	[0.023]	[0.023]	[0.024]	[0.024]	[0.024]
Population (in millions)	−0.002	−0.003	−0.003	−0.003	−0.001	−0.001	−0.002
	[0.003]	[0.003]	[0.003]	[0.003]	[0.003]	[0.003]	[0.003]
Constant	0.028*	0.021*	0.021*	0.021*	0.025*	0.028*	0.033*
	[0.007]	[0.008]	[0.008]	[0.008]	[0.009]	[0.007]	[0.007]
R-squared	0.984	0.985	0.985	0.985	0.985	0.985	0.984
N	3,109	3,109	3,109	3,109	3,102	3,102	3,109

Cell entries are least squares regression coefficients with standard errors clustered at the state level in parentheses. The models also include fixed effects for states. * $p < 0.05$.

Sources: Crowd Counting Consortium (protests); *New York Times* (COVID-19 infections and deaths); Kantar Media (advertising); American Community Survey (demographics); and CQ Voting and Elections Collection (election returns).

Model 1 includes only Clinton's vote share and the demographic attributes. It shows the expected results—that is, that Clinton's vote share was strongly correlated with Biden's and that the percent of a county that was Latino was associated with a decline in Biden's performance, relative to Clinton's.

Model 2 adds an indicator for whether the county experienced a racial justice protest. The result suggests that Biden did almost 1 percentage point better than Clinton ($b = 0.009$) in counties that did experience a protest, compared to those that did not. Models 3 and 4 disaggregate protests into those where there were (1) arrests, injuries, or property damage or (2) specifically injuries to police or property damage. This provides two ways to differentiate protests where violence occurred from those where it did not. But again, Biden did about equally well in counties with either type of protest.

Models 5 and 6 include the cumulative number of COVID-19 infections or deaths per capita. There was no significant association between COVID infections and county-level election outcomes. There was a negative association with COVID deaths, however. This implies that in counties with more COVID-19 deaths, Biden did worse than Clinton did in 2016 and Trump did better than he did in 2016. Specifically, the coefficient implies that Biden did about 1.5 points worse (relative to Clinton in 2016) in the county with the most COVID deaths (0.0068 per capita) than counties with no deaths.

Finally, model 7 includes a measure of Biden's advertising advantage. This is the number of ads supporting Biden (from his campaign or allied groups) minus the number of ads supporting Trump that were aired in each county in the last two months. We measure this by locating counties within media markets. We added to each county's total the number of ads aired nationally over this period. This coefficient is negatively signed, which means that a 1,000-ad advantage was associated with a −0.04-point shift in Biden's vote share relative to Clinton's—that is, four-hundredths of a percentage point. This suggests that Biden did slightly worse than Clinton did in the areas where he advertised the most.

MODELS OF THE EFFECT OF RACIAL JUSTICE PROTESTS
AND VOTE INTENTIONS

To analyze the effect of the racial protest data on vote intentions, we merge the protest data described above with the Nationscape survey data. For each respondent, we record whether there was a racial justice protest in their county in one or more of the three weeks before their interview. We analyze all Nationscape survey data from June 1, 2020, until Election Day.

The dependent variable is vote intention in the presidential election. From June 1 to June 18, 2020, vote choice was measured by asking, "If the general election for president of the United States was a contest between Joe Biden and Donald Trump, who would you support?" Respondents could answer Biden, Trump, or "don't know." After June 18, the vote intention question was, "If the election for president were going to be held now and the Democratic nominee was Joe Biden and the Republican nominee was Donald Trump, who would you vote for?" Respondents could answer Biden, Trump, someone else, or "don't know," or say that they would not vote. There was a period where both questions were asked (until September 18, 2020), allowing us to assess whether the change in question wordings and outcomes affected the results. No significant changes derived from the switch.

The models include the individual-level controls described in the appendix to chapter 6: age, education, race or ethnicity, gender, Hispanic identification, party identification, and the interaction between race and education. As in the chapter 6 models, these also include fixed effects for respondents' county of residence and for the week of the respondent's interview.

The results do not suggest any significant association between racial justice protests and vote intentions (see table A8.3).

TABLE A8.3. Models of the Effects of Local Racial Justice Protests on Vote Intentions

	Vote intentions
Protest 1–7 days before interview	−0.001
	(0.003)
Protest 8–14 days before interview	−0.001
	(0.003)
Protest 15–21 days before interview	−0.002
	(0.003)
Individual-level controls	Yes
County fixed effects	Yes
Survey wave fixed effects	Yes
N	104,002

Cell entries are least squares regression coefficients, with standard errors in parentheses. The dependent variables are coded 1 = intend to vote for Biden and 0 = intend to vote for Trump.

Source: Crowd Counting Consortium and Democracy Fund + Nationscape Survey.

MODELS OF THE EFFECT OF TELEVISION ADVERTISING ON VOTE INTENTIONS

To examine the relationship between Trump's and Biden's televised advertising, we merged daily advertising data licensed to us by Kantar Media with weekly Nationscape surveys. Specifically, we matched each respondent in the survey to the number of advertisements aired by and for both candidates. To analyze public safety issues in particular, we categorized the advertisements by content as determined by Kantar Media (see chapter 7).

For each Nationscape respondent, we summed the total number of ads for each candidate in the respondent's media market in two unique periods of time: the seven days *prior* to their interview and the seven days *after* their interview. We use the prior seven days to reflect previous research showing that the effects of advertising tend to decay quickly. We use the later seven days as a "placebo test." The notion is that ads before the interview have the potential to affect a person's vote choice, while ads aired after they are interviewed should not be able to affect respondents' vote choice (although these two quantities are highly correlated).

The advertising models examine the relationship between vote intentions and advertising overall, as well as ads divided into those that mentioned issues related to public safety and those that did not mention public safety issues (i.e., all other ads).

In the analyses that follow, we analyze only respondents who reported being registered to vote and indicated an intention to vote for Biden or Trump (coded as described above). The models include a set of individual-level controls for age, education, race or ethnicity, gender, Hispanic identification, party identification, and the interaction between race and education. The models also include fixed effects for respondents' state of residence, media market, and the week of the respondent's interview (since each survey wave took place over a week). The first group of fixed effects accounts for characteristics of states or media markets that may themselves be correlated with votes for one of the candidates or with the candidates' decisions about whether to advertise in that place. The last set of fixed effects accounts for the potential for attitudes to change over time, regardless of where respondents lived or what ads they could have seen.

The results show little evidence that the overall balance of advertising was associated with vote intentions (model 1 of table A8.4). The same is true if we separate the balance of advertising into measures of pro-Biden and pro-Trump ads (not shown).

The results also show little evidence that advertisements about public safety in the wake of George Floyd's murder and the ensuing protests affected respondents' vote intention (table A8.4). Biden's public safety advertisements appeared to boost his vote share by a small amount: 1,000 additional public safety ads were associated with an increase in his vote share of 0.03, or three-hundredths of a percentage point. But Trump's ads about public safety had no perceptible effect on people's decisions to vote for him; this effect was no different from the near-zero effect of his other advertising during this period.

As a placebo test, we investigated whether ads aired after the respondent's date of interview also affected their vote choice, something that should be impossible. Finding no effects for ads aired after the respondent was interviewed provides confidence that significant effects found

TABLE A8.4. Models of the Relationship between Campaign Advertising and Vote Intentions, June–November 2020

	Model 1	Model 2	Model 3	Model 4
	(all ads)	(all ads)	(public safety)	(public safety placebo)
Balance of ads in past week	0.003 (0.003)			
Biden ads in past week		0.002 (0.003)		
Trump ads in past week		0.002 (0.006)		
Biden public safety in past week			0.033 (0.010)	
Trump public safety ads in past week			0.004 (0.007)	
Biden all other ads in past week			−0.003 (0.004)	
Trump all other ads in past week			0.0004 (0.008)	
Biden public safety in next week				0.008 (0.011)
Trump public safety ads in next week				0.004 (0.007)
Biden all other ads in next week				−0.002 (0.004)
Trump all other ads in next week				0.0004 (0.008)
Individual-level controls	Yes	Yes	Yes	Yes
State fixed effects	Yes	Yes	Yes	Yes
Media market fixed effects	Yes	Yes	Yes	Yes
Survey wave fixed effects	Yes	Yes	Yes	Yes
N	92,130	92,130	92,130	90,183

Cell entries are least squares regression coefficients, with standard errors in parentheses. The dependent variables are coded so that 1 indicates an intention to vote for Biden and 0 an intention to vote for Trump. The advertising measures are denominated in 1,000 of ad airings.

Source: Kantar Media and The Democracy Fund + Nationscape Project.

for ads aired before the interview date are not being driven by candidates' expectations about their vote share, which would lead them to advertise more in places where they were already ahead. Placebo tests produced no statistically significant relationship between vote intention and public safety (or other) advertising. This provides some confirmation that the small relationship between Biden's public safety advertising and vote intentions is not spurious.

RELATIONSHIP BETWEEN VOTE CHOICE AND VIEWS OF THE POLICE AND BLACK LIVES MATTER, 2016–20

To assess the relationship between views of the police and vote choice, we rely on VOTER Survey interviews conducted with the same respondents in November 2016 and September 2020. In both waves of interviewing, respondents were asked to rate the police and Black Lives Matter (BLM) on a 0–100 scale, where 100 equals the most favorable feeling. We rescaled this to the 0–1 interval. Respondents were also asked whom they voted for in the 2016 presidential election and whom they intended to vote for in the 2020 election. We coded those variables into a dichotomy (1 = Clinton/Biden, 0 = Trump).

We estimated regression models of both 2020 vote intention and 2020 attitudes toward the police or BLM. Each model includes a lagged value of the dependent variable as well as the 2016 value of the other variable. For example, the model of 2020 vote intention includes 2016 vote intention and 2016 attitudes toward the police or BLM. Table A8.5 presents the results.

The results show a very strong relationship between 2016 and 2020 voting behavior. There is, however, a small and statistically insignificant relationship between 2020 vote intention and 2016 police attitudes, suggesting that people's prior view of the police did not affect any changes in voting behavior over this period. By contrast, 2020 views of the police were less strongly related to 2016 values (b = 0.653), largely because of the changes between the two interviews. These changes were related to 2016 vote choice: relative to Trump voters, Clinton voters' views of the police were about 16 points lower on the 0–100 scale (b = −0.159).

TABLE A8.5. Models of the Relationships between Presidential Vote Choice and Views of the Police and Black Lives Matter, 2016 and 2020

	2020 Vote intention	2020 Views of the police
2016 Vote choice	0.939	−0.149
(1 = Clinton, 0 = Trump)	(0.007)	(0.007)
2016 Views of the police	−0.013	0.610
	(0.014)	(0.015)
N	2,998	

	2020 Vote intention	2020 Views of BLM
2016 Vote choice	0.896	0.359
(1 = Clinton, 0 = Trump)	(0.009)	(0.010)
2016 Views of the BLM	0.080	0.545
	(0.013)	(0.014)
N	2,830	

Cell entries are coefficients from least squares regression models, with standard errors in parentheses. *Source*: VOTER Survey.

A similar pattern emerges for vote choice and views of BLM. There is a statistically significant relationship between 2020 vote choice and 2016 views of BLM (b = 0.08), but it is much smaller than the relationship between 2020 views of BLM and 2016 vote choice (b = 0.359).

People's partisan predispositions appear to have affected their views of the police and BLM much more than their views of the police or BLM affected their vote choice in 2020.

APPENDIX TO CHAPTER 9

Figures A9.1 and A9.2 report the results of the revealed importance experiment carried out in a separate Nationscape survey conducted from January 21 to February 3, 2021. The results show that Democrats and Republicans disagreed about voting by mail but both prioritized it. Republicans also prioritized voter identification, which most favored. Democrats, fewer of whom favored voter identification, prioritized it less.

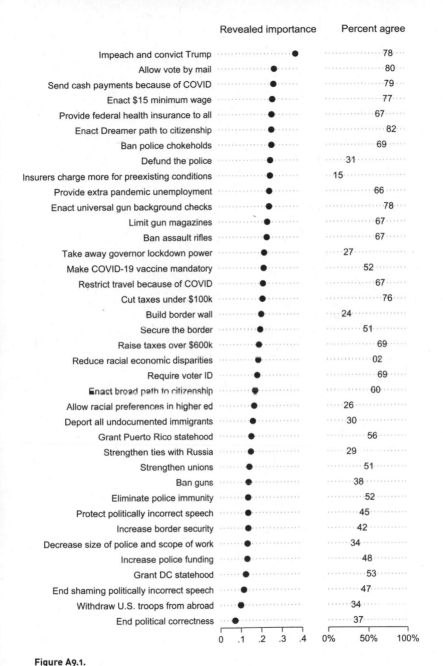

	Revealed importance	Percent agree
Impeach and convict Trump		78
Allow vote by mail		80
Send cash payments because of COVID		79
Enact $15 minimum wage		77
Provide federal health insurance to all		67
Enact Dreamer path to citizenship		82
Ban police chokeholds		69
Defund the police		31
Insurers charge more for preexisting conditions		15
Provide extra pandemic unemployment		66
Enact universal gun background checks		78
Limit gun magazines		67
Ban assault rifles		67
Take away governor lockdown power		27
Make COVID-19 vaccine mandatory		52
Restrict travel because of COVID		67
Cut taxes under $100k		76
Build border wall		24
Secure the border		51
Raise taxes over $600k		69
Reduce racial economic disparities		02
Require voter ID		69
Enact broad path to citizenship		60
Allow racial preferences in higher ed		26
Deport all undocumented immigrants		30
Grant Puerto Rico statehood		56
Strengthen ties with Russia		29
Strengthen unions		51
Ban guns		38
Eliminate police immunity		52
Protect politically incorrect speech		45
Increase border security		42
Decrease size of police and scope of work		34
Increase police funding		48
Grant DC statehood		53
End shaming politically incorrect speech		47
Withdraw U.S. troops from abroad		34
End political correctness		37

Figure A9.1.

Revealed Importance of Political Issues among Democrats. *Source*: Democracy Fund + UCLA Nationscape Survey, January 21–February 3, 2021.

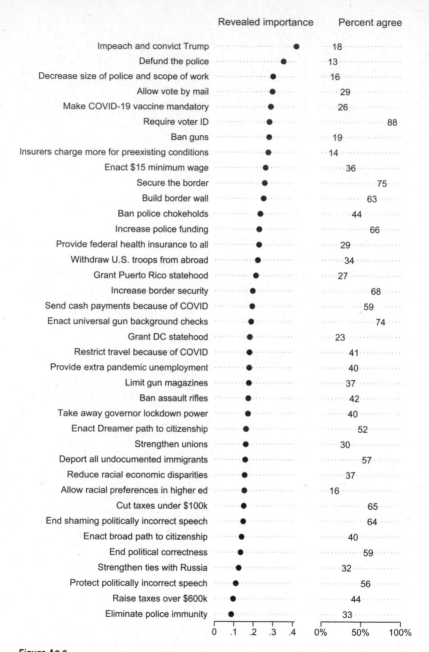

Figure A9.2.
Revealed Importance of Political Issues among Republicans. *Source*: Democracy Fund + UCLA Nationscape Survey, January 21–February 3, 2021.

CHAPTER 1: THE STORM IS HERE

1. Ellen Barry, Nicholas Bogel-Burroughs, and Dave Philipps, "Woman Killed in Capitol Embraced Trump and QAnon," *New York Times*, January 7, 2021, https://www.nytimes.com /2021/01/07/us/who-was-ashli-babbitt.html.

2. Paul Gattis, "Mo Brooks: Today Patriots Start 'Kicking Ass' in Fighting Vote Results," AL .com, January 6, 2021, https://www.al.com/news/2021/01/mo-brooks-today-patriots-start -kicking-ass-in-fighting-vote-results.html. The Giuliani quote was recorded by Vox reporter Aaron Rupar: https://twitter.com/atrupar/status/1346847382768676864. The Donald Trump Jr. quote is cited in Ashley Parker, Josh Dawsey, and Philip Rucker, "Six Hours of Paraly- sis: Inside Trump's Failure to Act after a Mob Stormed the Capitol," *Washington Post*, January 11, 2021, https://www.washingtonpost.com/politics/trump-mob-failure/2021/01/11/36a46e2e -542e-11eb-a817-e5e7f8a406d6_story.html. The Trump quotes are cited in Charlie Savage, "Incitement to Riot? What Trump Told Supporters before Mob Stormed Capitol," *New York Times*, January 10, 2021, https://www.nytimes.com/2021/01/10/us/trump-speech-riot.html.

3. U.S. Attorney of the District of Columbia, "Department of Justice Closes Investigation into the Death of Ashli Babbitt," April 14, 2021, https://www.justice.gov/usao-dc/pr/department -justice-closes-investigation-death-ashli-babbitt.

4. Robert A. Pape and Keven Ruby, "The Capitol Rioters Aren't Like Other Extremists," *The Atlantic*, February 2, 2021, https://www.theatlantic.com/ideas/archive/2021/02/the-capitol -rioters-arent-like-other-extremists/617895/; Rachel Weiner, Spencer S. Hsu, Tom Jackman, and Sahana Jayaraman, "Desperate, Angry, Destructive: How Americans Morphed into a Mob," *Washington Post*, November 9, 2021, https://www.washingtonpost.com/dc-md-va/2021/11/09 /rioters-charges-arrests-jan-6-insurrection/.

5. The phrase "initially pleased" is from Peter Baker and Maggie Haberman, "Capitol Attack Leads Democrats to Demand That Trump Leave Office," *New York Times*, January 7, 2021,

https://www.nytimes.com/2021/01/07/us/politics/trump-leave-office-resignation.html. That Trump did not want to include "stay peaceful" is in Parker, Dawsey, and Rucker, "Six Hours of Paralysis."

6. Parker, Dawsey, and Rucker, "Six Hours of Paralysis."

7. Michael S. Schmidt and Luke Broadwater, "Officers' Injuries, Including Concussions, Show Scope of Violence at Capitol Riot," *New York Times*, February 11, 2021, https://www.nytimes.com/2021/02/11/us/politics/capitol-riot-police-officer-injuries.html.

8. Shaun Bowler, Todd Donovan, Ola Listhaug, Christopher J. Anderson, and André Blais, *Losers' Consent: Elections and Democratic Legitimacy* (New York: Oxford University Press, 2007).

9. The estimate of COVID-19 deaths in 2020 is here: https://ourworldindata.org/explorers/coronavirus-data-explorer?zoomToSelection=true&time=2020-03-01..latest&facet=none&pickerSort=desc&pickerMetric=new_deaths_per_million&Metric=Confirmed+deaths&Interval=Cumulative&Relative+to+Population=false&Align+outbreaks=false&country=~USA. On the unemployment numbers, see Rakesh Kochhar, "Unemployment Rose Higher in Three Months of COVID-19 than It Did in Two Years of the Great Recession," Pew Research Center, June 11, 2020, https://www.pewresearch.org/fact-tank/2020/06/11/unemployment-rose-higher-in-three-months-of-covid-19-than-it-did-in-two-years-of-the-great-recession/. Note that for both COVID-19 deaths and unemployment, the numbers are likely underestimated, given that the death statistics reflect only confirmed deaths and traditional measures of unemployment understated it because of measurement challenges during the pandemic.

10. David Ignatius, "Coronavirus Will Test Whether the Planet Can Unite in the Face of a Global Crisis," *Washington Post*, February 25, 2020, https://www.washingtonpost.com/opinions/coronavirus-will-test-whether-the-planet-can-unite-in-the-face-of-a-global-crisis/2020/02/25/f44195c8-5818-11ea-9000-f3cffee23036_story.html; Ron Elving, "Will This Be the Moment of Reckoning on Race That Lasts?," NPR, June 13, 2020, https://www.npr.org/2020/06/13/876442698/will-this-be-the-moment-of-reckoning-on-race-that-lasts.

11. A transcript of Biden's inaugural address is here: https://www.whitehouse.gov/briefing-room/speeches-remarks/2021/01/20/inaugural-address-by-president-joseph-r-biden-jr/.

12. The trend in partisan ideological identification from 1994 to 2020 is depicted in Lydia Saad, "Americans' Political Ideology Held Steady in 2020," Gallup, January 11, 2021, https://news.gallup.com/poll/328367/americans-political-ideology-held-steady-2020.aspx. On the trend from 1972 to 2012, see Lilliana Mason, *Uncivil Agreement: How Politics Became Our Identity* (Chicago: University of Chicago Press, 2018), 35, figure 3.4. See also Matthew Levendusky, *The Partisan Sort: How Liberals Became Democrats and Conservatives Became Republicans* (Chicago: University of Chicago Press, 2009), and Morris Fiorina, *Unstable Majorities: Polarization, Party Sorting, and Political Stalemate* (Palo Alto, CA: Hoover Institution Press, 2017).

13. Data on the partisanship of demographic groups from approximately 1994 to 2019 is depicted in Carroll Doherty, Jocelyn Kiley, and Nida Asheer, "In Changing U.S. Electorate, Race and Education Remain Stark Dividing Lines," Pew Research Center, June 2, 2020, https://www.pewresearch.org/politics/2020/06/02/democratic-edge-in-party-identification-narrows-slightly/#gender-gap-in-party-affiliation-widens#generational-divides-in-partisanship#religious-divides-in-partisanship. The trend in African American partisanship from 1952 to 2016 is presented in Ismail K. White and Chryl N. Laird, *Steadfast Democrats: How Social Forces Shape Black Political Behavior* (Princeton: Princeton University Press, 2020), 4, figure 0.1. On the trend

in religiosity, see Mason, *Uncivil Agreement,* and Alan I. Abramowitz, *The Great Alignment: Race, Party Transformation, and the Rise of Donald Trump* (New Haven: Yale University Press, 2018), 54, figure 3.4. On the earlier trend in the partisanship of men, see Karen M. Kaufman and John R. Petrocik, "The Changing Politics of American Men: Understanding the Source of the Gender Gap," *American Journal of Political Science* 43, no. 3 (1999): 864–87.

14. Delia Baldassarri and Barum Park, "Was There a Culture War? Partisan Polarization and Secular Trends in U.S. Public Opinion," *Journal of Politics* 82, no. 3 (2020): 809–27. See especially figures 3 and 5. For other evidence for the 1973–2008 period, see Joseph Daniel Ura and Christopher R. Ellis, "Partisan Moods: Polarization and the Dynamics of Mass Party Preferences," *Journal of Politics* 74, no. 1 (2012): 277–91. Note that this pattern does not characterize all issues. On social issues related to gender roles and the rights of gay and lesbian people, the parties have been moving in the same direction—although not always at the same rate—rather than moving apart. This reflects the secular trend toward more liberal views on those issues.

15. Daniel Q. Gillion, Jonathan M. Ladd, and Marc Meredith, "Party Polarization, Ideological Sorting and the Emergence of the US Partisan Gender Gap," *British Journal of Political Science* 50 (2020): 1217–43.

16. On the declining correlation between Catholicism and party identification, see Mason, *Uncivil Agreement.*

17. Party polarization among members of Congress is well documented in the Voteview project, built on the work of political scientists Keith Poole and Howard Rosenthal with additional effort by Nolan McCarty and Jeffrey Lewis. See https://voteview.com/parties/all. On polarization among activists, see Geoffrey C. Layman, Thomas M. Carsey, John C. Green, Richard Herrera, and Rosalyn Cooperman, "Activists and Conflict Extension in American Party Politics," *American Political Science Review* 104, no. 2 (2010): 324–46. On the link between elite polarization and mass polarization, see Levendusky, *The Partisan Sort,* and Marc Hetherington, "Resurgent Mass Partisanship: The Role of Elite Polarization," *American Journal of Political Science* 95 (2001): 619–31. A good comparison of polarization among members of Congress and voters is Seth J. Hill and Chris Tausanovitch, "A Disconnect in Representation? Comparison of Trends in Congressional and Public Polarization," *Journal of Politics* 77, no. 4 (2015): 1058–75.

18. The increase in the percentage of Americans who perceived differences is not due to changes in the survey mode within the ANES, which included both online and face-to-face modes in the 2012 and 2016 surveys and then was almost exclusively online in 2020, when the COVID-19 pandemic made face-to-face interviewing untenable. For example, from 2008 to 2016 there were increases in the percentage of people who perceived differences only among face-to-face respondents. There were also increases from 2012 to 2020 among online respondents. In addition, this increase in the perception of important differences is present among all kinds of people, including partisans and independents as well as those who pay more or less attention to politics. See this ANES table (https://electionstudies.org/resources/anes-guide/second-tables/?id=109) as well as Corwin Smidt, "Polarization and the Decline of the American Swing Voter," *American Journal of Political Science* 61, no. 2 (2016): 365–81.

19. On basic accuracy, see Levendusky, *The Partisan Sort,* 41. On increasing distance, see John Sides, Michael Tesler, and Lynn Vavreck, *Identity Crisis: The 2016 Presidential Campaign and the Battle for the Meaning of America* (Princeton: Princeton University Press, 2018), 168. On perceiving the opposing party as more distant, see Abramowitz, *The Great Alignment,* 59.

20. There is some debate, however, about the extent to which people's evaluations toward the other party reflect policy differences as opposed to dislike per se. See Lilla V. Orr and Gregory A. Huber, "The Policy Basis of Measured Partisan Animosity in the United States," *Journal of Politics* 64, no. 3 (2020): 569–86; and Nicholas Dias and Yphtach Lelkes, "The Nature of Affective Polarization: Disentangling Policy Disagreement from Partisan Identity," *American Journal of Political Science*, forthcoming.

21. Shanto Iyengar, Yphtach Lelkes, Matthew Levendusky, Neil Malhotra, and Sean J. Westwood, "The Origins and Consequences of Affective Polarization in the United States," *Annual Review of Political Science* 22 (2019): 129–46; Alan I. Abramowitz and Steven Webster, "The Rise of Negative Partisanship and the Nationalization of U.S. Elections in the 21st Century," *Electoral Studies* 41, no. 1 (2016): 12–22.

22. Scott Keeter, "From Telephone to Web: The Challenge of Mode of Interview Effects in Public Opinion Polls," Pew Research Center, May 13, 2015, https://www.pewresearch.org /methods/2015/05/13/from-telephone-to-the-web-the-challenge-of-mode-of-interview -effects-in-public-opinion-polls/.

23. On exaggerating policy differences, see Matthew S. Levendusky and Neil Malhotra, "(Mis)perceptions of Partisan Polarization in the American Public," in "Party Polarization," ed. Shanto Iyengar, special issue, *Public Opinion Quarterly* 80, no. S1 (2016): 378–91. On exaggerating demographic differences, see Douglas J. Ahler and Gaurav Sood, "The Parties in Our Heads: Misperceptions about Party Composition and Their Consequences," *Journal of Politics* 80, no. 3 (2018): 964–81. On exaggerating perceptions of partisan prejudice and dehumanization, see Samantha L. Moore-Berg, Lee-Or Ankori-Karlinsky, Boaz Hameiri, and Emile Bruneau, "Exaggerated Meta-Perceptions Predict Intergroup Hostility between American Political Partisans," *PNAS* 117, no. 26 (2020): 14864–872. On what party favorability ratings measure, see James N. Druckman and Matthew S. Levendusky, "What Do We Measure When We Measure Affective Polarization?," *Public Opinion Quarterly* 83, no. 1 (2019): 114–22; and James N. Druckman, Samara Klar, Yanna Krupnikov, Matthew Levendusky, and John Barry Ryan, "(Mis-)Estimating Affective Polarization," *Journal of Politics*, forthcoming.

24. On the increasing polarization in presidential approval and increasing party loyalty in presidential elections, see Gary Jacobson, "Driven to Extremes: Donald Trump's Extraordinary Impact on the 2020 Elections," *Presidential Studies Quarterly* 51, no. 3 (September 2021): 492–521. On the decline in split-ticket voting, see https://electionstudies.org/resources/anes-guide/top -tables/?id=111.

25. On the weakening relationship between the economy and presidential approval, see Sides, Tesler, and Vavreck, *Identity Crisis*, and Paul. M. Kellstedt, Ellen M. Key, and Matthew J. Lebo, "Motivated Reasoning, Public Opinion, and Presidential Approval," *Political Behavior* 42 (2020): 1201–21. On polarization, economic outcomes, and presidential elections, see Christopher R. Ellis and Joseph Daniel Ura, "Polarization and the Decline of Economic Voting in American National Elections," *Social Science Quarterly* 102, no. 1 (2021): 83–89.

26. On the increase in continuity across elections and the declining magnitude of electoral shocks, see Larry M. Bartels, "Trench Warfare: The 2020 Election in Historical Perspective," Vanderbilt Project on Unity and American Democracy, February 9, 2021, https://www .vanderbilt.edu/unity/2021/02/09/trench-warfare/.

27. The ANES statistics are here: https://electionstudies.org/resources/anes-guide/top
-tables/?id=22. On increasing partisan parity, see Fiorina, *Unstable Majorities*, and Frances E.
Lee, *Insecure Majorities: Congress and the Perpetual Campaign* (Chicago: University of Chicago
Press, 2016). On the dwindling number of battleground states and the importance of winner-take-
all rules, see David A. Hopkins, *Red Fighting Blue: How Geography and Electoral Rules Polarize
American Politics* (New York: Cambridge University Press, 2017).

28. On the origins of this measure, see Donald R. Kinder and Lynn M. Sanders, *Divided by
Color: Racial Politics and Democratic Ideals* (Chicago: University of Chicago Press, 1996). On its
meaning, see Cindy D. Kam and Camille D. Burge, "Uncovering Reactions to the Racial Resentment Scale across the Racial Divide," *Journal of Politics* 80, no. 1 (2018): 314–20.

29. On the preexisting partisan gap in attributions of racial inequality, see Michael Tesler,
Post-Racial or Most-Racial? Race and Politics in the Obama Era (Chicago: University of Chicago
Press, 2016), chap. 7; Abramowitz, *The Great Alignment*, 131; and Adam M. Enders and Jamil S.
Scott, "The Increasing Racialization of American Electoral Politics, 1988–2016," *American Politics
Research* 47, no. 2 (2019): 275–303. On the increase in liberal racial attitudes among Democrats,
see Sides, Tesler, and Vavreck, *Identity Crisis*, 213, figure 9.4, and Baldassarri and Park, "Was
There a Culture War?" On changing attitudes toward Islam and Muslims, see again Sides, Tesler,
and Vavreck, *Identity Crisis*, 213, figure 9.4.

30. John Sides, Michael Tesler, and Lynn Vavreck, "Gender Attitudes and American Public
Opinion in the Trump Era," in *Dynamics of American Democracy: Partisan Polarization, Political
Competition, and Government Performance*, ed. Eric M. Patashnik and Wendy J. Schiller (Law-
rence: University Press of Kansas, 2021), 156–83.

31. These are results from the November 2016 and November 2020 waves of the Views of the
Electorate Research (VOTER) Survey. A more systematic analysis shows a similar pattern. We
compared party polarization in the December 2011 and November 2020 VOTER Survey interviews on these measures: the abortion question; a scale that captures economic attitudes (views
of the government's role in health care and taxing the wealthy); a scale that captures immigration attitudes (views of a path to citizenship for undocumented immigrants, whether undocumented immigrants make a contribution to the United States, and whether legal immigration
should be easier or harder); and a scale that captures racial attitudes (the "racial resentment"
battery). Each scale ranges from 0 to 1, so the maximum level of partisan polarization would be
1. The increase in partisan polarization on economic attitudes between 2011 and 2016 was 0.06
(from 0.58 to 0.64) and the increase in polarization on abortion was 0.08. Party polarization on
immigration increased by 0.21 and polarization on racial resentment increased by 0.21.

32. One important historical account of party divisions on civil rights is Eric Schickler, *Racial
Realignment: The Transformation of American Liberalism, 1932–1965* (Princeton: Princeton University Press, 2016). An account that shows the connection between elite and public views of
civil rights is Edward G. Carmines and James A. Stimson, *Issue Evolution: Race and the Transformation of American Politics* (Princeton: Princeton University Press, 1989). The party break-
down on the 1986 immigration bill is here: https://www.govtrack.us/congress/votes/99-1986
/h872.

33. On Obama's rhetoric on race, see Daniel Q. Gillion, *Governing with Words: The Political
Dialogue on Race, Public Policy, and Inequality in America* (Cambridge: Cambridge University

Press, 2016). The findings about Obama and racial attitudes are detailed extensively in Tesler, *Post-Racial or Most-Racial?*

34. Jennifer Steinhauer, Jonathan Martin, and David M. Herszenhorn, "Paul Ryan Calls Donald Trump's Attack on Judge 'Racist,' but Still Backs Him," *New York Times*, June 7, 2016, https://www.nytimes.com/2016/06/08/us/politics/paul-ryan-donald-trump-gonzalo-curiel.html.

35. See Sides, Tesler, and Vavreck, *Identity Crisis*; Brian F. Schaffner, Matthew MacWilliams, and Tatishe Nteta, "Understanding White Polarization in the 2016 Vote for President: The Sobering Role of Racism and Sexism," *Political Science Quarterly* 133, no. 1 (2018): 9–34; Nicholas Valentino, Carly Wayne, and Marzia Oceno, "Mobilizing Sexism: The Interaction of Emotion and Gender Attitudes in the 2016 US Presidential Election," in "The Psychology of Politics and Elections," ed. Cindy D. Kam, special issue, *Public Opinion Quarterly* 82, no S1 (2018): 213–35; and Daniel J. Hopkins, "The Activation of Prejudice and Presidential Voting: Panel Evidence from the 2016 U.S. Election," *Political Behavior* 43 (2021): 663–86.

36. Stephen P. Nicholson, "Polarizing Cues," *American Journal of Political Science* 56, no. 1 (2012): 52–66.

37. Michael Tesler, "Donald Trump Is Making the Border Wall Less Popular," *The Monkey Cage* (blog), August 16, 2016, https://www.washingtonpost.com/news/monkey-cage/wp/2016/08/16/donald-trump-is-making-the-border-wall-less-popular/.

38. There has been extensive research on attitude or issue importance, its origins, and its consequences for politics. See, for example, Jon A. Kronick, "The Role of Attitude Importance in Social Evaluation: A Study of Policy Preferences, Presidential Candidate Evaluations, and Voting Behavior," *Journal of Personality and Social Psychology* 55, no. 2 (1988): 196–210; Vincent L. Hutchings, *Public Opinion and Democratic Accountability: How Citizens Learn about Politics* (Princeton: Princeton University Press, 2003); and Seth J. Hill, *Frustrated Majorities: How Issue Intensity Enables Smaller Groups of Voters to Get What They Want* (New York: Cambridge University Press, 2022).

39. Thomas J. Leeper and Joshua Robison, "More Important, but for What Exactly? The Insignificant Role of Subjective Issue Importance in Vote Decisions," *Political Behavior* 42 (2020): 239–59.

40. This kind of experiment is known in the academic literature as a "conjoint experiment." For an overview, see Kirk Bansak, Jens Hainmueller, Daniel J. Hopkins, and Teppei Yamamoto, "Conjoint Survey Experiments," in *Advances in Experimental Political Science*, ed. James N. Druckman and Donald P. Green (New York: Cambridge University Press, 2021), 19–40. We introduced results from this experiment in Lynn Vavreck, John Sides, and Chris Tausanovitch, "What Is Voters' Highest Priority? There's a Way to Find Out," *New York Times*, December 5, 2019, https://www.nytimes.com/2019/12/05/upshot/impeachment-biggest-issue-voters-poll.html. On the use of conjoint experiments to measure issue importance, see Chris Hanretty, Benjamin E. Lauderdale, and Nick Vivyan, "A Choice-Based Measure of Issue Importance in the Electorate," *American Journal of Political Science* 64, no. 3 (2020): 519–35.

41. Zoe Greenberg, "2020 Is One of the Top 5 Contenders for Craziest Year in American History," *Boston Globe*, October 2, 2020, https://www.bostonglobe.com/2020/10/06/nation/were-one-top-5-contenders-craziest-year-american-history/; Reid Wilson, "Why 2020 Really Was the Worst Year Ever," *The Hill*, December 27, 2020, https://thehill.com/homenews/state-watch/531279-why-2020-really-was-the-worst-year-ever.

42. Jon Reid, "House GOP's Poverty Push Overshadowed by Their Nominee," *Morning Consult*, June 7, 2016, https://morningconsult.com/2016/06/07/paul-ryan-house-gop-agenda-donald-trump/.

CHAPTER 2: THE FIGHT

1. David A. Fahrenthold, "A Time Magazine with Trump on the Cover Hangs in His Golf Clubs," *Washington Post*, June 27, 2017, https://www.washingtonpost.com/politics/a-time-magazine-with-trump-on-the-cover-hangs-in-his-golf-clubs-its-fake/2017/06/27/0adf96de-5850-11e7-ba90-f5875b7d1876_story.html; Jenna Johnson, "Donald Trump Is (Finally) Named Time's 'Person of the Year,'" *Washington Post*, December 7, 2016, https://www.washingtonpost.com/news/post-politics/wp/2016/12/07/donald-trump-is-finally-named-times-person-of-the-year/.

2. Michael Scherer, "2016 Person of the Year: Donald Trump," *Time*, December 2016, https://time.com/time-person-of-the-year-2016-donald-trump/.

3. See B. Dan Wood, *The Myth of Presidential Representation* (New York: Cambridge University Press, 2009).

4. Amita Kelly, "Here Is What Donald Trump Wants to Do in His First 100 Days," NPR, November 9, 2016, https://www.npr.org/2016/11/09/501451368/here-is-what-donald-trump-wants-to-do-in-his-first-100-days; Sarah A. Binder, "Legislative Stalemate in Postwar America, 1947–2018," in *Dynamics of American Democracy*, ed. Eric M. Patashnik and Wendy J. Schiller (Lawrence: University Press of Kansas, 2020), 65–86; Andrew W. Barrett and Matthew Eshbaugh-Soha, "Presidential Success on the Substance of Legislation," *Political Research Quarterly* 57, no. 1 (2007): 100–112.

5. A good overview of the challenges confronting Trump is George C. Edwards III, "'Closer' or Context? Explaining Donald Trump's Relations with Congress," *Presidential Studies Quarterly* 48, no. 3 (2018): 456–79. The Ryan quote is from Craig Gilbert, "Speaker Paul Ryan's Status and Agenda at Risk in Obamacare Repeal Vote," *USA Today*, March 22, 2017, https://www.usatoday.com/story/news/politics/2017/03/22/speaker-paul-ryans-status-and-agenda-risk-obamacare-repeal-vote/99509786/. The "Better Way" plan is here: http://www.gop.gov/wp-content/uploads/2016/07/ABetterBooklet_update.pdf.

6. James M. Curry and Frances E. Lee, *The Limits of Party: Congress and Lawmaking in a Polarized Era* (Chicago: University of Chicago Press, 2020).

7. On the logic of appealing directly to the public, see Samuel Kernell, *Going Public: New Strategies of Presidential Leadership* (Washington, DC: CQ Press, 1997). For the data and findings on public appeals, see Brandice Canes-Wrone, *Who Leads Whom? Presidents, Policy, and the Public* (Chicago: University of Chicago Press, 2006). On executive actions, see Dino P. Christenson and Douglas R. Kriner, *The Myth of the Imperial Presidency: How Public Opinion Checks the Unilateral Executive* (Chicago: University of Chicago Press, 2020).

8. Richard Neustadt, *Presidential Power: The Politics of Leadership* (New York: Wiley and Sons, 1960), 34.

9. For the data underlying the figure, see Frank Newport, "Trump Family Leave, Infrastructure Proposals Widely Popular," Gallup, April 7, 2017, https://news.gallup.com/poll/207905/trump-family-leave-infrastructure-proposals-widely-popular.aspx.

10. John Sides, Michael Tesler, and Lynn Vavreck, *Identity Crisis: The 2016 Presidential Campaign and the Battle for the Meaning of America* (Princeton: Princeton University Press, 2018), 211; Emily Ekins, "Americans Used to Support a Border Wall. What Changed Their Minds?," Cato Institute, January 14, 2019, https://www.cato.org/publications/commentary/americans -used-support-border-wall-what-changed-their-minds.

11. Steve Benen, "Trump Brags about Executive Orders He Used to Condemn," MSNBC, April 25, 2017, https://www.msnbc.com/rachel-maddow-show/trump-brags-about-executive -orders-he-used-condemn-msna983871. On how dynamics in Congress affect the president's decision to issue executive orders, see William G. Howell, *Power without Persuasion: The Politics of Direct Presidential Action* (Princeton: Princeton University Press, 2003).

12. Quoted in Christenson and Kriner, *The Myth of the Imperial Presidency*, 165, 166.

13. The Quinnipiac poll is available here: https://poll.qu.edu/national/release-detail ?ReleaseID=2488. For additional polling data, see Alec Tyson, "Public Backs Legal Status for Immigrants Brought to U.S. Illegally as Children, but Not a Bigger Border Wall," Pew Research Center, January 19, 2018, https://www.pewresearch.org/fact-tank/2018/01/19/public-backs-le gal-status-for-immigrants-brought-to-u-s-illegally-as-children-but-not-a-bigger-border-wall/; and Philip Bump, "With DACA, Trump Again Prioritizes His Base Over What's Politically Popular," *Washington Post*, September 5, 2017, https://www.washingtonpost.com/news/politics/wp/2017 /09/05/with-daca-trump-again-prioritizes-his-base-over-whats-politically-popular/.

14. These quotes are cited in Edwards, "'Closer' or Context?," 470.

15. On Trump's downplaying the conversation with Democrats, see Maggie Haberman and Yamiche Alcindor, "Pelosi and Schumer Say They Have Deal with Trump to Replace DACA," *New York Times*, September 13, 2017, https://www.nytimes.com/2017/09/13/us/politics /trump-dinner-schumer-pelosi-daca-obamacare.html. On the "shithole" comment, see Tal Kopan and Lauren Fox, "Trump Says Some Immigrants from 'Shithole Countries' As He Rejects Bipartisan Deal," CNN, January 11, 2018, https://www.cnn.com/2018/01/11/politics/daca -deal-obstacles-flake-white-house/index.html.

16. James Hohmann, "The Daily 202: Freewheeling Immigration Debate in Senate Will Test Power of Conservative Outside Groups," *Washington Post*, February 12, 2018, https://www .washingtonpost.com/news/powerpost/paloma/daily-202/2018/02/12/daily-202-freewheeling -immigration-debate-in-senate-will-test-power-of-conservative-outside-groups/5a81116930 fb041c3c7d77e7/.

17. Tal Kopan and Lauren Fox, "Bipartisan DACA, Border Security Deal Fails in Senate, Putting Immigration Bill's Future in Doubt," CNN, February 15, 2018, https://www.cnn.com /2018/02/15/politics/trump-immigration-veto/index.html; Tal Kapon, "A Timeline of DACA Offers Trump Has Rejected," CNN, March 23, 2018, https://www.cnn.com/2018/03/23 /politics/daca-rejected-deals-trump/index.html.

18. On the contrast between Trump's policy and Obama's, see Dara Lind, "What Obama Did with Migrant Families vs. What Trump Is Doing," Vox, June 21, 2018, https://www.vox.com /2018/6/21/17488458/obama-immigration-policy-family-separation-border. The John Kelly quote is from this May 11, 2018, interview with National Public Radio: https://www.npr.org /2018/05/11/610116389/transcript-white-house-chief-of-staff-john-kellys-interview-with-npr. The 5,500 figure is cited in Caitlin Dickerson, "Parents of 545 Children Separated at the Border Cannot Be Found," *New York Times*, October 21, 2020, https://www.nytimes.com/2020/10/21

/us/migrant-children-separated.html. The government report is Joanne Chiedi, "Care Provider Facilities Described Challenges Addressing Mental Health Needs of Children in HHS Custody," Office of the Inspector General, Department of Health and Human Services, September 2019, https://www.documentcloud.org/documents/6380666-Inspector-General-Report-from -HHSOIG.html. On the deaths of children, see Nicole Goodkind, "Trump Officials Acknowl- edge Sixth Migrant Child Death in U.S. Custody in 6 Months after None the Previous Decade," *Newsweek*, May 23, 2019, https://www.newsweek.com/border-family-separation-child-death -democrats-investigate-1434591. The 545 estimate is cited in Dickerson, "Parents of 545 Children Separated."

19. Christenson and Kriner, *The Myth of the Imperial Presidency*, 148–55, 169.

20. Paul Pierson, *Dismantling the Welfare State? Reagan, Thatcher, and the Politics of Retrench- ment* (New York: Cambridge University Press, 2010).

21. On the survey of GOP donors and voters, see David Broockman and Neil Malhotra, "What Do Partisan Donors Want?," *Public Opinion Quarterly* 84, no. 1 (2020): 104–18. On the link between support for government involvement in health care and support for Trump in the Republican primary, see Sides, Tesler, and Vavreck, *Identity Crisis*, 79–80. The Boehner quote is from Darius Tahir, "Boehner: Republicans Won't Repeal and Replace Obamacare," *Politico*, February 23, 2017, https://www.politico.com/story/2017/02/john-boehner-obamacare -republicans-235303.

22. Mike DeBonis, Ed O'Keefe, and Robert Costa, "GOP Health-Care Bill: House Repub- licans Abruptly Pull Their Rewrite of the Nation's Health-Care law," *Washington Post*, March 24, 2017, https://www.washingtonpost.com/powerpost/house-leaders-prepare-to-vote-friday-on -health care reform/2017/03/24/736f1cd6-1081-11e7-9d5a-a83e627dc120 story.html?tid=a _inl_manual. The Trump quote is cited in Erik Wemple, "Trump Rewards Maria Bartiromo with a Scoop of Chocolate Cake," *Washington Post*, April 12, 2017, https://www.washingtonpost .com/blogs/erik-wemple/wp/2017/04/12/trump-rewards-maria-bartiromo-with-a-scoop-of -chocolate-cake/.

23. Dan Merica, Jim Acosta, Lauren Fox, and Phil Mattingly, "Trump Calls House Health Care Bill 'Mean,'" CNN, June 14, 2017, https://www.cnn.com/2017/06/13/politics/trump -senators-health-care-white-house-meeting/index.html.

24. For the Rosen quote and more detail on the GOP's failure to repeal Obamacare, see Jonathan Cohn, "The Real Reason Republicans Couldn't Kill Obamacare," *The Atlantic*, March 22, 2021, https://www.theatlantic.com/politics/archive/2021/03/why-trump -republicans-failed-repeal-obamacare/618337/.

25. Ben Schreckinger and Nick Gass, "Trump: My Tax Plan Is 'Going to Cost Me a Fortune,'" *Politico*, September 28, 2015, https://www.politico.com/story/2015/09/donald-trump-2016 -tax-plan-214139; Peter Eavis, "Donald Trump's Plan to Raise Taxes on the Rich: Just Kidding," *New York Times*, May 11, 2016, https://www.nytimes.com/2016/05/12/upshot/donald-trumps -plan-to-raise-taxes-on-rich-just-kidding.html; Jonathan Swan, "Scoop: Bannon Pushes Tax Hike for Wealthy," Axios, July 2, 2017, https://www.axios.com/scoop-bannon-pushes-tax-hike -for-wealthy-2452197801.html. On public opinion about taxing the wealthy, see Karlyn Bow- man, Heather Sims, and Eleanor O'Neill, "Public Opinion on Taxes: 1937 to Today," American Enterprise Institute Public Opinion Studies, April 2015, https://www.aei.org/research-products /report/aei-public-opinion-study-on-taxes-1937-to-today/. On views of taxing the wealthy and

Trump's primary support, see Sides, Tesler, and Vavreck, *Identity Crisis*, 79–80. On views of GOP donors and voters, see Broockman and Malhotra, "What Do Partisan Donors Want?"

26. Joint Committee on Taxation, "Distributional Effects of the Conference Agreement for H.R. 1, the 'Tax Cuts and Jobs Act," December 18, 2017, https://www.jct.gov/publications/2017/jcx-68-17/; Tax Policy Center, "Distribution Analysis of the Conference Agreement for the Tax Cuts and Jobs Act," December 18, 2017, https://www.taxpolicycenter.org/publications/distributional-analysis-conference-agreement-tax-cuts-and-jobs-act; Heather Long, "The Final GOP Tax Bill Is Complete. Here's What Is in It," *Washington Post*, December 15, 2017, https://www.washingtonpost.com/news/wonk/wp/2017/12/15/the-final-gop-tax-bill-is-complete-heres-what-is-in-it/.

27. John Wagner, "Trump Signs Sweeping Tax Bill into Law," *Washington Post*, December 22, 2017, https://www.washingtonpost.com/news/post-politics/wp/2017/12/22/trump-signs-sweeping-tax-bill-into-law/.

28. The data in figure 2.3 represents averages of public polls conducted in the months during the debate over the legislative initiatives. All data comes from the Roper Center's archive of polls. Most of this data was originally gathered by Christopher Warshaw, and we thank him very much for sharing them.

29. Paul Kane, "Infrastructure Was Trump's Shot at a Bipartisan Deal, but He Left Democrats Waiting by the Phone," *Washington Post*, June 6, 2017, https://www.washingtonpost.com/powerpost/infrastructure-was-trumps-shot-at-a-bipartisan-deal-he-left-democrats-waiting-by-the-phone/2017/06/06/2bdce7de-4a30-11e7-9669-250d0b15f83b_story.html; Mallory Shelbourne, "Trump's Infrastructure Plan Hits a Dead End," *The Hill*, May 17, 2018, https://thehill.com/policy/transportation/388071-trumps-infrastructure-plan-hits-a-dead-end; Alexander Bolton, "Lawmakers Say Trump's Infrastructure Vision Lacks Political Momentum," *The Hill*, February 6, 2019, https://thehill.com/homenews/senate/428666-lawmakers-say-trumps-infrastructure-vision-lacks-political-momentum; Tanya Snyder and Nancy Cook, "Trump to Democrats: No Infrastructure without Trade Deal," *Politico*, May 21, 2019, https://www.politico.com/story/2019/05/21/trump-infrastructure-deal-1464437. The "Groundhog Day" quote is from Katie Rogers, "How 'Infrastructure Week' Became a Long-Running Joke," *New York Times*, May 22, 2019, https://www.nytimes.com/2019/05/22/us/politics/trump-infrastructure-week.html.

30. On the congressional response on trade, see Edwards, "'Closer' or Context?," 467, and also Jennifer Steinhauer, "G.O.P. Senators Pull Away from Trump, Alarmed at His Volatility," *New York Times*, May 14, 2017, https://www.nytimes.com/2017/05/14/us/politics/trump-republican-senators.html; Jeffrey M. Jones, "Americans Say U.S.-China Tariffs More Harmful than Helpful," Gallup, July 26, 2018, https://news.gallup.com/poll/238013/americans-say-china-tariffs-harmful-helpful.aspx; Jeremy Diamond, "Trump Sides with Putin Over U.S. Intelligence," CNN, July 16, 2018, https://www.cnn.com/2018/07/16/politics/donald-trump-putin-helsinki-summit/index.html; Abby Phillip, "Trump Signs What He Calls 'Seriously Flawed' Bill Imposing New Sanctions on Russia," *Washington Post*, August 2, 2017, https://www.washingtonpost.com/news/post-politics/wp/2017/08/02/trump-signs-bill-imposing-new-sanctions-on-russia-but-issues-a-statement-with-concerns/; Sarah D. Wire, "'Disgraceful': Republicans Sharply Criticize Trump's Behavior at News Conference with Putin," *Los Angeles Times*, July 16, 2018, https://www.latimes.com/politics/la-na-pol-washington-reacts-helsinki

-20180716-story.html. Significant GOP opposition to Trump's Russia policy continued into 2019 as well, when many Republicans voted against lifting sanctions on three companies tied to a Russian oligarch. See Kenneth P. Vogel, "136 House Republicans Join Democrats in Vote against Russia Sanctions Relief," *New York Times*, January 17, 2019, https://www.nytimes.com/2019/01/17/us/politics/trump-house-russia-sanctions.html; Kelsey Snell and Karoun Demirjian, "Capitol Hill Republicans Not On Board with Trump Budget," *Washington Post*, March 16, 2017, https://www.washingtonpost.com/powerpost/capitol-hill-republicans-not-on-board-with-trump-budget/2017/03/16/9952d63e-0a6b-11e7-b77c-0047d15a24e0_story.html. Damian Paletta and Steven Mufson, "Trump Federal Budget 2018: Massive Cuts to the Arts, Science, and the Poor," *Washington Post*, March 16, 2017, https://www.washingtonpost.com/business/economy/trump-federal-budget-2018-massive-cuts-to-the-arts-science-and-the-poor/2017/03/15/0a0a0094-09a1-11e7-a15f-a58d4a988474_story.html. For a later example, see Jeff Mason and Richard Cowan, "Trump's $4.8 Trillion Budget Gets Chilly Reception from Congress," Reuters, February 10, 2020, https://www.reuters.com/article/us-usa-trump-budget/trumps-4-8-trillion-budget-gets-chilly-reception-from-congress-idUSKBN204174. The figures about spending on education and scientific research are based on the authors' calculations from the General Social Survey.

31. Manu Raju, "Hill Republicans Revolt over Trump's Plans to Build Border Wall," CNN, February 6, 2017, https://www.cnn.com/2017/02/03/politics/border-wall-republicans/index.html; BBC, "Trump Says He Is Willing to 'Close Government' to Build Mexico Wall," BBC, August 23, 2017, https://www.bbc.com/news/world-us-canada-41020779; Burgess Everett, Sarah Ferris, and Caitlin Oprysko, "Trump Says He's 'Proud' to Shut Down Government during Fight with Pelosi and Schumer," *Politico*, December 11, 2018, https://www.politico.com/story/2018/12/11/trump-border-wall-congress-budget-1055433.

32. Polls about the shutdown are here: https://www.pollingreport.com/budget.htm. The polling averages of presidential approval are from FiveThirtyEight: https://projects.fivethirtyeight.com/trump-approval-ratings/.

33. GOP opposition is discussed in Jacob Pramuk and Christina Wilkie, "Trump Declares National Emergency to Build Border Wall, Setting Up Massive Legal Fight," CNBC, February 15, 2019, https://www.cnbc.com/2019/02/15/trump-national-emergency-declaration-border-wall-spending-bill.html. On the lack of new wall construction, see Silvia Foster-Frau, "Trump's Border Wall Falls Short of His Campaign Promise—But Leaves Behind a Legacy," *San Antonio Express-News*, December 4, 2020, https://www.expressnews.com/news/politics/texas_legislature/article/Trump-s-border-wall-falls-short-of-his-campaign-15776386.php. For more on the Trump administration's aggressive use of budgetary powers, see Eloise Pasachoff, "The President's Budget Powers in the Trump Era," in *Executive Policymaking: The Role of OMB in the Presidency*, ed. Meena Bose and Andrew Rudalevige (Washington, DC: Brookings Institution Press, 2020), 69–100.

34. Sarah Binder, "How to Waste a Congressional Majority," *Foreign Affairs*, January/February 2018, https://www.foreigncaffairs.com/articles/united-states/2017-11-22/how-waste-congressional-majority; Annie Lowrey, "The Party of No Content," *The Atlantic*, August 24, 2020, https://www.theatlantic.com/ideas/archive/2020/08/party-no-content/615607/. Edwards, "'Closer' or Context?," 467, notes "the relative absence of passage of significant legislation" in Trump's first year.

35. John Gramlich, "How Trump Compares with Other Recent Presidents in Appointing Federal Judges," Pew Research Center, July 15, 2020, https://www.pewresearch.org/fact-tank /2020/07/15/how-trump-compares-with-other-recent-presidents-in-appointing-federal -judges/.

36. Sarah Kliff, "Republicans Killed the Obamacare Mandate. New Data Shows It Didn't Really Matter," *New York Times*, September 21, 2020, https://www.nytimes.com/2020/09/18 /upshot/obamacare-mandate-republicans.html.

37. See Curry and Lee, *The Limits of Party*, on how internal party divisions were the central reason behind the party's challenges in repealing Obamacare and cutting government spending.

38. See this ABC News interview: https://abcnews.go.com/Politics/video/president-trump -white-house-interview-part-45052454.

39. This is based on first identifying *Washington Post* stories that mentioned the president, using key terms such as "Donald Trump" or "President Trump" or "Trump administration" and the word "scandal" in the headline or lead paragraph of the stories, and then eliminating op-eds as well as news stories that were not actually about an administration scandal. Our search parameters and coding strategy, as well as the choice of the *Washington Post*, is modeled on Brendan Nyhan, "Scandal Potential: How Political Context and News Congestion Affect the President's Vulnerability to Media Scandal," *British Journal of Political Science* 45, no. 2 (2015): 435–66. We cannot fully replicate his data because it was based on searches within the LexisNexis database, which no longer houses *Washington Post* content. We relied on Factiva instead. For Trump, we do not include coverage of Brett Kavanaugh's confirmation and the accusations of sexual assault because Kavanaugh was not part of the administration. We do, however, include coverage of scandals related to Trump's campaign, such as the one related to Cambridge Analytica. For Obama, we do not include coverage of Secretary of State Hillary Clinton's use of a private email server because these stories were framed in terms of her presidential campaign rather than the Obama administration itself.

40. Katie van Syckle, "Five Years, Thousands of Insults: Tracking Trump's Invective," *New York Times*, January 26, 2021, https://www.nytimes.com/2021/01/26/insider/Trump-twitter -insults-list.html. A visualization of the list is here: https://www.nytimes.com/interactive/2021 /01/19/upshot/trump-complete-insult-list.html#.

41. Louis Nelson and Madeline Conway, "Trump Escalates Attacks on McConnell," *Politico*, August 10, 2017, https://www.politico.com/story/2017/08/10/trump-attacks-mitch-mcconnell -twitter-241476; Rebecca Savransky, "Trump: 'Can You Believe' McConnell Couldn't Repeal, Replace Obamacare?," *The Hill*, August 10, 2017, https://thehill.com/homenews/administration /345999-trump-can-you-believe-mcconnell-couldnt-repeal-replace-obamacare. In YouGov surveys, McConnell was viewed favorably by 32 percent of Republicans and unfavorably by 35 percent as of August 5, 2017; his −3 net favorability rating was roughly where he had been since mid-July. After his fight with Trump, his net favorability rating dropped to −19 (29% favorable, 48% unfavorable) in a single week. The YouGov polls are here: https://today.yougov.com /topics/politics/trackers/mitch-mcconnell-favorability?crossBreak=republican.

42. David Sanger and Charlie Savage, "U.S. Says Russia Directed Hacks to Influence Elections," *New York Times*, October 7, 2016, https://www.nytimes.com/2016/10/08/us/politics

/us-formally-accuses-russia-of-stealing-dnc-emails.html; Office of the Director of National Intelligence, "Assessing Russian Activities and Intentions in Recent U.S. Elections," January 6, 2017, https://www.dni.gov/files/documents/ICA_2017_01.pdf; Adam Entous and Ellen Nakashima, "Trump Asked Intelligence Chiefs to Push Back against FBI Collusion Probe after Comey Revealed Its Existence," *Washington Post*, May 22, 2017, https://www.washingtonpost.com/world/national-security/trump-asked-intelligence-chiefs-to-push-back-against-fbi-collusion-probe-after-comey-revealed-its-existence/2017/05/22/394933 b.c.-3f10-11e7-9869-bac8b446820a_story.html; Josh Dawsey, "Behind Comey's Firing: An Enraged Trump, Fuming about Russia," *Politico*, May 10, 2017, https://www.politico.com/story/2017/05/10/comey-firing-trump-russia-238192; Matt Apuzzo, Maggie Haberman, and Matthew Rosenberg, "Trump Told Russians That Firing 'Nut Job' Comey Eased Pressure from Investigation," *New York Times*, May 19, 2017, https://www.nytimes.com/2017/05/19/us/politics/trump-russia-comey.html. The Mueller report is here: https://www.justice.gov/storage/report.pdf. See also Zachary B. Wolf, "Trump Has Already Said He's OK Working with Foreign Governments against His US Rivals," CNN, October 2, 2019, https://edition.cnn.com/2019/10/02/politics/foreign-dirt-campaigns-trump/index.html.

43. The whistle-blower complaint is here: https://www.cnn.com/2019/09/26/politics/read-whistleblower-complaint-trump-ukraine/index.html. The White House's transcript of the call is here, although it may not be complete: https://www.washingtonpost.com/context/official-readout-president-trump-s-july-25-phone-call-with-ukraine-s-volodymyr-zelensky/4b228f51-17e7-45 b.c.-b16c-3b2643f3fbe0/?itid=lk_inline_manual_7. See also Karoun Demirjian, Josh Dawsey, Ellen Nakashima, and Carol D. Leonig, "Trump Ordered Hold on Military Aid Days before Calling Ukrainian President, Officials Say," *Washington Post*, September 23, 2019, https://www.washingtonpost.com/national-security/trump-ordered-hold-on-military-aid-days-before-calling-ukrainian-president-officials-say/2019/09/23/df93a6ca-de38-11e9-8dc8-498eabc129a0_story.html; Pamela Brown, Jeremy Diamond, Kaitlan Collins, and Kevin Liptak, "Inside the White House's Effort to Contain Ukraine Call Fallout," CNN, October 8, 2019, https://www.cnn.com/2019/10/08/politics/donald-trump-ukraine-call-details-aftermath/index.html; Julian E. Barnes, Michael S. Schmidt, and Matthew Rosenberg, "Schiff Got Early Account of Accusations as Whistle-Blower's Concerns Grew," *New York Times*, October 2, 2019, https://www.nytimes.com/2019/10/02/us/politics/adam-schiff-whistleblower.html; Rachael Bade, Mike DeBonis, and Karoun Demirjian, "Pelosi Announces Impeachment Inquiry, Says Trump's Courting of Foreign Political Help Is a 'Betrayal of National Security,'" *Washington Post*, September 24, 2019, https://www.washingtonpost.com/powerpost/pelosi-top-democrats-privately-discuss-creation-of-select-committee-for-impeachment/2019/09/24/af6f735a-dedf-11e9-b199-f638bf2c340f_story.html; Tim Efrink, "Trump Suggests Pelosi, Schiff Committed 'Treason,' Should Be Impeached," *Washington Post*, October 7, 2019, https://www.washingtonpost.com/nation/2019/10/07/trump-pelosi-schiff-impeach-treason-tweet/.

44. The articles (H. Res. 755) are here: https://www.congress.gov/116/bills/hres755/BILLS-116hres755rh.pdf.

45. Glenn Kessler, "Trump's Outrageous Claim That 'Thousands' of New Jersey Muslims Celebrated the 9/11 Attacks," *Washington Post*, November 22, 2015, https://www.washingtonpost.com/news/fact-checker/wp/2015/11/22/donald-trumps-outrageous-claim-that-thousands

-of-new-jersey-muslims-celebrated-the-911-attacks/; German Lopez, "Donald Trump's Long History of Racism, from the 1970s to 2020," Vox, August 13, 2020, https://www.vox.com/2016 /7/25/12270880/donald-trump-racist-racism-history.

46. The Spencer quote is from David A. Graham, Adrienne Green, Cullen Murphy, and Parker Richards, "An Oral History of Trump's Bigotry," The Atlantic, June 2019, https://www .theatlantic.com/magazine/archive/2019/06/trump-racism-comments/588067/.

47. Jenna Johnson and John Wagner, "Trump Condemns Charlottesville Violence but Doesn't Single Out White Nationalists," Washington Post, August 12, 2017, https://www .washingtonpost.com/politics/trump-condemns-charlottesville-violence-but-doesnt-single -out-white-nationalists/2017/08/12/933a86d6-7fa3-11e7-9d08-b79f191668ed_story.html. The Gardner quote is noted in Tara Golshan, "GOP Senators React to Trump's Charlottesville Comments: 'Mr. President—We Must Call Evil by Its Name,'" Vox, August 12, 2017, https://www .vox.com/2017/8/12/16139144/gop-senators-react-trump-charlottesville. The Anglin quote is in Maya Oppenheim, "Neo-Nazis and White Supremacists Applaud Donald Trump's Response to Deadly Violence in Virginia," The Independent, August 13, 2017, https://www.independent.co .uk/news/world/americas/neo-nazis-white-supremacists-celebrate-trump-response-virginia -charlottesville-a7890786.html. See also Glenn Thrush and Maggie Haberman, "Trump Gives White Supremacists an Unequivocal Boost," New York Times, August 15, 2017, https://www .nytimes.com/2017/08/15/us/politics/trump-charlottesville-white-nationalists.html.

48. A transcript of Trump's August 15 remarks is here: https://www.latimes.com/politics/la -na-pol-trump-charlottesville-transcript-20170815-story.html. On the Phoenix rally, see Gregory Krieg, "Rally Trump vs. Teleprompter Trump," CNN, August 23, 2017, https://www.cnn .com/2017/08/23/politics/comparing-donald-trump-speeches-afghanistan-phoenix/index .html.

49. See Brian F. Schaffner, The Acceptance and Expression of Prejudice during the Trump Era (New York: Cambridge University Press, 2020), and Benjamin Newman, Jennifer L. Merolla, Sono Shah, Danielle Casarez Lemi, Loren Collingwood, and S. Karthick Ramakrishnan, "The Trump Effect: An Experimental Investigation of the Emboldening Effect of Racially Inflammatory Elite Communication," British Journal of Political Science 51, no. 3 (2020): 1138–59. At the same time, other research did not find any increase in hate speech or white nationalist rhetoric on Twitter during and immediately after the 2016 presidential campaign. See Alexandra Siegel et al., "Trumping Hate on Twitter? Online Hate Speech in the 2016 U.S. Election Campaign and Its Aftermath," Quarterly Journal of Political Science 16, no. 1 (2021): 71–104.

50. One example of this behavior by Trump supporters is described in Brianna Sacks, "A Trump Supporter Attacked Journalists after the President Blasted the Media at His Texas Rally," BuzzFeed, February 12, 2019, https://www.buzzfeednews.com/article/briannasacks/trump -supporter-shoved-journalists-el-paso-rally. The Trump quote is here: https://twitter.com /atrupar/status/1308567182436118528.

51. Veronica Stracqualursi and Liz Stark, "Trump Claims Media to Blame for 'Anger' after Bombs Sent to CNN, Dems," CNN, October 25, 2018, https://www.cnn.com/2018/10/25 /politics/trump-blames-media-for-anger-after-attacks/index.html; Adam Edelman, "Trump Hails Quick Arrest of Pipe Bomb Suspect, Vows 'Swift and Certain Justice,'" NBC News, October 26, 2018, https://www.nbcnews.com/politics/donald-trump/trump-hails-quick-arrest -pipe-bomb-suspect-vows-swift-certain-n924871.

52. Gregory Krieg, "Trump Threatens to Jail Clinton if He Wins Election," CNN, October 10, 2016, https://www.cnn.com/2016/10/09/politics/eric-holder-nixon-trump-presidential -debate/index.html; Kyle Cheney, "'Where Are All of the Arrests?' Trump Demands Barr Lock Up His Foes," *Politico*, October 6, 2020, https://www.politico.com/news/2020/10/07/trump -demands-barr-arrest-foes-427389.

53. Jake Tapper, "Trump Told CBD Head He'd Pardon Him if He Were Sent to Jail for Violating Immigration Law," CNN, April 13, 2019, https://www.cnn.com/2019/04/12/politics/trump -cbp-commissioner-pardon/index.html; Sides, Tesler, and Vavreck, *Identity Crisis*, 1–2.

54. These are a few examples among many. See Chris Cillizza and Brenna Williams, "15 Times Donald Trump Praised Authoritarian Rulers," CNN, July 2, 2019, https://www.cnn.com /2019/07/02/politics/donald-trump-dictators-kim-jong-un-vladimir-putin/index.html. On Duterte, see Louis Nelson, "Trump Praises Duterte for 'Unbelievable Job' Cracking Down on Drugs in the Philippines," *Politico*, May 24, 2017, https://www.politico.com/story/2017/05/24 /trump-rodrigo-duterte-call-transcript-238758.

55. Gregory Krieg, "CPAC Goes Full Trump for 2018," CNN, February 23, 2018, https://www .cnn.com/2018/02/23/politics/cpac-trump-takeover-2018/index.html.

CHAPTER 3: SOMEWHERE BETWEEN "LANDSLIDE" AND "OH, SHIT"

Epigraph: Brian Bennett, "'My Whole Life Is a Bet.' Inside President Trump's Gamble on an Untested Reelection Strategy," *Time*, June 20, 2019, https://time.com/longform/donald-trump -2020/.

1. A transcript of Trump's remarks is here: https://www.cbsnews.com/news/trump-cia -speech-transcript/. See also Shane Goldmacher and Matthew Nussbaum, "At CIA Headquarters, Trump Boasts about Himself, Denies Feud," *Politico*, January 21, 2017, https://www.politico .com/story/2017/01/trump-cia-langley-233971; Lori Robertson and Robert Farley, "The Facts on Crowd Size," FactCheck.org, January 23, 2017, https://www.factcheck.org/2017/01/the-facts -on-crowd-size/.

2. On presidents and polling, see James N. Druckman and Lawrence R. Jacobs, *Who Governs? Presidents, Public Opinion, and Manipulation* (Chicago: University of Chicago Press, 2015). On Trump's exaggerating his poll standing, one example is John Wagner, "Trump Shares an Inaccurate Graphic on Twitter That Overstates His Job Approval by 12 points," *Washington Post*, April 11, 2019, https://www.washingtonpost.com/politics/trump-shares-an-inaccurate-graphic -on-twitter-that-overstates-his-job-approval-by-12-points/2019/04/11/167d9ad6-5c4a-11e9 -9625-01d48d50ef75_story.html. Trump's attacks on polls and pollsters are many. See https:// www.nytimes.com/interactive/2021/01/19/upshot/trump-complete-insult-list.html#.

3. See https://news.gallup.com/poll/189299/presidential-election-2016-key-indicators .aspx#pcf-image; and Lydia Saad, "Trump and Clinton Finish with Historically Poor Images," Gallup, November 8, 2016, https://news.gallup.com/poll/197231/trump-clinton-finish -historically-poor-images.aspx.

4. Jeffrey M. Jones, "Trump Job Approval 21 Points below Average at One-Month Mark," Gallup, February 17, 2017, https://news.gallup.com/poll/204050/trump-job-approval-points -below-average-one-month-mark.aspx.

5. The questions that make up the index are the following: "We are interested in how people are getting along financially these days. Would you say that you (and your family living there) are better off or worse off financially than you were a year ago?"; "Now looking ahead—do you think that a year from now you (and your family living there) will be better off financially, or worse off, or just about the same as now?"; "Now turning to business conditions in the country as a whole—do you think that during the next twelve months we'll have good times financially, or bad times, or what?"; "Looking ahead, which would you say is more likely—that in the country as a whole we'll have continuous good times during the next five years or so, or that we will have periods of widespread unemployment or depression, or what?"; and "About the big things people buy for their homes—such as furniture, a refrigerator, stove, television, and things like that. Generally speaking, do you think now is a good or bad time for people to buy major household items?" For evidence of the historical reliability and validity of the index, see Paul M. Kellstedt, Suzanna Linn, and A. Lee Hannah, "The Usefulness of Consumer Sentiment: Assessing Construct and Measurement," *Public Opinion Quarterly* 79, no. 1 (2015): 181–203.

6. Peter K. Enns, Paul M. Kellstedt, and Gregory E. McAvoy, "The Consequences of Partisanship in Economic Perceptions," *Public Opinion Quarterly* 76, no. 2 (2012): 287–310; Kathleen Donovan, Paul M. Kellstedt, Ellen M. Key, and Matthew J. Lebo, "Motivated Reasoning, Public Opinion, and Presidential Approval," *Political Behavior* 42 (2020): 1201–21.

7. John Sides, Michael Tesler, and Lynn Vavreck, *Identity Crisis: The 2016 Presidential Campaign and the Battle for the Meaning of America* (Princeton: Princeton University Press, 2018).

8. Pew Research Center, "Trump Begins Third Year with Low Job Approval and Doubts about His Honesty," January 18, 2019, https://www.pewresearch.org/politics/2019/01/18/trump-begins-third-year-with-low-job-approval-and-doubts-about-his-honesty/; Amina Dunn, "Trump's Approval Ratings So Far Are Unusually Stable—and Deeply Partisan," Pew Research Center, August 24, 2020, https://www.pewresearch.org/fact-tank/2020/08/24/trumps-approval-ratings-so-far-are-unusually-stable-and-deeply-partisan/.

9. The Gallup polls underlying these statistics are here: https://news.gallup.com/poll/1732/presidential-ratings-personal-characteristics.aspx. Presidential approval ratings from the same time period were obtained here: https://news.gallup.com/interactives/185273/presidential-job-approval-center.aspx. See also Megan Brenan, "Americans' Views of Trump's Character Firmly Established," Gallup, June 18, 2020, https://news.gallup.com/poll/312737/americans-views-trump-character-firmly-established.aspx.

10. For more on Barack Obama's notably high personal approval, see John Sides and Lynn Vavreck, *The Gamble: Choice and Chance in the 2012 Presidential Election* (Princeton: Princeton University Press, 2013); and Pew Research Center, "Obama: Weak Job Ratings, but Positive Personal Image," January 19, 2012, https://www.pewresearch.org/politics/2012/01/19/section-1-barack-obamas-performance-and-image/.

11. The racism questions are from August 2018 and July 2019 Quinnipiac polls.

12. These figures come from the Crowd Counting Project, which is run by political scientists Erica Chenoweth and Jeremy Pressman. See Erica Chenoweth, Tommy Leung, Nathan Perkins, Jeremy Pressman, and Jay Ulfelder, "The Trump Years Launched the Biggest Sustained Protest Movement in U.S. History. It's Not Over," *The Monkey Cage* (blog), February 8, 2021, https://www.washingtonpost.com/politics/2021/02/08/trump-years-launched-biggest-sustained

-protest-movement-us-history-its-not-over/; and Erica Chenoweth and Jeremy Pressman, "Millions of Protestors Turned Out in June—More Than in Any Other Month Since Trump's Inauguration," *The Monkey Cage* (blog), August 31, 2018, https://www.washingtonpost.com/news /monkey-cage/wp/2018/08/31/millions-of-protesters-turned-out-in-june-more-than-in-any -month-since-trumps-inauguration/.

13. The data on Indivisible is from Lara Putnam and Gabriel Perez-Putnam, "Grassroots Blossom across America, Reshaping Country's Political Geography," American Communities Project, September 13, 2019, https://www.americancommunities.org/grassroots-blossom -across-america-reshaping-countrys-political-geography/. On local organizing, see Lara Putnam and Theda Skocpol, "Middle America Reboots Democracy," *Democracy*, February 20, 2018, https://democracyjournal.org/arguments/middle-america-reboots-democracy/; and Gideon Lewis-Kraus, "How the 'Resistance' Helped Democrats Dominate Virginia," *New York Times Magazine*, November 13, 2017, https://www.nytimes.com/2017/11/13/magazine/how-the -resistance-helped-democrats-dominate-virginia.html.

14. Gary Jacobson, "Extreme Referendum: Donald Trump and the 2018 Midterm Elections," *Political Science Quarterly* 134, no. 1 (2019): 9–38.

15. Erika Franklin Fowler, Michael Franz, and Travis N. Ridout, "The Big Lessons of Political Advertising in 2018," *The Conversation*, December 3, 2018, https://theconversation.com/the-big -lessons-of-political-advertising-in-2018-107673; Austin Bussing, Will Patton, Jason M. Roberts, and Sarah A. Treul, "The Electoral Consequences of Roll Call Voting: Health Care and the 2018 Election," *Political Behavior*, May 8, 2020, https://doi.org/10.1007/s11109-020-09615-4; Brian F. Schaffner, "The Heightened Importance of Racism and Sexism in the 2018 U.S. Midterm Election," *British Journal of Political Science*, September 16, 2020, https://doi.org/10.1017 /S0007123420000319; Sides, Tesler, and Vavreck, *Identity Crisis*, 224–25; Andrew O. Ballard, Hans J. G. Hassell, and Michael Heseltine, "Be Careful What You Wish For: The Impacts of Presidential Trump's Midterm Endorsements," *Legislative Studies Quarterly*, May 19, 2020, https://doi.org/10.1111/lsq.12284.

16. Catherine Lucey, Jonathan Lemire, and Zeke Miller, "Trump Tells AP He Won't Accept Blame if GOP Loses House," Associated Press, October 16, 2018, https://apnews.com/article /8f4baf7aaddc442dad0a726f3ebe7fff.

17. Jeremy Diamond, "Trump: I Could 'Shoot Somebody and I Wouldn't Lose Voters,'" CNN, January 24, 2016, https://www.cnn.com/2016/01/23/politics/donald-trump-shoot -somebody-support/index.html.

18. The McHenry quote is from Jonathan Martin and Maggie Haberman, "Fear and Loyalty: How Donald Trump Took Over the Republican Party," *New York Times*, December 21, 2019, https://www.nytimes.com/2019/12/21/us/politics/trump-impeachment-republicans.html.

19. Michael Tesler, "Why Are Republicans Silent about the Ukraine Whistleblower Scandal? This One Chart Explains," *The Monkey Cage* (blog), September 24, 2019, https://www .washingtonpost.com/politics/2019/09/24/why-are-republicans-silent-about-ukraine -whistleblower-scandal-this-one-chart-explains/. The Graham quote is from Michael D. Shear and Sheryl Gay Stolberg, "As Other Republican Senators Bolt, Lindsey Graham Cozies Up to Trump," *New York Times*, October 26, 2017, https://www.nytimes.com/2017/10/26/us/politics /trump-lindsey-graham-best-friends.html.

20. The YouGov tracking polls for Trump among Republicans are here: https://today.yougov
.com/topics/politics/trackers/donald-trump-approval?crossBreak=republican and https://
today.yougov.com/topics/politics/trackers/donald-trump-favorability?crossBreak=republican.
The YouGov tracking polls for Obama among Democrats are here: https://today.yougov.com
/topics/politics/trackers/president-obama-job-approval-rating?crossBreak=democrat and
https://today.yougov.com/topics/politics/trackers/barack-obama-favorability?crossBreak
=democrat. Larry Bartels, "Partisanship in the Trump Era," *Journal of Politics* 80, no. 4 (2018):
1483–94.

21. Frank Newport, "Americans Evaluate Trump's Character across 13 Dimensions," Gallup,
June 25, 2018, https://news.gallup.com/poll/235907/americans-evaluate-trump-character
-across-dimensions.aspx.

22. Megan Brenan, "Tax Day Update: Americans Still Not Seeing Tax Cut Benefit," Gallup,
April 12, 2019, https://news.gallup.com/poll/248681/tax-day-update-americans-not-seeing-tax
-cut-benefit.aspx.

23. Pew Research Center, "Most Border Wall Opponents, Supporters Say Shutdown Concessions Are Unacceptable," January 16, 2019, https://www.pewresearch.org/politics/2019/01
/16/most-border-wall-opponents-supporters-say-shutdown-concessions-are-unacceptable
/#partisans-differ-over-whether-shutdown-is-a-very-serious-problem.

24. On cross-pressures and defection in elections, see D. Sunshine Hillygus and Todd G.
Shields, *The Persuadable Voter: Wedge Issues in Presidential Campaigns* (Princeton: Princeton
University Press, 2008). On cross-pressured Obama voters in 2016, see Sides, Tesler, and
Vavreck, *Identity Crisis*.

25. Shane Croucher, "Republicans Chant 'Four More Years' at Trump's State of the Union
Address, Democrats Call It a 'Trump Rally,'" *Newsweek*, February 5, 2020, https://www
.newsweek.com/trump-sotu-pelosi-republicans-2020-election-1485756.

26. Ben White, "Trump Will Try to Spook Voters into Sticking with Him," *Politico*, February 3, 2020, https://www.politico.com/news/2020/02/03/trump-state-of-the-union-address
-110618; Ben White and Steven Shepard, "How Trump Is on Track for a 2020 Landslide," *Politico*, March 21, 2019, https://www.politico.com/story/2019/03/21/trump-economy-election
-1230495; Anita Kumar, "Trump Was Acquitted. But Didn't Get Exactly What He Wanted,"
Politico, February 5, 2020, https://www.politico.com/news/2020/02/05/trumps-impeachment
-test-tv-exoneration-109856.

27. On the incumbency advantage, see David R. Mayhew, "Incumbency Advantage in U.S.
Presidential Elections: The Historical Record," *Political Science Quarterly* 123, no. 2 (2008):
201–28. On how incumbency conditions the impact of economic growth and presidential ap-
proval, see James E. Campbell, Bryan J. Dettrey, and Hongxing Yin, "The Theory of Conditional
Retrospective Voting: Does the Presidential Record Matter Less in Open-Seat Elections?,"
Journal of Politics 72, no. 4 (2010): 1083–95. On the effect of the incumbent party's tenure in the
White House, see Alan I. Abramowitz, "Forecasting the 2008 Presidential Election with the
Time-for-Change Model," *PS: Political Science and Politics* 41, no. 4 (2008): 691–95; Christopher
Wlezien, "Policy (Mis)Representation and the Costs of Ruling: U.S. Presidential Elections in
Comparative Perspective," *Comparative Political Studies* 50, no. 6 (2017): 711–38. Notably, the
accuracy of forecasting models does not seem to have declined over time: see Richard Nadeau,
Ruth Dassonneville, Michael S. Lewis-Beck, and Philippe Mongrain, "Are Election Results

More Unpredictable? A Forecasting Test," *Political Science Research and Methods* 8 (2020): 764–71.

28. Substituting the equivalent change in real disposable income per capita for the change in gross domestic product generates a forecast a bit less favorable to Trump (48.6% of the major-party vote).

29. Stephanie Murray, "'You Have No Choice but to Vote for Me,' Trump Tells N.H. Rally," *Politico*, August 15, 2019, https://www.politico.com/story/2019/08/15/trump-new-hampshire -rally-manchester-1466285.

CHAPTER 4: A HOUSE UNITED

Epigraph: Carville's comments on MSNBC are here: https://www.msnbc.com/the-beat -with-ari/watch/-wake-up-dem-vet-calls-for-party-to-be-more-relevant-diverse-after-iowa -chaos-78129221946.

1. A transcript of the debate is here: https://abcnews.go.com/US/read-full-transcript-abc -news-3rd-democratic-debate/story?id=65587810.

2. Ryan Cooper, "Democrats' 2020 Battle Royale Is Going to Be Brutal, Dirty, and Totally Worthwhile," *The Week*, December 10, 2018, https://theweek.com/articles/811382/democrats -2020-battle-royale-going-brutal-dirty-totally-worthwhile.

3. "Toxic distrust" is from Jonathan Allen and Amie Parnes, *Lucky: How Joe Biden Barely Won the Presidency* (New York: Crown, 2021), xxii.

4. Quoted in Seth Masket, *Learning from Loss: The Democrats 2016–2020* (New York: Cambridge University Press, 2020), 1.

5. Masket, *Learning from Loss*. That Biden believed Clinton was not a good candidate is reported in Allen and Parnes, *Lucky*, xx.

6. The 60 percent and 80 percent figures are from John Sides, Michael Tesler, and Lynn Vavreck, *Identity Crisis: The 2016 Presidential Campaign and the Battle for the Meaning of America* (Princeton: Princeton University Press, 2018), 111, 160.

7. On the notion of a Democratic Tea Party, see Tom Davis, "Are Democrats Facing Their Own Tea Party–Style Reckoning?," *Politico*, March 18, 2019, https://www.politico.com /magazine/story/2019/03/18/democrats-aoc-ocasio-cortez-socialists-pelosi-congress-left-tea -party-225813/. The data on primary challengers and outside groups comes from Robert Boatright and Zachary Albert, "Factional Conflict and Independent Expenditures in the 2018 Democratic House Primaries," *Congress and the Presidency* 48, no. 1 (2021): 50–77.

8. On the invisible primary and its importance, see Marty Cohen, David Karol, Hans Noel, and John Zaller, *The Party Decides: Presidential Nominations before and after Reform* (Chicago: University of Chicago Press, 2008).

9. Glenn Thrush, "Party of Two," *Politico* magazine, July/August 2016, https://www.politico .com/magazine/story/2016/07/2016-barack-obama-hillary-clinton-democratic-establishment -campaign-primary-joe-biden-elizabeth-warren-214023/.

10. Alexander Burns and Jonathan Martin, "Joe Biden Announces 2020 Run for President, after Months of Hesitation," *New York Times*, April 25, 2019, https://www.nytimes.com/2019 /04/25/us/politics/joe-biden-2020-announcement.html.

11. Cohen et al., *The Party Decides*.

12. Most state legislators also did not endorse a presidential candidate in 2020. Among those who did, there was even less consensus on a favored candidate. See data collected by the political scientist Boris Shor: https://twitter.com/bshor/status/1224366104715366401 and https://twitter.com/bshor/status/1224386863504424960.

13. On Biden's courting of Sharpton and Abrams, see Allen and Parnes, *Lucky*, 4–6, 24–26. On Obama's stance toward Biden's campaign, see Allen and Parnes, *Lucky*, 32, 86, 113.

14. On changes in presidential primary fund-raising, see Marty Cohen, David Karol, Hans Noel, and John Zaller, "Party versus Faction in the Reformed Presidential Nominating System," *PS: Political Science and Politics* 49, no. 4 (2016): 701–8. The 2016 fund-raising numbers are from the Campaign Finance Institute: http://www.cfinst.org/pdf/federal/HistoricalTables/pdf/CFI_Federal-CF_18_Table1-03.pdf and http://www.cfinst.org/pdf/federal/HistoricalTables/pdf/CFI_Federal-CF_18_Table1-04a.pdf.

15. The 2007 data is here: http://www.cfinst.org/pdf/federal/HistoricalTables/pdf/CFI_Federal-CF_18_Table1-06c.pdf. They have been adjusted for inflation to compare to 2019.

16. Maggie Severns, "Why Biden Is Getting Crushed in the All-Important Money Race," *Politico*, October 24, 2019, https://www.politico.com/news/2019/10/24/obama-clinton-donors-biden-fundraising-056246. The quote from the Democratic fund raiser is in this article.

17. On increasing media coverage of the invisible primary, see Cohen et al., "Party versus Faction." On the importance of media coverage in the 2016 primaries, see Sides, Tesler, and Vavreck, *Identity Crisis*. On the 2016 Republican primary, see also Kevin Reuning and Nick Dietrich, "Media Coverage, Public Interest, and Support in the 2016 Republican Invisible Primary," *Perspectives on Politics* 17, no. 2 (2018): 326–39.

18. On discovery, scrutiny, and decline in the 2012 and 2016 presidential primaries, see John Sides and Lynn Vavreck, *The Gamble: Choice and Chance in the 2012 Election* (Princeton: Princeton University Press, 2013); Sides, Tesler, and Vavreck, *Identity Crisis*.

19. To document trends in news coverage in 2020, we rely on transcripts of cable network coverage gathered by the Internet Archive's Television News Archive. For each day, we calculated the total number of mentions of all the Democratic candidates and then each candidate's share of those mentions. This provides a very sensitive measure of exactly how much attention the candidates were getting. We then compare their share of news coverage to their average share in national polls. The cable networks are Fox News, CNN, MSNBC, C-SPAN, Fox Business, C-SPAN 2, Bloomberg, C-SPAN 3, and CNBC. The Internet Archive's Television News Archive is here: https://archive.org/details/tv. The data is accessible here: https://api.gdeltproject.org/api/v2/summary/summary?d=iatv. The polling data is from FiveThirtyEight: https://projects.fivethirtyeight.com/polls/president-primary-d/national/. We place each poll at the midpoint of its field period, calculate a daily average when there is more than one poll on the same day, and then smooth the daily numbers using local regression with a bandwidth of 0.05.

20. Astead W. Herndon, "Kamala Harris Is Accused of Lying about Listening to Tupac. Here's What Actually Happened," *New York Times*, February 13, 2019, https://www.nytimes.com/2019/02/13/us/politics/kamala-harris-snoop-tupac.html; Katie Zernike, "'Progressive Prosecutor': Can Kamala Harris Square the Circle?," *New York Times*, February 11, 2019, https://www.nytimes.com/2019/02/11/us/kamala-harris-progressive-prosecutor.html; Matt Flegenheimer

and Alexander Burns, "Kamala Harris Makes the Case That Joe Biden Should Pass That Torch to Her," *New York Times*, June 27, 2019, https://www.nytimes.com/2019/06/27/us/politics /kamala-harris-busing-joe-biden.html; Jonathan Martin, Astead W. Herndon, and Alexander Burns, "How Kamala Harris's Campaign Unraveled," *New York Times*, November 29, 2019, https://www.nytimes.com/2019/11/29/us/politics/kamala-harris-2020.html.

21. Isaac Stanley-Becker, "'He Knows Better': Pete Buttigieg Has Made Mike Pence His Target, and the Vice-President Isn't Pleased," *Washington Post*, April 11, 2019, https://www .washingtonpost.com/nation/2019/04/11/he-knows-better-pete-buttigieg-has-made-mike -pence-his-target-vice-president-isnt-pleased/; Mark Z. Barabak, "Mayor Pete Buttigieg Is the Hottest Thing in Politics. Can It Last?," *Los Angeles Times*, April 12, 2019, https://www.latimes .com/politics/la-na-pol-mayor-pete-buttegieg-democrats-president-2020-20190412-story .html; Michael M. Grynbaum, "Fox News Welcomes Pete Buttigieg. Trump and 'Fox & Friends' Aren't Pleased," *New York Times*, May 20, 2019, https://www.nytimes.com/2019/05/20 /business/media/fox-news-pete-buttigieg-chris-wallace.html; John Wagner, "Buttigieg Steps Off Campaign Trail after Deadly Police Shooting in South Bend," *Washington Post*, June 17, 2019, https://www.washingtonpost.com/politics/buttigieg-steps-off-campaign-trail-following -deadly-police-shooting-in-south-bend/2019/06/17/6c8ae536-90e9-11e9-b58a-a6a9afaa0e3e _story.html; Tom Perkins, "Pete Buttigieg: Police Killing Exposes Mayor's Troubled History with Minorities," *The Guardian*, June 27, 2019, https://www.theguardian.com/us-news/2019 /jun/27/pete-buttigieg-police-shooting-south-bend-indiana. The Marcia Fudge quote is from Hanna Trudo, "'Pete Has a Black Problem': Top Black Leaders Say Buttigieg Is 'Naive' on Race," *Daily Beast*, June 24, 2019, https://www.thedailybeast.com/pete-buttigieg-has-a-black-problem -top-african-american-leaders-say-he-is-naive-on-race. See also Trip Gabriel and Richard A. Oppel Jr., "Pete Buttigieg Was Rising. Then Came South Bend's Policing Crisis," *New York Times*, August 30, 2019, https://www.nytimes.com/2019/08/30/us/politics/pete-buttigieg-south -bend-police.html.

22. Scot Lehigh, "Pete Buttigieg Wins the Night," *Boston Globe*, October 16, 2020, https:// www.bostonglobe.com/opinion/2019/10/16/pete-buttigieg-wins-night/2DLyzB8s0Dqtsf p0y7VC2I/story.html; Quint Forgey, "Biden Surges in Iowa Poll," *Politico*, October 21, 2019, https://www.politico.com/news/2019/10/21/pete-buttigieg-iowa-poll-053145; Michael Harriott, "Pete Buttigieg Is a Lying MF," *The Root*, November 25, 2019, https://www.theroot.com /pete-buttigieg-is-a-lying-mf-1840038708; and Reid J. Epstein and Sydney Ember, "Pete Buttigieg Responds to Uproar over Past Comments on Minority Students," *New York Times*, November 26, 2019, https://www.nytimes.com/2019/11/26/us/politics/pete-buttigieg-the-root -michael-harriot.html.

23. David P. Redlawsk, Caroline J. Tolbert, and Todd Donovan, *Why Iowa? How Caucuses and Sequential Elections Improve the Presidential Nominating Process* (Chicago: University of Chicago Press, 2011). Some commentators wondered whether Buttigieg might have benefited more if the Iowa outcome had not taken days to finalize. Buttigieg's bump in New Hampshire was smaller than that of some other Iowa winners. For example, John Kerry's standing in the New Hampshire polls increased by 16 points after he won the 2004 Iowa caucus, and Obama's increased by 16 points in 2008. At the same time, Buttigieg's Iowa win was narrower than either Kerry's or Obama's and not a dramatic "upset" of a favored candidate (Howard Dean in 2004,

Hillary Clinton in 2008). Moreover, other Iowa winners have seen smaller polling bumps in New Hampshire (for example, in the 2012 Republican primary, Rick Santorum got a 6-point bump). Thus, it is hard to know exactly how much the Iowa delay hurt Buttigieg.

24. Jim Tankersley, "Warren's Plan Is Latest Push by Democrats to Raise Taxes on the Rich," *New York Times*, January 24, 2019, https://www.nytimes.com/2019/01/24/us/politics/wealth -tax-democrats.html; Isaac Stanley-Becker and Tony Romm, "Facebook Deletes, and Then Restores, Elizabeth Warren's Ads Criticizing the Platform, Drawing Her Rebuke," *Washington Post*, March 12, 2019, https://www.washingtonpost.com/nation/2019/03/12/facebook-deletes -then-restores-elizabeth-warrens-ads-criticizing-platform-drawing-her-rebuke/. The "play catch-up" line is from Thomas Kaplan and Jim Tankersley, "Elizabeth Warren Has Lots of Plans. Together, They Would Remake the Economy," *New York Times*, June 10, 2019, https://www .nytimes.com/2019/06/10/us/politics/elizabeth-warren-2020-policies-platform.html; Greg- ory Krieg, "Five Takeaways from Elizabeth Warren's CNN Town Hall," CNN, March 19, 2019, https://www.cnn.com/2019/03/18/politics/elizabeth-warren-townhall-takeaways; Cat Fergu- son, "6,500 Turn Out for Elizabeth Warren's Oakland Town Hall," *San Jose Mercury News*, May 31, 2019, https://www.mercurynews.com/2019/05/31/elizabeth-warrens-laney-town-hall -delayed-by-huge-crowd/.

25. David Gutman, "Elizabeth Warren Tells Crowd of 15,000 in Seattle, 'Nobody Gets to Stay on the Sidelines,'" *Seattle Times*, August 25, 2019, https://www.seattletimes.com/seattle-news /politics/elizabeth-warren-tells-crowd-of-15000-in-seattle-nobody-gets-to-stay-on-the -sidelines/; Joseph Zeballos-Roig, "Thousands Flooded a Manhattan Park to See Elizabeth Warren in Her Biggest Rally to Date, and Her Selfie Line after Lasted Almost 4 Hours," *Business Insider*, September 17, 2019, https://www.businessinsider.com/elizabeth-warren-drew-a-crowd -of-thousands-campaign-stop-2019-9; Chris Cillizza, "What Elizabeth Warren's Massive Crowds Tell Us," CNN, August 26, 2019, https://www.cnn.com/2019/08/26/politics/elizabeth -warren-crowd-size-2020.

26. Madeleine Carlisle, Mahita Gajanan, Abigail Abrams, Abby Vesoulis, and Rachel E. Greenspan, "October Democratic Debate Highlights: Elizabeth Warren Takes Punches from Buttigieg, Biden, and More," *Time*, October 15, 2019, https://time.com/5701382/democratic -debate-live-updates/; Alexander Burns and Jonathan Martin, "Warren Draws Fire from All Sides, Reflecting a Shift in Fortunes in Race," *New York Times*, October 15, 2019, https://www .nytimes.com/2019/10/15/us/politics/october-democratic-debate-recap.html; Jacob Pramuk, "Elizabeth Warren Says She Would Not Raise Middle-Class Taxes for $52 Trillion Health-Care Plan," CNBC, November 1, 2019, https://www.cnbc.com/2019/11/01/elizabeth-warren -releases-plan-to-pay-for-medicare-for-all.html. Relevant reporting includes Alice Miranda Oll- stein, "5 Ways Opponents Are Going After Warren's 'Medicare for All Plan,'" *Politico*, Novem- ber 4, 2019, https://www.politico.com/news/2019/11/04/five-ways-opponents-warren -medicare-065740; Ronald Brownstein, "Can Warren Actually Avoid Taxing the Middle Class?," *The Atlantic*, November 3, 2019, https://www.theatlantic.com/politics/archive/2019/11/warren -medicare-all-taxes/601315/. The *Washington Post* column is Jennifer Rubin, "Elizabeth War- ren's Biggest Political Decision May Be Her Worst," *Washington Post*, November 7, 2019, https:// www.washingtonpost.com/opinions/2019/11/07/warrens-biggest-political-decision-may-be -her-worst/.

27. The analysis of invisible primary news coverage from the 2016 campaign is Thomas E. Patterson, "Pre-Primary News Coverage of the 2016 Presidential Race: Trump's Rise, Sanders' Emergence, Clinton's Struggle," Shorenstein Center on Media, Politics and Public Policy, June 2016, https://shorensteincenter.org/pre-primary-news-coverage-2016-trump-clinton -sanders/#The_Democratic_Race. On Sanders's tax returns, see Thomas Kaplan, "Bernie Sanders Released His Tax Returns. He's Part of the 1%," *New York Times*, April 15, 2019, https://www .nytimes.com/2019/04/15/us/politics/bernie-sanders-taxes.html. On the socialism speech, see Sean Sullivan, "Sen. Bernie Sanders Defends Democratic Socialism, Reflecting Internal Democratic Battle over the Party's Philosophy," *Washington Post*, June 12, 2019, https://www .washingtonpost.com/politics/sen-bernie-sanders-defends-democratic-socialism-reflecting -internal-democratic-battle-over-the-partys-philosophy/2019/06/12/bd8cb660-8c95-11e9 -b08e-cfd89bd36d4e_story.html. On Sanders's heart attack, see Sydney Ember and Jonathan Martin, "Bernie Sanders Is Hospitalized, Raising Questions about His Candidacy," *New York Times*, October 2, 2019, https://www.nytimes.com/2019/10/02/us/politics/bernie-sanders -health.html.

28. Sydney Ember and Jonathan Martin, "Joe Biden Scrambles to Stem Crisis after Lucy Flores' Allegation," *New York Times*, March 31, 2019, https://www.nytimes.com/2019/03/31/us /politics/joe-biden-flores.html; Lisa Lerer, "Joe Biden Jokes about Hugging in a Speech, then Offers a Mixed Apology," *New York Times*, April 5, 2019, https://www.nytimes.com/2019/04 /05/us/politics/joe-biden-controversy.html; Amber Phillips, "Joe Biden Picked a Bad Week to Have a Bad Week," *Washington Post*, June 21, 2019, https://www.washingtonpost.com/politics /2019/06/21/just-how-bad-has-joe-bidens-week-been-hes-defending-his-record-civil-rights/.

29. Matt Viser and Greg Jaffe, "As He Campaigns for President, Joe Biden Tells a Moving but False War Story," *Washington Post*, August 29, 2019, https://www.washingtonpost.com /politics/as-he-campaigns-for-president-joe-biden-tells-a-moving-but-false-war-story/2019 /08/29/b5159676-c9aa-11e9-a1fe-ca46e8d573c0_story.html; Stephen Collinson, "New Biden Gaffe Raises Question of Truth in Trump's Post-Fact Era," CNN, August 30, 2019, https://www .cnn.com/2019/08/30/politics/joe-biden-donald-trump-truth-2020-campaign; Colby Itkow- itz, "'He Knows I'll Beat Him Like a Drum': Biden Accuses Trump of Abusing Power to Smear Him," *Washington Post*, September 21, 2019, https://www.washingtonpost.com/politics/he -knows-ill-beat-him-like-a-drum-biden-accuses-trump-of-abusing-power-to-smear-him/2019 /09/21/49bf62de-dc93-11e9-a688-303693fb4b0b_story.html; Maeve Reston, "Analysis: What Biden's 'Damn Liar' Exchange Shows When It Comes to His Candidacy," CNN, Decem- ber 6, 2020, https://www.cnn.com/2019/12/06/politics/joe-biden-iowa-voter-confrontation -analysis; Margaret Talev, "Biden Promises Restrictions on Hunter, Family if Elected," Axios, December 8, 2019, https://www.axios.com/joe-biden-hunter-family-restrictions-impeachment -c13a3832-b501-43e9-8709-de6243c9d21d.html; Eric Levitz, "Joe Biden Still Can't Answer Basic Questions about Hunter and Burisma," *New York*, December 9, 2019, https://nymag.com /intelligencer/2019/12/joe-biden-hunter-burisma-axios-iowa-disqualifying.html. On Clin- ton's entering the race, see Allen and Parnes, *Lucky*, 117–18.

30. The Plouffe quote is from Glenn Thrush, "Party of Two," *Politico* magazine, July/Au- gust 2016, https://www.politico.com/magazine/story/2016/07/2016-barack-obama-hillary -clinton-democratic-establishment-campaign-primary-joe-biden-elizabeth-warren-214023/.

31. On the reshuffling of Biden's campaign staff and money problems, see Allen and Parnes, *Lucky*, chap. 8. On the shift in forecasting models after the Iowa caucus, see Nate Silver, "Our Post-Iowa Primary Forecast Is Up, and Biden's Chances Are Down," FiveThirtyEight, February 5, 2020, https://fivethirtyeight.com/features/our-post-iowa-primary-forecast-is-up-and -bidens-chances-are-down/.

32. Natasha Korecki and David Siders, "Sanders Sends Democratic Establishment into Panic Mode," *Politico*, February 23, 2020, https://www.politico.com/news/2020/02/23 /sanders-democratic-establishment-panic-mode-117065; Jonathan Allen, "Bloomberg Storms to the Center of the 2020 Presidential Fray," NBC News, February 12, 2020, https:// www.nbcnews.com/politics/2020-election/bloomberg-storms-center-2020-presidential -fray-n1135111.

33. Quoted in Allen and Parnes, *Lucky*, 35.

34. On Clyburn's initial skepticism of a Biden candidacy, see Allen and Parnes, *Lucky*, 13. On the alleged impact of Clyburn's endorsement, see Donna M. Owens, "Jim Clyburn Changed Everything for Joe Biden's Campaign. He's Been a Political Force for a Long Time," *Washington Post*, April 1, 2020, https://www.washingtonpost.com/lifestyle/style/jim-clyburn-changed -everything-for-joe-bidens-campaign-hes-been-a-political-force-for-a-long-time/2020/03/30 /7d054e98-6d33-11ea-aa80-c2470c6b2034_story.html.

35. In the FiveThirtyEight polling average, Biden had 38.4 percent of the vote in South Carolina but won 48.7 percent of the vote (a 29-point margin over Sanders). In the seven South Carolina polls conducted after the New Hampshire primary but before the Nevada caucus, Biden led by an average of 3 to 4 points. In the three South Carolina polls conducted after Nevada but before the Clyburn endorsement, Biden led by an average of 14 points. This shows that his upward swing predated Clyburn's decision.

36. The survey firm Data for Progress graciously provided this data to us. The appendix provides more details on how we arrived at this finding.

37. Allen and Parnes, *Lucky*, 223–25.

38. Sean Sullivan, "Sanders Faces Growing Pressure to Withdraw from Presidential Race," *Washington Post*, March 17, 2020, https://www.washingtonpost.com/politics/sanders-faces -growing-pressure-to-withdraw-from-presidential-race/2020/03/17/1e17b57a-687d-11ea -b313-df458622c2cc_story.html; Sydney Ember, "Bernie Sanders Drops Out of 2020 Democratic Race for President," *New York Times*, April 8, 2020, https://www.nytimes.com/2020/04 /08/us/politics/bernie-sanders-drops-out.html.

39. Matt Flegenheimer and Katie Glueck, "Joe Biden Is Poised to Deliver the Biggest Surprise of 2020: A Short, Orderly Primary," *New York Times*, March 10, 2020, https://www.nytimes .com/2020/03/10/us/politics/joe-biden-democratic-primaries.html.

40. Zachary Evans, "Biden Campaign: We 'Don't Have to Win in Iowa,'" Yahoo, November 4, 2019, https://www.yahoo.com/now/biden-campaign-don-t-win-125338850.html.

41. For more on the role of age, race, and partisanship in the 2016 Democratic primary, see Sides, Tesler, and Vavreck, *Identity Crisis*, chap. 6.

42. On political activation in primaries, see Larry Bartels, *Presidential Primaries and the Dynamics of Public Choice* (Princeton: Princeton University Press, 1988).

43. Allen and Parnes, *Lucky*, 48.

44. On how partisanship constrains voting based on ideology or policy, see Stephen A. Jessee, "Partisan Bias, Political Information and Spatial Voting in the 2008 Presidential Election," *Journal of Politics* 72, no. 2 (2010): 327–40.

45. See Sides, Tesler, and Vavreck, *Identity Crisis*, chap. 5.

46. On the 1984 primary, see Bartels, *Presidential Primaries*, 86–88. On the 2008 primary, see Michael Tesler and David O. Sears, *Obama's Race: The 2008 Election and the Dream of a Post Racial America* (Chicago: University of Chicago Press, 2010), 43–44. On the 2016 primary, see Sides, Tesler, and Vavreck, *Identity Crisis*, chap. 6.

47. These results are based on statistical models of Democratic primary voters who reported voting for Biden or Sanders or intended to vote for Biden or Sanders in the March 5–April 2 Nationscape surveys. The models control for the strength of Democratic party identification, age, gender, and race or ethnicity. Among those who placed Sanders to Biden's left, this correlation was much larger: someone who identified as moderate was about 42 points more likely to vote for Biden than someone who identified as very liberal. Among the voters who saw no difference between Biden and Sanders, there was no correlation between their own ideological identification and their vote. And among the 10 percent who placed Biden to Sanders's left, the direction of the effect was reversed: compared to moderates, stronger liberals were more likely to support Biden, not Sanders. Among those who could not place Biden or Sanders (or either) on the ideological spectrum, there was a modest correlation between their own ideological identification and their primary vote: someone who identified as moderate was about 19 points more likely to vote for Biden than someone who identified as very liberal.

48. We rely on 2019 surveys to capture the period of the most contestation among the Democratic front-runners—that is, before candidates like Warren were winnowed out and before Biden's surge and Sanders's exit. In the table, Republicans include independents who lean Republican.

49. Astead W. Herndon, "Progressive Ideas Remain Popular. Progressive Presidential Candidates Are Losing. Why?," *New York Times*, March 18, 2020, https://www.nytimes.com/2020/03/18/us/politics/bernie-sanders-progressives-elizabeth-warren.html.

50. German Lopez, "The Controversial 1994 Crime Law That Joe Biden Helped Write, Explained," *Vox*, September 29, 2020, https://www.vox.com/policy-and-politics/2019/6/20/18677998/joe-biden-1994-crime-bill-law-mass-incarceration.

51. Jonathan Martin, Astead W. Herndon, and Alexander Burns, "How Kamala Harris's Campaign Unraveled," *New York Times*, November 29, 2019, https://www.nytimes.com/2019/11/29/us/politics/kamala-harris-2020.html.

52. On Jackson's campaign, see Katherine Tate, *From Protest to Politics: The New Black Voters in American Elections* (Cambridge, MA: Harvard University Press, 1994), 12, 138–43.

53. The analysis of Obama's standing among Black voters is based on data from the 2008 National Annenberg Election Study. In this survey, African Americans interviewed before the Iowa caucus were roughly evenly split between Obama and the other candidates, but his support jumped 10 points among African Americans interviewed after Iowa but before the New Hampshire primary. A similar pattern emerges in the 2008 Cooperative Campaign Analysis Project, which reinterviewed the same African American respondents on December 17, 2017, January 25,

2018 (the day before the South Carolina primary), and March 21, 2018. Across these interviews, African American support for Obama increased from 52 percent to 59 percent to 75 percent.

54. On the intersection of race and gender—especially the voting behavior of Black women—see Tasha S. Philpot and Hanes Walton Jr., "One of Our Own: Black Female Candidates and the Voters Who Support Them," *American Journal of Political Science* 51, no. 1 (2007): 49–62.

55. Ismail K. White and Chryl N. Laird, *Steadfast Democrats: How Social Forces Shape Black Political Behavior* (Princeton: Princeton University Press, 2020).

56. Relevant research on the nature and role of ideology among African Americans includes White and Laird, *Steadfast Democrats*, and Tasha S. Philpot, *Conservative but Not Republican: The Paradox of Party Identification and Ideology Among African Americans* (New York: Cambridge University Press, 2017). There is also evidence that a measure of ideological self-identification is not necessarily a valid measure of ideology for African Americans. See Hakeem Jefferson, "The Curious Case of Black Conservatives: Construct Validity and the 7-point Liberal-Conservative Scale," Stanford University working paper, https://www.dropbox.com/s/rh33nhu5m55e01k/Curious%20Case%20of%20Black%20Conservatives_Short.pdf?dl=0.

57. On Obama and public opinion toward Biden and other figures, see Michael Tesler, *Post-Racial or Most-Racial? Race and Politics in the Obama Era* (Chicago: University of Chicago Press, 2016); and Michael Tesler, "The Obama Effect Has Helped Joe Biden with Black Voters. Will It Last?," *The Monkey Cage* (blog), October 8, 2019, https://www.washingtonpost.com/politics/2019/10/08/obama-effect-has-helped-joe-biden-with-black-voters-will-it-last/. On Sanders's potential primary challenge, see Edward-Isaac Dovere, "The Hidden History of Sanders's Plot to Primary Obama," *The Atlantic*, February 19, 2020, https://www.theatlantic.com/politics/archive/2020/02/sanders-obama-primary-challenge/606709/.

58. Amina Dunn and Jocelyn Kiley, "Some Democrats Are Bothered Nominee Is an Older White Man—And They Solidly Back Biden in November," Pew Research Center, April 20, 2020, https://www.pewresearch.org/fact-tank/2020/04/20/some-democrats-are-bothered-nominee-is-an-older-white-man-and-they-solidly-back-biden-in-november/.

59. Juliana Menasce Horowitz, Ruth Igielnik, and Kim Parker, "Women and Leadership 2018," Pew Research Center, September 20, 2018, https://www.pewresearch.org/social-trends/2018/09/20/women-and-leadership-2018/.

60. M. J. Lee, "Bernie Sanders Told Elizabeth Warren in Private 2018 Meeting That a Woman Can't Win," Sources Say," CNN, January 13, 2020, https://www.cnn.com/2020/01/13/politics/bernie-sanders-elizabeth-warren-meeting/index.html; Veronica Stracqualursi and Gregory Krieg, "Clinton Says 'Nobody Likes' Sanders and Won't Commit to Backing Him if He's the Democratic Nominee," CNN, January 21, 2020, https://www.cnn.com/2020/01/21/politics/hillary-clinton-bernie-sanders-documentary/index.html.

61. Allen and Parnes, *Lucky*, 54.

62. On this measure, see Janet K. Swim, Kathryn J. Aikin, Wayne S. Hall, and Barbara A. Hunter, "Sexism and Racism: Old-Fashioned and Modern Prejudices," *Journal of Personality and Social Psychology* 68, no. 2 (1995): 199–214; Janet K. Swim and Laurie Cohen, "Overt, Covert, and Subtle Sexism: A Comparison between the Attitude toward Women and Modern Sexism Scales," *Psychology of Women Quarterly* 21, no. 1 (1997): 103–18. On gender attitudes in 2016 and beyond, see Sides, Tesler, and Vavreck, *Identity Crisis*; John Sides, Michael Tesler, and Lynn

Vavreck, "Gender Attitudes and American Public Opinion in the Trump Era," in *Dynamics of American Democracy: Partisan Polarization, Political Competition, and Government Performance,* ed. Eric M. Patashnik and Wendy J. Schiller (Lawrence: University Press of Kansas, 2021), 156–83; and Nicholas A. Valentino, Carly Wayne, and Marzia Oceno, "The Interaction of Emotion and Gender Attitudes in the 2016 U.S. Presidential Election." *Public Opinion Quarterly* 82 (2018): 213–35. There is related evidence using a different measure of gender attitudes called "hostile sexism." See Brian F. Schaffner, Matthew MacWilliams, and Tatishe Nteta, "Understanding White Polarization in the 2016 Vote for President: The Sobering Role of Racism and Sexism," *Political Science Quarterly* 133, no. 1 (2018): 9–34; and Brian F. Schaffner, "The Heightened Importance of Racism and Sexism in the 2018 U.S. Midterm Election," *British Journal of Political Science* (2020), doi:10.1017/S0007123420000319.

63. These findings confirm those from surveys conducted earlier in the primary campaign. See Sam Luks and Brian Schaffner, "New Polling Shows How Much Sexism Is Hurting the Democratic Women Running for President," *The Monkey Cage* (blog), July 11, 2019, https://www .washingtonpost.com/politics/2019/07/11/women-candidates-must-overcome-sexist -attitudes-even-democratic-primary/; Brian Schaffner and Jon Green, "Sexism Is Probably One Reason Why Elizabeth Warren Didn't Do Better," Data for Progress, March 5, 2020, https:// www.dataforprogress.org/blog/3/5/sexism-one-reason-why-warren-didnt-do-better; and Kjersten Nelson, "You Seem Like a Great Candidate, but . . . : Race and Gender Attitudes and the 2020 Democratic Primary," *Journal of Race, Ethnicity, and Politics* 6, no. 3 (2021): 642–66.

64. The 97 percent figure is from Ryan Pougiales, "The Question of 'Electability,'" Third Way, September 12, 2019, https://www.thirdway.org/memo/the-question-of-electability; Kathy Frankovic, "In 2020, Winning Is Everything for Most Democratic Voters," YouGov, June 11, 2019, https://today.yougov.com/topics/politics/articles-reports/2019/06/11/democrats -2020-winning-poll. The same trend was visible in other polls. See Nathaniel Rakich and Dhrumil Mehta, "Democrats Care More about Winning than Usual," FiveThirtyEight, March 8, 2019, https://fivethirtyeight.com/features/democrats-care-more-about-winning -than-usual/.

65. Lisa Lerer, "It's a Question No One Says They Want to Ask. But the Women Running for President Keep Hearing It," *New York Times*, July 3, 2019, https://www.nytimes.com/2019 /07/03/us/politics/women-presidential-candidates-2020.html; Jonathan Martin, "Many Democrats Love Elizabeth Warren. They Also Worry about Her," *New York Times*, August 15, 2019, https://www.nytimes.com/2019/08/15/us/politics/elizabeth-warren-2020-campaign .html. See also Aaron Blake, "Elizabeth Warren Is Surging. This One Big Question Looms over Her," *Washington Post*, August 8, 2019, https://www.washingtonpost.com/politics/2019/08/08 /elizabeth-warren-all-important-electability-question/. For evidence that Democratic primary voters evaluated hypothetical 2020 candidates in ways that suggest they considered women candidates and Black candidates less electable, see Jon Green, Brian Schaffner, and Sam Luks, "Strategic Discrimination in the 2020 Democratic Primary," working paper, 2021, https://osf.io /xj6ba/. Voters' preferences in the 2020 primary also shifted to favor male or white candidates in experiments when they were told that candidates needed to appeal to male voters or white voters, respectively, or were primed to think about whether general election voters would support Black or women candidates. See Regina Bateson, "Strategic Discrimination," *Perspectives on Politics* 18, no. 4 (2020): 1068–87.

66. On how people change their perceptions of electability to match their views of the candidates, see the discussion in Bartels, *Presidential Primaries*, 53. On an experimental test of electability in the 2012 Republican primary, see Sides and Vavreck, *The Gamble*, 93–94.

67. Other data showed similar gains for Warren. For example, surveys with voters before and after the June 2019 primary debate showed that both Warren and Harris did better on the "magic wand" question after the debate: https://www.filesforprogress.org/memos/pre_post_debate1.pdf).

68. For other polling data showing these trends, see Eli Yokley, "Democratic Primary Voters Flock Back to Biden after South Carolina Victory," Morning Consult, March 2, 2020, https://morningconsult.com/2020/03/02/post-south-carolina-poll-joe-biden/.

69. Reid J. Epstein, Lisa Lerer, and Thomas Kaplan, "Joe Biden Wins Primaries in Florida, Illinois, and Arizona," *New York Times*, March 17, 2020, https://www.nytimes.com/2020/03/17/us/politics/march-17-democratic-primary.html.

70. This pattern of general favorability was also visible in the December 2019 VOTER Survey. See Robert Griffin and John Sides, "The Great Wide Open," Voter Study Group, January 2020, https://www.voterstudygroup.org/publication/the-great-wide-open.

71. The 2020 findings are based on an analysis of likely Democratic primary voters in the pooled Nationscape surveys conducted between July 2019 and January 2020. Among these voters, views of Biden were positively correlated with views of Sanders ($r = 0.20$), Warren ($r = 0.29$), and Buttigieg ($r = 0.37$). Views of Sanders were positively correlated with views of Buttigieg ($r = 0.22$) and especially Warren ($r = 0.42$). The 2008 findings are based on the National Annenberg Election Study, which showed that throughout the spring of 2008, Democratic primary voters' views of Clinton were slightly negatively correlated with their views of Obama. And by June 2016, Democratic primary voters' views of Sanders and Clinton were even more negatively correlated ($r = -0.23$) in YouGov/*Economist* polls. By comparison, when Sanders dropped out in April 2020, the correlation between views of Sanders and views of Biden was +0.14.

72. In the 2008 data, favorability is coded on a 0 to 10 scale. We calculated the percent on the favorable side of that scale (6/10) and the unfavorable side (0/4), including those without an opinion in the denominator. In the 2016 and 2020 data, favorability was coded on a 1 to 4 scale, ranging from strongly unfavorable to strongly favorable. We calculated percentages similarly. Thus, the comparisons between 2008 and the other years should be interpreted cautiously.

CHAPTER 5: "DEADLY STUFF"

1. Steven H. Woolf, Derek A. Chapman, and Jong Hyung Lee, "COVID-19 as the Leading Cause of Death in the United States," *JAMA* 325, no. 2 (2021): 123–24, doi:10.1001/jama.2020.24865. The COVID casualty figures are from https://ourworldindata.org/covid-deaths.

2. Donald F. Kettl, "States Divided: The Implications of American Federalism for COVID-19," *Public Administration Review* 80, no. 4 (2020): 595–602.

3. The World Health Organization declaration is here: https://www.who.int/publications/m/item/covid-19-public-health-emergency-of-international-concern-(pheic)-global-research-and-innovation-forum.

4. The O'Brien and Trump quotes are from Bob Woodward, *Rage* (New York: Simon & Schuster, 2020).

5. Michael D. Shear, Sheri Fink, and Noah Weiland, "Inside Trump Administration, Debate Raged over What to Tell Public," *New York Times*, March 7, 2020, https://www.nytimes.com /2020/03/07/us/politics/trump-coronavirus.html; Fred Imbert and Eustance Huang, "Dow Plunges 1,000 Points on Coronavirus Fears, 3.5% Drop Is Worst in Two Years," CNBC, February 24, 2020, https://www.cnbc.com/2020/02/24/us-futures-coronavirus-outbreak.html. Trump's February 26 remarks are here: https://www.c-span.org/video/?469747-1/president -trump-announces-vice-president-pence-charge-coronavirus-response. On Trump's February 29 remark, see Kathryn Watson, "A Timeline of What Trump Has Said on Coronavirus," CBS News, April 3, 2020, https://www.cbsnews.com/news/timeline-president-donaldtrump -changing-statements-on-coronavirus/, and Lena H. Sun, "CDC, the Top U.S. Public Health Agency, Is Sidelined during Coronavirus Pandemic," *Washington Post*, March 19, 2020, https:// www.washingtonpost.com/health/2020/03/19/cdc-top-us-public-health-agency-is-sidelined -during-coronavirus-pandemic/.

6. For examples from the debate about border closure, see Sharmila Devi, "Travel Restrictions Hampering COVID-19 Response," *The Lancet* 395, no. 10233 (2020): 1331–32; Julia Belluz and Steven Hoffman, "The Evidence on Travel Bans for Diseases like Coronavirus Is Clear: They Don't Work," Vox, January 23, 2020, https://www.vox.com/2020/1/23/21078325/wuhan -china-coronavirus-travel-ban; Matthew Yglesias, "The Road Not Traveled," Slow Boring, December 3, 2020, https://www.slowboring.com/p/the-road-not-traveled. On the porous restrictions on travelers from China, see Steve Eder, Henry Fountain, Michael H. Keller, Muyi Xiao, and Alexandra Stevenson, "430,000 People Have Traveled from China to U.S. Since Coronavirus Surfaced," *New York Times*, April 4, 2020, https://www.nytimes.com/2020/04/04/us /coronavirus-china-travel-restrictions.html. On the prevalence of transmission from Europe, see Carl Zimmer, "Most New York Coronavirus Cases Came from Europe, Genomes Show," *New York Times*, April 8, 2020, https://www.nytimes.com/2020/04/08/science/new-york -coronavirus-cases-europe-genomes.html. On a "lost February" and the problems with the coronavirus test, see Alexis C. Madrigal and Robinson Meyer, "How the Coronavirus Became an American Catastrophe," *The Atlantic*, March 21, 2020, https://www.theatlantic.com/health /archive/2020/03/how-many-americans-are-sick-lost-february/608521/; Robert P. Baird, "What Went Wrong with Coronavirus Testing in the U.S.," *New Yorker*, March 16, 2020, https:// www.newyorker.com/news/news-desk/what-went-wrong-with-coronavirus-testing-in-the-us; David Willman, "The CDC's Failed Race against COVID-19: A Threat Underestimated and a Test Overcomplicated," *Washington Post*, December 26, 2020, https://www.washingtonpost.com /investigations/cdc-covid/2020/12/25/c2b418ae-4206-11eb-8db8-395dedaaa036_story .html. The Trump quote is cited in Watson, "A Timeline of What Trump Has Said." The CDC official's quote is from Willman, "The CDC's Failed Race against COVID-19."

7. Lev Facher, "President Trump Just Declared the Coronavirus Pandemic a National Emergency. Here's What That Means," Stat, March 13, 2020, https://www.statnews.com/2020/03/13 /national-emergency-coronavirus/; Ben Gittleson and Jordyn Phelps, "Government Response Updates: Trump Issues Stricter Guidelines to Stop Virus Spread," ABC News, March 16, 2020, https://abcnews.go.com/Politics/white-house-grapples-coronavirus-guidelines-markets

-plummet/story?id=69620218. The story about Barron is in Watson, "A Timeline of What Trump Has Said."

8. Paul Farhi and Sarah Ellison, "On Fox News, Suddenly a Very Different Tune about the Coronavirus," *Washington Post,* March 16, 2020, https://www.washingtonpost.com/lifestyle /media/on-fox-news-suddenly-a-very-different-tune-about-the-coronavirus/2020/03/16 /7a7637cc-678f-11ea-9923-57073adce27c_story.html/.

9. The research on state emergency declarations is Luke Fowler, Jaclyn J. Kettler, and Stephanie L. Witt, "Pandemics and Partisanship: Following Old Paths into Uncharted Territory," *American Politics Research,* 49, no. 1 (2021): 3–16. The research on social distancing policies is Christopher Adolph, Kenya Amano, Bree Bang-Jensen, Nancy Fullman, and John Wilkerson, "Pandemic Politics: Timing State-Level Social Distancing Responses to COVID-19," *Journal of Health Politics, Policy, and Law,* 46, no. 2 (2021), 211–33.

10. On Trump's praise of Xi, see Myah Ward, "15 Times Trump Praised China as Coronavirus Was Spreading across the Globe," *Politico,* April 15, 2020, https://www.politico.com/news/2020 /04/15/trump-china-coronavirus-188736. On the trend in the use of "China virus," see Sean Darling-Hammond et al., "After 'The China Virus' Went Viral: Racially Charged Coronavirus Coverage and Trends in Bias against Asian Americans," *Health Education and Behavior* 47, no. 6 (2020), 870–79. The March 16–30 figure for Trump's use of "Chinese virus" is from Jérôme Viala-Gaudefroy and Dana Lindaman, "Donald Trump's 'Chinese Virus': The Politics of Naming," The Conversation, April 21, 2020, https://theconversation.com/donald-trumps-chinese -virus-the-politics-of-naming-136796. On Trump's March 19 remarks, see Anne Gearan, "Trump Takes Direct Aim at China as Known U.S. Infections Double and Criticism Mounts," *Washington Post,* March 19, 2020, https://www.washingtonpost.com/politics/trump-takes -direct-aim-at-china-as-known-us-infections-double-and-criticism-mounts/2020/03/19 /6df10828-6a06-11ea-abef-020f086a3fab_story.html.

11. Emily Badger and Alicia Parlapiano, "Government Orders Alone Didn't Close the Economy. They Probably Can't Reopen It," *New York Times,* May 7, 2020, https://www.nytimes.com /2020/05/07/upshot/pandemic-economy-government-orders.html?smid=tw-share; Clare Malone and Kyle Bourassa, "Americans Didn't Wait for Their Governors to Tell Them to Stay Home Because of COVID-19," FiveThirtyEight, May 8, 2020, https://fivethirtyeight.com /features/americans-didnt-wait-for-their-governors-to-tell-them-to-stay-home-because-of -covid-19/; David Gonzalez and Sinna Nasseri, "'Patients Have Panic in Their Eyes': Voices from a Covid-19 Unit," *New York Times,* April 29, 2020, https://www.nytimes.com/2020/04/29 /nyregion/coronavirus-nyc-hospitals.html.

12. Philip Ball, "The Lightning-Fast Quest for COVID Vaccines—and What It Means for Other Diseases," *Nature,* December 18, 2020, https://www.nature.com/articles/d41586-020 -03626-1.

13. The exchange between Trump and Inslee is reported in Lawrence Wright, "The Plague Year," *New Yorker,* December 28, 2020, https://www.newyorker.com/magazine/2021/01/04 /the-plague-year.

14. The Baker story is in Wright, "The Plague Year." One story among many about the states' bidding war is Jeanne Whalen, Tony Romm, Aaron Gregg, and Tom Hamburger, "Scramble for Medical Equipment Descends into Chaos as U.S. States and Hospitals Compete for Rare

Supplies," *Washington Post*, March 24, 2020, https://www.washingtonpost.com/business/2020
/03/24/scramble-medical-equipment-descends-into-chaos-us-states-hospitals-compete-rare
-supplies/. See also Kathryn Watson, "Trump Says States Need to 'Work Out' Competing Bids
for Medical Equipment for Themselves," CBS News, April 3, 2020, https://www.cbsnews.com
/news/trump-states-bids-medical-equipment-ventilators-supplies/.

15. Mike DeBonis, Chris Mooney, and Juliet Eilperin, "White House Issues Coronavirus
Testing Guidance That Leaves States In Charge," *Washington Post*, April 27, 2020, https://www
.washingtonpost.com/politics/white-house-issues-coronavirus-testing-guidance-that-leaves
-states-in-charge/2020/04/27/c465cc9c-88a2-11ea-8ac1-bfb250876b7a_story.html; Katherine Eban, "How Jared Kushner's Secret Testing Plan 'Went Poof into Thin Air,'" *Vanity Fair*,
July 30, 2020, https://www.vanityfair.com/news/2020/07/how-jared-kushners-secret-testing
-plan-went-poof-into-thin-air; Reuters Staff, "Trump Urges Slowdown in COVID-19 Testing,
Calling It a 'Double-Edged Sword,'" Reuters, June 21, 2020, https://www.reuters.com/article
/us-health-coronavirus-trump-testing/trump-urges-slowdown-in-covid-19-testing-calling-it-a
-double-edge-sword-idUSKBN23S0B4; Erica Werner and Jeff Stein, "Trump Administration
Pushing to Block New Money for Testing, Tracing, and CDC in Upcoming Coronavirus Relief
Bill," *Washington Post*, July 18, 2020, https://www.washingtonpost.com/us-policy/2020/07/18
/white-house-testing-budget-cdc-coronavirus/.

16. Wei Lyu and George L. Wehby, "Community Use of Face Masks and COVID-19: Evidence from a Natural Experiment of State Mandates in the U.S.," *Health Affairs* 39, no. 8 (2020),
https://doi.org/10.1377/hlthaff.2020.00818; Gery P. Guy Jr et al., "Association of State-Issues
Mask Mandates and Allowing On-Premises Restaurant Dining with County-Level COVID-19
Case and Death Growth Rates—United States, March 1–December 31, 2020," Centers for Disease Control and Prevention, March 5, 2021, https://www.cdc.gov/mmwr/volumes/70/wr
/mm7010e3.htm.

17. Aaron Blake, "Trump's Dumbfounding Refusal to Encourage Wearing Masks," *Washington Post*, June 25, 2020, https://www.washingtonpost.com/politics/2020/06/25/trumps
-dumbfounding-refusal-encourage-wearing-masks/; Michael Scherer, "Trump's Mockery of
Wearing Masks Divides Republicans," *Washington Post*, May 27, 2020, https://www
.washingtonpost.com/politics/trumps-mockery-of-wearing-masks-divides-republicans/2020
/05/26/2c2bdc02-9f61-11ea-81bb-c2f70f01034b_story.html; Philip Rucker and Seung Min
Kim, "Republican Leaders Now Say Everyone Should Wear a Mask—Even as Trump Refuses
and Has Mocked Some Who Do," *Washington Post*, June 30, 2020, https://www.washingtonpost
.com/politics/republican-leaders-now-say-everyone-should-wear-a-mask--even-as-trump
-refuses-and-mocks-those-who-do/2020/06/30/995a32d0-bae9-11ea-80b9-40ece9a701dc
_story.html; Toluse Olorunnipa, "Trump Dons Mask in Public for the First Time, Months after
Public Health Experts Said Everyone Should," *Washington Post*, July 11, 2020, https://www
.washingtonpost.com/politics/trump-dons-mask-in-public-for-the-first-time-months-after
-public-health-experts-said-everyone-should/2020/07/11/8d948b64-c3ca-11ea-b4f6
-cb39cd8940fb_story.html.

18. The April 3 quote is from Kathryn Watson, "A Timeline of What Trump Has Said on
Coronavirus," CBS News, April 3, 2020, https://www.cbsnews.com/news/timeline-president
-donald-trump-changing-statements-on-coronavirus/. The others are from Glenn Kessler,

"Trump Kept Saying Victory over the Coronavirus Was Near. Then He Got Sick," *Washington Post*, October 5, 2020, https://www.washingtonpost.com/politics/2020/10/05/trump-kept -saying-victory-over-coronavirus-was-near-then-he-got-sick/.

19. Maggie Haberman and David E. Sanger, "Trump Says Coronavirus Cure Cannot 'Be Worse than the Problem Itself,'" *New York Times*, March 23, 2020, https://www.nytimes.com /2020/03/23/us/politics/trump-coronavirus-restrictions.html; Matt Zapotosky, Josh Dawsey, Jose A. Del Real, and William Wan, "Trump Administration Pushing to Reopen Much of the U.S. Next Month," *Washington Post*, April 9, 2020, https://www.washingtonpost.com/national /trump-reopen-us-economy/2020/04/09/10d42b4a-7a7b-11ea-9bee-c5bf9d2e3288 _story.html.

20. On the economic consequences of pandemics, see Òscar Jordà, Sanjay R. Singh, and Alan M. Taylor, "Longer-Run Economic Consequences of Pandemics," Federal Reserve Bank of San Francisco, https://www.frbsf.org/economic-research/files/wp2020-09.pdf. On the effect of restrictions in the 1918–19 flu pandemic, see Sergio Correia, Stephan Luck, and Emil Verner, "Pandemics Depress the Economy, Public Health Interventions Do Not: Evidence from the 1918 Flu," Social Science Research Network, June 2020, https://papers.ssrn.com/sol3 /papers.cfm?abstract_id=3561560. The study of state restrictions and consumer traffic is Austan Goolsbee and Chad Syverson, "Fear, Lockdown, and Diversion: Comparing Drivers of Pandemic Economic Decline 2020," National Bureau of Economic Research, June 2020, https:// www.nber.org/papers/w27432. See also their update here: https://bfi.uchicago.edu/insight /research-update-drivers-of-economic-decline/. And see Sangmin Aum, Sang Yoon Lee, and Yongseok Shin, "COVID-19 Doesn't Need Lockdowns to Destroy Jobs: The Effect of Local Outbreaks in Korea," National Bureau of Economic Research, May 2020, https://www.nber.org /papers/w27264.

21. On restrictions during the 1918–19 pandemic, see Martin C. J. Bootsma and Neil M. Ferguson, "The Effect of Public Health Measures on the 1918 Influenza Pandemic in U.S. Cities," *Proceedings of the National Academy of Sciences* 104, no. 18 (2007): 7588–93; Howard Markel, Harvey B. Lipman, J. Alexander Navarro, Alexandra Sloan, Joseph R. Michalsen, Alexandra Minna Stern, and Martin S. Cetron, "Nonpharmaceutical Interventions Implemented by US Cities During the 1918–1919 Influenza Pandemic," *JAMA* 298, no. 6 (2007): 644–54; and Robert J. Barro, "Non-Pharmaceutical Interventions and Mortality in U.S. Cities during the Great Influenza Pandemic, 1918–19," National Bureau of Economic Research, April 2020, https://www .nber.org/papers/w27049. On restrictions during the COVID-19 pandemic, see James H. Fowler, Seth J. Hill, Remy Levin, and Nick Obradovich, "The Effect of Stay-at-Home Orders on COVID-19 Cases and Fatalities in the United States," working paper, May 2020, https://www .medrxiv.org/content/10.1101/2020.04.13.20063628v3; Charles Courtemanche, Joseph Garuccio, Anh Le, Joshua Pinkston, and Aaron Yelowitz, "Strong Social Distancing Measures in the United States Reduced the COVID-19 Growth Rate," *Health Affairs* 39, no. 7 (2020): 1237–46; Solomon Hsiang et al., "The Effect of Large-Scale Anti-Contagion Policies on the COVID-19 Pandemic," *Nature* 584 (2020): 262–67; and Wei Lyu and George L. Wehby, "Shelter-in-Place Orders Reduced COVID-19 Mortality and Reduced the Rate of Growth in Hospitalizations," *Health Affairs* 39, no. 9 (2020): 1615–23. For similar evidence from China, see Hanming Fang, Long Wang, and Yang Yang, "Human Mobility Restrictions and the Spread of the Novel

Coronavirus (2019-NCoV) in China," National Bureau of Economic Research, March 2020, https://www.nber.org/system/files/working_papers/w26906/w26906.pdf.

22. Peter Baker and Michael D. Shear, "Trump Says States Can Start Reopening While Acknowledging the Decision Is Theirs," *New York Times*, April 16, 2020, https://www.nytimes.com/2020/04/16/us/politics/coronavirus-trump-guidelines.html; Jason Slotkin, "Protestors Swarm Michigan Capitol amid Showdown over Governor's Emergency Powers," NPR, May 1, 2020, https://www.npr.org/sections/coronavirus-live-updates/2020/05/01/849017021/protestors-swarm-michigan-capitol-amid-showdown-over-governors-emergency-powers; Steve Neavling, "Gov. Whitmer Becomes Target of Dozens of Threats on Private Facebook Groups ahead of Armed Rally in Lansing," *Detroit Metro Times*, May 11, 2020, https://www.metrotimes.com/news-hits/archives/2020/05/11/whitmer-becomes-target-of-dozens-of-threats-on-private-facebook-groups-ahead-of-armed-rally-in-lansing; Nicholas Bogel-Burroughs, Shaila Dewan, and Kathleen Gray, "FBI Says Michigan Anti-Government Group Plotted to Kidnap Gov. Gretchen Whitmer," *New York Times*, October 8, 2020, https://www.nytimes.com/2020/10/08/us/gretchen-whitmer-michigan-militia.html.

23. Griff Witte and Katie Zezima, "Ohio Gov. Mike DeWine's Coronavirus Response Has Become a National Guide to the Crisis," *Washington Post*, March 16, 2020, https://www.washingtonpost.com/national/coronavirus-ohio-dewine-outbreak/2020/03/16/9bdc6b1e-67b2-11ea-9923-57073adce27c_story.html; Associated Press, "Ohio Republicans Criticize Gov. Mike DeWine on Election, Pandemic," CBS, June 28, 2020, https://pittsburgh.cbslocal.com/2020/06/28/ohio-republicans-mike-dewine-covid-election/; Jeremy Pelzer, "Articles of Impeachment Drawn Up against Gov. Mike DeWine over Coronavirus Orders," Cleveland.com, https://www.cleveland.com/open/2020/08/articles-of-impeachment-drawn-up-against-gov-mike-dewine-over-coronavirus-orders.html; Manny Fernandez and J. David Goodman, "Red vs. Red in Texas, with Republicans Battling One Another after Mask Order," *New York Times*, July 23, 2020, https://www.nytimes.com/2020/07/23/us/coronavirus-texas-abbott-republicans.html.

24. Sheryl Gay Stolberg, Noah Weiland, Sarah Mervosh, and David E. Sanger, "With the Federal Health Megaphone Silent, States Struggle with a Shifting Pandemic," *New York Times*, June 17, 2020, https://www.nytimes.com/2020/06/17/us/politics/coronavirus-pandemic-federal-response.html?action=click&module=Top%20Stories&pgtype=Homepage; Mike Pence, "There Isn't a Coronvirus 'Second Wave,'" *Wall Street Journal*, June 16, 2020, https://www.wsj.com/articles/there-isnt-a-coronavirus-second-wave-11592327890; Michael D. Shear, Maggie Haberman, and Astead W. Herndon, "Trump Rally Fizzles as Attendance Falls Short of Campaign's Expectations," *New York Times*, June 20, 2020, https://www.nytimes.com/2020/06/20/us/politics/tulsa-trump-rally.html.

25. Stolberg et al., "With the Federal Health Megaphone Silent."

26. Lindsey Cormack, "The Ebola Outbreak Generated Greater Response from Republican Lawmakers," *The Monkey Cage* (blog), November 14, 2014, https://www.washingtonpost.com/news/monkey-cage/wp/2014/11/14/the-ebola-outbreak-generated-greater-response-from-republican-lawmakers/. The Cruz staffer tweet (later deleted) is noted here: https://sts-news.medium.com/the-gop-has-a-boehner-for-your-ebola-fears-f022a3973f8c. The

Trump tweets are noted here: https://www.theroot.com/donald-trumps-old-ebola-tweets -reveal-his-incompetence-1842383794. See also Jonathan Martin, "Republicans Hint at Ebola as an Election Issue," *New York Times*, October 15, 2014, https://www.nytimes.com/politics /first-draft/2014/10/15/republicans-hint-at-ebola-as-an-election-issue/?searchResultPosi- tion=7.

27. Michael Tesler, "Republicans Were More Concerned about Ebola than They've Been about Coronavirus. Here's Why," *The Monkey Cage* (blog), March 27, 2020, https://www .washingtonpost.com/politics/2020/03/27/republicans-were-more-concerned-about-ebola -than-theyve-been-about-coronavirus-heres-why/.

28. See the Nationscape figures here: https://www.voterstudygroup.org/covid-19-updates#. For similar evidence of polarization in concern about the virus, see Joshua Clinton, Jon Cohen, John S. Lapinski, and Marc Trussler, "Partisan Pandemic: How Partisanship and Public Health Concerns Affect Individuals' Social Mobility during COVID-19," *Science Advances* 7, no. 2 (2021), https://www.science.org/doi/10.1126/sciadv.abd7204. Polling by Civiqs showed similar polarization: https://civiqs.com/results/coronavirus_concern?uncertainty=true&annotations =true&zoomIn=true&sumTotals=true&trendline=true.

29. For leader approval ratings, see Morning Consult's tracking data: https://morningconsult .com/form/global-leader-approval/. In Italy, Giuseppe Conte also saw his approval rating in- crease. See Rick Noack, "For Some World Leaders, Popularity Grows along with Coronavirus Case Numbers," *Washington Post*, May 13, 2020, https://www.washingtonpost.com/world/2020 /05/13/some-world-leaders-popularity-grows-along-with-coronavirus-case-numbers/. John- son's May 10 address announcing the shift in policy is here: https://www.gov.uk/government /speeches/pm-address-to-the-nation-on-coronavirus-10-may-2020. The "growing revolt" quote is from Toby Helm, Mark Townsend, Julian Coman, and Robin McKie, "Revolt over Easing of Coronavirus Lockdown Spreads as Poll Slump Hits Boris Johnson," *The Guardian*, May 17, 2020, https://www.theguardian.com/business/2020/may/16/revolt-over-easing -lockdown-spreads-as-poll-slump-hits-prime-minister.

30. We are grateful to Morning Consult for supplying the gubernatorial approval data. Due to data processing issues, there is not complete data for Kentucky.

31. In Nationscape surveys, large majorities of Americans, including both Democrats and Republicans, also reported washing their hands more often and stocking up on food or other essential items. For similar evidence on the relationship between partisanship and COVID behaviors, see Shana Kushner Gadarian, Sara Wallace Goodman, and Thomas B. Pepinsky, "Partisanship, Health Behavior, and Policy Attitudes in the Early Stages of the COVID-19 Pan- demic," working paper, March 2020, https://papers.ssrn.com/sol3/papers.cfm?abstract_id =3562796; Mark Blumenthal, "On Coronavirus Social Distancing, Americans Not So Divided," YouGov, April 16, 2020, https://today.yougov.com/topics/politics/articles-reports/2020/04 /16/coronavirus-social-distancing-americans-not-so-div.

32. Ariel Edwards-Levy, "Here's How Most Americans Really Feel about Wearing Face Masks," *Huffington Post*, May 20, 2020, https://www.huffpost.com/entry/face-masks-poll -partisan-culture-war_n_5ec584fcc5b642a7d150e103; Megan Brenan, "Americans' Face Mask Usage Varies Greatly by Demographics," Gallup, July 13, 2020, https://news.gallup.com/poll /315590/americans-face-mask-usage-varies-greatly-demographics.aspx.

33. Hunt Allcott, Levi Boxell, Jacob Conway, Matthew Gentzkow, Michael Thaler, and David Yang, "Polarization and Public Health: Partisan Differences in Social Distancing during COVID-19," National Bureau of Economic Research, 2020, https://www.nber.org/papers/w26946; Anton Gollwitzer, Cameron Martel, William J. Brady, Philip Pärnamets, Isaac G. Freedman, Eric D. Knowles, and Jay J. Van Bavel, "Partisan Differences in Physical Distancing Are Linked to Health Outcomes During the COVID-19 Pandemic," *Nature Human Behaviour* 4 (2020): 1186–97; Keena Lipsitz and Grigore Pop-Eleches, "The Partisan Divide in Social Distancing," Social Science Research Network, May 2020, https://papers.ssrn.com/sol3/papers.cfm?abstract_id=3595695; Elliott Ash, Sergio Galletta, Dominik Hangartner, Yotam Margalit, and Matteo Pinna, "The Effect of Fox News on Health Behavior during COVID-19," Social Science Research Network, 2020, https://papers.ssrn.com/sol3/papers.cfm?abstract_id=3636762; Daniel A. N. Goldstein and Johannes Wiedemann, "Who Do You Trust? The Consequences of Political and Social Trust for Public Responsiveness to COVID-19 Orders," Social Science Research Network, 2020, https://papers.ssrn.com/sol3/papers.cfm?abstract_id=3580547.

34. The Crowd Counting Consortium data is here: https://sites.google.com/view/crowdcountingconsortium/view-download-the-data?authuser=0. The numbers reported here are based on our own coding and analysis. On media coverage of the anti-lockdown protests, see Erica Chenoweth, Lara Putnam, Tommy Leung, Jeremy Pressman, and Nathan Perkins, "Media Coverage Has Blown Anti-Lockdown Protests Out of Proportion," Vox, May 10, 2020, https://www.vox.com/2020/5/10/21252583/coronavirus-lockdown-protests-media-trump.

35. See Clinton et al., "Partisan Pandemic," and John Sides, Chris Tausanovitch, and Lynn Vavreck, "The Politics of COVID-19: Partisan Polarization about the Pandemic Has Increased, but Support for Health Care Reform Hasn't Moved at All," *Harvard Data Science Review*, November 30, 2020, https://doi.org/10.1162/99608f92.611350fd.

36. John Zaller, *The Nature and Origins of Mass Opinion* (New York: Cambridge University Press, 1992).

37. Political attentiveness is measured by asking people factual questions about basic political rules and institutions. On the value of measuring attentiveness in this way, see Vincent Price and John Zaller, "Who Gets the News? Alternative Measures of News Reception and Their Implications for Research," *Public Opinion Quarterly* 5, no. 2 (1993): 133–64. The Nationscape surveys ask people two questions: what is the number of years in one full Senate term (six) and who is the chief justice of the U.S. Supreme Court (where respondents must choose from a list including John Roberts, Sandra Day O'Connor, William Rehnquist, Paul Ryan, and Elena Kagan). On average, 39 percent of Nationscape respondents knew the answer to the first question and 45 percent to the second question. In figure 5.8, the dashed lines represent the 46 percent of respondents who got neither question correct; the solid lines represent the 29 percent of respondents who got both questions correct.

38. On mask mandates, see Ariel Edwards-Levy, "Most Americans Favor Mask Requirements, Poll Finds," *Huffington Post*, June 30, 2020, https://www.huffpost.com/entry/mask-requirements-huffpost-yougov-poll_n_5efbb870c5b6ca9709163993. In the April 23–29 Nationscape survey, 76 percent of Americans, including 64 percent of Republicans, agreed that "To limit the spread of coronavirus, state and local governments should be able to limit people's

right to attend religious services in person" as opposed to "People's right to attend religious services in person should be protected, even if it means people are increasing the risk of exposing themselves and others to coronavirus." For similar evidence that the majority of Americans, including Republicans, wanted either not to allow in-person religious services or allow them only with restrictions, see Elana Schor and Emily Swanson, "Poll Shows a Partisan Split over Virus-Era Religious Freedom," Associated Press, May 13, 2020, https://apnews.com/article/1d 8cc0e0b8343b4bda5de88b843bec3b.

39. Robin Hanson, "Why Openers Are Winning," Overcoming Bias, May 5, 2020, https:// www.overcomingbias.com/2020/05/why-openers-are-winning.html; Tyler Cowen, "On Reopening, Robin Hanson Suggests a Political Economy Hypothesis," Marginal Revolution, https://marginalrevolution.com/marginalrevolution/2020/05/on-reopening-robin-hanson-is -exactly-correct.html; Keith Humphreys, "Widespread Testing Might Not Work in America. We Love Our 'Freedom' Too Much," *Washington Post*, May 14, 2020, https://www.washingtonpost .com/outlook/widespread-testing-might-not-work-in-america-we-love-our-freedom-too -much/2020/05/14/4904d6a4-9556-11ea-9f5e-56d8239bf9ad_story.html; Ross Douthat, "What Isn't Trump's Fault," *New York Times*, September 12, 2020, https://www.nytimes.com /2020/09/12/opinion/sunday/trump-coronavirus.html.

40. Rebecca Sanders and Jack Mewhirter, "New Survey: Yes, Americans Will Give Up Liberties to Fight the Coronavirus," *The Monkey Cage* (blog), September 28, 2020, https://www .washingtonpost.com/politics/2020/09/28/new-survey-yes-americans-will-give-up-liberties -fight-coronavirus/.

41. See https://www.cdc.gov/eis/field-epi-manual/chapters/Communicating-Investigation .html.

42. Aaron Rupar, "'They Are Dying. That's True. It Is What It Is.' Trump's Axios Interview Was a Disaster," *Vox*, August 4, 2020, https://www.vox.com/2020/8/4/21354055/trump-axios -interview-jonathan-swan.

CHAPTER 6: GEORGE FLOYD

Epigraph: Daniel Q. Gillion, *The Loud Minority: Why Protests Matter in American Democracy* (Princeton: Princeton University Press, 2020), 34.

1. Larry Buchanan, Quoctrung Bui, and Jugal K. Patel, "Black Lives Matter May Be the Largest Movement in U.S. History," *New York Times*, July 3, 2020, https://www.nytimes.com /interactive/2020/07/03/us/george-floyd-protests-crowd-size.html.

2. Dan Balz, "The Politics of Race Are Shifting, and Politicians Are Struggling to Keep Pace," *Washington Post*, July 5, 2020, https://www.washingtonpost.com/graphics/2020/politics/race -reckoning/?hpid=hp_hp-banner-low_reckoning-2p%3Ahomepage%2Fstory-ans&itid=hp _hp-banner-low_reckoning-2p%3Ahomepage%2Fstory-ans.

3. Michael Wines, "'Looting' Comment from Trump Dates Back to Racial Unrest of the 1960s," *New York Times*, May 29, 2020, https://www.nytimes.com/2020/05/29/us/looting -starts-shooting-starts.html. Trump's comment about Tiananmen Square is noted here: https://twitter.com/michikokakutani/status/709570919463780353. Maggie Astor, "What Trump, Biden, and Obama Said about the Death of George Floyd," *New York Times*, May 29,

2020, https://www.nytimes.com/2020/05/29/us/politics/george-floyd-trump-biden-obama
.html.

4. Frederick Melo, "Arson Suspects Face Federal Charges in Connection with Unrest after
Death of George Floyd," *Pioneer Press*, October 10, 2020, https://www.twincities.com/2020/10
/10/federal-charges-arson-george-floyd-protests-minneapolis-st-paul/.

5. Jason Hoffman, "More than 60 Secret Service Officers and Agents Were Injured Near the
White House This Weekend," CNN, May 31, 2020, https://www.cnn.com/us/live-news/george
-floyd-protests-05-31-20/h_cb459ab077b164295d8d61d80987e3fb; Peter Baker, Maggie
Haberman, Katie Rogers, Zolan Kanno-Youngs, and Katie Benner, "How Trump's Idea for a
Photo Op Led to Havoc in a Park," *New York Times*, June 2, 2020, https://www.nytimes.com
/2020/06/02/us/politics/trump-walk-lafayette-square.html. The U.S. Park Police said that the
protestors who were cleared were acting violently, but this was disputed by reporters on the
scene as well as one officer of the DC National Guard. See Tom Jackman and Carol Leonig,
"National Guard Officer Says Police Suddenly Moved on Lafayette Square Protestors, Used 'Excessive Force' before Trump Visit," *Washington Post*, July 27, 2020, https://www.washingtonpost
.com/nation/2020/07/27/national-guard-commander-says-police-suddenly-moved-lafayette
-square-protesters-used-excessive-force-clear-path-trump/.

6. Katie Rogers, "Protestors Dispersed with Tear Gas So Trump Could Pose at Church," *New
York Times*, June 1, 2020, https://www.nytimes.com/2020/06/01/us/politics/trump-st-johns
-church-bible.html; Marianne Levine, Andrew Desiderio, and Burgess Everett, "Republicans
Chastise Trump for Ousting Protestors, Church Photo-Op," *Politico*, June 2, 2020, https://www
.politico.com/news/2020/06/02/republican-criticism-trump-ousting-protesters-church
-photo-op-296521. Examples of polls showing disapproval of Trump's handling of the protests
include Grant Smith, Joseph Ax, and Chris Kahn, "Exclusive: Most Americans Sympathize with
Protests, Disapprove of Trump's Response," Reuters, June 2, 2020, https://www.reuters.com
/article/us-minneapolis-police-poll-exclusive/exclusive-most-americans-sympathize-with
-protests-disapprove-of-trumps-response-reuters-ipsos-idUSKBN239347; Candice Jaimungal,
"Majority Disapprove of Trump's Handling of Black Lives Matter Protests," YouGov, July 1, 2020,
https://today.yougov.com/topics/politics/articles-reports/2020/07/01/majority-disapprove
-trumps-handling-protests; and Scott Clement and Dan Balz, "Big Majorities Support Protests
over Floyd Killing and Say Police Need to Change, Poll Finds," *Washington Post*, June 9, 2020,
https://www.washingtonpost.com/politics/big-majorities-support-protests-over-floyd-killing
-and-say-police-need-to-change-poll-finds/2020/06/08/6742d52c-a9b9-11ea-9063
-e69bd6520940_story.html.

7. Gillion, *The Loud Minority*.

8. John Sides, Michael Tesler, and Lynn Vavreck, *Identity Crisis: The 2016 Presidential Campaign and the Battle for the Meaning of America* (Princeton: Princeton University Press, 2018), 114.

9. See https://twitter.com/LeaderMcConnell/status/1273283161984839681 and https://
twitter.com/JakeSherman/status/1270434560334012417.

10. Jamie Ballard, "Most Americans Say the Officer Involved in George Floyd's Death Should
Be Arrested," YouGov, May 29, 2020, https://today.yougov.com/topics/politics/articles-reports
/2020/05/29/george-flyd-chauvin-arrest-poll-survey-data. The data from the June 2020 You-
Gov poll is here: https://docs.cdn.yougov.com/ngcg634q9k/econTabReport.pdf#page=56. See
also Tim Alberta, "Is This the Last Stand of the 'Law and Order' Republicans?," *Politico*, June 8,

2020, https://www.politico.com/news/magazine/2020/06/08/last-stand-law-and-order
-republicans-306333.

11. On the trends in Nationscape surveys, see also Michael Tesler, "The Floyd Protests Have
Changed Public Opinion about Race and Policing. Here's the Data," *The Monkey Cage* (blog),
June 9, 2020, https://www.washingtonpost.com/politics/2020/06/09/floyd-protests-have
-changed-public-opinion-about-race-policing-heres-data/; Tyler T. Reny and Benjamin J. Newman, "The Opinion Mobilizing Effect of Social Protest against Police Violence: Evidence
from the 2020 George Floyd Protests," *American Political Science Review* 115, no. 4 (2021):
1499–1507.

12. Soumyajit Mazumder, "The Persistent Effect of the US Civil Rights Movement on Po-
litical Attitudes," *American Journal of Political Science* 62, no. 4 (2018): 922–35; Ryan D. Enos,
Aaron R. Kaufman, and Melissa L. Sands, "Can Violent Protest Change Local Policy Support?
Evidence from the Aftermath of the 1992 Los Angeles Riot," *American Political Science Review*
113, no. 4 (2019): 1012–28; and Soumyajit Mazumder, "Black Lives Matter for Whites' Racial
Prejudice: Assessing the Role of Social Movements in Shaping Racial Attitudes in the United
States," working paper, last updated May 5, 2019, https://osf.io/preprints/socarxiv/ap46d/.

13. The Civiqs polling trend is available here: https://civiqs.com/results/black_lives_matter.
In Nationscape surveys, a similar question about BLM was not added until mid-July 2020, but
it showed a similar decline in support throughout the rest of the election year. See also Jennifer
Chudy and Hakeem Jefferson, "Support for Black Lives Matter Surged Last Year. Did It Last?,"
New York Times, May 22, 2021, https://www.nytimes.com/2021/05/22/opinion/blm-movement
-protests-support.html.

14. See Robert Griffin, Mayesha Quasem, John Sides, and Michael Tesler, "Racing Apart:
Partisan Shifts on Racial Attitudes over the Last Decade," Voter Study Group, October 2021,
https://www.voterstudygroup.org/publication/racing-apart.

15. The term "issue attention cycle" is from Anthony Downs, "Up and Down with Ecology—
the 'Issue-Attention Cycle,'" *Public Interest* 28 (1972): 38–50. On the issue attention cycle and
mass shootings, see Danny Hayes, "Why It's So Hard to Pass Gun Control Laws (in One
Graph)," *Washington Post*, October 2, 2017, https://www.washingtonpost.com/news/monkey
-cage/wp/2015/08/26/why-its-so-hard-to-pass-gun-control-laws-in-one-graph/; and Nathaniel Rakich, "How Views on Gun Control Have Changed in the Last 30 Years," FiveThirtyEight,
August 7, 2019, https://fivethirtyeight.com/features/how-views-on-gun-control-have-changed
-in-the-last-30-years/. On civil rights protests and news attention, see Omar Wasow, "Agenda
Seeding: How the 1960s Black Protests Moved Elites, Public Opinion and Voting," *American
Political Science Review* 114, no. 3 (2020): 638–59.

16. Results from the TV News Archive are available here: https://tinyurl.com/2p87r5z2.
This analysis builds on Michael Tesler, "Support for Black Lives Matter Surged during Protests,
but Is Waning among White Americans," FiveThirtyEight, August 19, 2020, https://
fivethirtyeight.com/features/support-for-Black-lives-matter-surged-during-protests-but-is
-waning-among-white-americans/. The Crowd Counting Consortium is here: https://sites
.google.com/view/crowdcountingconsortium/home.

17. On the geography of the protests, see Lara Putnam, Erica Chenoweth, and Jeremy Pressman, "The Floyd Protests Are the Broadest in U.S. History—and Are Spreading to White,

Small-Town America," *The Monkey Cage* (blog), June 6, 2020, https://www.washingtonpost
.com/politics/2020/06/06/floyd-protests-are-broadest-us-history-are-spreading-white-small
-town-america/.

18. Buchanan et al., "Black Lives Matter."

19. David Nakamura, "In Trump's New Version of American Carnage, the Threat Isn't Immigrants or Foreign Nations. It's Other Americans," *Washington Post*, July 4, 2020, https://www
.washingtonpost.com/politics/in-trumps-new-version-of-american-carnage-the-threat-isnt
-immigrants-or-foreign-nations-its-other-americans/2020/07/04/f1354fa6-be10-11ea-8cf5
-9c1b8d7f84c6_story.html. For the volume of "defund" content by cable news channel, see
https://tinyurl.com/4h2nk6vd. For the volume of "Portland" content by cable news channel,
see https://tinyurl.com/4n3zkuzw. Many more examples are documented here: https://tinyurl
.com/2p8d3xaw.

20. Aris Folley, "Barr Says Cases of Floyd, Blake Not 'Interchangeable,'" *The Hill*, September 2, 2020, https://thehill.com/homenews/administration/514906-barr-says-cases-of-floyd
-blake-not-interchangeable. These polling results are from an August 27–28, 2020, YouGov poll:
https://docs.cdn.yougov.com/trcdohan8j/20200828_yahoo_coronavirus_crosstabs.pdf.

21. Other polling also showed Republican attitudes reverting to their pre-Floyd levels. See,
for example, declines in Republicans' belief that racial discrimination was a big problem, in
Monmouth University polls: https://www.monmouth.edu/polling-institute/reports
/monmouthpoll_us_070820/. There was also a decline in Republicans' belief that police killings of African Americans are a broader problem. See Emily Guskin, Scott Clement, and Dan
Balz, "Americans Support Black Lives Matter but Resist Shifts of Police Funds or Removal of
Statues of Confederate Generals or Presidents Who Were Enslavers," *Washington Post*, July 21,
2020, https://www.washingtonpost.com/politics/americans-support-black-lives-matter-but
-resist-shifts-of-police-funds-or-removal-of-statues-of-confederate-generals-or-presidents-who
-were-enslavers/2020/07/21/02d22468-cab0-11ea-91f1-28aca4d833a0_story.html.

22. These results are from a June 7–9, 2020, YouGov/*Economist* poll: https://docs.cdn
.yougov.com/ngcg634q9k/econTabReport.pdf#page=56. See also Michael Tesler, "Republicans and Democrats Agree on the Protests but Not Why People Are Protesting," FiveThirtyEight, June 17, 2020, https://fivethirtyeight.com/features/republicans-and-democrats
-increasingly-agree-on-the-protests-but-not-why-people-are-protesting/.

23. Christopher D. DeSante and Candis Watts Smith, *Racial Stasis* (Chicago: University of
Chicago Press, 2020). On the development of the measure of racial resentment, see Donald R.
Kinder and Lynn M. Sanders, *Divided by Color* (Chicago: University of Chicago Press, 1996).
On the prior stability of racial resentment and other racial attitude measures, see Michael Tesler,
Post-Racial or Most-Racial? Race and Politics in the Obama Era (Chicago: University of Chicago
Press, 2016). On the meaning of the racial resentment scale, see Cindy D. Kam and Camille D.
Burge, "Uncovering Reactions to the Racial Resentment Scale across the Racial Divide," *Journal
of Politics* 80, no. 1 (2019): 314–20.

24. On the earlier trends, see Sides, Tesler, and Vavreck, *Identity Crisis*. On the trend in the
2011–16 VOTER Survey, see Sean McElwee, "The Rising Racial Liberalism of Democratic Voters," *New York Times*, May 23, 2018, https://www.nytimes.com/2018/05/23/opinion/democrats
-race.html.

25. Adam M. Enders and Jamil S. Scott, "The Increasingly Racialization of American Electoral Politics, 1988–2016," *American Politics Research* 47, no. 2 (2019): 275–303.

26. To be sure, public opinion on affirmative action is sensitive to how the program is described. See, for example, Laura Stoker, "Understanding Whites' Resistance to Affirmative Action: The Role of Principled Commitments and Racial Prejudice," in *Perception and Prejudice: Race and Politics in the United States*, ed. Jon Hurwitz and Mark Peffley (New Haven: Yale University Press, 2019), 135–70. Thus, we do not claim that these numbers are canonical estimates of support for affirmative action in the absolute; our claim is merely that opinions have changed over time in ways that mirror party polarization on racial issues more generally.

27. For more evidence, see Andrew M. Engelhardt, "Racial Attitudes through a Partisan Lens," *British Journal of Political Science* 51, no. 3 (2021): 1062–79.

28. Ian Haney Lopez, *Dog Whistle Politics* (New York: Oxford University Press, 2014), 4; Tali Mendelberg, *The Race Card* (Princeton: Princeton University Press, 2001).

29. Anne Gearan, "Trump Promotes Video of a Supporter Saying 'White Power,'" *Washington Post*, June 28, 2020, https://www.washingtonpost.com/politics/2020/06/28/trump -promotes-video-supporter-saying-white-power/. For more, see Greg Miller, "Allegations of Racism Have Marked Trump's Presidency and Become Key Issue as Election Nears," *Washington Post*, September 23, 2020, https://www.washingtonpost.com/national-security/trump-race -record/2020/09/23/332b0b68-f10f-11ea-b796-2dd09962649c_story.html.

30. John Zaller, *The Nature and Origins of Mass Opinion* (New York: Cambridge University Press, 1992); Adam J. Berinsky, *In Time of War: Understanding American Public Opinion from World War II to Iraq* (Chicago: University of Chicago Press, 2009); Gabriel S. Lenz, *Follow the Leader? How Voters Respond to Politicians' Policies and Performance* (Chicago: Chicago University Press, 2012); Stephen P. Nicholson, "Polarizing Cues," *American Journal of Political Science* 56, no. 1 (2012): 52–66; and Michael Tesler, "Donald Trump Is Making the Border Wall Less Popular," *The Monkey Cage* (blog), August 16, 2016, https://www.washingtonpost.com/news /monkey-cage/wp/2016/08/16/donald-trump-is-making-the-border-wall-less-popular/.

31. Dean Knox, Will Lowe, and Jonathan Mummolo, "Administrative Records Mask Racially Biased Policing," *American Political Science Review* 114, no. 3 (2020): 619–37; Dean Knox and Jonathan Mummolo, "Making Inferences about Racial Disparities in Police Violence," *Proceedings of the National Academy of Sciences* 117, no. 3 (2020): 1261–62.

32. Maya King, "'The World Is Looking at Us': Minneapolis Puts 'Defund the Police' to a Vote," *Politico*, September 22, 2021, https://www.politico.com/news/2021/09/22/minneapolis -reckoning-defund-the-police-513568. The cable news data is based on the number of mentions of "defund" or "defunds" and "choke hold" or "choke holds" on CNN, Fox News, and MSNBC: see https://tinyurl.com/3nuhupps. Note that this is not just a function of Fox News coverage of defunding. The same pattern was true on CNN and MSNBC.

33. Scott Detrow and Barbara Sprunt, "'He Thinks Division Helps Him': Biden Condemns Trump's Protest Response," NPR, June 2, 2020, https://www.npr.org/2020/06/02/867671792 /biden-to-condemn-trumps-protest-response-in-speech.

34. Thomas B. Edsall and Mary D. Edsall, *Chain Reaction: The Impact of Race Rights and Taxes on American Politics* (New York: Norton, 1991); Paul M. Sniderman and Edward G. Carmines, *Reaching beyond Race* (Cambridge, MA: Harvard University Press, 1997); and

Nicholas A. Valentino and David O. Sears, "Old Times There Are Not Forgotten: Race and Partisan Realignment in the Contemporary South," *American Journal of Political Science* 49, no. 3 (2005): 672–88.

CHAPTER 7: THE DEATH STAR AND THE BASEMENT

1. Mark Urquiza's obituary is here: https://www.legacy.com/obituaries/azcentral/obituary .aspx?n=mark-anthony-urquiza&pid=196459145. On Kristin Urquiza's speech at the Democratic National Convention, see Matt Stevens, Isabella Grullón, and Jennifer Medina, "Kristin Urquiza, Whose Father Died of Covid, Denounces Trump at D.N.C.," *New York Times*, August 17, 2020, https://www.nytimes.com/2020/08/17/us/politics/kristin-urquiza-dad-covid -trump.html?searchResultPosition=1.

2. Alex Thompson, "The Biden Campaign Faces a Mind-Boggling Challenge: How to Make Joe Go Viral," *Politico*, May 3, 2020, https://www.politico.com/news/2020/05/03/can-joe -bidens-team-make-him-go-viral-228706; Eric Wilson, "COVID-19 Has Made the 2020 Campaign Virtual. That's a Disaster for Biden," Fast Company, May 13, 2020, https://www .fastcompany.com/90504199/covid-19-has-made-the-2020-campaign-virtual-thats-a-disaster -for-biden; Zeke Miller, "Trump Knocks Biden for Campaigning from Basement amid Virus," Associated Press, May 8, 2020, https://apnews.com/article/michael-pence-politics-joe-biden -virus-outbreak-donald-trump-d95718bfff3e5c7b07d58ab49bdb1e16.

3. The 2016 campaign finance figures are here: https://www.opensecrets.org/pres16/. Romney's primary election spending is here: http://www.cfinst.org/pdf/federal/HistoricalTables /pdf/CFI_Federal_CF_18_Table1-03.pdf. The 2019 campaign finance figures are here: https:// ballotpedia.org/Presidential_election_campaign_finance,_2020. The anxious Democrat quote and the May 2020 cash-on-hand figures are from Katie Glueck, "How the Biden Campaign Aims to Win Battleground States," *New York Times*, May 15, 2020, https://www.nytimes.com/2020 /05/15/us/politics/joe-biden-campaign-2020.html. The Parscale tweet is here: https://twitter .com/parscale/status/1258388669544759296?lang=en.

4. The comparison between Trump and Obama is here: https://ballotpedia.org/Presidential _election_campaign_finance,_2020.

5. The details about the Trump campaign's spending and Stepien's comment are in Shane Goldmacher and Maggie Haberman, "How Trump's Billion-Dollar Campaign Lost Its Cash Advantage," *New York Times*, September 7, 2020, https://www.nytimes.com/2020/09/07/us /politics/trump-election-campaign-fundraising.html.

6. An example of where Trump contravened the preferences of state authorities is Nevada. See https://www.cnbc.com/2020/09/14/in-defiance-of-nevada-governor-trump-holds -indoor-rally.html. The "double standard" quote is from Will Steakin and Ben Gittleson, "Trump Heads into Flu Season amid Pandemic Mocking Masks, Holding Packed Campaign Rallies," ABC News, September 11, 2020, https://abcnews.go.com/Politics/trump-heads-flu-season -amid-pandemic-mocking-masks/story?id=72950584. The number of rallies is tabulated in Adrian Blanco, "Amid the Pandemic, Trump and Biden Traveled Most Often to Pennsylvania and Florida," *Washington Post*, November 2, 2020, https://www.washingtonpost.com/elections

/2020/11/02/campaign-rallies-covid/. The Trump quote is from Brian Bennett and Tessa Berenson, "An Election Day Upset Hangs on Donald Trump's Formidable Ground Game," *Time*, November 2, 2020, https://time.com/5906581/donald-trump-campaign-ground-game/.

7. The number of field offices is from Joshua Darr, "In 2020, the Ground Game Is All Trump," *Mischiefs of Faction* (blog), October 9, 2020, https://www.mischiefsoffaction.com/post/2020 -ground-game. On Biden, see Steve Peoples, "After Pandemic Delay, Biden Launching In-Person Canvassing," Associated Press, October 1, 2020, https://apnews.com/article/election-2020 -virus-outbreak-joe-biden-donald-trump-elections-1e4e392fff3fed0a7925ef9cd9ca33e1. On the effectiveness of in-person and telephone contacting, see Donald P. Green, Mary C. Mc-Grath, and Peter M. Aronow, "Field Experiments and the Study of Voter Turnout," *Journal of Elections, Public Opinion, and Parties* 23, no. 1 (2013): 27–48.

8. John Sides, Lynn Vavreck, and Chris Warshaw, "The Effect of Television Advertising in United States Elections," *American Political Science Review*, forthcoming.

9. See figure 4 in Travis N. Ridout, Erika Franklin Fowler, and Michael M. Franz, "Spending Fast and Furious: Political Advertising in 2020," *The Forum* 18, no. 4 (2021): 465–92.

10. On the 2016 expenditures, see Christine B. Williams and Girish J. Gulati, "Digital Advertising Expenditures in the 2016 Presidential Election," *Social Science Computer Review* 36, no. 4 (2018): 406–21. On 2020 expenditures, see Ridout et al., "Spending Fast and Furious."

11. Joe Biden, "'We Are Living through a Battle for the Soul of This Nation,'" *The Atlantic*, August 27, 2017, https://www.theatlantic.com/politics/archive/2017/08/joe-biden-after -charlottesville/538128/. The Anzalone quote is from Jonathan Allen and Amie Parnes, *Lucky: How Joe Biden Barely Won the Presidency* (New York: Crown, 2021), 180.

12. This discussion draws from Lynn Vavreck, *The Message Matters: The Economy and Presidential Campaigns* (Princeton: Princeton University Press, 2007).

13. See John Sides and Lynn Vavreck, *The Gamble: Choice and Chance in the 2012 Presidential Campaign* (Princeton: Princeton University Press, 2013), 110–111.

14. The issue codes were provided by Kantar/CMAG, the company that collected the advertising data. Health care ads include those coded as mentioning health care generally, the Affordable Care Act, prescription drugs, or Medicaid. See also Ridout et al., "Spending Fast and Furious," table 4. The Biden ad "Dignity" is here: https://www.youtube.com/watch?v=gqZgy _ucCy0. The Biden ad "Personal" is here: https://www.youtube.com/watch?v=vi4bcatoFns.

15. In figure 7.2, the category "economy" includes ads that Kantar/CMAG categorized as discussing the economy or "manufacturing/construction." The category "jobs" includes the categories "jobs/unemployment" and "jobs/unemployment/outsourcing." The "Backbone" ad is here: https://www.youtube.com/watch?v=y_dxotPTrXE.

16. Ridout et al., "Spending Fast and Furious."

17. The data on concern about the coronavirus is from Nationscape surveys. See also https:// projects.fivethirtyeight.com/coronavirus-polls/. The data on trust in Biden and Trump to handle the pandemic is from an October 15–19 *New York Times*/Siena College poll. See https:// int.nyt.com/data/documenttools/us101520-crosstabs1/016bc5d8ae03038c/full.pdf. Similar findings from a late August poll are in Eli Yokeley, "Trump Says 'No One Will Be Safe' under His Opponent. But More Voters Trust Biden on Public Safety," Morning Consult, September 2, 2020, https://morningconsult.com/2020/09/02/public-safety-biden-trump-polling/.

18. On trust to handle the economy, see again the October 15–19 *New York Times*/Siena College poll, https://int.nyt.com/data/documenttools/us101520-crosstabs1/016bc5d8ae03038c/full.pdf.

19. Nick Corasaniti and Maggie Haberman, "'Geriatric,' 'China's Puppet': Trump Campaign Unleashes Ads Attacking Biden," *New York Times*, May 15, 2020, https://www.nytimes.com/2020/05/15/us/politics/trump-ads-joe-biden.html; Alexander Burns, Maggie Haberman, Jonathan Martin, and Nick Corasaniti, "A Sitting President, Riling the Nation during a Crisis," *New York Times*, May 15, 2020, https://www.nytimes.com/2020/05/15/us/politics/president-trump-coronavirus-pandemic-response.html.

20. The "rounded the final turn" comment is cited in Steakin and Gittleson, "Trump Heads into Flu Season."

21. On themes in Trump's ads, see Ridout et al., "Spending Fast and Furious," table 4. The "Great American Comeback" ad is here: https://www.youtube.com/watch?v=de10uQej6sA.

22. Ads attacking Biden on taxes include https://www.youtube.com/watch?v=zjgQlzlZfGA and https://www.youtube.com/watch?v=H1nIO5I2bO4. An ad attacking Biden on Social Security and Medicare is here: https://www.youtube.com/watch?v=z7dLYLTsJZ0. The immigration ad is here: https://www.youtube.com/watch?v=H1nIO5I2bO4.

23. The two ads are here: https://www.youtube.com/watch?v=AOOlOMLaFho and https://www.youtube.com/watch?v=moZOrq0qL3Q. See also Linda Qiu, "Trump Ads Attack Biden through Deceptive Editing and Hyperbole," *New York Times*, August 15, 2020, https://www.nytimes.com/2020/08/15/us/politics/trump-campaign-ads-biden.html; Matthew Yglesias, "Trump's Tweets about Saving the 'Suburban Lifestyle Dream,' Explained," *Vox*, August 3, 2020, https://www.vox.com/2020/8/3/21347565/suburban-lifestyle-dream-trump-tweets-fair-housing.

24. On the 2020 crime rate, see Lois Beckett and Abené Clayton, "How Bad Is the Rise in US Homicides? Factchecking the 'Crime Wave' Narrative Police Are Pushing," *The Guardian*, June 30, 2021, https://www.theguardian.com/us-news/2021/jun/30/us-crime-rate-homcides-explained. The Gallup poll data is here: https://news.gallup.com/poll/1603/crime.aspx.

25. Joe Biden, "We Must Urgently Root Out Systematic Racism, from Policing to Housing to Opportunity," *USA Today*, June 10, 2020, https://www.usatoday.com/story/opinion/2020/06/10/biden-root-out-systemic-racism-not-just-divisive-trump-talk-column/5327631002/. On polling on police reform, see Nathanial Rakich, "How Americans Feel about 'Defunding the Police,'" FiveThirtyEight, June 19, 2020, https://fivethirtyeight.com/features/americans-like-the-ideas-behind-defunding-the-police-more-than-the-slogan-itself/. Biden's "Be Not Afraid" ad is here: https://www.youtube.com/watch?v=LgHXJ3rdOn0.

26. The "cautious line" story is Jonathan Martin, Alexander Burns, and Thomas Kaplan, "Biden Walks a Cautious Line as He Opposes Defunding the Police," *New York Times*, June 8, 2020, https://www.nytimes.com/2020/06/08/us/politics/biden-defund-the-police.html. See also Glenn Kessler, "The Continuing GOP Fiction That President Biden Supports Defunding the Police," *Washington Post*, June 29, 2021, https://www.washingtonpost.com/politics/2021/06/29/continuing-gop-fiction-that-president-biden-supports-defunding-police/.

27. The Pew Research Center results are here: https://www.pewresearch.org/politics/2020/06/30/publics-mood-turns-grim-trump-trails-biden-on-most-personal-traits-major-issues/.

The Morning Consult results are described in Yokeley, "Trump Says 'No One Will Be Safe.'" The *New York Times* results are here: https://int.nyt.com/data/documenttools/us101520 -crosstabs1/016bc5d8ae03038c/full.pdf. See also Giovanni Russonello, "Which Candidate Do Voters Trust to Handle the Unrest?," *New York Times*, September 4, 2020, https://www.nytimes .com/2020/09/04/us/politics/trump-biden-protests-polling.html; and Shannon Pettypiece, "Trump Doubles Down on Crime Message as Polls Suggest It's a Risky Gamble," NBC News, September 8, 2020, https://www.nbcnews.com/politics/2020-election/trump-doubles-down -crime-message-polls-suggest-it-s-risky-n1239268.

28. One articulation of this view is Kevin M. Kruse, "Law and Order Won't Help Trump Win Reelection," *Washington Post*, June 2, 2020, https://www.washingtonpost.com/outlook /2020/06/02/law-order-wont-help-trump-win-reelection/. The DNC ad is here: https:// twitter.com/DNCWarRoom/status/1300820598445219840.

29. This is reported in Alexander Burns, Jonathan Martin, and Maggie Haberman, "In Final Stretch, Biden Defends Lead against Trump's Onslaught," *New York Times*, September 6, 2020, https://www.nytimes.com/2020/09/06/us/politics/trump-biden-2020.html.

30. Ashley Parker and Josh Dawsey, "Seven Days: Following Trump's Coronavirus Trail," *Washington Post*, December 5, 2021, https://www.washingtonpost.com/politics/trump -coronavirus-positive/2021/12/05/b1a55fda-544f-11ec-8927-c396fa861a71_story.html.

31. Damian Paletta and Yasmeen Abutaleb, "Inside the Extraordinary Effort to Save Trump from COVID-19," *Washington Post*, June 25, 2021, https://www.washingtonpost.com/politics /2021/06/24/nightmare-scenario-book-excerpt/; Maeve Reston and Gregory Krief, "White House Sows Confusion about Trump's Condition as Source Tells Reporters Next 48 Hours Will Be Critical," CNN, October 4, 2020, https://edition.cnn.com/2020/10/03/politics /donald-trump-coronavirus-walter-reed/index.html.

32. Peter Baker and Maggie Haberman, "Trump Leaves Hospital, Minimizing Virus and Urging Americans 'Don't Let It Dominate Your Lives,'" *New York Times*, October 5, 2020, https://www.nytimes.com/2020/10/05/us/politics/trump-leaves-hospital-coronavirus.html. The Trump campaign football tweet is here: https://twitter.com/TeamTrump/status/131324 7460458926080. The campaign quote is here: https://twitter.com/Olivianuzzi/status/13131 54949115793409.

33. On the three cable networks combined, the median number of fifteen-second segments about COVID was 707 in August, 634 in September, and 881 in October. Toluse Olorunnipa, Amy B. Wang, and Josh Dawsey, "Second Trump-Biden Debate Has Fewer Interruptions but More Counterpunches," *Washington Post*, October 23, 2020, https://www.washingtonpost.com /politics/debate-trump--biden/2020/10/23/5b67a0d2-1478-11eb-bc10-40b25382f1be_story .html; Caitlin O'Kane, "'We're About to Go into a Dark Winter': Biden Says Trump Has No Plan for Coronavirus," CBS News, October 23, 2020, https://www.cbsnews.com/news/biden -trump-coronavirus-plan-vaccine-winter/. Trump's diagnosis also led to the cancellation of a debate previously scheduled for October 15. Trump refused to participate when the commission that organizes presidential debates moved the event to a virtual format, and instead the candidates held competing townhalls broadcast at the same time on different networks.

34. Matt Friedman, "New Jersey Officials Fear Trump Fundraiser in Bedminster Could Turn into Super Spreader," *Politico*, October 2, 2020, https://www.politico.com/states/new-jersey

/story/2020/10/02/trump-looked-100-percent-normal-during-bedminster-fundraiser
-attendee-says-1319744; Annie Karni and Maggie Haberman, "A White House Long in Denial
Confronts Reality," *New York Times*, October 3, 2020, https://www.nytimes.com/2020/10/03
/us/politics/white-house-coronavirus.html; Carol D. Leonig, "Secret Service Agents Outraged
by Trump's Drive outside Hospital," *Washington Post*, October 4, 2020, https://www
.washingtonpost.com/elections/2020/10/04/trump-covid-live-updates/#link-UIJECVECJ
VGR5CRF2EASH3Z4UM; Maggie Haberman and Annie Karni, "Trump's Return Leaves
White House in Disarray as Infections Jolt West Wing," *New York Times*, October 6, 2020,
https://www.nytimes.com/2020/10/06/us/politics/white-house-coronavirus.html.

35. The reaction of Redfield is reported in Paletta and Abutaleb, "Inside the Extraordinary
Effort."

36. A compilation of results from the CNN/Michigan/Georgetown project is here: https://
s3mc.org/political-communication/election-2020-project/. See also Jennifer Agiesta, "In News
about the Presidential Race, Coronavirus Overtakes Nearly All Else," CNN, October 8, 2020,
https://www.cnn.com/2020/10/08/politics/the-breakthrough-trump-biden-coronavirus
-debate/index.html; and Grace Sparks, "As the Campaign Closes, Coronavirus Remains the
Main Event," CNN, November 3, 2020, https://www.cnn.com/2020/11/03/politics/the
-breakthrough-coronavirus-trump-biden/index.html. The *Huffington Post*/YouGov poll is discussed in Ariel Edwards-Levy, "Here Are Voters' Top Issues for 2020," *Huffington Post*, October 30, 2020, https://www.huffpost.com/entry/voters-top-issues-2020-biden-trump-poll_n
_5f9c7db5c5b616c2f31490a8.

37. Pew Research Center, "Public's Mood Turns Grim; Trump Trails Biden on Most Personal
Traits, Major Issues," June 30, 2020, https://www.pewresearch.org/politics/2020/06/30
/publics-mood-turns-grim-trump-trails-biden-on-most-personal-traits-major-issues/.

38. For Clinton's polling average, see https://projects.fivethirtyeight.com/2016-election
-forecast/national-polls/.

39. For example, see Sides, Tesler, and Vavreck, *Identity Crisis*, on similar partisan rallies in 2016.

40. The same trend in Trump's favorability was visible in YouGov polls: https://today.yougov
.com/topics/politics/trackers/donald-trump-favorability?period=5yrs.

41. Maureen Dowd, "Trump Does It His Way," *New York Times*, April 2, 2016, https://www
.nytimes.com/2016/04/03/opinion/sunday/trump-does-it-his-way.html. Trump's comment
about hitting Biden was noted by CNN's Daniel Dale: https://twitter.com/ddale8/status
/1323132334946816000. Katie Shepherd, "Trump Cheers Supporters Who Swarmed a Biden
Bus in Texas: 'These Patriots Did Nothing Wrong,'" *Washington Post*, November 2, 2020, https://
www.washingtonpost.com/nation/2020/11/02/trump-caravan-biden-bus/.

42. "Reality Check: Did Millions Vote Illegally in the US?," BBC News, January 25, 2017,
https://www.bbc.com/news/world-us-canada-38744612; Alicia Victoria Lozano, "Trump Accuses Democrats of 'Rigging' the November Election during November Rally," NBC News,
September 13, 2020, https://www.nbcnews.com/politics/2020-election/trump-accuses
-democrats-rigging-november-election-during-nevada-rally-n1239969; Quint Forgey, Zach
Montellaro, and Caitlin Oprysko, "Trump Refuses to Back Down on Suggestion of Election
Delay," *Politico*, July 30, 2020, https://www.politico.com/news/2020/07/30/trump-suggests
-delaying-2020-election-387902.

43. Jonathan Swan, "Scoop: Trump's Plan to Declare Premature Victory," Axios, November 1, 2020, https://www.axios.com/trump-claim-election-victory-ballots-97eb12b9-5e35-402f-9ea3 -0ccfb47f613f.html; Ryan Lizza and Daniel Lippman, "Republicans Publicly Silent, Privately Disgusted by Trump's Election Threats," *Politico*, November 3, 2020, https://www.politico.com /news/2020/11/03/republicans-trump-election-threats-433910.

CHAPTER 8: CHANGE (AND MORE OF THE SAME)

1. In 2016, seven electors attempted to vote for candidates other than Trump or Clinton, which is why the total does not sum to 538.

2. Scott Detrow and Asma Khalid, "Biden Wins Presidency, According to AP, Edging Trump in Turbulent Race," Associated Press, November 7, 2020, https://www.npr.org/2020/11/07 /928803493/biden-wins-presidency-according-to-ap-edging-trump-in-turbulent-race; David Siders, Anita Kumar, and Christopher Cadelago, "Biden Wins," *Politico*, November 7, 2020, https://www.politico.com/news/2020/11/07/joe-biden-wins-presidential-election-results -2020-434654.

3. David R. Mayhew, "Incumbency Advantage in U.S. Presidential Elections: The Historical Record," *Political Science Quarterly* 123, no. 2 (2008): 201–28.

4. Biden's average lead in national polls was 8.4 points at the end of the campaign, according to FiveThirtyEight: https://projects.fivethirtyeight.com/polls/president-general/national/. FiveThirtyEight's Senate forecast average indicated that Democrats would control about 52 seats: https://projects.fivethirtyeight.com/2020-election-forecast/senate/. The FiveThirtyEight House forecast average suggested that Democrats would win 239 seats (vs. the 235 they controlled after the 2018 election); they won 222. Another forecast suggested even larger gains for the Democrats in Congress: Michael Lewis-Beck and Charles Tien, "The Political Economy Model: A Blue Wave Forecast for 2020," *PS: Political Science and Politics* 54, no. 1 (2021): 59–62.

5. On the Electoral College bias in favor of the GOP, see Geoffrey Skelley, "Even Though Biden Won, Republicans Enjoyed the Largest Electoral College Edge in 70 Years. Will That Last?," FiveThirtyEight, January 19, 2021, https://fivethirtyeight.com/features/even-though -biden-won-republicans-enjoyed-the-largest-electoral-college-edge-in-70-years-will-that -last/.

6. Jake Sherman and Anna Palmer, "Politico Playbook: What Blue Wave?," Politico, November 4, 2020, https://www.politico.com/newsletters/playbook/2020/11/04/what-blue-wave -490798.

7. George Packer, "America's Plastic Hour Is Upon Us," *The Atlantic*, October 2020, https:// www.theatlantic.com/magazine/archive/2020/10/make-america-again/615478/.

8. J. Scott Armstrong and Andreas Graefe, "The PollyVote Popular Vote Forecast for the 2020 US Presidential Election," *PS: Political Science and Politics* 54, no. 1 (2021): 96–98.

9. For more evidence, see John Sides, Michael Tesler, and Lynn Vavreck, *Identity Crisis: The 2016 Presidential Campaign and the Battle for the Meaning of America* (Princeton: Princeton University Press, 2018), chap. 8.

10. Katie Glueck, Shade Goldmacher, and Glenn Thrush, "Now Comes the Hard Part for Joe Biden," *New York Times*, April 8, 2020, https://www.nytimes.com/2020/04/08/us/politics/biden-sanders-campaign-policy.html.

11. See Sides, Tesler, and Vavreck, *Identity Crisis*, table 8.1, 160.

12. This is based on survey interviews conducted in September 2020 (which asked whether respondents had voted in a Democratic primary or caucus and, if so, for whom) and then again after the election in November and December 2020.

13. The 3-point and 8-point estimates for Black and Latino voters, respectively, are from Yair Ghitza and Jonathan Robinson, "What Happened in 2020," Catalist, 2021, https://catalist.us/wh-national/. See also Michael Power, "Liberals Envisioned a Multiracial Coalition. Voters of Color Had Other Ideas," *New York Times*, November 15, 2020, https://www.nytimes.com/2020/11/16/us/liberals-race.html.

14. The data is available here: https://today.yougov.com/topics/politics/trackers/donald-trumps-ideology.

15. For each issue, respondents placed the candidates on a 7-point scale ranging from more liberal to more conservative. We made this scale range from 0 (most liberal) to 100 (most conservative) to be more intuitive. The scales measured ideology on the basic liberal-conservative spectrum, whether the government should provide more or fewer services and spending, whether the government should provide health insurance or whether we should rely on private insurance; whether the government should provide a guaranteed job and standard of living as opposed to letting people get ahead on their own; whether the government should spend more or less on national defense; whether the government should help improve the economic and social position of Black Americans and other minority groups or whether those groups should get ahead on their own; and whether there should be tougher regulations on business to protect the environment or whether regulations are already too much of a burden on business.

16. The 2016 and 2020 Cooperative Election Survey also showed a similar pattern to the ANES. On a similar 1–7 scale that we converted to range from 0 to 100, respondents rated Clinton at 25 and Trump at 67 in 2016. In 2020, they rated Biden at 25 and Trump at 79. Further analysis of the ANES also shows that the shifts in perceptions of Biden and Trump were present among Republicans, independents, and Democrats. Thus, these shifts were not just cases of partisan projection, where Democrats perceived Biden as closer to them and Trump further away, and Republicans perceived Trump as closer and Biden further away.

17. For evidence of these longer-term shifts in placements of the Democratic and Republican candidates, see Sides, Tesler, and Vavreck, *Identity Crisis*, 167–69. On the comparison between Biden and Clinton, see Alex Roarty, "Biden Is Labeled a Moderate. But His Agenda Is Far More Liberal than Hillary Clinton's," McClatchy, March 4, 2020, https://www.mcclatchydc.com/news/politics-government/election/campaigns/article234890482.html.

18. Ideological identification is measured with a five-category scale ranging from very liberal to very conservative. Abortion attitudes are measured a scale that combines attitudes on whether women should be able to obtain an abortion always as a matter of choice; whether to allow abortion only in cases of rape, incest, or risk to the mother's life; whether to prohibit abortion after the twentieth week of pregnancy; whether to allow employers to decline health

insurance coverage for abortion; whether to prohibit the use of federal funds for abortion; and whether to prohibit abortion entirely. Gun attitudes are measured with a scale that combines attitudes on whether to prohibit state and local governments from publishing the names and addresses of all gun owners; ban assault rifles; and make it easier to obtain a concealed carry permit. Racial attitudes are measured with agreement or disagreement with two statements: "White people in the U.S. have certain advantages because of the color of their skin" and "Racial problems in the U.S. are rare, isolated situations." We divide the abortion, gun, and racial attitude scales into rough terciles in order to present results for conservatives, moderates, and liberals.

19. See, for example, Sides, Tesler, and Vavreck, *Identity Crisis*, chap. 8; Brian F. Schaffner, Matthew MacWilliams, and Tatishe Nteta, "Understanding White Polarization in the 2016 Vote for President: The Sobering Role of Racism and Sexism," *Political Science Quarterly* 133, no. 1 (2018): 9–34; Daniel J. Hopkins, "The Activation of Prejudice and Presidential Voting: Panel Evidence from the 2016 U.S. Election," *Political Behavior* 43 (2021): 663–86.

20. Sides, Tesler, and Vavreck, *Identity Crisis*, chap. 9; Peter K. Enns and Ashley Jardina, "Complicating the Role of White Racial Attitudes and Anti-Immigrant Sentiment in the 2016 U.S. Presidential Election," *Public Opinion Quarterly* 85, no. 2 (Summer 2021): 539–70.

21. Ideological identification is a 5-point scale that ranges from very liberal to very conservative. Immigration attitudes are a scale based on respondents' views of a path to citizenship for undocumented immigrants, whether these immigrants are a benefit or burden to the United States, and whether it should be easier or harder to immigrate legally to the United States. Views of racial inequality is a scale based on the four items discussed in chapter 6 (see figure 6.5). Abortion attitudes are measured with a question asking whether abortion should be legal in all circumstances, legal in some circumstances and illegal in others, or illegal in all circumstances. Views of economic policy is based on respondents' views of the 2010 health care law, raising taxes on the wealthy, and whether the government should guarantee that everyone has health insurance.

22. Sabrina Rodriguez, "How Miami Cubans Disrupted Biden's Path to a Florida Win," *Politico*, November 4, 2020, https://www.politico.com/news/2020/11/04/biden-miami-cubans-election-2020-433999; Elizabeth Findell, "Why Democrats Lost So Many South Texas Latinos—The Economy," *Wall Street Journal*, November 8, 2020, https://www.wsj.com/articles/how-democrats-lost-so-many-south-texas-latinosthe-economy-11604871650.

23. On the overall effect of military casualties in the Korean and Vietnam Wars on presidential elections outcomes, see Douglas A. Hibbs Jr., "Bread and Peace Voting in U.S. Presidential Elections," *Public Choice* 104, no. 1 (2000): 149–80. On the local effects of the Iraq War, see David Karol and Edward Miguel, "The Electoral Cost of War: Iraq Casualties and the 2004 U.S. Presidential Election," *Journal of Politics* 69, no. 3 (2007): 633–48; and Douglas L. Kriner and Francis X. Shen, "Iraq Casualties and the 2006 Senate Elections," *Legislative Studies Quarterly* 33, no. 4 (2007): 507–30. On the effects of local COVID-19 deaths on vote intentions, see Christopher Warshaw, Lynn Vavreck, and Ryan Baxter-King, "Fatalities from COVID-19 Are Reducing Americans' Support for Republicans at Every Level of Federal Office," *Science Advances* 6, no. 44 (2020), https://www.science.org/doi/10.1126/sciadv.abd8564.

24. Christopher H. Achen and Larry M Bartels, *Democracy for Realists* (Princeton: Princeton University Press, 2016), 139–42.

25. John Sides, Lynn Vavreck, and Christopher Warshaw, "The Effect of Television Advertising in U.S. Elections," *American Political Science Review*, forthcoming.

26. Rachael Bade and Erica Werner, "Centrist House Democrats Lash Out at Liberal Colleagues, Blame Far-Left Views for Costing the Party Seats," *Washington Post*, November 5, 2020, https://www.washingtonpost.com/politics/house-democrats-pelosi-election/2020/11/05/1ddae5ca-1f6e-11eb-90dd-abd0f7086a91_story.html. See also https://twitter.com/mkraju/status/1324445099430940673?lang=en.

27. See, for example, Marc Caputo, "Culture Wars Fuel Trump's Blue-Collar Latino Gains," *Politico*, November 21, 2020, https://www.politico.com/news/2020/11/21/culture-wars-latinos-trump-438932.

28. Daniel Q. Gillion, *The Loud Minority: Why Protests Matter in American Democracy* (Princeton: Princeton University Press, 2020).

29. Omar Wasow, "Agenda Seeding: How the 1960s Black Protests Moved Elites, Public Opinion and Voting," *American Political Science Review*, 114, no. 3 (2020): 638–59.

30. Tobi Thomas, Adam Gabbatt, and Caelainn Barr, "Nearly 1,000 Instances of Police Brutality Recorded in US Anti-racism Protests," *The Guardian*, October 29, 2020, https://www.theguardian.com/us-news/2020/oct/29/us-police-brutality-protest.

31. Good windows into the "Is 2020 like 1968?" debate include David Weigel, "The Trailer: This Election Isn't 1968 or 1992 or 2016," *Washington Post*, May 31, 2020, https://www.washingtonpost.com/politics/paloma/the-trailer/2020/05/31/the-trailer-this-election-isn-t-1968-or-1992-or-2016/5ed2f3ee602ff12947e7ffac/; Kevin Kruse, "Law and Order Won't Help Trump Win Reelection," *Washington Post*, June 2, 2020, https://www.washingtonpost.com/outlook/2020/06/02/law-order-wont-help-trump-win-reelection/; and Omar Wasow, "The Protests Started out Looking Like 1968. They Turned into 1964," *Washington Post*, June 11, 2020, https://www.washingtonpost.com/outlook/2020/06/11/protests-started-out-looking-like-1968-they-turned-into-1964/. The study of the Rodney King riots is Ryan D. Enos, Aaron R. Kaufman, and Melissa L. Sands, "Can Violent Protest Change Local Policy Support? Evidence from the Aftermath of the 1992 Los Angeles Riot," *American Political Science Review* 113, no. 4 (2019): 1012–28.

32. On Kenosha, see also "Rioting amid Demonstrations for Racial Justice May Have Helped Donald Trump," *The Economist*, May 22, 2021, https://www.economist.com/graphic-detail/2021/05/22/rioting-amid-demonstrations-for-racial-justice-may-have-helped-donald-trump.

33. Andrew M. Engelhardt, "Racial Attitudes through a Partisan Lens," *British Journal of Political Science* 51, no. 3 (2021): 1062–79; Enns and Jardina, "Complicating the Role of White Racial Attitudes."

34. Amber Phillips, "Joe Biden's Victory Speech, Annotated," *Washington Post*, November 7, 2020, https://www.washingtonpost.com/politics/2020/11/07/annotated-biden-victory-speech/.

CHAPTER 9: SUBVERSION

1. James Oliphant and Nathan Layne, "Georgia Republicans Purge Black Democrats from County Election Boards," Reuters, December 9, 2021, https://www.reuters.com/world/us/georgia-republicans-purge-black-democrats-county-election-boards-2021-12-09/.

2. Domenico Montanaro, "Biden Eschews Anger, Hoping 'Unity' Can Lift Him to the Presidency," NPR, May 19, 2019, https://www.npr.org/2019/05/19/724708438/biden-eschews-anger-hoping-unity-can-lift-him-to-the-presidency; Alexander Burns, Jonathan Martin, and Katie Glueck, "How Joe Biden Won the Presidency," *New York Times*, November 7, 2020, https://www.nytimes.com/2020/11/07/us/politics/joe-biden-president.html. The Biden ad ("Heal America") is here: https://www.youtube.com/watch?v=kCYN5MY5BHg. See also Maggie Haberman, "Trump Departs Vowing, 'We Will Be Back in Some Form,'" *New York Times*, January 20, 2021, https://www.nytimes.com/2021/01/20/us/politics/trump-presidency.html.

3. Jeffrey M. Jones, "Biden Begins Term with 57% Job Approval," Gallup, February 4, 2021, https://news.gallup.com/poll/329348/biden-begins-term-job-approval.aspx.

4. Perry Bacon Jr., "Biden's Initial Batch of Executive Actions Is Popular," FiveThirtyEight, January 27, 2021, https://fivethirtyeight.com/features/bidens-initial-batch-of-executive-actions-is-popular/. On Biden's legislative initiatives, see https://www.economist.com/president-joe-biden-polls.

5. A good and balanced discussion of popularism is Ezra Klein, "David Shor Is Telling Democrats What They Don't Want to Hear," *New York Times*, October 8, 2021, https://www.nytimes.com/2021/10/08/opinion/democrats-david-shor-education-polarization.html.

6. Jon Cohen, "Fact Check: No Evidence Supports Trump's Claim That COVID-19 Vaccine Result Was Suppressed to Sway Election," *Science*, November 11, 2020, https://www.science.org/content/article/fact-check-no-evidence-supports-trump-s-claim-covid-19-vaccine-result-was-suppressed.

7. Jim Acosta and Caroline Kelly, "Donald and Melania Trump Received Covid Vaccine at the White House in January," CNN, March 1, 2021, https://www.cnn.com/2021/03/01/politics/trump-melania-vaccinated-white-house/index.html; Jack Brewster, "Trump: I 'Don't Know' Why Republicans Are Vaccine Hesitant, Again Floats Pfizer Conspiracy," *Forbes*, April 20, 2021, https://www.forbes.com/sites/jackbrewster/2021/04/20/trump-i-dont-know-why-republicans-are-vaccine-hesitant-again-floats-pfizer-conspiracy-theory/?sh=5f7ec0776b34; Azi Paybarah and Lauren McCarthy, "Donald Trump Said He Got a Booster Shot and His Supporters Booed," *New York Times*, December 20, 2021, https://www.nytimes.com/2021/12/20/world/trump-supporters-booster-shots.html.

8. Chris Cillizza, "Donald Trump's Latest Dangerous Vaccine Pronouncement," CNN, July 19, 2021, https://www.cnn.com/2021/07/19/politics/donald-trump-covid-19-vaccines/index.html; Allan Smith, "Trump Booed at Alabama Rally after Telling Supporters to Get Vaccinated," NBC News, August 22, 2021, https://www.nbcnews.com/politics/donald-trump/trump-booed-alabama-rally-after-telling-supporters-get-vaccinated-n1277404; Jack Healy, Noah Weiland, and Richard Fausset, "As Omicron Spreads and Cases Soar, the Unvaccinated Remain Defiant," *New York Times*, December 25, 2021, https://www.nytimes.com/2021/12/25/us/omicron-unvaccinated.html.

9. Tiffany Hsu, "Despite Outbreaks among Unvaccinated, Fox News Hosts Smear Shots," *New York Times*, July 11, 2021, https://www.nytimes.com/2021/07/11/business/media/vaccines-fox-news-hosts.html.

10. The YouGov poll is here: https://docs.cdn.yougov.com/pnu6yfcz0j/econTabReport.pdf. See also the Kaiser Family Foundation polling: https://www.kff.org/coronavirus-covid-19

/dashboard/kff-covid-19-vaccine-monitor-dashboard/?utm_source=web&utm_medium
=trending&utm_campaign=COVID-19-vaccine-monitor. There were similar partisan gaps in
respondents' willingness to vaccinate their children. As of the November 2021 Kaiser Family
Foundation poll, conducted about five months after the vaccine was available to children age
twelve and older, 80 percent of Democrats with children this age said that they had been vaccinated, compared to just 25 percent of Republican parents.

11. The July 2021 YouGov results are here: https://docs.cdn.yougov.com/w2zmwpzsq0
/econTabReport.pdf. The poll results on vaccine misinformation are here: https://www.kff
.org/coronavirus-covid-19/poll-finding/kff-covid-19-vaccine-monitor-media-and-misin
formation/.

12. Gaby Galvin, "White House's COVID-19 Vaccination Mandates Have the Support of
about 3 in 5 Americans," Morning Consult, September 13, 2021, https://morningconsult.com
/2021/09/13/white-house-covid-vaccination-mandates-poll/.

13. Daniel Wood and Geoff Brumfiel, "Pro-Trump Counties Now Have Far Higher COVID
Death Rates. Misinformation Is to Blame," NPR, December 5, 2021, https://www.npr.org
/sections/health-shots/2021/12/05/1059828993/data-vaccine-misinformation-trump
-counties-covid-death-rate; Samira Sadeque, "Nearly All Fox Staffers Vaccinated for COVID
Even as Hosts Cast Doubt on Vaccine," The Guardian, September 15, 2021, https://www
.theguardian.com/media/2021/sep/15/fox-news-vaccines-testing-tucker-carlson.

14. Lev Facher, "GOP Opposition to Vaccine Mandates Extends Far beyond COVID-19,"
Stat, November 17, 2021, https://www.statnews.com/2021/11/17/gop-opposition-to-vaccine
-mandates-extends-far-beyond-covid-19/. The July 2013 YouGov poll results are here: http://
cdn.yougov.com/cumulus_uploads/document/63g3p232e0/tabs_Vaccines_0716172013.pdf.
The July 2021 YouGov poll results are here: https://docs.cdn.yougov.com/w2zmwpzsq0
/econTabReport.pdf.

15. Biden's statement is here: https://www.whitehouse.gov/briefing-room/speeches
-remarks/2021/04/20/remarks-by-president-biden-on-the-verdict-in-the-derek-chauvin-trial
-for-the-death-of-george-floyd/. See also Jennifer Agiesta, "CNN Poll: Most Satisfied with
Chauvin Verdict, but Partisans Divide," CNN, April 27, 2021, https://www.cnn.com/2021/04
/27/politics/cnn-poll-chauvin-trial/index.html. The DeSantis and Carlson comments are
quoted in Steve Benen, "Following Chauvin's Conviction, Many on the Right Slam Jurors,"
MSNBC, April 22, 2021, https://www.msnbc.com/rachel-maddow-show/following-chauvin-s
-conviction-many-right-slam-jurors-n1264914. There was also a large partisan divide in
response to the acquittal of Kyle Rittenhouse, who was charged after killing two men in the
racial justice protests in Kenosha, Wisconsin. See John Sides and Michael Tesler, "Racially
Charged Trials Were Less Politically Polarized in the Past," Washington Post, November 30,
2021, https://www.washingtonpost.com/outlook/2021/11/30/arbery-rittenhouse-partisan
-polarization/.

16. See Sides and Tesler, "Racially Charged Trials."

17. The Ipsos poll is here: https://www.ipsos.com/en-us/news-polls/reuters-ipsos-poll
-critical-race-theory-07152021. Similar findings are in this November 4–8, 2021, Monmouth
University poll: https://www.monmouth.edu/polling-institute/reports/monmouthpoll_us
_111021/.

18. Matthew Choi, "Trump Declines to Commit to a Peaceful Transition of Power after Election," *Politico*, September 23, 2020, https://www.politico.com/news/2020/09/23/trump-peaceful-transition-of-power-420791; Evan Osnos, "Can Biden's Center Hold?," *New Yorker*, August 31, 2020, https://www.newyorker.com/magazine/2020/08/31/can-bidens-center-hold.

19. Jim Rutenberg, Jo Becker, Eric Lipton, Maggie Haberman, Jonathan Martin, Matthew Rosenberg, and Michael S. Schmidt, "77 Days: Trump's Campaign to Subvert the Election," *New York Times*, January 31, 2021, https://www.nytimes.com/2021/01/31/us/trump-election-lie.html. Brann's opinion is here: https://pacer-documents.s3.amazonaws.com/147/127057/15517440654.pdf.

20. Katie Benner, "Meadows Pressed Justice Dept. to Investigate Election Fraud Claims," *New York Times*, June 5, 2021, https://www.nytimes.com/2021/06/05/us/politics/mark-meadows-justice-department-election.html; Rutenberg et al., "77 Days."

21. Jacqueline Alemany, Emma Brown, Tom Hamburger, and Jon Swaine, "Ahead of Jan. 6, Willard Hotel in Downtown D.C. Was a Trump Team 'Command Center' for Effort to Deny Biden the Presidency," *Washington Post*, October 23, 2021, https://www.washingtonpost.com/investigations/willard-trump-eastman-giuliani-bannon/2021/10/23/c45bd2d4-3281-11ec-9241-aad8e48f01ff_story.html.

22. For more, see Edward B. Foley, "The Repugnant Plan Brewing for State Legislatures to Steal the Election Must Be Stopped," *Washington Post*, November 6, 2020, https://www.washingtonpost.com/opinions/2020/11/06/state-legislatures-electoral-college-steal/.

23. Peter Baker, Maggie Haberman, and Annie Karni, "Pence Reached His Limit with Trump. It Wasn't Pretty," *New York Times*, January 12, 2021, https://www.nytimes.com/2021/01/12/us/politics/mike-pence-trump.html; Isaac Stanley-Becker, "Top General Was So Fearful Trump Might Spark War That He Made Secret Calls to His Chinese Counterpart, New Book Says," *Washington Post*, September 14, 2021, https://www.washingtonpost.com/politics/2021/09/14/peril-woodward-costa-trump-milley-china/.

24. Robert Griffin and Mayesha Quasem, "Crisis of Confidence," Voter Study Group, June 2021, https://www.voterstudygroup.org/publication/crisis-of-confidence. A similar drop in Republican trust in the election system was visible in Morning Consult polls: https://morningconsult.com/form/tracking-voter-trust-in-elections/. The Pew Research Center polls are presented in Karlyn Bowman and Samantha Goldstein, "Voices on the Vote," Voter Study Group, May 2021, https://www.voterstudygroup.org/publication/voices-on-the-vote. The Public Religion Research Institute poll is here: https://www.prri.org/research/competing-visions-of-america-an-evolving-identity-or-a-culture-under-attack/. For experimental evidence that Trump's tweets attacking the integrity of the election actually changed his supporters' views, see Katherine Clayton, Nicholas T. Davis, Brendan Nyhan, Ethan Porter, Timothy J. Ryan, and Thomas J. Wood, "Elite Rhetoric Can Undermine Democratic Norms," *PNAS* 118, no. 3 (June 8, 2021), https://doi.org/10.1073/pnas.2024125118.

25. The Suffolk University polls are here: https://www.suffolk.edu/academics/research-at-suffolk/political-research-center/polls/national. See also Jeffrey M. Jones, "In U.S., 84% Accept Trump as Legitimate President," Gallup, November 11, 2016, https://news.gallup.com/poll/197441/accept-trump-legitimate-president.aspx; Scott Clement, "One-Third of Clinton Supporters Say Trump Election Is Not Legitimate, Poll Finds," *Washington Post*, November 13, 2016, https://www.washingtonpost.com/news/the-fix/wp/2016/11/13/one-third-of-clinton-supporters-say-trump-election-is-not-legitimate-poll-finds/. Polls in 2017 showed an increase

in the percentage of Democrats who said that Trump was illegitimate, but this appears to reflect more his conduct as president than the circumstances of his election. See Lydia Saad, "Trump Mostly Performing to Americans' Expectations," Gallup, April 27, 2017, https://news.gallup.com /poll/209222/trump-mostly-performing-americans-expectations.aspx. For additional 2020 polling, see: https://pollingreport.com/2020wh.htm.

26. Lane Cuthbert and Alexander Theodoridis, "Do Republicans Really Believe Trump Won the 2020 Election? Our Research Suggests They Do," *The Monkey Cage* (blog), January 7, 2022, https://www.washingtonpost.com/politics/2022/01/07/republicans-big-lie-trump/.

27. Daniel Dale, "Trump Is Doing More Lying about the Election than Talking about Any Other Subject," CNN, June 12, 2021, https://www.cnn.com/2021/06/12/politics/analysis -trump-election-lies-blog-post-presidency.

28. Rosalind S. Helderman and Josh Dawsey, "'A Real Conflagration': Wisconsin Emerges as Front Line in War over the 2020 Vote," *Washington Post*, December 16, 2021, https://www .washingtonpost.com/politics/wisconsin-2020-vote-battle/2021/12/16/6c585248-5931-11ec -9a18-a506cf3aa31d_story.html.

29. The overall drop in Trump's approval rating is visible in FiveThirtyEight's polling averages: https://projects.fivethirtyeight.com/trump-approval-ratings/. The polling on arresting participants in the insurrection is here: https://civiqs.com/reports/2021/8/2/report-repub licans-increasingly-oppose-arresting-us-capitol-attackers.

30. Michael Tesler, "How the Capitol Riot Solidified Trump's Stranglehold on the GOP," Five ThirtyEight, January 5, 2022, https://tinyurl.com/2f9n9wc7.

31. Alan Feuer, "Debunking the Pro-Trump Right's Claims about the Jan. 6 Riot," *New York Times*, September 17, 2021, https://www.nytimes.com/2021/09/17/us/politics/capitol-riot -pro-trump-claims.html. The Trump quote is in Barton Gellman, "Trump's Next Coup Has Already Begun," *The Atlantic*, December 6, 2021, https://www.theatlantic.com/magazine /archive/2022/01/january-6-insurrection-trump-coup-2024-election/620843/.

32. The Pew Research Center poll is here: https://www.pewresearch.org/politics/2021/09 /28/declining-share-of-republicans-say-it-is-important-to-prosecute-jan-6-rioters/.

33. Meryl Kornfield and Mariana Alfaro, "1 in 3 Americans Say Violence against Government Can Be Justified, Citing Fears of Political Schism, Pandemic," *Washington Post*, January 1, 2022, https://www.washingtonpost.com/politics/2022/01/01/1-3-americans-say-violence against -government-can-be-justified-citing-fears-political-schism-pandemic/; Noam Lupu, Luke Plutowski, and Elizabeth J. Zechmeister, "Would Americans Ever Support a Coup? 40 Percent Now Say Yes," *The Monkey Cage* (blog), January 6, 2022, https://www.washingtonpost.com/politics /2022/01/06/us-coup-republican-support/. On the challenges of measuring public attitudes toward political violence, see Sean J. Westwood, Justin Grimmer, Matthew Tyler, and Clayton Nall, "Current Research Overstates American Support for Political Violence," *PNAS*, forthcoming.

34. Republican National Committee, "Growth and Opportunity Project," 2013. An archived copy of the report is here: https://online.wsj.com/public/resources/documents/RNCreport 03182013.pdf.

35. Brennan Center for Justice, "Voting Laws Roundup: July 2021," https://www.brennan center.org/our-work/research-reports/voting-laws-roundup-july-2021.

36. On voter identification laws and turnout, see Robert S. Erikson and Lorraine C. Minnite, "Modeling Problems in the Voter Identification–Voter Turnout Debate," *Election Law Journal* 8, no. 2 (2009): 85–101; Bernard L. Fraga, *The Turnout Gap: Race, Ethnicity, and Political*

Inequality in a Diversifying America (Cambridge: Cambridge University Press, 2018); and Enrico Cantoni and Vincent Pons, "Strict ID Laws Don't Stop Voters: Evidence from a U.S. Nationwide Panel, 2008–2018," *Quarterly Journal of Economics* 136, no. 4 (2021): 2615–60. On mail voting in 2020, see Jesse Yoder, Sandy Handan-Nader, Andrew Myers, Toby Nowacki, Daniel M. Thompson, Jennifer Wu, Chenoa Yorgason, and Andrew B. Hall, "How Did Absentee Voting Affect the 2020 U.S. Election?," Stanford University working paper, 2021, https://stanforddpl.org/papers /yoder_et_al_2020_turnout/. On how mail voting advantages neither party, see Daniel M. Thompson, Jennifer A. Wu, Jesse Yoder, and Andrew B. Hall, "Universal Vote-by-Mail Has No Impact on Partisan Turnout or Vote Share." *PNAS* 117, no. 25 (2020): 14052–56.

37. The report is here: https://protectdemocracy.org/update/protect-democracy-releases -report-on-election-interference-schemes-by-state-legislators/. See also Gellman, "Trump's Next Coup," and Richard L. Hasen, "Republicans Aren't Done Messing with Elections," *New York Times*, April 23, 2021, https://www.nytimes.com/2021/04/23/opinion/republicans-voting -us-elections.html. A letter from political scientists raising similar concerns is here: https://www .newamerica.org/political-reform/statements/statement-of-concern/.

38. The count of 163 is from Ashley Parker, Amy Gardner, and Josh Dawsey, "How Republicans Became the Party of Trump's Election Lie after January 6," *Washington Post*, January 5, 2022, https://www.washingtonpost.com/politics/republicans-jan-6-election-lie/2022/01/05 /82f4cad4-6cb6-11ec-974b-d1c6de8b26b0_story.html. See also Tim Reid, Nathan Layne, and Jason Lange, "Special Report: Backers of Trump's False Fraud Claims Seek to Control Next Elections," Reuters, September 22, 2021, https://www.reuters.com/world/us/backers-trumps -false-fraud-claims-seek-control-next-us-elections-2021-09-22/; Isaac Arnsdorf, Doug Bock Clark, Alexandra Berson, and Anjeanette Damon, "Heeding Bannon's Call, Election Deniers Organize to Seize Control of the GOP—and Reshape America's Elections," *ProPublica*, September 2, 2021, https://www.propublica.org/article/heeding-steve-bannons-call-election -deniers-organize-to-seize-control-of-the-gop-and-reshape-americas-elections.

39. Sonam Vashi, "After a Wave of Violent Threats against Election Workers, Georgia Sees Few Arrests," *ProPublica*, March 3, 2021, https://www.propublica.org/article/after-a-wave-of -violent-threats-against-election-workers-georgia-sees-few-arrests?mc_cid=da765bbb92&mc _eid=bdbe3095e5; Linda So, "Trump-Inspired Death Threats Are Terrorizing Election Workers," Reuters, June 11, 2021, https://www.reuters.com/investigates/special-report/usa-trump -georgia-threats; Jason Szep and Linda So, "Trump Campaign Demonized Two Georgia Election Workers—and Death Threats Followed," Reuters, December 1, 2021, https://www.reuters .com/investigates/special-report/usa-election-threats-georgia; Linda So and Jason Szep, "Reuters Unmasks Trump Supporters Who Terrified U.S. Election Officials," Reuters, November 9, 2021, https://www.reuters.com/investigates/special-report/usa-election-threats/. The survey of local election officials is here: https://www.brennancenter.org/sites/default/files /2021-06/Local_Election_Officials_Survey_0.pdf. See also Zack Beauchamp, "'We Are Going to Make You Beg for Mercy': America's Public Servants Face a Wave of Threats," Vox, November 18, 2021, https://www.vox.com/22774745/death-threats-election-workers-public-health -school.

40. Susan Dominus and Luke Broadwater, "The Scars of January 6," *New York Times Magazine*, January 9, 2022, https://www.nytimes.com/2022/01/04/magazine/jan-6-capitol-police -officers.html. Anton is the officer's middle name, which was used to protect his privacy.

41. The vulnerability of state governments to democratic erosion is noted in Frances E. Lee, "Populism and the American Party System: Opportunities and Constraints," *Perspectives on Politics* 18, no. 2 (2020): 370–88. For a full treatment, see Jacob M. Grumbach, *Laboratories against Democracy* (Princeton: Princeton University Press, 2022).

42. See Milan Svolik, "When Polarization Trumps Civic Virtue: Partisan Conflict and the Subversion of Democracy by Incumbents," *Quarterly Journal of Political Science* 15, no. 1 (2020): 3–31; Matthew H. Graham and Milan W. Svolik, "Democracy in America? Partisanship, Polarization, and the Robustness of Support for Democracy in the United States," *American Political Science Review* 114, no. 2 (2020): 392–409; Robert R. Kaufman and Stephan Haggard, "Democratic Decline in the United States: What Can We Learn from Middle-Income Backsliding?," *Perspectives on Politics* 17, no. 2 (2019): 417–32; Robert C. Lieberman, Suzanne Mettler, Thomas B. Pepinsky, Kenneth M. Roberts, and Richard Vallely, "The Trump Presidency and American Democracy: A Historical and Comparative Analysis," *Perspectives on Politics* 17, no. 2 (2019): 470–79; Suzanne Mettler and Robert C. Lieberman, *Four Threats: The Recurring Crises of American Democracy* (New York: St. Martin's Press, 2020).

43. For more on how contemporary polarization may continue rather than self-correct, see Paul Pierson and Eric Schickler, "Madison's Constitution under Stress: A Developmental Analysis of Political Polarization," *Annual Review of Political Science* 23 (2020): 37–58.

44. On the centrality of leaders' choices to democratic decline or "backsliding," see Steven Levitsky and Daniel Ziblatt, *How Democracies Die* (New York: Crown, 2019), and Aziz Huq and Tom Ginsburg, "How to Lose a Constitutional Democracy," *UCLA Law Review* 65 (2018), https://www.uclalawreview.org/lose-constitutional-democracy/.

APPENDIX TO CHAPTER 1

1. Andrew Mercer, Arnold Lau, and Courtney Kennedy, "For Weighting Online Opt-In Samples, What Matters Most?," Pew Research Center, January 26, 2018, https://www.pewresearch.org/methods/2018/01/26/for-weighting-online-opt-in-samples-what-matters-most/.

2. Derek Holliday, Tyler Reny, Alex Rossell-Hayes, Aaron Rudkin, Chris Tausanovitch, and Lynn Vavreck, "Democracy Fund + UCLA Nationscape Methodology and Representativeness Assessment," updated December 2021, https://www.voterstudygroup.org/uploads/reports/Data/NS-Methodology-Representativeness-Assessment.pdf.

APPENDIX TO CHAPTER 2

1. For more on the original construction of this data, see Sarah A. Binder, *Stalemate: Causes and Consequences of Legislative Gridlock* (Washington, DC: Brookings Institution Press, 2003).

APPENDIX TO CHAPTER 3

1. On this logarithmic transformation, see Christopher H. Achen and Larry M. Bartels, *Democracy for Realists* (Princeton: Princeton University Press, 2016), 150n4.

2. This follows Alan I. Abramowitz, "Forecasting the 2008 Presidential Election with the Time-for-Change Model," *PS: Political Science and Politics* 41, no. 4 (2008): 691–95.

3. The logic of the Clarify package is presented in Gary King, Michael Tomz, and Jason Wittenberg, "Making the Most of Statistical Analyses: Improving Interpretation and Presentation," *American Journal of Political Science* 44, no. 2 (2000): 341–55.

APPENDIX TO CHAPTER 4

1. On the challenge of estimating the effects of policy, see Gabriel Lenz, *Follow the Leader? How Voters Respond to Politicians' Policies and Performance* (Chicago: University of Chicago Press, 2012).

2. For more on this type of model, see Joshua D. Clinton, Simon Jackman, and Douglas Rivers, "The Statistical Analysis of Roll Call Data," *American Political Science Review* 98, no. 2 (2004): 355–70. For details of the estimation routine, see Jeffrey B. Lewis and Chris Tausanovitch, "gpuideal: Fast Fully Bayesian Estimation of Ideal Points with Massive Data," working paper, August 2018, https://ctausanovitch.com/gpuideal.pdf.

APPENDIX TO CHAPTER 8

1. Another survey that compared 2016 vote choice to vote intentions in the late summer of 2020 also found high levels of stability. See Pew Research Center, "Election 2020: Voters Are Highly Engaged, but Nearly Half Expect to Have Difficulties Voting," August 13, 2020, https://www.pewresearch.org/politics/wp-content/uploads/sites/4/2020/08/PP_2020.08.13_Voter-Attitudes_FINAL1.pdf.

ACKNOWLEDGMENTS

ONE OF THE LAST TIMES the three of us were together in the same place, we were in the lobby of the Marriott Hotel in Des Moines, Iowa. It was February 3, 2020, and the Iowa Democratic caucuses had just concluded. Pete Buttigieg was declaring victory, and Joe Biden had come in fourth place. The U.S. Senate was about to acquit Donald Trump on all impeachment charges brought against him—the first time.

A lot has changed since that day, more than two years ago now.

We left Iowa and six weeks later, like many people, we retreated to our homes during the COVID-19 pandemic. We taught courses from our spare bedrooms and watched one of the strangest presidential elections in modern history come to an extraordinarily bitter and violent end on January 6, 2021.

In writing about this election, we have much to be grateful for, not the least of which is our health and the health of our families and friends. We are also grateful to many people for supporting this project.

We especially thank Michael Tesler, who coauthored our book about the 2016 election, *Identity Crisis*, and coauthored chapter 6 of this book. Michael pushed us to think carefully about the challenges to American democracy that were revealed by the 2020 election and urged us to confront them head-on. He also lent us his expertise as a scholar of racial attitudes, public opinion, and voting behavior to help tell the story of how the murder of George Floyd affected the election. There is no finer colleague or collaborator.

We are deeply indebted to the Democracy Fund, its Voter Study Group, and in particular Joe Goldman, Robert Griffin, Alicia Prevost, Mayesha Quasem, and Lauren Strayer. Their support enabled two data collections that inform the analyses in this book: the Democracy Fund + UCLA Nationscape Project, which completed roughly 500,000 interviews between 2019 and 2021, and the Views of the Electorate Research (VOTER) Survey, an amazing panel of interviews that began in 2011 and still continues. The Democracy Fund recognized the need for innovative surveys to help us better understand the values and beliefs of ordinary Americans. Without their generosity and insights, our work would not have been possible.

We also would like to thank our partners at the market research firm Lucid, who brainstormed with us about project possibilities and worked tirelessly to field our Nationscape surveys: Eli Ackerman, Lauren Astrachan, Ashley Burkardt, Kyle Cousans, Wiley Davis, Mary Kate Hutchinson, and Allison St. Martin.

Several graduate students at UCLA helped us along the way. We are grateful for the hard work of Alex Rossell Hayes, Derek Holliday, Tyler Reny, and Aaron Rudkin in fielding the Nationscape Project. Nothing stopped or slowed this team down—not even the sudden move to fielding the project remotely. Adam Bakr, Ryan Baxter-King, Jacques Courbe, and Brian Hamel helped us gather and analyze other data. Similarly, we appreciate the work of undergraduate students William Lewis (Hobart and William Smith Colleges) and Sophie Simcox (UCLA). We also thank two Vanderbilt University graduate students, Mary Catherine Sullivan and Sierra Wiese, for their help in collecting data.

We are also grateful to the many people who provided us with data. These include Sarah Binder, Jim Gimpel, and Chris Warshaw; Dan Hopkins and Diana Mutz for access to the ISCAP Panel; Jason Ganz and Sean McElwee at Data for Progress; Parker Howell and Andreas Katsouris at Aristotle International; and Ellissa Brown, Nick Laughlin, and Olivia Peterson at Morning Consult. We thank the Internet Archive and Kalev Leetaru for providing publicly accessible data on television news coverage; Erica Chenoweth, Jeremy Pressman, and the Crowd Counting Consortium for providing publicly accessible data on protest activity; FiveThirtyEight and the Roper Center for Public Opinion Research for their important collections of survey and other data; the American National Election Studies and the Cooperative Election Study for their ongoing survey projects, both of which are vital to the study of the American electorate; and Kantar Media and the Campaign Media Analysis Group for data on the candidates' advertising buys.

We have benefited from the feedback of many friends and colleagues who read and commented on chapter drafts or who helped us with analyses. This includes Allison Anoll, Larry Bartels, John Dearborn, Cindy Kam, Eunji Kim, Dave Lewis, Jeff Lewis, Meredith McClain, Leah Rosenstiel, Dan Thompson, Sharece Thrower, Alan Wiseman, and John Zaller. Jeff Lewis deserves particular thanks for helping us solve every data emergency that emerged in real time.

We also benefited from presenting this research to various audiences, including at Vanderbilt University, George Washington University, Harvard University, Yale University, the Harris School at the University of Chicago, UCLA, UCSD, the University of Toronto, the University of Pennsylvania, and Florida State University.

An early version of our argument in chapter 5 was published in the *Harvard Data Science Review*. We thank Ryan Enos for the invitation to publish our work there, and the founding editor of the journal, Xiao-Li Meng, for the opportunity. An early version of our argument in chapter 6 was published by the Democracy Fund Voter Study Group, and we again thank Robert Griffin, Mayesha Quasem, and Michael Tesler for their collaboration.

Obviously, this project would not have been possible without the ongoing support and extraordinary patience of Princeton University Press, which dates back to the publication of Sides and Vavreck's *The Gamble*. We thank them for continuing to be interested in our ideas and in publishing a more academic account of a presidential election for a wider audience. We especially thank Bridget Flannery-McCoy, John Donohue, and Alena Chekanov, all of whom helped make the book better.

This project, like so much else that happened to us in the past two years, depended on the support and patience of our families: Jeff Lewis; Stephanie Carrie and Max and Ian Tausanovitch; and Serena, Ethan, and Hannah Sides. We are sure the last thing any of them wanted was to spend the pandemic cooped up with someone writing a book about the state of U.S. politics. Through the loss of day care, homeschooling, and our endless Zoom meetings with Max and Ian echoing in the background, our families made it possible for us to write this book. Jeff will surely be glad not to hear the words, "So, do you think you can scrape that data off the web?" Hannah and Ethan will be happy to have their dad back full time.

The pandemic only made the importance of our families clearer to us, and we dedicate this book to them.

John dedicates this book to his parents, Rick and Elizabeth Sides. Would that our political leaders could more fully embody their values: self-sacrifice for the good of others; grace and kindness toward those with whom they disagree; and a deep concern for the less fortunate.

Chris dedicates this book to his wife, Stephanie. She is everything that our calcified politics is not: broad-minded, enthusiastic, loving, kind, creative, and inspired. Find yourself a partner like Stephanie and years like 2020 will be a joy.

Lynn dedicates this book to her niece and nephew, Abigail and William Lewis. On the cusp of solving some of the problems we lay out in these pages, they—and their generation—will do better. With them, there are no bitter ends, only beginnings.

INDEX

Note: Page numbers followed by "f" or "t" indicate figures and tables, respectively.

Also by

JOHN SIDES
AND LYNN VAVRECK

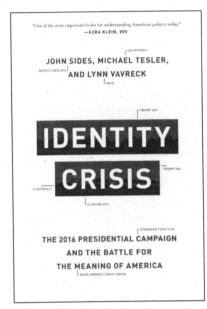

"One of the most important books for understanding American politics today."
—EZRA KLEIN, *VOX*

JOHN SIDES, MICHAEL TESLER,
AND LYNN VAVRECK

IDENTITY
CRISIS

THE 2016 PRESIDENTIAL CAMPAIGN
AND THE BATTLE FOR
THE MEANING OF AMERICA

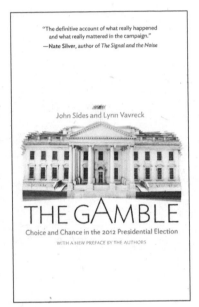

"The definitive account of what really happened
and what really mattered in the campaign."
—Nate Silver, author of *The Signal and the Noise*

John Sides and Lynn Vavreck

THE GAMBLE

Choice and Chance in the 2012 Presidential Election

WITH A NEW PREFACE BY THE AUTHORS

PRINCETON UNIVERSITY PRESS

Available wherever books are sold.
For more information visit us at www.press.princeton.edu